Cities, Slums and Gen
in the Global South

Developing regions are set to account for the vast majority of future urban growth, and women and girls will become the majority inhabitants of these localities in the Global South. This is one of the first books to detail the challenges facing poorer segments of the female population who commonly reside in 'slums'. It explores the variegated disadvantages of urban poverty and slum-dwelling from a gender perspective.

Cities, Slums and Gender in the Global South revolves around conceptualisation of the 'gender–urban–slum interface' which explains key elements to understanding women's experiences in slum environments. It has a specific focus on the ways in which gender inequalities can be entrenched but also alleviated. Included is a review of the demographic factors which are increasingly making cities everywhere 'feminised spaces', such as increased rural–urban migration among women, demographic ageing, and rising proportions of female-headed households in urban areas. Discussions focus in particular on education, paid and unpaid work, access to land, property and urban services, violence, intra-urban mobility, and political participation and representation.

This book will be of use to researchers and professionals concerned with gender and development, urbanisation and rural–urban migration.

Sylvia Chant is Professor of Development Geography at the London School of Economics and Political Science, UK.

Cathy McIlwaine is Professor of Geography at Queen Mary University of London, UK.

Cities, Slums and Gender in the Global South

Towards a feminised urban future

Sylvia Chant and Cathy McIlwaine

Routledge
Taylor & Francis Group

LONDON AND NEW YORK

First published 2016
by Routledge
2 Park Square, Milton Park, Abingdon, Oxon OX14 4RN

and by Routledge
711 Third Avenue, New York, NY 10017

Routledge is an imprint of the Taylor & Francis Group, an informa business

British Library Cataloguing in Publication Data
A catalogue record for this book is available from the British Library

Library of Congress Cataloging in Publication Data
A catalog record for this book has been requested

ISBN: 978-0-415-72164-6 (hbk)
ISBN: 978-1-138-19278-2 (pbk)
ISBN: 978-1-315-86299-6 (ebk)

Typeset in Times New Roman
by Keystroke, Station Road, Codsall, Wolverhampton

Contents

Figures

Plates

Tables

Boxes

Foreword

At present there is a profound conjuncture between cities of the Global South and academics and practitioners concerned with gender and urban development, thus making it a highly propitious time to focus on the relationship between the two. With decades of research and programmatic interventions to address aspects of women's lives in cities, why is this specific context so important? First, there is the completion of the dramatic demographic transition from rural to urban, with the majority of the world's population now living in cities. While such changing demographics are not homogeneous, with Africa and Asia now catching up with long-term Latin American trends in urbanisation rates, nevertheless, for the first time, this is a global phenomenon. Second, linked, but by no means automatically predicted, more women than ever before are now living in cities, rather than in rural areas of the Global South, with a so-called 'feminised urban future' anticipated – in which many households will be headed by women.

In parallel with this fundamental demographic change are a number of important related milestones in the global international development community, most important of which is the ratification of the Sustainable Development Goals (SDGs) – with two, namely urban and gender equality, included among the seventeen proposed. This provides an exceptional opportunity to put the interests and needs of marginalised, excluded and poor urban women in the Global South firmly on the international research, policy and practice agenda. However, to achieve this, there is still a need for robust evidence-based research that makes the case conclusively and comprehensively on an issue that has a long political history of being invisibilised.

Sylvia Chant and Cathy McIlwaine, each in her own way, are ideally placed to address the challenge that this presents. As academics they are both extensively grounded in gendered urban poverty and inequality research, with differences in emphasis, focus and region that complement and strengthen each other. Indeed, my own professional relationship with both authors, which goes back some thirty years to a time when far fewer feminist researchers focused on cities in the Global South, makes it a very special honour to contribute a foreword for this book. Among Sylvia's extensive portfolio is fieldwork-based research first on household headship and housing, which included collaborating with me in 1985 on a UN-Habitat report on *The Role of Women in the Execution of Low-Income*

Housing Projects (Moser and Chant, 1985), then her extensive work on women-headed households, and more recently her critical contribution to the 'feminisation of poverty' debates. Her range is global, but with detailed research in cities in the Philippines, Mexico, Costa Rica and The Gambia.

Of particular relevance in Cathy's primary research for me has been our collaboratively undertaken participatory urban appraisal of violence in the 1990s in Colombia and Guatemala, culminating in a co-authored book, *Encounters with Violence in Latin America: Urban Poor Perceptions from Colombia and Guatemala* (Moser and McIlwaine, 2004), and ten years later in our co-editorship of a special issue of *Environment and Urbanization* on 'Conflict and Violence in Twenty-first Century Cities' (Moser and McIlwaine, 2014). Over the past decade Cathy has also undertaken path-breaking policy-focused research on Latin American transnational women migrants who move primarily from cities of the Global South to those in the Global North.

As the name suggests, *Cities, Slums and Gender in the Global South* provides a comprehensive, ethnographically rich panorama of urban gender issues. However, the book's unique contribution relates to the fact that it goes beyond the perennial 'add women and stir' descriptions of 'women in cities' (Moser, 1993), to develop and ground it in a new theoretical framework involving the 'gender–urban–slum interface'. The shift from a city-level focus to one that specifically positions gender issues within slums, both in terms of land and housing, as well as economic activities, acknowledges the increasingly important connection between slums and informality in urban areas of Africa, Asia and Latin America. This demographic and theoretical construct not only reflects a post-Mike Davis (2006) problematisation of slums as 'dumping grounds', recapturing earlier conceptualisations of informal settlements as spaces of promise and aspiration as well as sites of resistance. In addition, as Parnell and Robinson (2012) have commented more generally, it reinforces the imperative of recalibrating urban theory from the standpoint of Global South cities, as well as being profoundly relevant to policy and planning.

Excellently complementing the transformative gender asset accumulation framework I developed recently (Moser, 2015), the 'gender–urban–slum interface' framework contextualises the interrelatedness between the diverse sites and scales women experience, whether it is the home, neighbourhood–settlement or city. Various chapters elaborate on this, examining distinct dimensions of gendered lives and livelihoods, including education, paid and unpaid work, access to land, property and urban services, health, violence, intra-urban mobility, and political participation and representation. Throughout, this multi-dimensional framework facilitates the identification of how and why gender inequalities exist, and the reasons for their frequent perpetuation in local slums, highlighting the fact that urbanisation does not always necessarily benefit women. Indeed, slums themselves, as 'spatial poverty traps' (see Chant and Datu, 2015), can obstruct the empowerment of women, so often assumed to occur in urban contexts. At the same time, on a more positive note, the book seeks to specify entry points where gender power relations are contested and challenged, either individually or through collective actions (Moser, 2009), both of which are vital for the achievement of gendered 'rights to the city'.

The current conjuncture of both demographic and policy agendas, mentioned at the outset of this foreword, undoubtedly guarantee the importance of this book for academics and practitioners alike.

Caroline O. N. Moser
Professor Emerita, University of Manchester,
formerly Director of the Global Urban Research Centre
and Professor of Urban Development

Preface and acknowledgements

The seeds of this volume derive in part from our joint contributions to the preparation of UN-Habitat's *State of Women in Cities 2012/13*, which was on the theme of gender and urban prosperity, with a major focus on fostering women's economic empowerment in cities. We thank the team at UN-Habitat for involving us in this venture and for inviting us to participate in the Gender Equality Action Assembly at the Sixth World Urban Forum in Naples in September 2012.

While elements of *Cities, Slums and Gender in the Global South* clearly draw on the vast amount of background research and writing we did for UN-Habitat, the present volume, commissioned initially by Natalie Tomlinson at Routledge, and thereafter managed by Robert Langham, with Lisa Thomson as editorial assistant, draws on our personal interests and experience in matters gender and urban which stretch back a long way – in Sylvia's case to the early 1980s, and in Cathy's to the end of that decade. Since this time our individual (and collaborative) research has embraced themes such as gender dimensions of housing, rural–urban migration, urban labour markets and female employment, urban poverty, urbanisation and household transitions, urban violence and civil society. While most of these issues have been explored in the context of field-based research in developing countries, Cathy has also diversified into the area of international migration from Latin America to London. Given this legacy, and an inevitable desire to complement rather than replicate our UN-Habitat work, the approach and emphasis in this book depart substantially from the thrust of *State of Women in Cities* in two main ways. First, we have written primarily for an academic readership. This allowed us considerably more scope to reflect on concepts and nuances which are often sacrificed in policy-oriented documentation, which is not to deny that we hope that planners, policy-makers, NGO personnel, activists and other stakeholders will find the empirical and theoretical material of use and interest in their applied work. Second, rather than concentrating primarily on urban prosperity and women's economic empowerment, we have attempted to provide a more holistic and arguably more critical analysis of the social, economic and political challenges to creating more gender equitable cities as urban populations in the Global South become increasingly 'feminised'.

It is impossible to name all the individuals who have helped us on our journey, but we owe particular debts to the following for background work and comments:

Gwendolyn Beetham, Marty Chen, Robin Dunford, Alice Evans, Steve Huxton, Michael Keith, Ralph Kinnear, Chloë Last, Julia Martin, Chris Mogridge, Isik Ozurgetem, Diane Perrons, Jeff Steller, Demetria Tsoutouras and Lindsay Walton. We would also like to extend particular gratitude to Yara Evans for her invaluable research assistance in relation to the figures and tables as well as for additional editorial help.

Although many of the photographs presented in the volume were taken by ourselves, acknowledgements are also due to several individuals for their kind permission to reproduce the following images: Marty Chen, for Figure 8.7; Andrew Fleming for Plate 6.1; Michael Keith for Plates 9.2 and 10.2; Carlosfelipe Pardo for Plates 2.5, 7.3 and 7.7; Taylor Barr for Plate 2.8; Belinda Fleischmann for Plate 8.12; Danielle Da Silva for Plates 5.2, 7.2 and 8.2; and Romi Savini for Plate 1.9, and for introducing Sylvia to Pepe Mateos, who kindly provided Plates 3.2 and 9.3.

Sylvia Chant
Cathy McIlwaine
London, July 2015

Abbreviations

ACE	African Coast to Europe
AfDB	African Development Bank
ART	Anti-Retroviral Therapy
BPFA	Beijing Platform for Action
CAMEBA	Carácas Slum Upgrading Project
CAP	Crosscutting Agra Programme
CAVIP	Advisory Programme for the Construction and Improvement of Low-income Housing
CCF	Community Credit Facility
CCT	Conditional Cash Transfer
CEDAW	Convention on the Elimination of All Forms of Discrimination Against Women
CEDOVIP	Centre for Domestic Violence Prevention
CEPAL	United Nations Economic Commission for Latin America
CMDs	Common Mental Disorders
COHRE	Centre on Housing Rights and Evictions
COPD	Chronic Obstructive Pulmonary Disorder
COTA	Children of the Andes
CPRC	Chronic Poverty Research Centre
CPTED	Crime Prevention Through Environmental Design
CSW	Commission on the Status of Women
CURE	Centre for Urban and Regional Excellence
DAMPA	Damyan ng Maralitang Pilipinong Api
DHS	Demographic and Health Surveys
FGC	Female Genital Cutting
GADN	UK's Gender and Development Network
GBV	Gender-Based Violence
GDP	Gross Domestic Product
GGGI	Global Gender Gap Index
GII	Gender Inequality Index
GLTN	Global Land Tools Network
GNI	Gross National Income
GNP	Gross National Product

GRB	Gender Responsive Budgeting
GROOTS	Grassroots Women Operating Together in Sisterhood
GWA	Gender and Water Alliance
HIV/AIDS	Human Immunodeficiency Virus/Acquired Immune Deficiency Syndrome
ICFTU	International Confederation of Free Trade Unions
ICPD	International Conference on Population and Development
ICT	Information and Communication Technology
ILO	International Labour Organisation
IMF	International Monetary Fund
IPL	International Poverty Line
IPV	Intimate Partner Violence
JMP	Joint Monitoring Programme
JNNURM	Jawarharlal Nehru National Urban Renewal Mission
LGBT	Lesbian, Gay, Bisexual and Transgender
MDGs	Millennium Development Goals
MDP	Multidimensional Poor
METRAC	Metropolitan Action Committee on Public Violence Against Women and Children
MHM	Menstrual Hygiene Management
NASVI	National Association of Street Vendors of India
NAWOU	National Association of Women's Organisations
NFHS	National Family Health Survey
NGOs	Non-Governmental Organisations
NSDF	National Slum Dwellers Federation
OD	Open Defecation
OECD	Organisation for Economic Cooperation and Development
OLPC	One Laptop Per Child
PTSDs	Post-Traumatic Stress Disorders
RAY	Rajiv Awas Yojana
SAPs	Structural Adjustment Programmes
SDGs	Sustainable Development Goals
SDI	Shack/Slumdwellers International
SEWA	Self-Employed Women's Association
SIGI	Social Institutions and Gender Index
SNA	System of National Accounts
SPARC	Society for the Promotion of Area Resources
STEM	Sciences, Mathematics and Technology
SWaCH	Solid Waste Collection Handling
TFR	Total Fertility Rate
TLA	Textile Labour Union
UN	United Nations
UN Women	United Nations Women
UNAIDS	Joint United Nations Programme on HIV/AIDS
UN-DESA	United Nations Department of Economic and Social Affairs

UNDP	United Nations Development Programme
UNFPA	United Nations Fund for Population Activities
UN-Habitat	United Nations Human Settlements Programme
UNHRC	United Nations Human Rights Council
UNICEF	United Nations Children's Fund
UNIFEM	United Nations Development Fund for Women
USAID	United States Aid
VAW	Violence Against Women
WACOL	Women's Aid Collective
WASH	Water, Sanitation and Hygiene
WCC	Women's Construction Collective
WEF	World Economic Forum
WHO	World Health Organisation
WIEGO	Women in Informal Employment: Globalising and Organising
WSSCC	Water Supply Sanitation Collaboration Council
YUW	Young Urban Women
ZAWA	Zanzibar Water Authority

1   Introduction

Cities and slums in the Global South – the importance of gender

Introduction

It is well known that over half the global population is now urban, and that despite some exceptions, mainly in sub-Saharan Africa (see Fox, 2011; Potts, 2012a, 2012b; Satterthwaite, 2010), the trend to greater concentration of people in towns and cities is likely to continue as the twenty-first century wears on. By 2030, for example, an anticipated two-thirds or more of the world's inhabitants will be urban, with the vast bulk of future growth accounted for by developing areas (UN-DESA, 2014a:1; UN-Habitat, 2012a:ix; see also Jones *et al.*, 2014; McGranahan and Satterthwaite, 2014).

What is perhaps less well known is that women will be the majority of urban citizens in the coming decades. This is partly due to increasing levels of female rural–urban migration (especially in regions where men have traditionally dominated population movements), and partly a result of demographic ageing – across the world women generally outlive their male counterparts, and many of these women are urban-based (see Chant, 2013; Chant and Datu, 2011a, 2011b, 2015; Kinyanjui, 2014; Tacoli, 2012). What is also suggested by current trajectories, particularly in Latin America but elsewhere too, is that greater proportions of urban dwellers will live in female-headed households. Global demographics are changing, and rapidly: a 'feminised urban future' beckons in which the women's share of city populations will be larger than that of men. Given the notion that urbanisation comprises the power to transform societies (see UN-Habitat, 2014a), and that through situating themselves in urban areas, '(w)omen in particular believe that they can improve their status, position, and their children's opportunities' (Meleis, 2011:1), is it possible that past and projected demographic change may add momentum to struggles for greater gender equality?

Certainly, a historic association of urbanisation with possibilities for 'female emancipation' (primarily on account of the 'breakdown' of patriarchal family systems and landholding, and greater opportunities for female education and economic autonomy) makes it tempting to think of the 'urban century' as offering prospects for narrowing gender disparities and injustices on an unprecedented scale. As UN-Habitat (2010c:3) contends: 'it is . . . in cities that societal progress such as the advancement of women and increasing levels of gender equality take place'.

Recognising that in some contexts gender divisions, along with various restrictions on women, may be more pronounced in urban than in rural settings (see Schütte, 2014, on Afghanistan), cities generally seem to offer women scope to escape some of demands on their time and labour associated with domesticity and subsistence provision in rural environments (see Bibler and Zuckerman, 2013; also Chant, 1996; Lees, 2004; McDowell, 1999). The particular characteristics of urban employment, such as greater possibilities for remuneration in women's own right and a broader range of occupational choices, also tend to be associated with some important shifts in women's independence and self-development (see Bradshaw, 2013b; Evans, 2013a, 2013b). Compounding these processes, evidence suggests that young male urban dwellers, especially those with exposure to secondary education, 'hold more equitable views than older men' (Barker, 2014:86). Indeed, as further noted by Barker, 'Given that the world is becoming more urban, and that young people in much of the world are staying in school for longer, young men are being pushed – or increasingly socialised – towards accepting gender equality' (ibid.; see also Plan International, 2011).

This said, the difficulties experienced by urban women vis-à-vis their rural counterparts may not be that dissimilar, especially where the former are poor and/ or reside in slums. As pointed out by Cecilia Tacoli and David Satterthwaite (2013:3), while urbanisation is often associated with greater independence among women as a result of better access to services and employment, lower fertility rates, and a degree of relaxation of patriarchal norms within and beyond the family, 'most urban women experience profound disadvantages compared to men in their daily lives' (see also Chant and McIlwaine, 2013b; Muñoz-Boudet *et al.*, 2012:37; Tacoli, 2014:1). As additionally emphasised by Afaf Ibrahim Meleis (2011:5): 'Urbanisation creates physical demands on women due to new waged work, urban stressors, limited convenient transportation, demands on their time, and new complexities in their lives.' These pressures conceivably weigh heaviest on female migrants to urban areas who may lack support networks and face social stigma alongside isolation (see Messias, 2011:156–7; also Lenoël, 2014; Tacoli *et al.*, 2015:25–6). This resonates for women migrants who originate internally from rural areas as well as those who have moved internationally between cities in other countries of the Global South (Bastia and Busse, 2011), or indeed to Global North cities (Wills *et al.*, 2010; see also Parnell and Robinson, 2012).

However, perhaps even more important than migrant status is where women live in cities. Generally speaking, women who are poorer (in income terms), and who reside in disadvantaged or marginalised urban communities (particularly 'slums') are those who are usually most at risk of the worst excesses of socio-economic and gender inequality. As part of its assessment of the Beijing Platform for Action+20 in 2015, for example, UN Women (2015a:9) has drawn attention to the fact that while urbanisation has helped to present new possibilities for gender equality, there are major challenges too, not least on account of the growth of informal settlements which produce 'new kinds of urban spaces marked by destitution and insecurity on a vast scale'. Indeed, given that cities seem to be associated with mounting social, political and economic inequality within their boundaries as well as in relation to rural areas, not to mention beyond borders to other cities globally, gender divisions and disparities persist, and in some instances are reconstituted or exacerbated. This is arguably one reason why neither quantitative nor qualitative data reveal any systematic relationship between the 'feminisation' of urban populations and substantially narrowed gender gaps in such arenas as education, employment, earnings, assets, health, vulnerability to violence, and political voice and representation (see below). This also explains why consideration of intra-urban heterogeneity and slums from a gender perspective constitutes a core element in our book, and is the basis of a framework which we have denominated the 'gender–urban–slum interface'.

In the 'gender–urban–slum interface', on which we expound in detail in Chapter 2, we identify a broad series of territorial and thematic domains through which gender disparities in cities can be most fruitfully approached and addressed. Among many influences, this draws inspiration from Caren Levy's (1996) model of a 'web of institutionalisation', which recognises the interplay of different elements and 'sites of power' in the framing, evolution and integration of gender in policy and planning.

We hope that this contribution will not only be empirically, methodologically and analytically useful for Global South cities per se, but also assist in the vital task of (re)theorising urbanisation and urban dynamics from a non-Northern vantage point (see Robinson, 2002, 2003, 2006; see also Myers, 2011; Parnell *et al.*, 2009; Parnell and Robinson, 2012; Vira and James, 2011; Williams *et al.*, 2009). In the interests of better informing what Ananya Roy (2009:820) has termed 'new geographies of urban theory', gender is paramount notwithstanding its comparative, not to mention notable, neglect in Global South city-making processes to date. As emphasised by Linda Peake and Martina Rieker (2013:2): '[W]omen are an important node in the constellations of power, and thus in the production of centre and margins, in imaginaries of the urban'.

Despite an already extensive, and burgeoning, literature on gender and cities, the main focus has been on advanced economies where many conditions and theoretical constructions are not easily mapped on to developing countries (Peake and Rieker, 2013). This is not to deny that in an ever more globalised world some fundamental gendered cleavages – especially in terms of the *position* of women in relation to men – do travel, and are arguably disturbingly widespread. These include the fact that cities are overwhelmingly designed *by* men, and *for* men, that women are often rendered less mobile than men in urban environments, that they are more vulnerable to violence, and that in general terms women are disadvantaged by gender roles and relations – economically, physiologically, psychologically, socially, sexually and politically. As summarised by the UK's Gender and Development Network: 'Gender is a universal structural inequality which affects all peoples in all countries and is not confined to developing countries alone' (GADN, 2013:24). In addition, the socio-economic processes underpinning the growth of cities in the Global North and Global South are increasingly intertwined, especially in relation to international migration. Not only do cities of the Global North often depend on the cheap labour of migrants from poorer countries, and invariably from developing nations (Wills *et al.*, 2010), but movement between cities of the South and North leads to complex changes in gender ideologies (McIlwaine, 2010).

This said, there is a real need to focus on the Global South in its own right, especially given that this is where the vast bulk of current and future urban growth is occurring. Here, we wish not only to rectify a tendency for debates around inclusive or transformative cities either to neglect gender altogether or to focus on only one or two aspects of women's experiences, such as violence (see Shrestha *et al.*, 2015; Whitzman *et al.*, 2013), but also to broaden our knowledge and appreciation of gender in relation to intra-urban heterogeneity by considering the socio-spatial significance of residence, especially as this pertains to slums (see also Peake and Rieker, 2013:13).

While not wishing to make a case for invidious comparisons between North and South, nor to suggest that urban women in developing countries are necessarily worse off than many of their counterparts in advanced economies (Peake and Rieker, 2013), we take on board UN-Habitat's (2012a:45) assertion that the 'everyday lives' of women and men in developing and developed countries differ to a substantial degree, and contend that treating women in the urban world as a homogeneous group is inappropriate.

Urban women in the Global South, especially those who reside in slums, are more likely than their Northern counterparts to suffer greater levels of extreme and relative monetary poverty, iniquitous unpaid labour burdens stemming from poorly consolidated shelter and absent or deficient urban services and infrastructure, sorely limited access to salaried employment, lack of welfare benefits, lack of protection from gender-sensitive legislation, and inability to seek the support of institutions in asserting claims, rights and justice, even where these are formally mandated. For some groups of female urban dwellers in the Global South, the intersecting vulnerabilities occasioned by such factors as age, conjugal and family status, and sexuality may render them largely powerless to carve out any kind of meaningful existence for themselves and their households.

In light of this, and in the interests of enriching and broadening current debates on gender in the city, we attempt in the present volume to sketch out an anatomy of 'where we are now' in terms of women in cities and slums of the Global South, and 'what of the future' in respect of how women might be better enabled to act by, and for, themselves, in shaping more gender-equitable urban environments in which they will be the majority stakeholders. We envisage a struggle in light of existing challenges, but hope to offer some pointers towards rendering cities spaces of equal rights, and a vanguard for creating possibilities for women and men of all generations to enjoy and benefit equally from the positive aspects of urbanisation – economic, political and social – at all levels.

While our dedicated introduction to core components in the 'gender–urban–slum interface' is reserved for Chapter 2, in order to establish context we provide brief background below to the term 'slum', how slums are defined and measured, and more detailed justification as to why consideration of this space is particularly relevant to poor women in cities of the South.

Introducing 'slums'

'Slum' terminology has only (re)entered the lexicon in discourse on Global South cities in any concerted manner since the beginning of this century, and it is not necessarily here to stay. Indeed not only has a plethora of alternative terms been used to define the most marginalised areas of cities over time, such as 'ghettoes', 'colonies', 'informal settlements' and 'peri-urban areas' (see, e.g., Hawkins *et al.*, 2013:9), but descriptors seem to go in and out of favour. In Kenya, for example, 'informal settlement' currently seems to be the preferred nomenclature (see Gulis *et al.*, 2014:219).

This is possibly not surprising given historical controversy around the term 'slum' which appears to have originated in Victorian England, and which in Global South and North alike has been viewed as homogenising, simplistic and denigrating, as noted by Alan Gilbert (2009:38) who states: 'The use of a word with as long and disreputable a history as the "slum" is risky and typifies the current tendency to generalise and trivialise' (see also Gilbert, 2007). In some quarters 'slums' (which are typically equated with informal self-build settlements) have been lauded as spaces of hope, promise and aspiration (e.g. Lloyd, 1979; Turner, 1976). They have also been regarded as sites of resistance capable of spawning significant urban social movements, as described by Castells (1978) among others (see also Appadurai, 2002; Chatterjee, 2004). However, such positive readings have commonly been eclipsed by associations with the 'apocalyptic anti-urbanism' (Angotti, 2006:961) characterising works such as Mike Davis's (2006) *Planet of Slums*, which portrays such spaces in the Global South as inherently problematic, dysfunctional, poor and representative of an informality that is separate from the rest of the city. As Davis's somewhat emotive rhetoric puts it, slums are 'dumping grounds' for 'surplus humanity' (ibid.:174–5), where people squat 'in squalor, surrounded by pollution, excrement, and decay' (ibid.:19). Such views, which portray slums as 'exceptional' and antithetical to twenty-first-century urbanism, have been widely problematised and critiqued (see e.g., Jones, 2011; Huchzermeyer, 2014), with Vyjayanthi Rao (2006:231) arguing that: 'The slum – as a demographic and theoretical construct – straddles the conceptual and material forms of city-making that are challenging the imaginary of the modern city.'

Yet, however contested and problematic the term 'slum' might be, there is a strong association with informality which increasingly characterises twenty-first-century metropoli and indeed in many developing countries forms the primary mode of production – whether in terms of land appropriation and housing construction, or in respect of economic activity more generally (Roy, 2005, 2009, 2015). Recognising that informality is by no means restricted to low-income groups (ibid.; see also Ghertner, 2008), the particular connection of slums and informality with the urban areas of Africa, Asia and Latin America not only reinforces the imperative of recalibrating urban theory from the standpoint of Global South cities (Parnell and Robinson, 2012) but is deeply relevant to policy and planning (ibid.; see also Yiftachel, 2006).

The latter is perhaps especially so since the launch of the Millennium Development Goals (MDGs), which, under the overarching rubric of reducing extreme poverty, included in MDG7 ('ensure environmental stability') a target (number 11) that called for 'a significant improvement in the lives of at least 100 million slumdwellers by 2020' (UN-Habitat, 2008b:3). That slums should have been specified in the MDG agenda highlights the fact that extreme poverty and slum residence are frequently correspondent, and even if 'it is rare for housing conditions to be considered within definitions of poverty' (Tacoli *et al.*, 2015:17), that they might be worthy of more dedicated investigation and intervention. According to UNICEF (2012:33) for instance: 'Slums are the physical manifestation of the urbanisation of poverty', and as asserted by Bipasha Baruah (2007:2102): 'Despite the significant contributions to the urban economy, slum communities exist on the fringes of society and occupy the lower rungs of social and economic hierarchies.' This said, it is equally important to underline the widely acknowledged observation that slums and poverty are not necessarily one and the same (see, e.g, Bapat, 2009; Chandrasekhar and Mukhopadhyay, 2008; Gupta *et al.*, 2009; Harpham, 2009; Khosla, 2009; Mitlin, 2005; Patel, 2002; Ruthven, 2002; Sabry, 2009). For example, while Barbara Harriss-White *et al.* (2013:408) profess that 'Slums are containers of marginalised people', they also caution that 'the equation of slums with homogeneous sinks of poverty and/or of dominant processes of marginalisation ... deserves interrogation'. It is accordingly important to acknowledge not only that there is often considerable social and economic heterogeneity in slum settlements (ibid.:399; Hawkins *et al.*, 2013:15), but that pathologising stereotypes around 'Third World' urban slums are frequently misleading as well as overdrawn (see Gilbert 2007, 2009; Jones, 2011; Jovchelovitch and Priego-Hernández, 2013; UN-Habitat, 2010c:8–9). Indeed, even as slums evolve over time, as they often do, into less obviously 'dystopian spaces' (Jones, 2011), the stigma and connotations of 'dirt, disease, toxicity and danger' (ibid.:696), as also reflected in Mike Davis's (2006) work, routinely endure.

Echoing such observations, in their dedicated discussion of slum nomenclature, Diana Mitlin and David Satterthwaite (2012:395n) assert: 'The term "slum" usually has derogatory connotations and can suggest that a settlement needs replacement or can legitimate the evictions of its residents.' By the same token, these authors also draw attention to the fact that some neighbourhood organisations and networks have appropriated the term 'slum' in their self-identification in an attempt to invert this negativity, further noting that in some contexts being designated a 'slum' (as in 'notified slums' in India) can actually provide lobbying power and access to assistance (ibid.). As echoed by Harriss-White *et al.* (2013:399) for India: 'Legally "notified slums" ... have greater legal protection and provide greater access to state resources for people.'

Defining and measuring slums

Beyond debates over the term 'slum' per se, it should also be noted that what earns a settlement this epithet has also been the subject of considerable discussion, with

---

Box 1.1   UN-Habitat's official definition of 'slum household'

Households lacking one or more of the following:

- Durable housing – a permanent structure providing protection from the elements.
- Adequate living area – no more than three people sharing a room, or notional floor area of four square metres per person.
- Access to improved water, which is sufficient (twenty litres per person per day), affordable (no more than 10 per cent of household income), and can be obtained without extreme effort on the part of women and children.
- Access to improved sanitation, notably a private toilet, or a public one shared with a reasonable number of people.
- Secure tenure and protection against forced evictions.

Sources: Arimah, 2007; Rakodi, 2014:24; UN-Habitat, 2006b, 2008a, 2014b.

UNICEF (2012:69), among others, emphasising the importance of 'clear definitions of "urban slums" that reduce conceptual confusion and enable meaningful comparison'.

The MDGs provided major impetus to this with Target 11 (see above) requiring a tool for monitoring and measuring purposes, to which the task fell to an inter-agency 'expert' coalition comprising UN-Habitat in partnership with the World Bank and UNDP. The definition devised by this consortium held that 'slumdwellers' consist of people residing in homes or communities suffering from one or more 'shelter deprivations', whether in respect of quality of building materials, degree of overcrowding, access to water and sanitation, or security of tenure (see Box 1.1). In turn, a settlement is classified as a 'slum' where 50% or more of its component households is affected by one or more of these deprivations (UN-Habitat, 2008a).

Although the definitional criteria itemised in Box 1.1 may in themselves seem narrow, in conjunction with one another they are conceivably impossibly broad, with Nyovani Madise *et al.* (2012:1146) pointing out that because strict application of all criteria 'leads to a large and rather heterogeneous slum community', stakeholders typically take the default position of a slum comprising only two or more elements.

'Strict application' of any element is of course doubtful, given vulnerability to localised and arbitrary interpretation, and the inevitable tensions between self-reporting by residents and the frequently different knowledges and agendas of 'outsiders' such as municipal or state officials. Indeed, given haziness around issues of 'secure tenure', this is frequently omitted from assessments (Chant, 2011a; Rakodi, 2014:24).

Plate 1.1 Comuna 13 slum on outskirts of Medellín, Colombia

Source: Cathy McIlwaine.

Beyond the fact that 'there are no data collected in nations each year on "slum" populations using the UN definitions' (Tacoli *et al.*, 2015:2), another reason why it is difficult to generalise about slums is their varied character and spatial location in cities. As pointed out by Eugenie Birch (2011:78), such settlements may be 'located either in interstices of inner cities or on peripheral, often vulnerable land in crowded, poorly planned neighbourhoods' (see also Myers, 2011:70–1). Indeed, in some contexts, such as Greater Banjul, the capital of The Gambia, for example, our own fieldwork has revealed there are few readily identifiable 'slum settlements', with slum housing often situated in the same street, and sometimes next door or on the same compound as non-slum and even elite housing.

While it is indeed the case that concentrated expanses of slum housing can be found in city centres, as in the case of Dharavi, which lies in the shadow of the central business district of Mumbai (where an estimated 55 per cent of the population resides in slums; Birch, 2011:78), more typically the Global South's largest slums are located on or towards the urban periphery where they originated from squatting or irregular commercial land transfers in the era of most rapid urban growth between the middle and late twentieth century. Although peri-urban (or formerly peri-urban) slums are typically prone to densification over time, there are many instances where these settlements may not be overcrowded but rather quite low-density, as noted on the fringes of towns such as Liberia, Cañas and Santa Cruz in Guanacaste, northwest Costa Rica (Chant and McIlwaine, 2009).

Plate 1.2 Slum dwelling on plot adjacent to elite house, Fajara, The Gambia

Source: Sylvia Chant.

Despite the caveats mentioned above, and that databases are usually less than robust, the criteria adopted by the inter-agency body remain the only effective basis for UN-Habitat's slum estimates (Mitlin and Satterthwaite, 2012). Relying on these albeit tenuous estimates, it appears that slum populations have been declining in relative terms since 1990 (see Figure 1.1; see also Harris, 2015:122), although in absolute terms, as of 2012, slums were still deemed to number nearly a billion urban inhabitants worldwide (see Figure 1.2). Over 90 per cent were concentrated in developing regions, ranging from almost one-quarter (23.5 per cent) of the urban population in Latin America and the Caribbean, to around one-third in Southeastern Asia (31 per cent) and Southern Asia (35 per cent), to nearly two-thirds in sub-Saharan Africa (61.7 per cent) (UN-Habitat, 2012b). Some individual countries in the latter region have especially high proportions of urban slum dwellers, such as the Central African Republic with 96 per cent (UN-Habitat, 2014b:2–3).

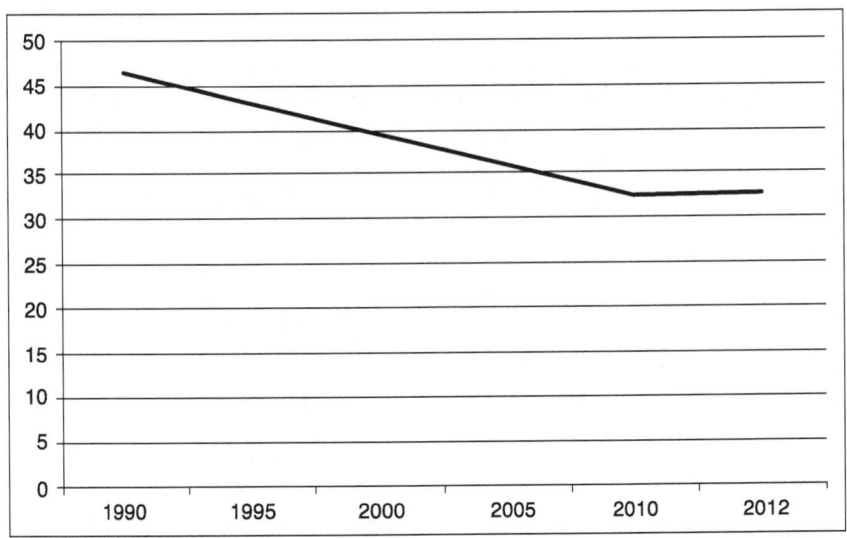

Figure 1.1 Proportion of developing region urban populations living in slums, 1990–2012
(percentage)

Source: Adapted from UN, 2014b:46 ('Population living in urban slums and proportion of urban
population living in slums, developing regions' figure).

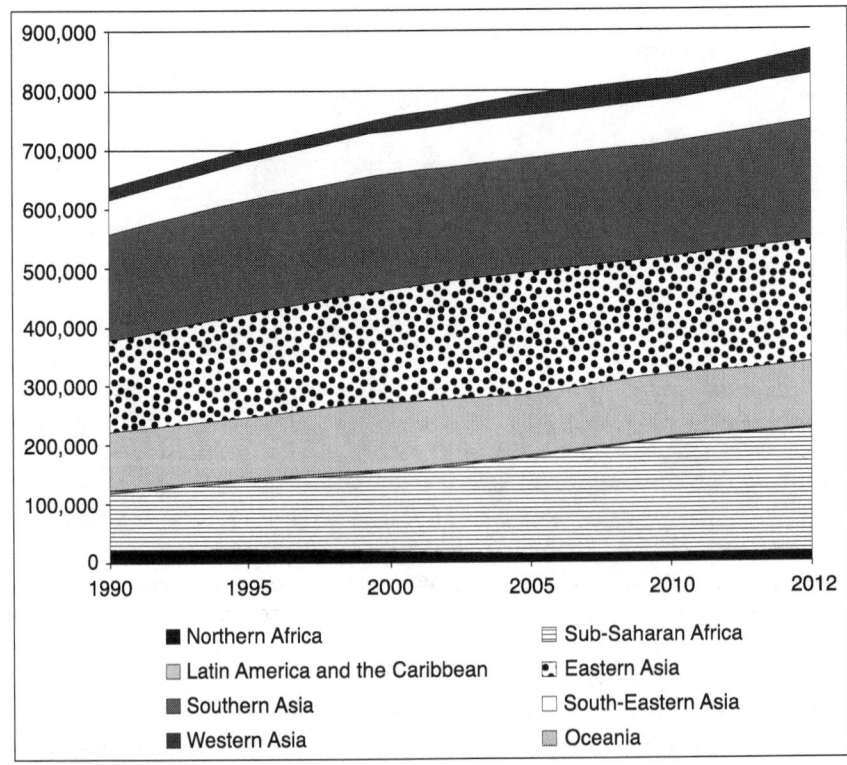

Legend:
- ■ Northern Africa
- ▤ Sub-Saharan Africa
- ▨ Latin America and the Caribbean
- ▨ Eastern Asia
- ■ Southern Asia
- □ South-Eastern Asia
- ■ Western Asia
- ▨ Oceania

Figure 1.2 Urban populations living in slums by region, 1990–2012 (thousands)

Source: Compiled from UN-Habitat, 2013:Table 3, 151.

Plate 1.3 Inner-city slum dwelling, Marrakech, Morocco

Source: Sylvia Chant.

Why emphasise slums in the analysis of gender in Global South cities?

Given that many of those who reside in slums are poor, coupled with the difficulties of pinning down the 'slum' as a distinct or indeed systematically distinctive type of urban space, it might have been more straightforward for us to talk simply about gender and poverty in cities of the Global South. However, although slums do vary widely in their scale and nature (see Mitlin and Satterthwaite, 2013), we feel that many of the archetypal shelter deprivations ascribed to them, individually or in combination, merit particular attention in the context of poor women's lives in developing world cities. As highlighted by Pushpha Arabindoo (2011:634), slums are important sites of everyday gendered practices among many urban dwellers in the Global South. Indeed, while women's homes and communities are critical in their negotiation of daily life in towns and cities everywhere, mainly on account of feminised responsibilities for domestic and unpaid carework (Chant, 2013; Jarvis *et al.*, 2009; Tacoli, 2014), it might also be said that urban slums in the Global South present particularly trenchant barriers to gender and other forms of equality.

Not only do the female occupants of slums often spend the bulk of their time in these settlements and thus bear the daily brunt of slum living, but the challenging circumstances of deficient housing, poor services and infrastructure, and inadequate connections to other parts of the city, can constrain livelihoods in several ways, and mire women in poverty over the long term. That slums may be tantamount to 'spatial poverty traps' (Unterhalter, 2009:16; see also Chant and

Datu, 2011b, 2015) is underlined by the fact that, for many women, home-based enterprise and production in a context of weak markets is their only viable means of generating income (Chant, 1996, 2014; Gondwe and Ayenagbo, 2013; Gough and Kellett, 2001). Moreover, questions of security, crime and violence are often more pronounced in slum settlements (see Moser, 2004; Moser and McIlwaine, 2004, 2014) and especially gender-based violence and violence against women and girls (ActionAid, 2011; Amnesty International, 2010; Kamndaya *et al.*, 2015; McIlwaine, 2013). While slum environments can also offer opportunities for women to organise socially and politically, and to improve their neighbourhoods, the odds of success are often stacked against them, not only because of the privations internal to slums, but because of 'male bias' in cities at large. In short, although poor women in slum and non-slum areas of cities experience a similar range of challenges in relation to gender inequalities, the greater concentration of poverty in slum neighbourhoods aggravated by overcrowding, insecurity, lack of access to security of tenure, water and sanitation, as well as limited recourse to and reproductive health services, often poses formidable barriers to women's attempts to exit privation. As asserted by Harriss-White *et al.* (2013:400) in relation to the Chennai metropolitan area, where just over one-quarter of its nine million inhabitants are slum dwellers:

> Compared with non-slum areas, slums have higher concentrations of people who are constrained by a reinforcing set of deprivations including low caste, less education, insecure work, limited economic resources, unenforceable rights, low and irregular incomes and malnutrition and other health deficits.

Harriss-White *et al.* (2013:422) further note that: 'The physical fabric of slums is by definition a series of sinks of infrastructural neglect, on top of which slumdwellers are vulnerable to many shocks' – both economic and environmental. Significantly, too, slums are not only home to a great number of the poor in the Global South, but women are frequently a disproportionate percentage of their residents (ibid.; see also Khosla, 2009).

Gender, space and other intersectionalities

Given the heterogeneity of women in urban areas within the Global South itself, attention is paid throughout the volume – where data and analysis permit – not only to differences between slums and non-slum areas, but to the intersections of gender with other axes of social difference such as age, socio-economic status, employment status and sexuality. Although scant information on these intersections for many cities prohibits systematic or comprehensive treatment, their relevance is paramount, as summarised by Rena Khosla (2009:7):

> Urban women, while generally sharing specific gender interests arising from a common set of responsibilities and roles, constitute a fairly diverse group. There are elderly women, working women and women whose major

Plate 1.4 Peri-urban slum housing, Cebu City, Philippines

Source: Sylvia Chant.

Plate 1.5 Mother and daughter in Mexican slum

Source: Sylvia Chant.

responsibility is in the domestic sphere. There are also women who balance multiple roles at the same time. Poor women living in slums and low resource areas face disadvantages which are very different from those faced by women from middle class families. Slum dwellers also experience an unequal level of service, women are doubly disadvantaged from poor access [*sic*]. Cities, especially large urban areas, also have more numbers of women-headed households, single women living by themselves, professional women who need to travel, etc., and urban development planning must respond to the needs of these diverse groups. Experience has shown that women not only bear the brunt of poverty, but their empowerment is key to its reduction.

Within this scenario, consideration of men and gender relations is paramount, and again forms as much of our discussion as possible. This befits a relational approach which regards subjects not as fixed and immutable, but as engaging in dynamic interactions and negotiations which are often co-constitutive of other types of change, be this in respect of urban growth, macro-economic shifts, and/or political and demographic transitions (Levy, 2009; see also Berry, 2011; Evans, 2013a; Jarvis *et al.*, 2009; Sassen, 2001, 2010; UN-Habitat, 2012a:20).

Gender and urban policy: a note on context and momentum

In addressing notable 'gender gaps' in cities and slums in the Global South, this volume draws on a wide range of legacies. These include long-standing academic interest in the field of gender and the urban, dating from analyses conducted by feminist sociologists and geographers and other social scientists of women's relations with the 'built environment' in the 1960s and 1970s (although, as previously identified, this was mainly confined to Global North cities; see UN-Habitat, 2012a:18), to more dedicated research on developing regions in the 1980s spearheaded most notably by the urban social anthropologist Caroline Moser (1986, 1995; discussed further in Chapter 2).

While much of this ground-breaking scholarship has been of an applied orientation, interest in the gender–urban nexus has taken rather longer to ferment in policy and advocacy circles. That said, the latter also provides a rich resource of knowledge and argument, with organisations such as UN-Habitat and the Huairou Commission playing major roles in taking the urban 'gender agenda' forward and providing considerable momentum for 'en-gendering' cities in the Global South, especially from the perspective of women from the grassroots (see, e.g., Huairou Commission, 2010a, 2010b, 2011; Kiwala, 2005; UN-Habitat, 2006a, 2007a, 2010b). Recent initiatives include UN-Habitat's 2008–2013 Gender Equality Action Plan, the flagship publication *State of Women in Cities 2012/13* (UN-Habitat, 2013), and the Policy and Plan for Gender Equality and the Empowerment of Women 2014–2019 (UN-Habitat, 2015) (see Box 1.2).

The Policy and Plan for Gender Equality and the Empowerment of Women builds on Habitat's 2008–2013 Gender Equality Action Plan, which aimed to progress attainment of the MDGs, especially MDG3 ('promote gender equality

---

Box 1.2   UN-Habitat's Policy and Plan for Gender Equality and the Empowerment of Women, 2014–2019

This policy and plan identifies how UN-Habitat will collaborate with national and city authorities as well as civil society in order that the experiences of women and men are included in all aspects of urban development. Issues of quality and equity are emphasised in the quest for inclusive and sustainable urban governance, planning, economic management and basic service delivery. The guiding principles are fourfold, as follows:

- Vision: UN-Habitat promotes the commitment to work towards the realisation of a world in which men and women are recognised as equal partners in development so that economically productive, socially inclusive and environmentally sustainable cities and other human settlements can be achieved.
- Mission: UN-Habitat supports a range of stakeholders to respond positively to the opportunities and challenges of urbanisation by providing advice and assistance on transforming cities and other human settlements into inclusive centres of vibrant economic growth, social progress, environmental safety and human security. This can only be achieved in the context of full gender equality and empowerment of women and youth.
- Goal: Well-planned and -governed efficient cities with adequate infrastructure and full access to employment, land, public space and basic services which include housing, water, sanitation, energy and transport. This is carried out on the basis of equality and non-discrimination among all social groups.
- Strategic result: 'Environmentally, economically and socially sustainable, gender-responsive, youth aware, rights-based and inclusive urban development policies implemented by national, regional and local authorities have improved the standard of living of the urban poor, male and female, young and old, and enhanced their full and equal participation in the socio-economic life of the city' (UN-Habitat, 2015:10)

Source: UN-Habitat, 2015.

---

and empower women') and MDG7 ('ensure environmental sustainability'), which included the targets of reducing by half the proportion of the population lacking sustainable access to water and sanitation by 2015 and achieving significant improvements in the lives of at least 100 million slum dwellers by 2020 (see above). The new plan focuses on various aspects of gender mainstreaming as well as updates of the MDGs through the Sustainable Development Goals (SDGs), to be rolled out in 2016 (UN-Habitat, 2015; UN Women, 2013). The proposed SDGs of most relevance to the plan are SDG5 – to 'achieve gender equality and empower all women and girls' – and SDG11, which aims to 'make cities and human settlements inclusive, safe, resilient and sustainable' by 2030. Although there is no mention of cities or urbanisation in SDG5, women and girls (along with children, people with disabilities and older persons) are specifically identified within SDG11, with objective 11.2 making reference to urban residents who are vulnerable to lack of safe, affordable and sustainable transport systems (see below).

It is welcome to see some, albeit incremental, gestures towards recognition of connections between gender and the urban in mainstream agenda-setting, even though this is arguably a far cry from the call made by UN-Habitat in its 2012 report on gender and urban planning that:

> Given the international commitment to achieving gender equality and the fact that cities are made up of gendered spaces and places, a new model for planning in the 21st century must integrate a gender perspective at each stage of the process and at each level of planning.
>
> (UN-Habitat, 2012a:x)

None the less, arguably every little helps in a context in which since the UN Decade for Women (1975–1985), a broad swathe of initiatives to advance gender-equitable development has been pursued by major organisations within the UN system, other multilaterals such as the World Bank, bilateral institutions, national governments, international and national NGOs, and grassroots women's movements and networks (see Benavides Llerena *et al.*, 2007; Chant and McIlwaine, 2009:chapter 8; Mitlin, 2008; Patel and Mitlin, 2004, 2010).

In light of the above, and drawing on the growing repository of gender expertise in academic and policy fora, this volume is organised around what are arguably the most crucial arenas for gender equality in cities and slums in the contemporary Global South. Following our detailed outline of the 'gender–urban–slum interface' in Chapter 2, the pivotal issues therein are the subject of dedicated individual discussion in Chapters 3–9. Finally, in our conclusion, we provide pointers to the main pathways to creating more gender-equitable cities of the South which we hope will resonate across a more global remit. In the remainder of the present chapter, we establish further context by setting out the core reasons for 'en-gendering' urban analysis, policy and planning, with particular reference to slums, in the twenty-first century.

Key rationales for 'en-gendering' urban analysis, policy and planning in the Global South

There are arguably two main reasons which urge contemporary analysis of cities and slums in the Global South from a gender perspective. The first, as mentioned earlier, is demographic: women are not only forming a progressively greater share of urban inhabitants, but a substantial constituency of slum dwellers, too. In India, for example, where cities are still predominantly male-populated spaces, gender gaps in numbers tend to be less marked in slums (Khosla, 2009:25). Departing from this rather practical *raison d'être*, our second major rationale hinges more on principle: namely, that there seems to be a range of gendered injustices in cities which form part of a process whereby, despite the wealth produced by urbanisation, poverty has failed to disappear and inequalities are rising (see Meleis, 2011:1). In the case of women, particularly disturbing is the hiatus between what they contribute to the 'urban prosperity' celebrated by UN-Habitat (2012b, 2013), among others, and what they derive in terms of rewards (Chant and Datu, 2015; Chant and McIlwaine, 2013a, 2013b).

A review follows, first of feminising urban demographics (a theme to which we return in the context of our conceptual model in Chapter 2, with particular reference to fertility and reproductive and sexual health and rights) and, second, of some of the paradoxes of socio-economic and gendered inequalities associated with urbanisation in Global South regions.

The feminisation of urban demographics

'Cities of women'?

As mentioned at the start of this chapter, in increasing numbers of developing countries cities are home to a growing and increasingly a majority population of women (see Chant, 2013; Tacoli and Chant, 2014). While feminised urban sex ratios reflect a combination of factors, including sex-differentiated demographic ageing, the impacts of war and conflict, as well as international population movements (many of which are discussed below), a major issue is the cumulative gender selectivity of rural–urban migration, with Latin America distinguished as a region in which more women than men have moved to towns and cities over the past several decades (Chant, 1998; Chant and McIlwaine, 2009:86–7). In the period 1965–75, for example, an estimated 109 women moved to urban destinations in Latin America for every 100 men (Gilbert and Gugler, 1982:59), whereas in sub-Saharan Africa, the ratio during the same period was only 92 female migrants per 100 males (ibid.). Female-selective urbanward migration has continued to be marked in Central and South America, along with some Southeast Asian countries, such as Cambodia, Thailand and Vietnam, with urban sex ratios notably feminised as a consequence (Chant and McIlwaine, 2009:86–7; see also Table 1.1). Such patterns are often attributed to the relatively greater labour opportunities for women in urban settings and to a degree of flexibility in women's freedoms to move in the context of prevailing household and kinship structures.

Although urban sex ratios in a range of countries in sub-Saharan Africa and South Asia are now beginning to display feminised patterns, traditionally lower levels of female rural–urban migration in these regions have been explained by such factors as socio-cultural restrictions on independent female movement, virilocal marriage, and the encouragement of young men to gain urban experience as a form of masculine 'rite of passage' (see Tacoli and Mabala, 2010). The historical dominance of men in rural–urban movement has also been attributed to the comparative lack of employment opportunities for women in towns and cities

Table 1.1 Urban sex ratios, selected countries in Global South regions

	Urban population (%)	Sex ratio (women per 100 men*)
Africa		
Benin (2011)	44.92	103
Botswana (2006)	56.42	111
Burkina Faso (2006)	22.70	100
Cape Verde (2003)	55.84	105
Cameroon (2005)	48.76	99
Ethiopia (2008)	16.69	101
Ghana (2010)	50.88	109
Kenya (2009)	32.34	99
Lesotho (2006)	22.61	117
Libyan Arab Jamahiriya (2006)	88.16	97
Malawi (2008)	15.32	97
Mauritius (2011)	40.37	104
Morocco (2007)	59.22	105
Namibia (2011)	42.75	105
Niger (2008)	19.22	100
Republic of South Sudan (2008)	17.01	86
Rwanda (2002)	16.89	89
Sao Tome and Principe (2001)	54.12	107
Senegal (2002)	45.38	106
Somalia (2002)	33.99	98
Sierra Leone (2010)	40.11	102
South Africa (2001)	57.20	105
Uganda (2002)	12.27	107
Swaziland (2013)	22.97	110
Zambia (2000)	35.85	101
Tanzania (2013)	27.39	102
Zimbabwe (2002)	34.64	103
Central America and the Caribbean		
Belize (2006)	50.45	107
Costa Rica (2013)	61.80	111
Bermudas (2010)	100	108
Cuba (2013)	76.82	105
Dominican Republic (2013)	68.36	102
El Salvador (2007)	62.65	115
Guatemala (2005)	49.97	107
Honduras (2007)	49.79	109
Jamaica (2011)	76.81	106
Mexico (2005)	76.49	106
Nicaragua (2009)	56.77	108
Panama (2013)	66.97	103
Saint Lucia (2001)	26.92	109
South America		
Argentina (2010)	91.23	105
Bolivia (2012)	67.49	105
Brazil (2010)	84.36	107
Chile (2013)	87.05	104

	Urban population (%)	Sex ratio (women per 100 men*)
Colombia (2013)	76.12	107
Ecuador (2013)	63.16	104
Guyana (2002)	28.45	107
Paraguay (2013)	59.22	104
Peru (2013)	75.65	102
Suriname (2004)	66.74	100
Uruguay (2011)	94.66	110
Venezuela (2011)	88.09	101
Asia		
Afghanistan (2012)	23.82	94
Armenia (2011)	63.31	113
Azerbaijan (2012)	53.11	103
Bangladesh (2011)	23.30	91
Bhutan (2013)	37.22	88
Brunei Darussalam (2001)	71.71	99
Cambodia (2013)	21.96	108
China (2010)	50.27	95
Cyprus (2001)	67.37	107
Georgia (2002)	52.27	118
India (2011)	31.14	93
Indonesia (2010)	49.79	99
Iran (2006)	71.39	99
Iraq (2013)	69.44	96
Israel (2012)	91.46	103
Japan (2010)	90.71	105
Jordan (2004)	78.32	94
Kazakhstan (2008)	53.15	115
Kyrgyzstan (2012)	33.50	112
Lao PDR (2005)	27.07	99
Malaysia (2011)	63.50	98
Maldives (2006)	34.68	99
Mongolia (2010)	67.92	106
Nepal (2011)	17.07	96
Oman (2009)	72.93	59
Pakistan (2007)	35.24	94
Republic of Korea (2010)	82.02	101
Sri Lanka (2001)	14.57	97
Syrian Arab Republic (2011)	53.48	95
Tajikistan (2011)	26.41	98
Thailand (2011)	34.50	109
Turkey (2012)	72.06	99
Uzbekistan (2001)	37.08	102
Viet Nam (2009)	29.63	106

Source: UNSD, 2013:Table 7, 150–245.

Note: * Rounded up to the nearest whole number.

(Chant and McIlwaine, 2009:chapter 3). The legacy of lower female mobility (especially as unaccompanied or unpartnered migrants) remains in evidence in India, for example. Here the contemporary sex ratio of 90 women per 100 men is lower than the all-India figure of 93.3, and in large – 'million plus' – Indian cities, which contain one-quarter of the country's urban population, there are only 86.1 women per 100 men (Khosla, 2009:18), while the figure is as low as 81.9 in the capital, Delhi (Gupta *et al.*, 2009:24).

Interestingly, as mentioned earlier, masculinised urban sex ratios in India are less pronounced in slums than they are in non-slum areas (Khosla, 2009:25). Indeed, as reported by Harriss-White *et al.* (2013:401), among the over-fifty age group in slums women outnumber men by an estimated ratio of five to one. Although there is some evidence that women in South Asia and sub-Saharan Africa are gaining ground in urban labour markets (see Kinyanjui, 2014), this is not always the case, with urban–rural earnings gaps in the latter being considerably more favourable for migrant men than women (Agesa, 2003:13; see also Hughes and Wickeri, 2011:800–1). Such discrepancies may help to account for Kenya's markedly masculinised urban sex ratio of only 68 women per 100 men (see Table 1.1).

In Africa more generally women's migration to towns is less likely to be induced by urban opportunities as compelled by rural pressures. The latter include growing reliance on female migration as a source of remittances to rural kin in the wake of economic deterioration in the countryside, rural women's cumulative disadvantage in land inheritance and acquisition, and mounting challenges attached to premature male death and desertion (see Tacoli, 2006, 2010; Tacoli and Chant, 2014; Tacoli *et al.*, 2015:25). In the specific context of South Africa, Debbie Budlender and Francine Lund (2011:935) maintain that rising numbers of female intra-national migrants to urban areas are due to women's increased financial responsibilities for children, which often mean that their older counterparts in rural localities take on the main duties of care. Additional factors, noted by Hughes and Wickeri (2011:837–8) for Tanzania, are that, aside from women being literally 'chased off their land' by relatives, including their own children (see also Huisman, 2005, on rural Zimbabwe), female movement is prompted by those who are HIV-positive to access medical treatment in cities, as well as to avoid stigmatisation. However, as reported by Kate Hawkins *et al.*(2013:25) on the basis of work by Chimaraoke Izugbara and Eliud Wekesa (2011) in the context of two major Nairobi slums – Viwandani and Korogocho – stigma, gossip and alienation by no means disappear in urban contexts. That said, the imperatives of escaping domestic violence and a range of other 'harmful traditional practices' that are often more common in rural areas can also be significant. These include female genital cutting (FGC), which remains more prevalent in villages than towns and cities, despite active campaigns to halt the practice (see Chant and Touray, 2013, on The Gambia).

Another potential set of factors explaining the general trend to feminising urban sex ratios, not only in sub-Saharan Africa but further afield, revolves around violence and conflict, which are particularly marked in urban areas (Moser and McIlwaine, 2014). In Latin America for example, violent deaths among men

Plate 1.6 Female circumcisors 'drop the knife' at a community declaration in Jarra Soma, Lower River Region, The Gambia, July 2011

Source: Sylvia Chant.

resulting from homicide, traffic accidents and suicide are four times those of women. In combination with declining rates of maternal mortality, this may also help to account for rising urban 'surpluses' of women (Tacoli, 2012:10; see also Chapter 6, this volume)

'Cities of older women'?

Stemming, to some degree, from the above-mentioned historical antecedents in migration, variations exist among regions with regard to age-related urban sex ratios. Yet regardless of the dynamics of gender-selective migration in different regions, demographic ageing appears to be more important still. In line with Harriss-White *et al.*'s (2013) observations for India, where feminised sex ratios are most pronounced among the elderly, this applies not only to all countries in Table 1.2, except Pakistan, but especially so among the 'older old' (over eighty years). In the sub-Saharan African and Latin American countries in Table 1.2, 'older old' women outnumber their male counterparts by around two to one, and this also appears to be the case in Malaysia.

That with few exceptions senior female citizens far outnumber their male peers raises major questions as to the prospects for women in general in urban environments in the immediate and longer-term future. In many places advanced

Table 1.2 Urban sex ratios by age group in the two most urbanised countries in major regions of the Global South

	Male	Female	Ratio (women per 100 men)*	Male	Female	Ratio (women per 100 men)*
Latin America and Caribbean						
Argentina				**Chile**		
0–9	3,047,061	2,910,666	96	1,110,867	1,072,012	97
10–19	3,141,694	3,036,252	97	1,142,531	1,142,531	100
20–29	3,053,037	2,995,716	98	1,255,638	1,240,935	99
30–39	2,746,545	2,761,572	101	1,074,927	1,089,617	101
40–49	2,074,678	2,158,838	104	1,056,274	1,093,370	104
50–59	1,723,552	1,927,332	112	890,296	961,310	108
60–69	1,234,502	1,486,135	120	537,721	625,795	116
70–79	416,654	1,062,550	255	273,258	375,538	137
80+	282,920	603,172	213	105,275	199,352	189
South Asia						
Pakistan				**India**		
0–9	6,268,896	6,252,086	100	33,070,904	29,869,728	90
10–19	7,026,712	6,458,385	92	38,342,516	34,186,179	89
20–29	5,042,054	4,736,979	94	33,694,701	35,520,621	105
30–39	3,061,395	3,133,043	102	30,520,302	29,240,847	96
40–49	2,619,642	2,403,447	94	24,253,995	22,233,208	92
50–59	1,660,107	1,437,958	87	15,973,202	14,348,805	90
60–69	945,657	771,223	82	9,506,172	9,405,003	99
70–79	407,480	336,385	83	4,050,499	4,199,529	104
80+	146,262	99,876	68	1,517,899	1,876,116	124

East Asia

Malaysia

Age	2008	2013	Index
0–9	1,581,328	1,508,210	96
10–19	1,703,714	1,607,301	97
20–29	1,475,142	1,450,249	98
30–39	1,480,706	1,547,310	101
40–49	1,303,076	1,289,925	104
50–59	936,058	889,306	112
60–69	450,406	430,573	120
70–79	166,115	190,475	255
80+	47,865	73,398	213

China

Age	2008	2013	Index
0–9	33,330,639	28,171,490	85
10–19	45,268,567	41,128,951	91
20–29	65,015,300	63,723,174	98
30–39	61,781,353	59,254,969	96
40–49	60,568,901	56,847,136	94
50–59	38,893,282	37,730,641	97
60–69	21,933,639	22,013,607	100
70–79	12,290,362	13,018,401	106
80+	3,958,740	5,076,394	128

Sub-Saharan Africa

Botswana

Age	2008	2013	Index
0–9	104,447	102,500	98
10–19	106,006	115,406	109
20–29	109,813	127,924	116
30–39	69,894	77,873	111
40–49	41,628	47,889	115
50–59	22,331	24,914	112
60–69	10,232	14,529	142
70+	8,695	16,200	186
80+	—	—	—

South Africa

Age	2008	2013	Index
0–9	2,239,013	2,245,532	100
10–19	2,415,481	2,494,414	103
20–29	2,605,192	2,615,933	100
30–39	2,136,640	2,197,267	103
40–49	1,516,133	1,604,555	106
50–59	864,085	936,059	108
60–69	442,785	593,123	134
70–79	201,473	315,431	157
80+	69,368	142,980	206

Sources: UNSD, 2008:Table 7, 155–253; 2013:Table 7, 150–245.

Notes: Table includes the two most urbanised countries for which data are available; * rounded up to nearest whole number.

age is associated with greater poverty, especially among women. In the context of research in low-income settlements in the southern Indian city of Chennai, for example, Penny Vera-Sanso (2010) notes that older women are not just vulnerable to poverty because of gender differentials in life expectancy, but because of large age gaps between husbands and wives and the stigmatisation of female remarriage, and because women tend to enter their later years with fewer resources than men due to multiple accumulated deprivations in education, incomes, property and social benefits.

As observed more generally by UN-Habitat (2012a:5):

> Globally, women earn less over a lifetime than men, yet they tend to live longer. Their lower earnings can be attributed to time out of the workforce for childbearing, caring and household responsibilities, and getting paid less for the same work as men. As a result, women in countries with limited social security may have little or no income when they reach retirement age. Some may continue to work or rely on other household members to provide for them. This is a growing concern in countries with ageing populations.

In some instances, such as Ghana and Costa Rica, greater filial support may be devoted to mothers on account of their more enduring presence in, and commitments to, children (see e.g., Aboderin, 2010; Chant, 2007a; Knodel and Ofstedal, 2003), or because older women may be particularly resource poor. The latter is exemplified by China, where research in the cities of Yiyang and Baoding in the interior provinces of Hunan and Hebei, respectively, indicates that only 43 per cent of elderly women are in receipt of pensions, compared with 91 per cent of their male counterparts (Zhan and Montgomery, 2003:224). Assistance in such contexts may entail co-residence with younger generations, as also observed in the context of the city of Salvador, Brazil, where many low-income households live in matrifocal arrangements comprising three or more generations (Sardenburg, 2010; see also Chant, 2007a, on Costa Rica; and Safa, 1995, on Cuba, Puerto Rico and the Dominican Republic). In other instances, however, older women may not only be widowed and in a situation of living alone, or heading their own households, but slip under the radar of mainstream – or even gender-specific – anti-poverty interventions (see Varley, 2013:131–2).

In whichever case, younger women may bear the fallout of feminised demographic ageing due to their routine position on the front line of duties of care for elderly (and infirm) relatives (Hawkins *et al.*, 2013:17), which in the context of China, may involve both personal care and financial assistance (see Zhan and Montgomery, 2003). By the same token, this should not detract from the fact that many older women continue working far into old age and/or play critical roles in performing unpaid domestic and care duties which have to be neglected by their younger counterparts as pressures mount upon them to engage in remunerated work (see Kelbert and Hossain, 2014; Pinn and Corry, 2011:171; Sardenburg, 2010; Vera-Sanso, 2010). In some cases, this may also involve grandmothers looking after their grandchildren directly, a phenomenon which is often especially marked in societies suffering huge losses of 'prime-age' female adults from HIV/ AIDS, as in South Africa, where fathers frequently shirk financial and other responsibilities for offspring (Budlender and Lund, 2011).

'Cities of female-headed households'?

The interrelationships between urbanisation and household structure are often very difficult to generalise, being heavily contingent on space, time, historical antecedents, migration and access to resources such as income and housing (Chant and McIlwaine, 2009:chapter 9; Tacoli and Chant, 2014). Indeed, despite a nominal tendency towards a nuclearisation of households in cities, compared with a purportedly greater prevalence of extended forms in rural areas, there is a very mixed bag of evidence supporting such a trajectory in different parts of the Global South, with extended household arrangements particularly common in many cities in Africa and Asia (see Adepoju and Mbugua, 1997; Chant and McIlwaine, 2009:chapter 9). One such case is South Africa, where, due to various phenomena such as the historical legacy of apartheid, long-term and long-distance male-selective migration, low levels of formal marriage, inadequate and inadequately enforced legislation governing paternal support, and high levels of AIDS-related deaths among prime-age adults, only around one-third of households conform to a 'nuclear norm', as many as one-fifth of households comprise three or more genera-tions, and several children (up to around one-third) live with neither biological parent (Budlender and Lund, 2011:926–7; see also Dubihlela and Dubihlela, 2014; Herselman, 2014:49–50; Rogan, 2013). Another, albeit contrasting, example is provided by China, where it is possible to see the maintenance of joint family ideals taking the form of multi-generational households, especially where senior citizens have retained public housing to which privatisation and commodification are making access more difficult among their children (see Li and Shin, 2013). Yet even if general trends in household composition remain elusive, headship is a different matter, with female-headed households seemingly widely on the rise, especially in towns and cities, and revealing important intersections with demo-graphic ageing. In many regions of the Global South, for example, the highest proportion of woman-headed households lies in the sixty-plus age group. In Latin America and the Caribbean aggregated data for seven countries suggest that 37 per cent of heads of household over sixty are female, and that women heads in the sixty-plus age bracket constitute well over one-third (39.8 per cent) of all female heads in the region, compared with a mere 18.1 per cent share of male heads in the sixty-plus category (Varley, 2014:401, Table 7.3.2). This is not only because women tend to outlive men, but because women are generally younger than their husbands, leading Varley (2013:131) to suggest that widowhood is 'above all a female experience, and one that will become increasingly common in the urban areas of less wealthy countries' (see also Lenoël, 2014:chapter 4, on Morocco; Weldegiorgis and Jayamohan, 2013:36, on Ethiopia).

This is not to deny that non-marriage, divorce and separation as routes to female household headship tend to be more prevalent in cities than in rural areas, and may outweigh widowhood despite demographic ageing (see Chant, 2015). This is even the case in patriarchally conservative countries such as Bangladesh, where in Rajshahi City Habib (2010:177, Table 1) found that only 32.9 per cent of female heads who were not presently married were widows, and the rest divorced, separated or 'abandoned'.

The feminisation of urban sex ratios is also undoubtedly significant in this equation, with numerous countries in Latin America, where these are most pronounced (see Table 1.1), indicating quite dramatic increases in the share of urban households headed by women over the past twenty to thirty years (see Table 1.3).

Between the early 1990s and the middle of the second decade of the twenty-first century, female-headed households as a proportion of all urban households in Latin America increased by a mean of 9.8 percentage points. Brazil saw the greatest rise with an 18-percentage-point increase, followed by Uruguay and Venezuela (both 16 percentage points). Overall, eight of the seventeen countries sampled witnessed a double-digit increase in the percentage of female-headed households. During the same period the average increase in urbanisation was 14.9 percentage points. Countries that were less urbanised at the outset, such as Costa Rica and the Dominican Republic, tended to experience the most dramatic rises (with increases of 25 and 20 percentage points, respectively), while those that were more urbanised at the beginning of this period, such as Argentina (increase of 5 percentage points), rose significantly less.

Yet, despite the general tendency for rising levels of female household headship in urban areas to parallel upward trends in urbanisation, there is no significant statistical relationship between the two (see Chant, 2011b). Lack of direct correspondence undoubtedly owes to the fact that the reasons driving both of these phenomena vary from country to country (including different starting points in levels of female household headship and/or urbanisation), as well as within countries and across metropolitan areas. What does seem to be the case, however, and bearing out the general point made earlier, is that female-headed households in several countries are more common in towns and cities than in the countryside. For example, in Costa Rica, a long-term and discernibly accentuating trend has led to female household headship in urban areas reaching 27 per cent, compared with 16 per cent in rural parts of the country (see Chant, 2007a). In Ecuador, 27.7 per cent of urban households are headed by women as against 21.5 per cent in rural areas (Benavides Llerena *et al.*, 2007:1.2), and in Brazil shares of female household headship are much higher in the metropolitan areas of the north and northeast of the country (at 35.2 per cent and 35.1 per cent, respectively, as of 2002), compared with 25.5 per cent at a national level (Sardenburg, 2010:91). Indeed, evidence from a survey of a low-income community in the metropolitan region of Salvador, where the proportion of households headed by women is 32.9 per cent, suggests an even greater incidence (44 per cent) among the poor (ibid.).

Outside Latin America, urban–rural differentials in household headship have also been observed. In Morocco, for example, where households headed by women increased to 18 per cent nationally in 2012 from 15 per cent in 1982, the share of female-headed households in urban areas is 20 per cent, compared with

Table 1.3 Female-headed households as a proportion of all households in urban areas of Latin America (selected countries), 1990–2014

	Years	Urban population as % of national population*	Percentage point change in urbanisation (earliest to latest year)	Percentage urban households headed by women (FHHs[†])[‡]	Percentage point change in FHHs (earliest to latest year)
Argentina	1990	87		21	
	2014	92	+5	(2012) 36	+15
Bolivia	1989	56		17	
	2014	68	+12	(2011) 23	+6
Brazil	1990	74		20	
	2014	85	+11	(2013) 38	+18
Chile	1990	83		21	
	2014	89	+6	(2011) 34	+13
Colombia	1991	66		24	
	2014	76	+10	(2013) 33	+9
Costa Rica	1990	51		23	
	2014	76	+25	(2013) 36	+13
Dominican Republic	1997	58		31	
	2014	78	+20	(2013)36	+5
Ecuador	1990	55		17	
	2014	64	+9	(2013) 26	+11
El Salvador	1995	54		31	
	2014	66	+12	(2012)36	+5
Guatemala	1987	39		20	
	2014	51	+12	(2006) 27	+7
Honduras	1990	41		27	
	2014	54	+13	(2010) 32	+5
Mexico	1989	71		16	
	2014	79	+8	(2012) 25	+9
Nicaragua	1993	54		35	
	2014	56	+2	(2009) 34	+1
Panama	1991	54		26	
	2014	66	+12	(2013) 32	+6
Paraguay	1990	49		20	
	2014	59	+10	(2013) 32	+12
Peru	2002	73		23	
	2014	78	+5	(2013) 26	+3
Uruguay	1990	89		25	
	2014	95	+6	(2013) 41	+16
Venezuela	1990	84		22	
	2014	89	+5	(2013) 38	+16

Sources: Chant, 2002:Table 1; 2013:Table 1; CEPAL, 2001:Table V.3, 151; 2010:Table 1.1.14, 36; 2013:Table 1.1.14; UN-DESA, 2014a:Table 1, 20–25; 2014b:150–245.

Notes:
* UN-DESA's World Urbanisation Prospects measures population at five-year intervals. When the year selected in the table is different from this, the closest available data point is used. The latest data point (for urbanisation) is 2014 for all countries. All values have been rounded to the nearest whole number.
† Female-headed housholds.
‡ Figures for 2000 and later have been rounded to the nearest whole number to match CEPAL data from earlier periods.

Plate 1.7 Four-generational female-headed household in a peri-urban slum in Santa Cruz, Costa Rica

Source: UN-Habitat/Sylvia Chant.

only 14 per cent in rural areas (see Lenoël, 2014:105). In Senegal, the proportion of households headed by women at a national level is 22.4 per cent, but is as much is 34 per cent in the capital Dakar (which houses 50 per cent of the country's urban population), and 39 per cent in other urban areas (Evans, 2015:79).

The tendency for female-headed households to be more prevalent in urban areas in Latin America, as well as in other parts of the developing world (see Tacoli and Chant, 2014:Table 48.2), is not just a function of demographics (see Chant, 1997; Habib, 2010; Momsen, 2002, 2010; Safa, 1995), but of a wide range of economic and social factors associated with urban environments. These include greater access to employment and independent earnings, diminished entanglement in, and control by, patriarchal kinship systems (e.g. Folbre, 1991; Lenoël, 2014:205), and higher levels of urban female land and property ownership (UNFPA, 2007:19; see also Chapter 3, this volume). Indeed, Bradshaw's (1995) research on Honduras points to inequitable land access in rural areas being a major factor in the intra-national transfer of female-headed households to towns and cities. And even where women may enjoy equal land rights in rural areas, they may be constrained in their ability to farm it because of lack of access to labour and capital, as well as cultural prohibitions, requiring the diversification of livelihood strategies that may be associated ultimately with permanent migration to urban centres (Tacoli and Chant, 2014).

This is not to suggest, however, that urban female-headed households are necessarily income-poor or otherwise disadvantaged. In fact, in many cases, experience of female household headship might be considered as a 'portable asset' (Bird *et al.*, 2010) insofar as it produces individual and collective momentum for addressing gender inequality (see Chant, 2015). That said, a continued and rather problematic sub-text, if not headline, in policy and popular discourse is that households headed by lone women (whether widowed, separated/divorced, or never married) are somehow inferior to a purported male-headed norm, and are either the 'poorest of the poor' or potentially more vulnerable to falling into this state (Chant, 1997; see also Chant, 2015; Chant and Brickell, 2013; Habib, 2010; Klasen *et al.*, 2015; Noh and Kim, 2015; Stewart-Withers, 2011; Varley, 2013; Weldegiorgis and Jayamohan, 2013).

Notwithstanding mixed and often contradictory evidence and interpretations, rising numbers of women (and women-headed households) in urban areas appear to give little guarantee that demographic momentum in itself will necessarily transform gendered hierarchies. This accordingly reaffirms the second of our justifications for an urgent 'en-gendering' of research on cities and slums in the contemporary Global South.

Urbanisation, gender, and the paradoxes of equality and inequality

Our second main rationale for considering gender in urban scholarship and policy in the Global South revolves around the major question as to whether urbanisation – which, in recent years, has come to be increasingly regarded in a favourable light – is necessarily a process that is associated with greater gender equality.

The new (or renewed) positive take on cities (discussed in more detail below) is due in large part to the idea that cities are responsible for generating a disproportionate share of the world's Gross National Product (GNP). Particularly popular with donors and international agencies such as the World Bank, this notion has recently been encapsulated in the concept of 'urban prosperity', which was the theme of both UN-Habitat's *State of the World's Cities 2012/13* and its *State of Women in Cities 2012/13*. As asserted in the original concept note for UN-Habitat's 2012/13 report, 'urban prosperity' is almost invariably a positive term, implying 'success, wealth, thriving conditions, wellbeing or good fortune' (UN-Habitat, 2010c:7).

While not denying that cities may well be vanguards of economic growth, and various other forms of well-being, it is vital to stress that they are also marked by extreme and often mounting inequalities. Gender is deeply implicated in this, such as in women bearing the brunt of poor living standards and livelihood possibilities, especially in slums. Also pertinent here is the mismatch between what women contribute to generating urban wealth, and what they stand to gain as stakeholders. Women play a significant role in contributing to the 'prosperity of cities' through providing essential services, contributing to urban housing stock, provisioning economically for households, and enhancing the 'quality of life' in their homes and communities. However, they are often the last to benefit in respect of 'decent work', equal pay, tenure rights, access to, and accumulation of, assets, personal safety and security, and representation in formal structures of urban governance. The persistent undervaluation of women's efforts, in terms of both inputs to and outcomes of the prosperity of cities, constitutes a compelling moral, economic, political and policy rationale to understand how prevailing inequalities between women and men play out in urban environments, and how these might most effectively be addressed. As summarised by UN-Habitat (2008d:2–3):

> The experience by men and women of a city is quite different. Spatial and organisational aspects of the city affect men and women in different ways. A gender-aware approach to urban development and its management would seek to ensure that both women and men obtain equal access to and control over the resources and opportunities offered by a city. It would also seek to ensure that the design, provision and management of public services benefits both women and men.

Prior to exploring in more detail some of the potential paradoxes between urbanisation and progress towards gender equality, it is important to flesh out in a little more detail the rationales behind conceptualising cities as 'arenas of prosperity', and how this might be especially pertinent in respect of gender.

Cities as arenas of 'prosperity': in what and whose terms?

As iterated above, the most common connotations of the 'prosperity of cities' are economic growth and material wealth.

Despite the unprecedented 'time–space compression' heralded by the 'digital revolution', and the ongoing integration of global markets, the spatial concentration, clustering and proximity characterising urban environments appear to remain crucial in the generation of prosperity (Keiner *et al.*, 2005; Perrons, 2004; Rodríguez-Pose and Crescenzi, 2008; Spence *et al.*, 2009). The link between cities and prosperity has been associated with something of a sea-change in attitudes to urbanisation in recent years. While neo-Malthusian perspectives highlighting the dangers of overly rapid growth and 'urban bias' were once (and in some circles continue to be) prominent in development discourse (Bryceson *et al.*, 2009; Chen and Ravallion, 2007; Jones and Corbridge, 2008, 2010), a more positive view of the potential for economic, social and human capital accumulation in cities has increasingly taken hold (see, e.g., Venables, 2009; World Bank, 2009b; also Beall *et al.*, 2010; Harris, 2015)(REFS). As proclaimed in the 2013 *Global Monitoring Report*, for example, 'Cities and towns are hubs of prosperity' (World Bank/IMF, 2013:8). Increasingly this seems to depend on direct foreign investment, with Arif Hasan *et al.* (2010:1) noting that most Asian agglomerations aiming to brand themselves as 'world-class cities' have tried to attract such investment through:

> a version of urban prosperity and aspiration consisting of communication networks, investment friendly infrastructure, iconic architecture and . . . tourism. This image has been aggressively promoted since the 1990s by international financial institutions, national and international corporate sectors and a number of UN agencies.

Even if the world's urban population has only just surpassed the 50 per cent 'tipping point', statistical data suggest that as much as 70 per cent of global Gross Domestic Product (GDP) is generated in cities (World Bank, 2009a; see also UN-Habitat, 2010c, 2012b). Although urban contributions to GDP tend to be greater absolutely and relatively in high-income economies, at a macro scale there is a broadly positive correlation between national levels of urbanisation and per capita GDP (Dobbs *et al.*, 2011; UN-Habitat 2010c, 2012b; World Bank, 2009b). This tendency has been linked with notions of cities not just being the outcome of 'development' but 'engines of growth' in their own right (Satterthwaite, 2007; McGranahan and Satterthwaite, 2014; UNFPA, 2007), even if there is rather less evidence of this in developing regions such as Africa and, to a slightly lesser extent, Latin America (UN-Habitat, 2010c:22–3).

Indeed, partly on account of geographically uneven evidence of the positive impacts of urbanisation, Ivan Turok and Gordon McGranahan (2013:465) are wary of subscribing to the view that urbanisation and 'development' necessarily go hand in hand, especially without systems of governance which 'seek out ways of enabling forms of urbanisation that contribute to growth, poverty reduction and environmental sustainability'. Leading on from the latter, there is also a big question around whether cities can be 'resilient' in the face of climate change, which often threatens the poorest groups of urban residents, especially those who live in slums (see Kovats *et al.*, 2014; Pinn and Corry, 2011:162–3; Satterthwaite and Dodman, 2013; Tacoli *et al.*, 2013), or who engage in outdoor work such as

Plate 1.8 Makati business district, Metro Manila, Philippines

Source: Sylvia Chant.

street-vending and construction (see Hoa *et al.*, 2013, on heat stress in the city of Da Nang, Vietnam).

Regional variations in urbanisation and 'prosperity'

Factors shaping the links between 'place' and 'prosperity', and specific urban places and prosperity (World Bank, 2009b), remain difficult to generalise, including, as they do, migratory flows, natural and social factor endowments, historical legacies (and anachronisms), and the logic of macro-economic shifts (see, e.g., Storper and Scott, 2009). It is also evident that '[h]igh levels of urbanisation alone are not sufficient to generate high levels of prosperity', and there may be a 'cut-off' point when societies are over 70 per cent urbanised, as applies to many parts of Latin America (UN-Habitat, 2010c:5).

Latin America

With an estimated urban population of 80 per cent as of 2014 (UN-DESA, 2014a:23), Latin America (and the Caribbean) has not only for some time had the highest share of people living in towns and cities in the world (see Rodgers *et al.*, 2011), but one of the most concentrated patterns of economic activity. Latin America's top-ten cities accounted for 35 per cent of GDP in the region in 2007

Plate 1.9 Panorama of northern Buenos Aires, Argentina

Source: Romi Savini.

(compared with 25–30 per cent in the USA and Europe; Dobbs *et al.*, 2011:13). As noted earlier, Latin America also has the lowest share of slum dwellers, at just under one-quarter of its urban population. However, while Latin American cities grew very rapidly in the past, and captured decided scale benefits, some analysts argue that they are running into trouble now for the same reason (Dobbs *et al.*, 2011). Among new 'diseconomies' are urban sprawl and hampered mobility. Another problem is that the physical expansion of some urban centres has engulfed neighbouring towns outside city jurisdictions. This has entailed the fragmentation of political boundaries, with the spread of management responsibilities among multiple bodies leading to uncoordinated planning and development (Campesi, 2010; Dobbs *et al.*, 2011:13; Moser, 2009). As a consequence the rate of population growth has already slowed in some of Latin America's major metropoli, inward migration has fallen, and people have begun moving to 'midsize cities' (Dobbs *et al.*, 2011:13). Considerations regarding environmental quality are a further factor in recent inter-urban migration in Latin America with evidence suggesting that concern about children's well-being has rendered women key drivers in decisions to move to smaller, less congested, and perceptibly less polluted, centres (see Izazola, 2004; Izazola *et al.*, 2006).

Asia

Although a far smaller proportion of the population in Asia is urban, at 48 per cent (UN-DESA, 2014a:21), the region houses half the world's urban population and the largest share of the world's mega cities (more than ten million inhabitants), with China (sometimes dubbed 'the new "workshop" or "factory" of the world') and India ('the new "office" of the world') (Ghosh, 2010:1) leading a distinctively novel wave of metropolitan expansion. On the heels of an average annual growth rate of 2.4 per cent, for example, India's urban inhabitants numbered 345 million in 2009, constituting 30 per cent of the national population (World Bank, 2011b: 167). By 2014, absolute numbers of urban dwellers had risen to over 410 million, representing 32 per cent of the total (UN-DESA, 2014a:21).

China's urban population is much larger than India's: 586 million people in 2009, equating to 44 per cent of the total population, compared with only 27 per cent ten years earlier, and 20 per cent in 1980, and reflecting an average annual urban population growth rate of 3.3 per cent (ibid.: 166; see also Yeh *et al.*, 2011). By 2011, the share of the Chinese population living in urban areas had surpassed 50 per cent (Turok and McGranahan, 2013:466), and in 2014 it had reached 54 per cent (UN-DESA, 2014a:21) This often takes dramatic forms in terms of individual urban trajectories. For example, Shenzhen in south-eastern coastal China was a village as recently as 1970, but it is now a mega city (Satterthwaite and Dodman, 2013:292). Moreover, by 2025, China is likely to have 225 cities with one million or more people residing in them, and a total urban population of a billion (Keith *et al.*, 2013:6).

Although urban per capita GDP is expected to rise by 9 per cent per year in India, and 10 per cent in China, and by 2025 China's cities will generate an anticipated 20 per cent of global GDP (Dobbs *et al.*, 2011:30), evidence remains mixed as to how such phenomenal economic growth rates intersect with increases in national or urban prosperity broadly defined. In China, on one hand, state investments in urban infrastructure (about seven times higher in per capita terms than India's) have been crucial in fuelling job growth, especially in industry. In turn this has produced a situation in which average household incomes in Chinese cities are nearly three times those in rural areas, which has plausibly 'helped to limit the socially disruptive effects of . . . massive population movement' (Turok and McGranahan, 2013:466). This differs substantially from India, 'where urban congestion, water shortages, squalid living conditions and public health conditions are rife' (ibid.). Indeed, although India's urban population in general grew at 3 per cent per annum between 1991 and 2001, and that in mega cities such as Chennai, Delhi, Mumbai and Kolkata at 4 per cent, the growth rate of slums was as high as 5 per cent (Gupta *et al.*, 2009:9). In light of this, India's recent launch of the Rajiv Awas Yojana (RAY) Programme, an initiative which follows on the heels of the Jawarharlal Nehru National Urban Renewal Mission (JNNURM), introduced in 2005, and which aimed to make India 'slum-free' between 2009 and 2014, may be somewhat overambitious, not to mention contentious, especially given that this often involves massive displacements of low-income inhabitants (Chaplin, 2011:67–8; see also Doshi, 2013; Meth, 2013; SEWA-IIHS, 2011). Indeed, although India's record on reducing poverty compares reasonably with those of other countries in Asia (Ghosh, 2010), poverty did not continue to decline significantly between 2004 and 2008, when India's annual GDP growth leapt to rates of between 7.1 and 9.3 per cent (ibid.:Table 2,13). This is possibly because post-1990 liberalisation in India has been accompanied by long-term trends towards mounting income inequalities, cutbacks in public expenditure, and rising shares of self-employment and informal work that have penalised the poor (ibid.:22; see also Chen, 2011). Thus, although Asia as a whole has been the most successful developing region to date in reducing the proportion of people living on less than $1.25 a day, which fell from 60 per cent to 16 per cent between 1990 and 2005 in Eastern Asia, and from 39 per cent to 19 per cent in Southeastern Asia, it is perhaps no surprise, given India's dominance within Southern Asia, that poverty incidence in this sub-region showed a much less impressive drop – from 49 per cent to 39 per cent (UN, 2010a:6–7). This leads Ghosh (2010) and Turok and McGranahan (2013), among others, to the conclusion that growth and global economic integration need to be more carefully managed.

Also important to bear in mind is that Gross National Income (GNI) per capita in the region remains substantially lower (less than half) than in Latin America and the Caribbean, at $3163 per capita in East Asia and the Pacific, and $1107 in South Asia (World Bank, 2011b:12; see also Table 1.4). None the less, and perhaps serving as a further caution against any automatic association between levels of urbanisation and 'prosperity' – and gender equality – East Asia and the Pacific has the highest aggregate regional score (0.467) on the UNDP's Gender Inequality Index (GII; see below).

Sub-Saharan Africa

Sub-Saharan Africa is still at a relatively early stage of urbanisation, with only around 40 per cent of its population settled in urban areas. While 143 of the region's cities which are included in the McKinsey Global Institute's 'Cityscope' database – comprising just over 2000 cities worldwide with populations of 150,000 or more in Western Europe and the USA, and 200,000 or more in the rest of the world – produce 50 per cent of the region's GDP, a figure that is anticipated to rise to 60 per cent by 2025 (Dobbs *et al.*, 2011:31), cities in sub-Saharan Africa, many of which are clustered on the west coast, but also on the eastern littoral, are beset by a range of challenges. These include high levels of poverty and informal economic activity, with the rate of slum growth more or less on a par with the regional urban growth rate of 4 per cent per annum (UNFPA, 2007; World Bank, 2011b:168). Indeed, as noted earlier, just over 60 per cent of sub-Saharan Africa's urban population resides in slums, and there is burgeoning and largely under-employed male youth bulge (UN-Habitat/UNECA, 2008). The common 'demonisation' of this group does little to counter potential threats to stability and development (see Mabala, 2011), nor to highlight the important gendered point that levels of unemployment among female youth are usually greater not only within this region but elsewhere (see Chant, forthcoming).

Although there may be some links between urbanisation and development in Africa (Turok and McGranahan, 2013:474–5), urbanisation may not so much reflect

Plate 1.10 Building and development in the 'Haven of Peace' (Dar es Salaam), Tanzania

Source: Sylvia Chant.

Table 1.4 GNI per capita, poverty, urbanisation and gender inequality in regions of the Global South

	Gross National Income (GNI) per capita ($)	Proportion of people living on less than $1.25 a day (International Poverty Line/IPL)	Distribution of the world's Multidimensional Poor (MDP)* living in developing countries	Level of urbanisation	Gender Inequality Index (GII)† (where 1 indicates equality according to selected indicators)	Global Gender Gap Index (GGGI)‡ (where 1 indicates equality according to selected indicators)	Social Institutions and Gender Index (SIGI)§ (where 0 indicates equality according to selected indicators)
Eastern Asia	3,163	16% (Eastern Asia)/19% (Southeastern Asia)	15%	45%	0.467	–	.0639
Southern Asia	1,107	39%	51%	30%	0.739	.655	.260
Latin America	7,007	8%	3%	79%	0.609	.691	.0178
Sub-Saharan Africa	1,125	51%	28%	37%	0.735	.645	.186
Middle East and Northern Africa	3,597	3% (Northern Africa)/6% (Western Asia)	2%	58%	0.699	.609	.203

Sources: Hausmann *et al.*, 2010; OECD, 2009; UN, 2010a), UNDP, 2010; World Bank, 2011b.

Notes:
Different sources define regions differently, which makes direct comparisons difficult. The World Bank and UNDP include data for Southeast Asian countries within their regional figure for Southern/Eastern Asia. Also, while UNDP provides data for 'Arab States', the UN differentiates between Northern African and Western Asian countries.
See also notes below.

* The UNDP's Multidimensional Poverty Index (MPI), which was introduced in 2010, has not been calculated for all countries as yet. Nor are regionally aggregated scores available, only the percentage distribution of the world's 1.75 billion multidimensionally poor as shown in the table. The MPI is a three-dimensional index comprising health (as measured by nutrition and child mortality), education (children enrolled and years of schooling) and living standards (comprising cooking fuel, toilet, water, electricity, floor material and basic assets, such as a radio or bicycle). 'Multidimensional poverty' is deemed to apply where people are deprived in at least 30 per cent of the ten weighted indicators. The score derived combines the percentage of the population who are multidimensionally poor with the average number of deprivations from which they suffer: the higher the score, the greater the level of multidimensional poverty.

† The UNDP's Gender Inequality Index (GII) aggregates inequalities in reproductive health (as measured by adolescent fertility and maternal mortality), 'empowerment' (share of parliamentary seats and higher education attainment levels) and labour market (labour force participation), produces a score between 0 and 1, with 0 representing the highest level of inequality, and 1 total equality. Note that the regional aggregate figure for the GII in this table is for East Asia and the Pacific.

‡ The World Economic Forum's Global Gender Gap Index (GGGI) is a composite of four 'pillars' consisting of fourteen variables. These include economic participation and opportunity (as quantified by measuring advancement, remuneration and participation gaps, where advancement is composed from the female to male ratio among legislators, senior officials and managers, and the female to male ratio among professional and technical workers), educational attainment (measured by primary, secondary and tertiary enrolment ratios and literacy rates), health and survival (sex ratio at birth and life expectancies) and political empowerment (female legislators and the ratio of female to male ministerial-level positions). Scores are produced through a four-step process, ranging from 0 to 1, with 1 representing the highest level of equality and 0 the greatest level of inequality. Note that the regional aggregate figure for the GGGI is for Asia and the Pacific.

§ The Organisation for Economic Cooperation and Development's Social Institutions and Gender Index is a measure of twelve social institutions variables categorised under five main areas: family code (early marriage, polygamy, parental authority and inheritance); physical integrity (violence against women and female genital mutilation); son preference (calculated from missing women); civil liberties (freedom of movement and freedom of dress); and ownership rights (women's access to land, women's access to property other than land and women's access to credit). Taken together, these produce a score between 0 and 1, with 0 representing the highest level of equality, and 1 very high inequality.

the 'pull of economic opportunities' as rural and frequently climate-change-related 'push factors' such as drought, falling agricultural prices and ethnic conflict.

Management and capacity problems for African cities are somewhat unsurprisingly presented as challenged by precipitate and rapid demographic expansion (Hughes and Wickeri, 2011; Poulsen, 2010). It is also important to note that a number of countries in the region are finding that economic growth is best assured through the export of primary commodities, whether mined or agricultural, which may not build the connection between urbanisation and development observed in other parts of the world (Turok and McGranahan, 2013:477). However, there are also new growth opportunities provided through the spread of telecommunications, which, coupled with better leadership and scale economies, has put African cities on the verge of productivity growth for the first time, notwithstanding that at various junctures in this volume it will be clear that the benefits have not yet reached women – or indeed many men – especially in the poorer segments of society.

As evidenced in the above discussion, prosperity is not an inevitable outcome of urbanisation: there are 'costs' to urbanisation as well as 'benefits' (Overman and Venables, 2010), and, in the absence of sound, growth-nurturing management, cities can just as readily become sinkholes of poverty and inequality. Indeed, despite the fact that urbanisation during the past six-plus decades has contributed to the creation of more wealth 'than in all previous history' (CLEP, 2008:1), rising levels of economic prosperity have been accompanied by mounting inequality in many parts of the world, not least in urban areas. As Cecilia Tacoli (2012:5) has commented: 'The unwelcome corollary of the shift in the distribution of the world's population towards urban areas is that poverty is increasingly located in cities and towns.' In addition, the existence of such large populations living in situations of shelter deprivation is scarcely justified when considering the wealth produced by, and within, cities.

Persistent poverty and poor living standards when compounded by glaring socio-economic disparities and lack of decent work are often associated with violence, crime, insecurity, and mental and physical ill-health, which are not only harmful to people's everyday lived experiences in cities, but can seriously impede potential for carving out successful livelihoods (see, e.g., Harpham, 2009; Jones and Rodgers, 2009; Krujit and Koonings, 2009; Loyka, 2011; Mitlin and Satterthwaite, 2013:chapter 3; Moser, 2004; Moser and McIlwaine, 2004, 2014; Rakodi, 2008; Rodgers *et al.*, 2011; UN-Habitat, 2010c:3; Wilkinson and Pickett, 2009). As summarised by the United Nations Fund for Population Activities: 'no country in the industrial age has ever achieved significant economic growth without urbanisation', but in developing countries in particular, '[t]he current concentration of poverty, slum growth and social disruption in cities does paint a threatening picture' (UNFPA, 2007:1).

'Urban prosperity' and 'smart' urban management

Awareness of the downsides of untrammelled urban growth – that prosperity does not automatically reduce poverty or inequality, and indeed can be compromised

Plate 1.11 Out-of-work members of a Gambian urban 'vous' (male social network) gather on the street

Source: UN-Habitat/Sylvia Chant.

by the latter – has spawned new ideas about concepts of urban prosperity and management. Until quite recently urban economic growth was prioritised in the belief that benefits would 'trickle down' from leading to lagging sectors, and many forms of inequality were tolerated in that light. However, it is now realised that favouring city management that prioritises social equitability, along with considerations of environment and employment, is best for growth, as proposed in 'smart growth' (Dierwechter, 2008; Duany *et al.*, 2010; Song and Ding, 2010) or 'smart cities' approaches (Filion, 2010; Geller, 2003).

The juxtaposition, and indeed frequent polarisation, of wealth and poverty in urban areas requires a concept of 'urban prosperity' that extends beyond economic growth and GDP. Too often economic development has led to gains for only a few, but high human and environmental costs for many. To be useful as a diagnostic and policy tool, the 'prosperity of cities' needs to be conceptualised as a broad, multi-dimensional entity which encompasses considerations of 'well-being' that extend to social, political and gender inclusivity and equity (UN-Habitat, 2010c; see also UN-Habitat, 2008b, 2010a). As summarised by UN-Habitat (2012b:v) in *State of the World's Cities 2012/13*, dedicated to urban prosperity:

> Prosperity . . . transcends narrow economic success to encompass a socially broad-based, balanced and resilient type of development . . . Cities can offer remedies to the worldwide crises. If only we put them in better positions to respond to challenges of our age, optimising resources and harnessing the potentialities of the future. This is the 'good' people-centred city.

Indeed, in UN-Habitat's recently launched 'City Prosperity Index', 'equity and social inclusion' ranks as one of five dimensions alongside productivity, quality of life, infrastructure development and environmental sustainability, with inequality deemed to be inconsistent with prosperity (ibid.:22).

Acknowledging the problems inherent in using such an 'all-embracing' definition of prosperity that can render it too broad to be useful (Wong, 2015), 'prosperous cities', as envisaged by UN-Habitat, are potentially capable not only of contributing to national economic growth but also of creating opportunities for employment and income for all citizens. As asserted by UNFPA (2007:1): 'Cities concentrate poverty, but they also represent the best hope of escaping it' (see also UN-Habitat, 2010c). In order to achieve this, 'prosperous cities' require equitable access to the necessities for building human capabilities and well-being such as services, infrastructure, livelihoods, housing and healthcare, alongside proper vehicles for civic engagement and multi-stakeholder governance. In its aspirations to greater social inclusivity and equality, the 'prosperous city' is also a space where women and men should enjoy equal rights and opportunities (ibid.:7).

An 'holistic' approach to urban prosperity is extremely welcome from a gender perspective, even if women and gender are actually rather seldom mentioned in *State of the World's Cities 2012/13*, and far from effectively 'mainstreamed'. None the less, the report does at least point out that 'cities that have removed impediments to the full engagement of women, youths and even the elderly have invariably enhanced overall prosperity' (UN-Habitat, 2012b:70). Moreover, the first ever *State of Women in Cities*, published shortly afterwards, makes the definitive point that reaping the benefits of urban prosperity should be a right for all women and men, and that a rounded concept of urban prosperity needs to countenance notions of 'rights to the city' (Lefebvre, 1986; Harvey, 2008), which are appropriately gender-conscious (UN-Habitat, 2013:6; see also Fenster, 2005a; Parnell and Pieterse, 2010; and Chapter 2, this volume).

An holistic and appropriately gender-sensitive concept of 'urban prosperity' also needs to go beyond the rhetoric of rights, to encourage deep analysis of why often poor women invest multidimensional inputs in generating urban prosperity, yet routinely suffer the brunt of multidimensional privations. Recent analyses of 'gendered poverty', and more particularly the so-called 'feminisation of poverty', for example, have demonstrated that women's poverty cannot be encapsulated by income alone (Chant, 2010; Fukuda-Parr, 1999; Johnsson-Latham, 2004; Rodenberg, 2004). Alternative formulations, such as the 'feminisation of responsibility and/or obligation' (Chant, 2007a, 2008, 2015), have stressed the importance of labour, time and assets, and the fact that privation is by no means primarily, let alone exclusively, associated with female household headship (see also Moser, 2010; Sassen, 2001, 2010). As such, this not only involves considering many non-economic phenomena, but acknowledgement that gendered privations in cities are not restricted to 'public spaces' such as polity and labour markets, but are often integrally related with the more 'private' space of the home. Indeed, neglect of the latter, which is often deeply infused with patriarchal power relations, has been a prominent criticism in feminist critiques of the gender blindness of the original Lefebvrian formulation of urban rights (see Fenster, 2005a). This is even if in some contexts the 'private' space of the home can be a site of security and belonging as well as of violence, oppression, alienation and asymmetrical gender relations, perhaps especially where women are under the jurisdiction of extended families as well as husbands (see Schütte, 2014, on Afghanistan).

Gender equality and 'smart' urban management

Thinking about gender in relation to prosperity arguably provides a sharper focus on the hiatus between women's inputs to and outcomes from the wealth-generating possibilities of cities. Indeed, insofar as more inclusive cities are good for growth, it has also been recognised that gender equality can make cities 'smarter' still (UN-Habitat, 2010b), albeit with the proviso that gender-aware and fair 'smart growth' clearly demands 'smart management' (Tsenkova, 2007). In 'prosperous cities' women may well achieve more equality with men, and the female (and male) working poor are likely to be able to pursue their livelihoods alongside larger, more formal economic activities. In turn, households, families, communities and local and national governments all allegedly gain from women's enhanced economic contributions, poverty is reduced and overall prosperity increases (Arbache *et al.*, 2010; Chen, 2010b). Since women lag behind men in key areas such as labour force participation, 'decent work', access to credit and infrastructure, and per capita

Plate 1.12 Generating urban prosperity on the rooftops of Marrakech, Morocco

Source: Sylvia Chant.

income (ibid.; see also Mukhopadhyay and Sudarshan, 2003; Song *et al.*, 2011), doing something about these disparities potentially puts an enormous amount back into the urban economy and fosters higher rates and quality of growth.

Recognition of this nexus chimes with the 'smart economics' approach to gender and development which proposes that investing in women's and girls' education and well-being makes sound developmental sense (Buvinic and King, 2007; World Bank, 2006b). As espoused in the *World Development Report 2012: Gender Equality and Development*, for example, 'Gender equality matters . . . as an instrument for development' (World Bank, 2011c:3). Notwithstanding cautions that 'smart economics' approaches may serve more to 'instrumentalise' women rather than promote their human rights (e.g. Chant, 2012a; Cornwall, 2014; Roberts, 2015; Zuckerman, 2007), it could well be the case that ends justify means, with all-round benefits for all stakeholders.

As discussed in greater detail later, poverty does tend to be lower, and per capita GDP higher, in countries with greater gender equality (Klein *et al.*, 2010; UMFPED, 2009; UN Women, 2011b:3), and economic growth can be positively linked with greater opportunities for levelling the playing field between women and men (Dollar and Gatti, 1999; Ellis *et al.*, 2006; Hovorka *et al.*, 2009; World Bank, 2006b, 2011c; World Bank and Ellis, 2007). As summarised by Morrison *et al.* (2010:103):

It is important to recognise that the relationship between economic development/growth and gender equality is two-way. The general view is that economic development and growth are good for gender equality, and conversely, that greater gender equality is good for development.

That said, it is important to recognise that 'two-way' does not necessarily mean 'reciprocal'. Naila Kabeer and Luisa Natali (2013:3) have raised concerns with regard to the 'asymmetrical' relationship between gender equality and economic growth, indicating that gender equality in education and employment contributes much more systematically to economic growth than economic growth does to reducing gender gaps in such arenas as health, well-being and rights. Juanita Elias (2013:159) also indicates, with particular reference to Singapore and Japan, that 'many top-ranking "competitive" economies perform exceptionally badly in terms of measures of gender equality and vice versa'.

In light of this, recent claims made by the World Bank/IMF (2013:101), such as 'the potential of urbanisation to close the gender gap in earnings and enhance women's empowerment is enormous', should undoubtedly be treated with some caution. While the space of the city in general might be regarded as presenting a series of opportunities for women to exit poverty and enjoy more gender-equitable shares of urban wealth, this is difficult to countenance for all women, especially those who live in slums.

Leading on from the above, and recognising that finer-grained analysis allowing for more precise determination of the links between gender and the urban (let alone intra-urban) situation remains elusive, even the broad-brush general data presented in Tables 1.4 and 1.5 indicate that there are some, but

Plate 1.13 Domestic-based piece workers in León's shoe industry, Mexico

Source: Sylvia Chant.

clearly no definitive, systematic correlations between levels of poverty, per capita GNI, urbanisation, equality and/or gender equality across developing regions.

Echoing the discussion earlier in this chapter, Table 1.4 reveals a strong fit between urbanisation and per capita GNI. We can also see a broad inverse relationship between per capita GNI and the incidence of poverty, despite some notable exceptions. For example, Northern Africa is less urbanised and has far lower average income than Latin America yet half its poverty incidence, which reflects marked inequality in the latter region. Although inequality now appears to be on the decline, thanks largely to substantial upturns in social spending in countries such as Brazil and Chile (see Loyka, 2011), as Table 1.5 indicates, Brazil, one of Latin America's most urbanised societies, suffers extreme polarisation. Similarly, although Sub-Saharan Africa has a higher average per capita GNI than South Asia, it has a far larger share of the population living in extreme poverty as measured by the International Poverty Line (see Table 1.4). This would appear to confirm earlier observations that economic prosperity does not always trickle down to the poor.

When it comes to the interrelationships of gender with these variables, results are also mixed. For example, the UNDP's Gender Inequality Index (GII) fails to correspond with any other of the selected indicators in Table 1.4, although some relationships can be found between its constituent components and dimensions of economic prosperity or urbanisation. While the World Economic Forum's Global Gender Gap Index (GGGI) does correlate with GNI to some degree, the relationship appears to be driven primarily by Latin America which, as already alluded to, is marked by pervasive inequality that appears to be associated with a pronounced gender gap in earned income. The Social Institutions and Gender Index (SIGI) exhibits more correlations with Table 1.4 indicators than the other gender inequality measures, showing a particularly strong relationship with GNI. As regional wealth increases, there is an accompanying increase in gender equality, as measured by the SIGI components. This may be due to the fact that wealthier countries have, on average, more and stronger social institutions which protect women. The SIGI also exhibits a strong positive correlation with the UNDP's Multidimensional Poverty Index (MPI). As a country decreases its share of multidimensional poverty (MDP), the SIGI moves closer towards equality.

While the indicators discussed above serve to highlight that there are some connections between gender equality, wealth, poverty and urbanisation, these cannot be precisely or consistently specified on the basis of quantitative measures. Regrettably, women are more often the 'losers' rather than the 'winners' in urban environments, as they are in societies more generally. Confounding factors include discrepancies in regional definitions among different organisations, as well as deficits in sex-disaggregated data.

Sex-disaggregated data, gender indicators and the post-2015 agenda

A dearth of comprehensive sex-disaggregated quantitative data, especially for poorer countries, compromises the full and/or reliable geographical coverage of

Table 1.5 Inequality (Gini coefficient),* percentage urban slum population, multi-dimensional poverty and gender inequality† in the three most urbanised countries in each major region of the Global South

	Percent urban UNSD, 2013	Percent urban slum population (2009, unless stated) UN-Habitat, 2013	Gini Coefficient World Bank, 2014	Multidimensional Poor (MPI) living in country UNDP, 2014	Gender Inequality Index (GII) (where 1 indicates equality according to selected indicators) UNDP, 2014; value 2013	Global Gender Gap Index (GGGI) (where 1 indicates equality according to selected indicators) Hausmann et al., 2014:Table 3	Social Institutions and Gender Index (SIGI) (where 0 indicates equality according to selected indicators) OECD, 2014
Latin America and Caribbean							
Argentina	91	20.8	44	0.015	0.381	0.732	0.0107
Chile	87	9 (2005)	51	–	0.355	0.698	–
Brazil	84	26.9	53	0.012	0.441	0.694	0.0458
South Asia							
Pakistan	35	46.6	30	30.237	0.563	0.552	0.3013
India	31	29.4	34	0.282	0.563	0.646	0.2650
Bangladesh	23	61.6	32	0.237	0.529	0.698	0.3900
East Asia							
Malaysia	64	–	46	0.026	0.210	0.652	–
China	50	29.1	37	0.186	0.202	0.683	0.1310
Lao PDR	27	79.3 (2005)	36	–	0.534	0.704	0.1445
Sub-Saharan Africa							
Gabon	–	38.7 (2005)	42	0.073	0.508	–	0.4022
Botswana	56	–	60	–	0.486	0.713	–
Cameroon	49	46.1	41	0.260	0.622	–	0.2803

Sources: Hausmann et al., 2014; OECD, 2014; UNDP, 2014; UN-Habitat, 2012b; UNSD, 2013; World Bank, 2014:Table 2.9.

Notes:

* The Gini Coefficient is a measure of the inequality of income or wealth distribution in a country. It is calculated from the ratio of two areas on a Lorenz curve. A value of 0 indicates total income equality: that is, all wealth is distributed equally among all members of the population. A value of 1 represents total inequality. So scores may range between 0 and 1. The Gini Coefficient has been criticised by some scholars who argue that it is not useful when comparing countries of very different population sizes. Furthermore, it says nothing of the absolute wealth of a country: a wealthy country and a poor country may have identical coefficients, but in the poor country many people may not have access to even basic necessities.

† For components of the GII, GGGI and SIGI, please refer to notes in Table 1.4.

aggregate gender indicators such as the GGGI and the SIGI (see Drechsler and Jütting, 2010). Although, accordingly, data on individual dimensions of gender are a more robust basis of comparison among countries (see Van Staveren, 2013), these are often narrow in scope.

The indicators for gender in MDG3, for example – notably the ratio of girls to boys enrolled in primary, secondary and tertiary education, women's share of non-agricultural employment, and proportion of seats held by national parliaments – exclude elements vital to women's lives such as quantification of gender-differentiated domestic labour and care burdens. They also fail to provide a picture of ordinary, and especially the poorest, women because data on female employment that is predominantly informal, among other things, are far from robust (Chant, 2006, 2007a; see also Buvinic and King, 2007). Although major progress in enhancing the quality and coverage of sex-disaggregated statistics on the informal economy has been achieved through collaborations between the ILO and other stakeholders such as WIEGO (Women in Informal Employment, Globalising and Organising) (see ILO, 2002; Williams and Lansky, 2013), it is no surprise that the lack of gender indicators in all MDGs, and the limited nature of MDG3 targets for women compared with the Beijing Platform for Action (BPFA) of 1995, provoked widespread debate and critique (e.g. Antrobus, 2004; Chant, 2007b; Johnsson-Latham, 2010; Saith, 2006; UNMP/TFEGE, 2005).

Feminist critiques of the MDGs have thus highlighted the problems not only of inadequate data but of crucial omissions in emphasis, leading to widespread consensus on the importance of prioritising hitherto neglected issues that encompass gender-differentiated domestic labour and care burdens, violence against women, wage discrimination, sexual and reproductive health and rights, asset and property ownership, and participation in private and public decision-making at all levels (UN Women, 2013:6). Notice has also been drawn to the lack of attention paid to transformation and the structural causes of gender inequalities which have obstructed advances (see GADN, 2013; Zuckerman, 2007). Despite some marked improvements in educational attainment and legislative change in recent years, for example, the MDGs and even the more far-reaching Beijing Platform for Action (BPFA) of 1995 have not brought about fundamental shifts in gender inequalities. As UN Women (2015a:9) point out in relation to latter: 'Overall progress . . . has been unacceptably slow with stagnation and even regress in some contexts. Change towards gender equality has not been deep enough; nor has it been irreversible.'

These critiques have fed directly into the 'post-2015 agenda' and the creation of the seventeen Sustainable Development Goals (SDGs) scheduled to replace the MDGs (see earlier). UN Women (2013) has called for a standalone goal of 'transformative change for gender equality, women's rights and women's empowerment', with a specific attempt to address the structural determinants of gender inequalities in relation to agency and human rights (see Box 1.3). Although the current iteration of the Open Working Group of the UN General Assembly on the SDGs has not taken all recommendations into account, violence, unpaid care and domestic work and reproductive rights have at least assumed greater visibility (UN Open Working Group, 2014; see also Box 1.4).

Box 1.3   UN Women's proposed SDG5 of 'transformative change for gender equality, women's rights and women's empowerment'

Component 1: Freedom from violence against women and girls

Targets:

- Prevent and respond to violence against women and girls.
- Change perceptions, attitudes and behaviours that condone and justify violence against women and girls.
- Ensure security, support services and justice for women and girls.

Component 2: Gender equality in capabilities and resources

Targets:

- Eradicate women's poverty.
- Promote decent work for women.
- Build women's access to, and control over, productive assets.
- Reduce women's time burdens.
- Promote education and skills for women and girls.
- Improve women's and girls' health.
- Reduce maternal mortality and ensure women's and girls' sexual and reproductive health, and reproductive rights.
- Ensure women's sustainable access to energy.
- Ensure women's sustainable access to water and sanitation.

Component 3: Gender equality in decision-making power in public and private institutions

Targets:

- Promote equal decision-making in households.
- Promote participation in public institutions.
- Promote women's leadership in the private sector.
- Strengthen women's collective action.

Source: UN Women, 2013.

Notwithstanding this broadened range of criteria, major problems include that they still fail overwhelmingly to differentiate among women and men in different circumstances, socially or geographically, especially in terms of rural–urban residence and intra-urban heterogeneity. This is undoubtedly partly a function of

---

Box 1.4   UN Open Working Group on Sustainable Development Goals (SDGs): Goal 5: 'Achieve gender equality and empower all women and girls'

- 5.1 End all forms of discrimination against all women and girls everywhere.
- 5.2 Eliminate all forms of violence against all women and girls in public and private spheres, including trafficking and sexual and other types of exploitation.
- 5.3 Eliminate all harmful practices, such as child, early and forced marriage and female genital mutilations.
- 5.4 Recognise and value unpaid care and domestic work through the provision of public services, infrastructure and social protection policies, and the promotion of shared responsibility within the household and the family as nationally appropriate.
- 5.5 Ensure women's full and effective participation and equal opportunities for leadership at all levels of decision-making in political, economic and public life.
- 5.6 Ensure universal access to sexual and reproductive health and reproductive rights as agreed in accordance with the Programme of Action of the ICPD and the Beijing Platform for Action and the outcome documents of their review conferences.
- 5.a Undertake reforms to give women equal rights to economic resources, as well as access to ownership and control over land and other forms of property, financial services, inheritance, and natural resources in accordance with national laws.
- 5.b Enhance the use of enabling technologies, in particular ICT, to promote women's empowerment.
- 5.c Adopt and strengthen sound policies and enforceable legislation for the promotion of gender equality and the empowerment of all women and girls at all levels.

Source: UN Open Working Group, 2014.

---

the fact that sex-disaggregated information for different groups of women (or men) beyond household headship, for example, along lines of age, ethnicity, migrant status and so on, is likely to remain scarce (see Chant, 2006). Some data pertinent to differences among women per se, and between women and men, may also be difficult to obtain due to their political sensitivity. For example, given that cities may harbour less discrimination and more opportunities for networking and community formation among LGBT people (see, e.g., Jarvis *et al.*, 2009; Storper and Scott, 2009; Williams, 2010), such data are important, but elusive. However, there are also cases where relatively little is known about more basic aspects of gender in urban environments, which are technically amenable to measurement, such as gender differences in land and property ownership (Chant, 2006; Deere and Doss, 2006; Miraftab, 2001; Morrison *et al.*, 2010; Rakodi, 2014). This is notwithstanding that widespread informal occupation of land in developing world cities presents barriers to the gathering of exact and/or verifiable information (see Rakodi, 2010; UN-Habitat, 2005).

Data are also paltry when it comes to comparing women and men in relation to the wealthier and poorer parts of cities, which usually correspond with 'non-slum' and 'slum' settlements, respectively. As pointed out by Chandrasekhar and Mukhopadhyay (2008:3), among others: 'Despite evidence suggesting the heterogeneity of living standards within a city, rigorous examination of intracity differences in well-being is lacking.' And even less is known about transient populations in the city, and those who live or spend the vast majority of their time 'on the streets' (see Jones and Thomas de Benítez, 2010).

In light of this, data gathering has been reaffirmed as central to monitoring progress of gender equality and women's empowerment for the post-2015 era, and indeed UN Women (2015a:57) has called for a 'data revolution' in order to assess gender equality in all its complex forms, which should include quantitative and qualitative dimensions. With due attention to differentiated spaces this would certainly forge a pathway to enhancing greater appreciation of gender disparities in cities and slums, and help to do away with often speculative, superficial and simplistic over-generalisations of the 'gender question' in urban areas generally, and in the Global South in particular.

Concluding comments

This chapter has established the importance of exploring the experiences of women in cities in the Global South with a particular focus on those living in slum communities. In light of the evolution towards a 'feminised urban future' where women will comprise the majority urban population, we argue that it is essential to consider their contributions to urbanisation processes empirically, conceptually and in policy terms. While acknowledging that gender inequalities are widespread in cities of the South, we also hope to explore how these cities and urban areas more generally can be potentially emancipatory arenas if appropriate conditions and interventions are nurtured. Having established the core rationales for the book, and the background to gender in cities in what Jo Beall and Sean Fox (2009) have described as the 'first urban century', the next chapter proceeds to outline some core conceptual building blocks for understanding the significance of variegated spaces and social processes in the context of the 'gender–urban–slum interface' in the Global South.

2 Analysing gender in cities of the South

Introducing the 'gender–urban–slum interface'

Gendered urban analysis and policy in the South: historical antecedents

Calls to 'en-gender' urban analysis, policy and planning stretch back several decades, with Manuel Castells being one of the first scholars to point out how the traditional of invisibility of women in and beyond the academy led to flawed assumptions about the working of cities. In his book *Cities, Class and Power*, published in the late 1970s, for example, Castells famously articulated that:

> the subordinate role of women ... enables the minimal maintenance of its [the city's] housing, transport and public facilities ... because women guarantee unpaid transportation [movement of people and merchandise)] because they repair their homes, because they make meals when there are no canteens, because they spend more time shopping around, because they look after others' children when there are no nurseries and because they offer 'free entertainment' to the producers when there is a social vacuum and an absence of cultural creativity ... if women who 'do nothing' ever stopped to do 'only that', the whole urban structure as we know it would become completely incapable of maintaining its functions.
>
> (Castells, 1978:177–8)

As part and parcel of growing scholarly and policy interest in gender associated with the UN Decade for Women (1975–1985), recognition has steadily mounted not only of women's under-valorised contributions to urban life, but also of their various forms of exclusion from urban public spaces – whether physical, cultural or economic – and how they are seriously disadvantaged in spheres such as housing, and urban services (see UN-Habitat, 2008d:3; see also Ortíz Guitart *et al.*, 2014). In turn, feminist analyses have exhorted acknowledgement that the urban built environment in general, and its multiple component spaces, are typically constituted by, as well as constitutive of, gender-discriminatory processes, which reinforce one another in a complex panoply of ways (see, e.g., Chant and Datu, 2011a, 2011b, 2015; Frye *et al.*, 2008; Jarvis *et al.*, 2009; Massey, 1994, 1995; McDowell, 1983, 1999; McIlwaine, 2011).

While many feminist scholars embarked on analysing cities from a gender perspective in the 1980s, most studies at that time were concentrated in the Global North, with one of the few exceptions being the path-breaking work of Caroline Moser (1986), who not only synthesised evidence for 'gender-blindness' in urban analysis and planning in southern cities – for example in relation to housing, services, transport and employment – but also adapted Maxine Molyneux's (1984) concept of 'practical' and 'strategic gender interests' as a diagnostic and policy tool for shaping gender interventions in urban environments. Retaining Molyneux's original theoretical distinction between 'practical' and 'strategic', but substituting the term 'interests' to 'needs', Moser drew attention to urban planning interventions which addressed 'practical gender needs' in the context of women's immediate, material concerns in their stereotyped roles as wives and mothers, whether in the form of improved water supply, sanitation, electrification and so on, but did not, in themselves, unsettle existing gender divisions of labour and power. This was in contrast to initiatives which were oriented to a set of 'strategic gender needs' which entailed transformations towards a more equitable gendered order – for example, through consciousness-raising, negotiation around, and resistance to, prevailing gendered norms.

While recognising that practical and strategic gender needs are not necessarily bipolar opposites, and that strategic gender needs (or interests) can evolve out of practical interventions, especially those which encourage collective action among women, the fact is that it has taken a remarkably long time for ideas relating to 'en-gendering' the urban environment to filter through into dedicated and systematic urban policies and programmes that even address, let alone transform, gender. In light of this, Moser's (1995:225) comment of twenty years ago could perhaps be as readily applied on the eve of the post-2015 agenda:

> Although more marked in the 1960s and 1970s than it is today, gender blindness still prevents many researchers from appreciating the pivotal nature of gender relations in determining women's participation in urban life, their roles in resolving urban problems, and planning for urban futures.

The historical invisibility of women in cities and urban policy is due, inter alia, to under-valorisation and undercounting of women's work, male bias and gender-blindness in design and planning (Greed, 1994; Little, 1994; Malaza *et al.*, 2009; Reeves, 2002). Gender discrimination in society at large is also relevant here, with a general sidelining of socially reproductive labour, and a false dichotomy between 'private' and 'public' spaces (Frye *et al.*, 2008:618). As summarised by Helen Jarvis, Jonathan Cloke and Paula Kantor (2009:23–4; see also Dunaway, 2014):

> The most enduring argument for why cities are gendered in their construction and spatial arrangement resides with the (false) separation of discrete functions of production, consumption and social reproduction. Production entails not only the 'making' of things but the whole chain of commodities and services bought and sold in a capitalist economy. Social reproduction

covers all of those activities that are fundamental to the continued maintenance of human life (subsequent generations) and social existence. In the urban survival economies of the poor in the global south the household itself is a vital source of production and here there is a complete erosion of the boundaries between livelihood and household, spatially, physically and economically. Thus, what it actually takes to reproduce cities and daily life for urban poor and rich alike goes far beyond biological reproduction to encompass all of the mundane, typically unpaid (and disregarded) activities of feeding, clothing, sheltering and caring for current and future wage workers and all those whom the wage economy no longer had or never had any intention of rewarding in exchange for productive labour.

In their recent review of forty years of academic scholarship on social justice and the city, Ruth Fincher and Kurt Iveson (2012:233) point out that over time there has been a shift away from concentrating mainly on economic inequalities (most notably between wealth and poverty) to embracing other 'axes of difference' in cities, such as gender, ethnicity, sexuality and age, in their own right. The same authors also observe a transition from normative/prescriptive theoretical thinking about justice, to focusing more on 'procedure, process and the hearing of multiple voices . . . especially in urban planning' (ibid.:232). Part and parcel of making the process of analysis and planning more participatory and gender-aware has involved drawing attention to the diversity of households in urban areas, including women-headed households (Moser, 1986; see also Chant, 1996; Greed, 1994; Malaza *et al.*, 2009; also see below).

While these are welcome developments, and notwithstanding considerable theoretical strides in understanding gender in cities (e.g. Beall, 1996; Bruce and Köhn, 1986; Castells, 1978; Chant, 1996, 2007b; Greed, 1994; Jarvis *et al.*, 2009; Khosla, 2009; Massey, 1994; McDowell, 1983, 1999; Moser, 1986, 1995), as Jarvis *et al.* (2009:1) contend: 'the systematic treatment of urban and gender studies, as co-constitutive subjects, remains long overdue'.

Moser (2014) further notes how gender planning in urban areas remains constrained in its ability to bring about genuine transformations in roles, relations and inequalities between women and men. This she attributes to the tensions between political and technical/instrumental forces, and the chasm between theory and practice. Despite rhetorical gestures to transforming social relations, new emphasis on results-based management and evidence-based policy and planning also constitute a major brake on progress.

Disturbingly too, while women's poverty and disadvantage remain the foci of analytical and policy work on the city, these issues are inadequately 'mainstreamed', and often fail to take into account the particular challenges of slum dwelling, which are deeply implicated in the imbalance between women's inputs to, and outcomes from, 'urban prosperity', as discussed in Chapter 1.

The 'gender–urban–slum interface': principles and parameters

Taking our lead from a growing body of feminist scholarship on cities in general, any framework for analysing the interrelations between gender and the urban has to be holistic in scope, comprising different issues and spaces while also recognising their connectivities and intersectionalities (Chant and Datu, 2011b, 2015). Figure 2.1 provides a graphic representation of our baseline schema for approaching our investigation into gender inequalities in cities through a multidimensional, multi-spatial and multi-scalar lens.

The key criteria in Figure 2.1 combine recognition of major gender divisions and inequalities with specification of potentially crucial entry points to addressing women's equal rights to the city. By including micro-level spaces as households, and issues such as reproductive and sexual health and rights, this extends classic but arguably rather gender-blind Lefevbrian and de Certeauesque analyses which have

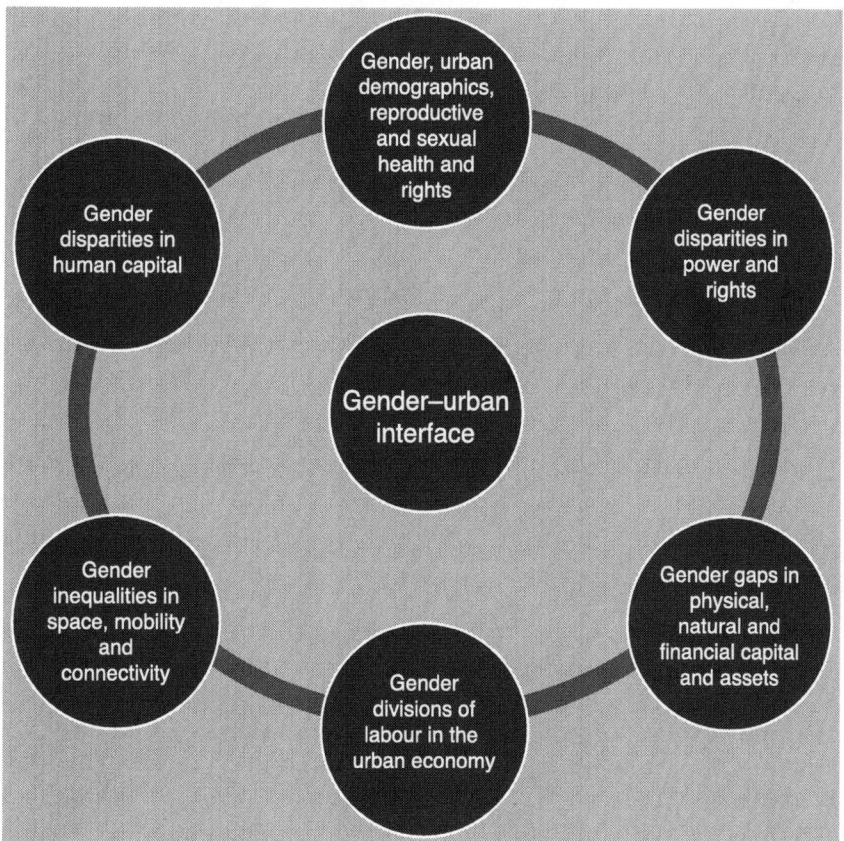

Figure 2.1 Conceptualising the gender–urban interface: critical dimensions and spaces

Source: Adapted from and elaborated on basis of Chant, 2011b:Figure 1.1.

historically dominated right to the city debates in mainstream literature (Fenster, 2005a, 2005b; Secor, 2004). Furthermore, it bolsters other important claims for a rights-based approach to the Southern city in ways that move beyond individual, so-called 'first-generation' rights that focus only on democracy, education and health, to include socio-economic rights at different scales (Parnell and Pieterse, 2010:149). While the issues identified in our schema do not map directly on the generations of rights, there is a high degree of resonance. Thus, 'second-generation' rights at the household level encompass housing, water, energy and waste services as well as 'third-generation' rights at the neighbourhood level linked with entitlements such as safety, social amenities and public transport (ibid.).

Our emphasis on rights not only aligns with the centrality of gender to rights-based development (Cornwall and Molyneux, 2006, 2008), but also resonates with the mounting importance of asset accumulation approaches for understanding well-being in cities. Underpinned by core theorisations of capabilities associated with, inter alia, Martha Nussbaum (2000) and Amartya Sen (1999), and building on earlier work by Moser (2009), and Moser and McIlwaine (2004, 2006) in relation to urban violence, the most recent iteration of a gender-sensitive urban asset framework has been presented by Moser (2015) in the context of 'just cities'. Here she pinpoints how the accumulation of a diverse range of assets can lead to female empowerment and gender transformation, albeit in variegated and often diffuse ways.

The main criteria pertinent to each of the major sets of dimensions in Figure 2.1 are summarised in Figure 2.2, which also highlights some of the cross-cutting issues that particularly affect female slum dwellers, such as time, income, health and well-being, violence and security, stability, politics and governance, and climate change. Collectively these constitute the core intersecting elements in the 'gender–urban–slum interface', which not only provides the framework for the present volume, but also offers a means for thinking through policy and programme interventions that can begin to address the widespread neglect or marginalisation of gender in urban planning to date. A brief introduction follows to each of the key components, which are then followed up in more detail in subsequent chapters.

Gender and urban demographics: fertility and reproductive rights

Chapter 1 highlighted how cities are becoming ever more feminised spaces in many developing countries, with rises in proportions of older women in urban populations, and increased shares of female-headed households. However, one demographic factor not covered in that discussion pertains to fertility and reproductive rights, which arguably have major significance in respect of gender in urban areas.

As background to this issue, the demographer Tim Dyson (2010) has contended (controversially, if persuasively) that the relationship between the purportedly global 'demographic transition' and urbanisation is even stronger than that between urbanisation and economic development. An integral aspect of the

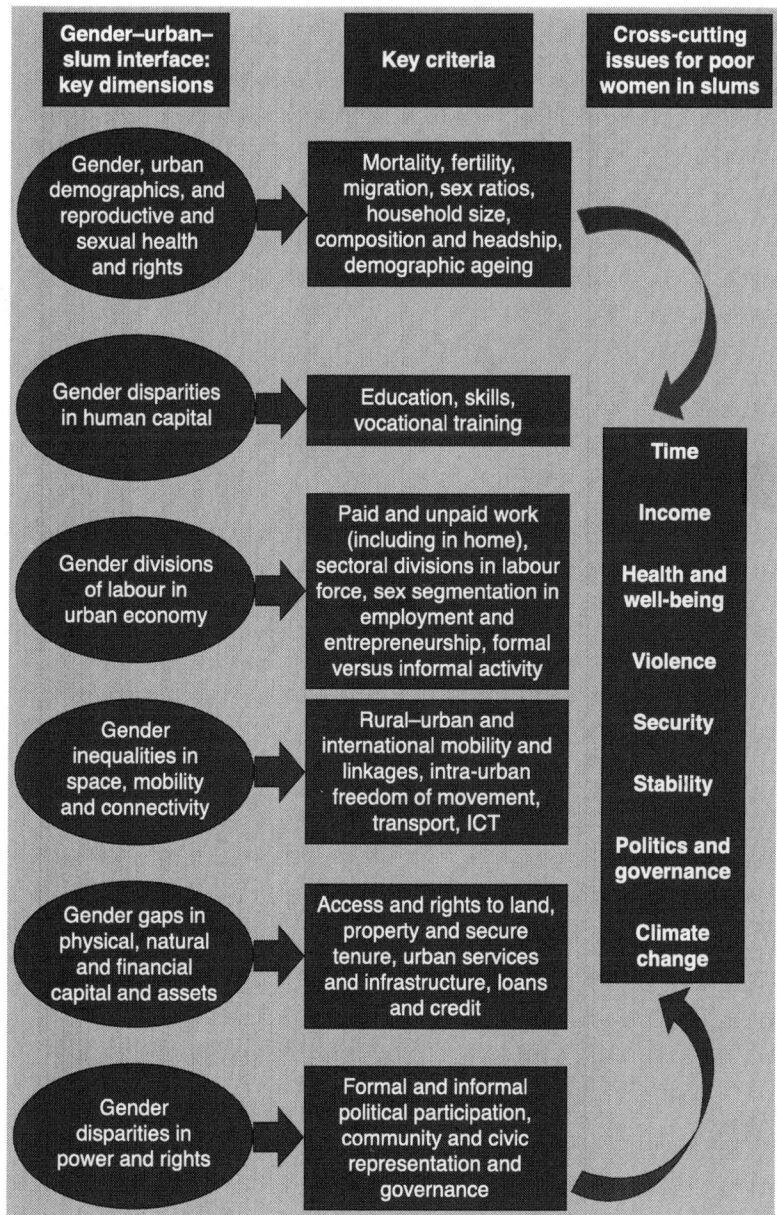

Figure 2.2 (De)constructing the 'gender–urban–slum interface': criteria and cross-cutting issues for understanding gendered inequalities in slums

demographic transition is lower fertility, which Dyson deems integral to women's progressive 'emancipation' (see also UNFPA, 2007).

Certainly there is considerable evidence that women in urban areas are likely to have lower birth rates, even where births in general remain high. In Senegal as a whole, for instance, the Total Fertility Rate (TFR, which refers to the average number of children a woman aged 15-49 is likely to bear in her lifetime) is 5.1, whereas it is only 3.7 in the capital city of Dakar, and 4.1 in other urban areas (Evans, 2015:91–2n). In neighbouring Gambia, the TFR is 5.6 nationally, but in urban areas only 4.7, compared with a rural rate of 6.8 (GBI/MDII, 2013:6). Although only 9 per cent of currently married women in the Gambia use a contraceptive method of any kind (and only 8 per cent a modern method such as the pill or Depo-Provera injections), contraceptive adoption by women is three times higher in urban as opposed to rural areas (ibid.:8).

Similar urban–rural differentials have been found in the multi-country grassroots survey carried out for the World Bank's *World Development Report 2012* on 'Gender Equality and Development' (World Bank, 2011c), with Ana Maria Muñoz-Boudet *et al.* (2012:90) concluding that 'Urban women – probably due to their exposure to relaxed norms, more certain supply of contraceptives, and better economic opportunities – were more likely than rural women to have less than three children.' In countries such as China, birth rates are also lower in urban areas: while son preference has long been common in a context of state-imposed restrictions on multiple births, urban couples tend to show weaker levels of discrimination against daughters than their rural counterparts (Murphy *et al.*, 2011).

However, despite generally lower TFRs in urban areas, access to safe and adequate contraception is uneven across individuals and urban spaces, as is its perceived relevance to people's lives, with the result that fertility is commonly higher among poorer groups of the population and in slums than in wealthier urban neighbourhoods (see Chant and McIlwaine, 2009:chapter 3; Martine *et al.*, 2013; Montgomery *et al.*, 2004). In Bangladesh, for instance, where an estimated 27 per cent of the population is urban, the TFR in slums is 2.5 (just under the national rate of 2.6), compared with 1.9 in non-slum settlements (Schuurman, 2009). As another example, in India's major cities the TFR is often higher by 0.2–0.5 births in slums than in non-slum areas (Gupta *et al.*, 2009:43). These disparities owe to a constellation of factors, including lack of information on reproductive health, unmet needs for family planning, and an above-average incidence of early pregnancy and marriage in deprived communities (ibid.). As many as 64 per cent of women aged 20–24 years in Bangladeshi slums, for instance, were mothers before the age of 20, as against 44 per cent in non-slum areas (Schuurman, 2009). Similar patterns obtain in a range of other countries for which data are available, and also show that this is often associated with early school dropout among girls (see Figure 2.3). This undoubtedly plays a part in undermining women's possibilities for attaining the socio-economic mobility so often associated with urban residence, and which is commonly regarded as vital in advancing gender equality. Indeed, in their extensive and critical review of the

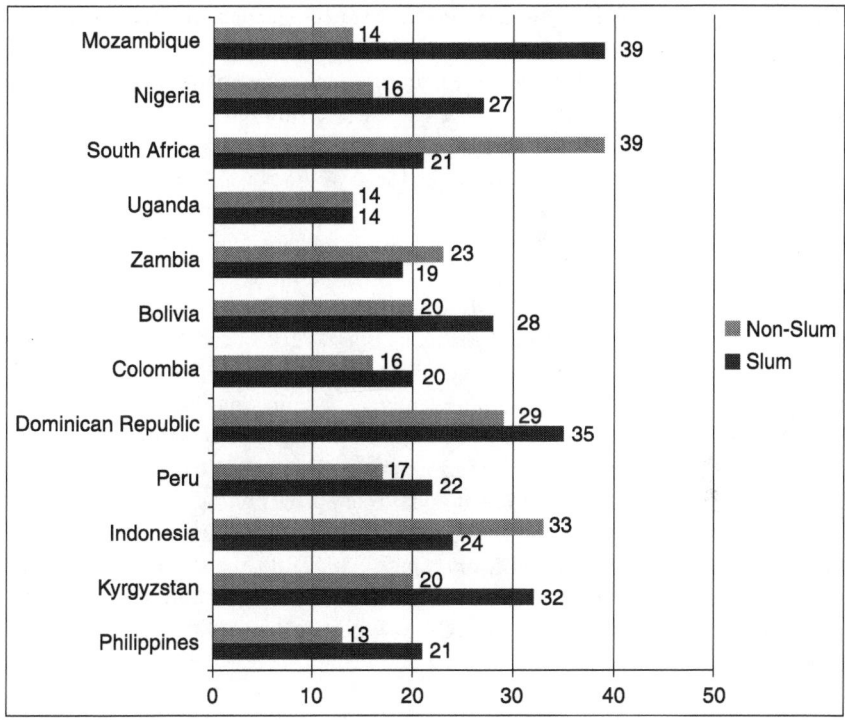

Figure 2.3 Female school dropout due to pregnancy and early marriage, slum and non-slum residence in selected countries of the Global South (percentage)

Source: Adapted from UN-Habitat, 2013e:Figure 2.9, 23.

interconnections between urbanisation and fertility decline, George Martine *et al.* (2013:38) conclude that only in cases where urbanisation is properly managed, and associated with progress towards socio-economic development which increases people's aspirations and their incentives to reduce birth rates, are there likely to be significant interrelations between urbanisation and fertility reduction. From the perspective of these authors, 'the exercise of citizenship is the best contraceptive' (ibid.), whether in rural or urban areas, even if urbanisation tends to accelerate the fertility transition.

Over and above the significance of place of residence in the city, the ability of some young urban women to exert control over their own fertility may be mediated by disparities between their age and economic status and those of male partners on whom they may rely for support (see Chant and Touray, 2013). As for women more generally, they may be dissuaded from, or denied rights to use, birth control where paternity is socially important to men and their natal kin and/or where as a marker of masculinity men not only forbid contraceptive adoption by their wives or female partners but also eschew personal use (Chant with Craske, 2003:chapter 4; Chant and McIlwaine, 2009:chapter 3; Touray, 2006). The role of coercive sex in situations of poverty should not be discounted either (see, e.g., Kamndaya *et al.*, 2015).

Notwithstanding that children are likely to be important economic, social and emotional resources for poor urban residents (e.g. Purewal, 2002; also Chant, 2007a; Smith, 2004), as well as a way of women legitimising their identities, women's lack of basic 'reproductive rights' such as the power to control their own bodies, or to determine the number and spacing of their pregnancies, is likely to be indicative of a lack of rights in other arenas, perhaps most notably sexual, as well as a barrier to the attainment of other rights (see, e.g., Cornwall *et al.* 2008; Corrêa, 2008; Petchesky and Judd, 1998). Moreover, while a potential 'care dividend' may accrue from lower births, it is critical to bear in mind that care needs and burdens are not so much determined by the ratio of young children to adults, as by social, political, cultural and economic factors, and by locally prevailing notions of 'good care' which are almost always gendered (UNRISD, 2010a:190). Indeed, in a context of ageing populations (see earlier) women are also predominantly in the front line of unpaid care provision for elderly people, as well as for the infirm (see, e.g., Bibler and Zuckerman, 2013; McNay, 2005; Ofstedal *et al.*, 2004; Zhan and Montgomery, 2003). In the context of contemporary demographic and economic trends, especially in urban areas, this clearly represents a major policy challenge (Chant with Craske, 2003:chapter 4; Varley and Blasco, 2000).

Plate 2.1 Male condom marketing, Greater Banjul, The Gambia

Source: Sylvia Chant.

Gendered divisions of labour in the urban economy

Another crucial element in the 'gender–urban–slum interface' relates to gender divisions of labour. Despite the primary role of employment in people's livelihoods (see Biles, 2008; Chen, 2010b; González de la Rocha, 2007; Moser, 2006, 2009; Rakodi, 2008:255), the health of urban economies owes as much to the unpaid 'reproductive' labour which goes on within households and communities as to the more formally acknowledged and valued arenas of human endeavour such as remunerated work which is registered in GDP and in the System of National Accounts (SNA) (see, e.g., Perrons, 2010; Razavi, 2007:4–5; UNRISD, 2010b). Indeed, for this reason, and recognising considerable overlap between various paid and unpaid activities relating to care (see Box 2.1), feminist scholars have increasingly used the term 'care economy' to underline the role of 'reproductive' activities in creating 'value' (e.g. Elson, 1999; Folbre, 1994).

Unpaid work burdens fall disproportionately upon women given a predominant and persistent divide in primary gendered responsibilities, with men's labour largely concentrated in 'productive'/income-generating work, and women's dedicated substantially to 'reproductive' labour which includes routine domestic

---

Box 2.1   Unpaid work, carework and unpaid carework: terminological distinctions

Although the terms 'unpaid work', 'care work' and 'unpaid care work' are often used interchangeably, there are important distinctions among them.

- Unpaid work comprises a wide range of activities, including unpaid work in family businesses, subsistence activities such as the collection of fuel or water, and care of persons with family or non-family connections. While the former two are now nominally included in the SNA, the unpaid care of children, the elderly, the sick and so on is not.
- Carework involves direct care of persons, including able-bodied adults, as well as children, elderly people, and those who are sick or disabled, on a paid or unpaid basis. Paid carers include nannies, nurses, childminders, careworkers for senior citizens and so on, who may work in the public, private or not-for-profit sector. Other people who provide care, although this may not be an explicit part of their work contract, include domestic workers. Parents, too, if on paid 'parental leave', are not technically doing 'unpaid carework'.
- Unpaid carework refers to the work of caring for persons with no explicit monetary reward. The vast bulk of unpaid carework is undertaken within the household or family context, but 'voluntary' unpaid carework may also extend to the neighbourhood or community level, or for institutions.

Source: Adapted from Razavi, 2007:Box 1, 6.

chores as well as more specialised carework (see Barker, 2014; Blackden and Wodon, 2006; Budlender, 2004, 2008, 2010; Chant, 1984, 1996; Esplen, 2009; Razavi, 2007; UN-DESA/UNDAW, 2009; UNRISD, 2010a; WHO, 2009). On top of this, it is also critical to bear in mind that women not only frequently perform a large amount of unpaid work in their own homes, but 'volunteer' work at the community level. As identified by Cecilia Tacoli (2014:4; see also Moser, 1992; Moser and Peake, 1987):

> Women's engagement in improving living conditions beyond the home is, to a large extent, an extension of their domestic responsibilities. The neighbour-hood is an extension of the home, and neighbourhood activities are consid-ered to be domestic, especially since domestic chores depend heavily on neighbourhood conditions.

Although women across developing regions are increasingly involved in paid as well as unpaid activities, this does not seem to have been matched by a commensurate increase in domestic labour and unpaid carework on the part of men (see, e.g., Chant, 2007a; ECLAC, 2004; Tacoli, 2012:18). As described by Debbie Budlender and Francine Lund (2011:942) in relation to South Africa, where enforcing paternal responsibility has been undermined over several years, not only by apartheid but by a long legacy of extra-marital births, a situation has emerged in which 'gendered patterns of care remain, in which men take little responsibility for financial or other forms of support, while women try and reconcile the need to be both carers and income-earners'. A similar pattern prevails even in countries such as Cuba, where legislative changes and political campaigns to encourage men to share domestic work have been in place for several decades (see Pearson, 1997; Safa, 1995). These inequities add up to a female-biased 'reproduction tax' (Palmer, 1992) which impinges upon women's productivity gains and their prospects of benefiting from 'urban prosperity' through widened job opportunities. As summarised by the World Bank (2011c:26): 'Gender differences in access to economic opportunities are driven in part by differences in time use that result from deep-rooted norms for the distribution of care and housework.' Moreover, as Ruth Pearson (2013:22) notes: 'paid work does not mean that women's primary responsibility for reproductive work within the family and community is diminished, and . . . for some women, waged work takes place within domestic settings where patriarchal control can be enforced'.

Owing to a combination of gender discrimination and enduring links between women and unpaid tasks, the women's market labour is frequently accorded lower value regardless of the work itself (Barker, 2014; Bibler and Zuckerman, 2013; Perrons, 2010; Perrons and Plomien, 2010). On top of this, and as discussed in more detail in Chapter 8, women are less likely to secure employment. As observed by Budlender and Lund (2011:936), for example: 'South African women are increasingly engaged in paid work, but many who would wish to do so – and, indeed, need to do so to cater to their own and their family's needs – are unable to find work.'

Plate 2.2 Poster compiled by low-income women detailing their multiple unvalued
responsibilities, Lihok Pilipina NGO, Cebu City, Philippines

Source: UN-Habitat/Sylvia Chant.

Major consequences of the increasing time women spend in remunerated labour while also continuing to undertake the bulk of unpaid domestic labour and carework, include the weighty overall burdens they bear in household livelihoods, as well as in the associated tasks of 'patching together' activities separated in urban space relating to shopping, childcare, employment and so on (McDowell *et al.*, 2006; see also Razavi, 2007:1). As discussed further in Chapter 7, it is important to highlight here that this 'space patching' is itself unpaid, adding support to Manuel Castells' argument that women's non-remunerated labour is vital to the functioning of cities (see earlier).

Yet women's remunerated activities are also integral to the generation of urban wealth, even if these tend to be informal rather than formal, and within the informal economy, home-based rather than extra-domestic. Women's income-generating ventures are also typically of a smaller, less capitalised scale than men's, and if not necessarily associated with lesser time commitments are almost always linked with poorer profits and remuneration (e.g. Chant, 2014; Chant and Pedwell, 2008; Chen, 2010a; Chen *et al.*, 2004; Kabeer, 2008a, 2008b; Meagher, 2010; see also below). Here it is vital to take into account the distinction between 'gender divisions of labour' and 'segmentation by sex' within urban labour markets. The former relates to the basic allocation of women's and men's time between paid and unpaid work based on gendered social norms, while the latter is associated with wage gaps (and other forms of inequality such as uneven access to health insurance and pensions) between women and men which are determined by a combination of social/gender norms and market forces (see Chen, 2010a; Chen *et al.*, 2004; Heintz, 2010; ILO, 2002; Razavi and Staab, 2010).

Another important consideration in analysing labour and productivity as a core component of the 'gender–urban–slum interface' in the Global South relates to the intergenerational effects of women's increasing involvement in remunerated work. Since reproductive labour displays a remarkably persistent association with women, and given major deficits in non-family forms of domestic and unpaid care support, as well as the challenges posed by slum residence, when mothers work, daughters often have to assume greater shares of reproductive labour which may provoke absenteeism from, or weaker performance at, school and sometimes early dropout, thereby inhibiting their own accumulation of human capital (see CPRC, 2010; González de la Rocha, 1994; Kelbert and Hossain, 2014; Moser, 1992).

Gender disparities in human capital

Related to a large degree, and often in mutually reinforcing ways, to gender divisions of labour is the question of gender disparities in human capital, including education, vocational training and skills. As another core element of the 'gender–urban–slum interface', human capital is not only critical in the terms of women's participation in labour markets and economic growth overall (Arbache *et al.*, 2010; Klasen, 2002; World Bank, 2006b, 2011c:210), but is also an integral aspect of 'personhood', affecting women's general capacities, their self-esteem, and their

Plate 2.3 Gambian girls draw water from a well in a residential compound in Old Jeswang, Greater Banjul

Source: Sylvia Chant.

ability to exert agency (see, e.g., Evans, 2013a; Plan International, 2010; Tjon-A-Ten *et al.*, 2011). Despite closing gender gaps in human capital, however, particularly in the sphere of education, the legacies of women's more limited access to various forms of human capital play a major part in shaping gender cleavages in livelihood opportunities (as discussed in Chapter 8) and asset acquisition (Chapter 3). This is particularly pertinent to slums, where a purported 'urban advantage' in education is compromised by a range of demand- and supply-side constraints such as poverty and ill-health, and lack of political will to cater to the poor's needs for educational provision, respectively (see Yorgancioglu, 2014:6).

Gender gaps in assets

Assets pertinent to gender (in)equality in cities include those of a physical, natural and financial nature, with gender gaps in land and property perhaps constituting one of the most important elements in the 'gender–urban–slum interface'. In most parts of the Global South women's access to these major assets is compromised through male-biased inheritance, discriminatory titling procedures, female disenfranchisement on death or desertion by spouses, whether through separation or divorce, and male control of property even where women possess legal or customary entitlements to conjugal or paternal holdings (CPRC, 2010; Cooper, 2010; Deere, 2010; Evans, 2015:78; Hughes and Wickeri, 2011; Moser, 2010; Sweetman, 2008; UN-Habitat, 2006a, 2007a; World Bank, 2011c:226ff.; Varley,

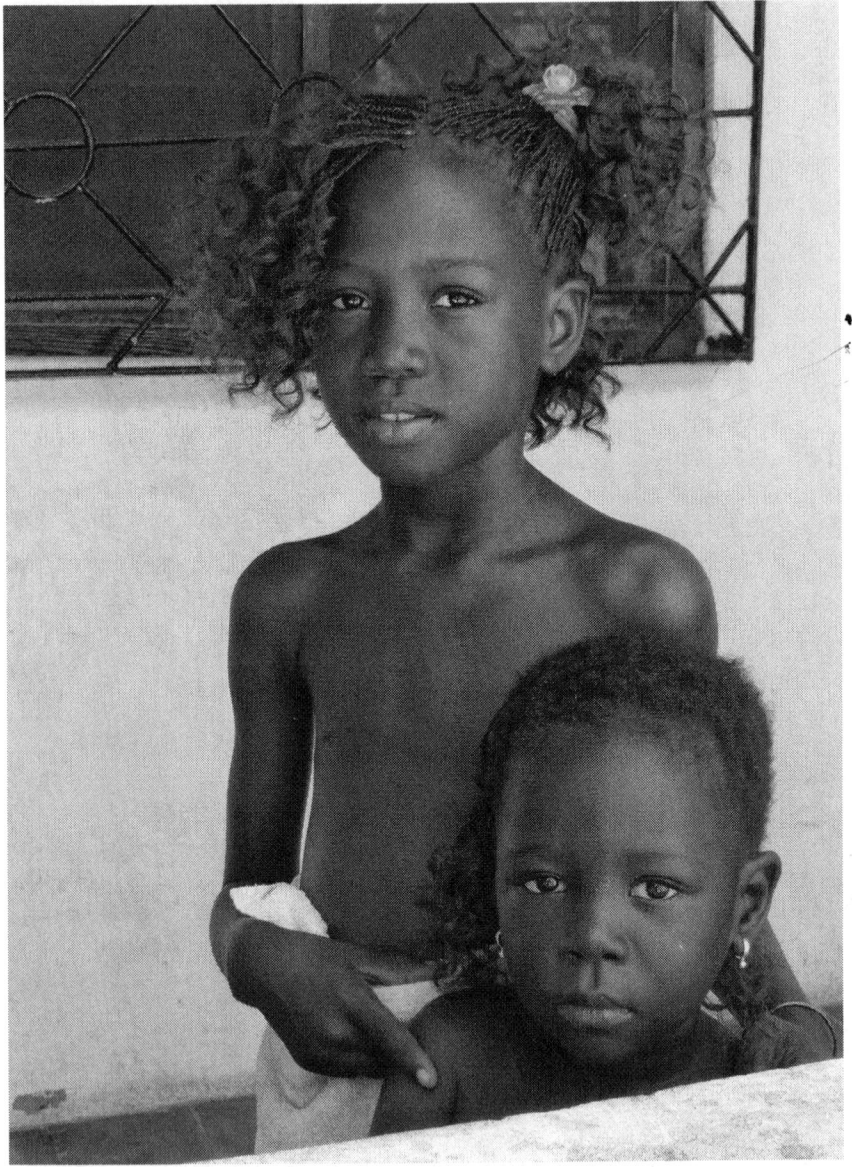

Plate 2.4 Gambian girl minding younger sister

Source: Sylvia Chant.

2007). On top of this, the location and quality of land and housing can exert major effects on the lives of women, given the disproportionate time they spend in the home in their roles as primary providers of domestic labour and unpaid carework. This is especially relevant to urban female slum dwellers from the point of view of hours spent in reproductive labour, security, stability, health status and general

Plate 2.5 The TransMilenio bus rapid transit system, Bogotá, Colombia
Source: Carlosfelipe Pardo.

well-being. While property might be described as a 'private' asset, access to public goods such as infrastructure and services, as well as access to public land for habitat and livelihoods, which again are limited for the residents of urban slums and poor people more generally, play an integral part in compounding shelter considerations, affecting women to a much greater degree than men. Housing and services are covered in Chapters 3 and 4, respectively, while some of the major ramifications in terms of health and violence are dealt with in Chapters 5 and 6. The subjects of the latter also intermesh in critical ways with our discussion in Chapter 7 of gendered urban space and mobility.

Gender divisions in space, mobility and connectivity

The assertion that 'planning policy tends to ignore the fact that women and men use space differently' (Burgess, 2008:112) is well founded in cities across the Global South, not to mention the world more generally, with women often considerably more constrained than men in terms of their physical access to, and social use, of urban space. This phenomenon not only reflects legacies of male bias in creating the built environment of the city, but can play an immensely important role in perpetuating gender differences and inequalities (Burgess, 2008; McDowell, 1983; Massey, 1994; Ortíz Guitart *et al.*, 2014).

One major constraint on women's access to public urban space is the association of reproductive labour with the home, which impinges upon women's time, proclivity and capacity to engage in extra-domestic activity. However, there are also strong symbolic dimensions surrounding the 'forbidden' and 'permitted' use of private as well as public spaces governed by patriarchal power relations and norms of female propriety, which may require certain modes of dress, behaviour and limitations on social interaction to render women 'invisible' or unapproachable (see Fenster, 1999, 2005; Jarvis *et al.*, 2009; Katz, 1993; Lessinger, 1990; Vera-Sanso, 1995, 2006). In the Pashtun-dominated city of Jalalabad, Afghanistan, for example, 'public life does not literally see any unveiled women' (Schütte, 2014:11), and as noted by Caren Levy (2013b:26–7) more generally:

> The significance of gender relations is at the heart of the distinction between public and private space, a false dichotomy between reproduction and consumption associated with women in the private sphere, and production and politics associated with men in the public sphere . . . in most societies women's mobility in public space is subject to a range of mechanisms of control, combined with decisions about travel – where, when and how – negotiated in the private sphere of the household and extended family networks.

Use of, and access to, space among women is also, unsurprisingly, cross-cut by time, not just in response to their multiple burdens, but also because of societal constraints on women's movements after dark. When 'traditional' norms are transgressed, as in the context of Indian cities such as Mumbai, Bangalore and Ahmedabad where new employment opportunities for women in call-centre work require time-zone synchronisation with advanced economies, strategies have to be established to cope with women's unprecedented entry into what Reena Patel (2010) has termed the 'urban nightscape'. One attempt to ensure women's safety (which also helps to obviate popular perceptions that 'call workers' are 'call girls') is for multinational companies to provide dedicated worker transport (ibid.). More generally, and as discussed in greater detail in Chapter 7, issues of access to, and provision, quality and affordability of, public transport are crucial in determining women's movement and access to opportunities within cities, including education, employment and social mixing and freedom from gender-based violence (e.g. Khosla, 2009:17; Kunieda and Gauthier, 2007; Levy, 2013a; McIlwaine and Moser, 2007; Moser, 2004; Titcombe, 2014).

It is also critical to note that even in the new 'digital age', where technology has the potential to diminish the constraints posed by physical limitations and 'frictions of distance', women's connectivity with others is commonly hampered by a gendered 'digital divide' (e.g. Perrons, 2004:chapter 6; ESCAP, 2002). This has knock-on effects in terms of the power of (poor) women to take advantage of new work opportunities, to build networks and develop 'social capital' (Jones and Chant, 2009; Willis, 2010; see also Langevang *et al.*, 2012). Although this applies largely to computing skills, hardware and software, and to internet access, in respect of more simple digital technology such as mobile phones, gender gaps are of a lesser magnitude. Preliminary evidence not only points to mobile telephony

Plate 2.6 A female pedestrian negotiates public space in Marrakech, Morocco

Source: Sylvia Chant.

being a relatively 'gender-neutral tool' (Scott *et al*., 2004:1), but also one which extends services to poor urban dwellers as well as to rural residents (Oestmann, 2007:1). Digital connectivity provides for smoothing rural–urban linkages by introducing changing perceptions of distance and permitting more frequent personal contact and resource flows between source and destination areas (de Bruijn, 2008; see also Donner, 2008:24). Mobile phones may also be used by families concerned about the safety of daughters working night shifts in India's urban call centres (Patel, 2010).

Yet neither virtual nor physical mobility necessarily transforms gender. Recognising that internal and international migration can reinforce, as well as challenge, gender roles and relations (see Bastia and Busse, 2011; Chant, 1998; Datta *et al*., 2009; Jolly and Reeves, 2005; McIlwaine, 2010), mobile telephony may subject female migrants, who are often under intense pressure normatively and pragmatically to remit money to relatives in source areas, to greater monitoring and surveillance, thereby making them less able to resist economic and other demands from rural kin. By the same token, the ability to remain in touch with family back home may also facilitate greater levels of independent female migration, including of mothers with young children, which detaches women from some of the physical, if not financial and emotional, investments they are expected to make in their maternal and other familial roles. What these diverse possibilities mean in terms of the potential gains to women from urban residence remains largely uncharted to date, but will undoubtedly benefit from dedicated investigation, as further identified in Chapter 7.

Plate 2.7 The River Gambia ferry crossing between Banjul and Barra, used by daily and weekly commuters and longer-term labour migrants

Source: Sylvia Chant.

Gender disparities in power and rights

A final critical component in the 'gender–urban–slum interface', to be dealt with in detail in Chapter 9, relates to gender differences in political power and rights. These differences obtain at all scales (personal, through household, community and city-wide spheres, and ultimately national levels) and are mediated by informal and formal mechanisms.

Although there is evidence of increased mobilisation and organisation of women at the grassroots, not least in the spate of popular uprisings in North Africa and the Middle East from 2011 onwards, this has not been without major costs in terms of violence, sexual harassment and other human rights violations against women. More generally, there remain major gender disparities in the more formal political realms of civic engagement and governance (UN-Habitat, 2008b:3; see also Patel and Mitlin, 2010).

Not only are women frequently under-represented in formal political structures in urban areas, including trade unions, cooperatives and workers' associations, which marginalise and invisibilise their economic roles (see Chen, 2010b), but where they do participate at the grassroots, they are often engaged in community-based struggles for basic services, with attendant problems attached to the frequent 'feminisation of responsibility' which this can imply (e.g. Beall, 2010; Lind, 2002, 2010; Miraftab, 2010). Such engagements may also bring about a privileging of domesticated concerns among women which reinforce

Plate 2.8 Two young women in Cairo's Tahrir Square play their part in the 2011 Egyptian Revolution

Source: UN-Habitat/Taylor Barr.

essentialising gender stereotypes (see Doshi, 2013). However, this should not detract from some considerable achievements made by grassroots women to organise collectively for change in a wide range of urban settings. As noted in Chapter 1, there is a long history of mobilisation among women slum dwellers either on their own or in strategic partnership with others as parts of broader coalitions (see, e.g., Patel and Mitlin, 2010). The latter also includes the work of such organisations as the Huairou Commission which have worked effectively in developing links between grassroots women's organisations and other actors to bring about political change that challenges gender inequalities in sustainable ways and ensures leadership roles for women from urban slum communities (Huairou Commission, 2010a, 2010b).

Concluding comments

This chapter has outlined the significance of including a gender perspective in analysing how cities, and especially slums, function, and the part played by both in perpetuating and potentially intensifying male–female inequalities. In delineating a broad-based framework for interrogating the 'gender–urban–slum interface', which encapsulates a range of gender disparities across different spaces and scales within cities, we hope not only to underline the conceptual importance of different dimensions of urban life from the micro- to the macro-level as they interact with gender, but also to highlight how cities can galvanise potential for promoting gender transformation individually and collectively. While we have presented the 'gender–urban–slum interface' as an holistic framework, balanced coverage of constituent issues in the chapters which follow is precluded by the fact that some elements of the schema have been more widely researched than others. Moreover, the relative recency of enquiry into climate change in relation to cities and slums, especially from a gender perspective (see Alber, 2011; Bradshaw and Linneker, 2014; Jabeen, 2014; Kovats *et al.*, 2014), means that we have had to omit this undoubtedly significant phenomenon from dedicated analysis. However, where possible, reference is made to less, as well as more, established debates in the field of gender and the urban, which we hope will serve as a platform for discussion and as a departure point for future empirical work and theorisation within the Global South, and across the world more generally.

3 Gendered access to land and housing in cities and slums

Introduction: gender, shelter and slums in the Global South

As pointed out in Chapter 2, land and housing form important elements under the rubric of assets (especially in terms of their natural, physical and financial aspects), and are central both to wider development goals and to understanding the 'gender–urban–slum interface'.

Housing in particular is widely regarded as an essential human need and right, as reflected, inter alia, in its incorporation into the Millennium Development Goals, with MDG7, Target 11 calling for improving the lives of at least 100 million slum dwellers by 2020 (see Chapter 1). This is likely to extend into the proposed Sustainable Development Goals (SDGs), with Goal 11, Target 11.1 specifying access for all to adequate, safe and affordable housing and basic services by 2030, in which slum upgrading constitutes a vital component (UN Open Working Group, 2014:17).

Interestingly, perhaps, the MDG target of slum improvement was one of the few that was achieved, and indeed surpassed a decade ahead of schedule, with 220 million people 'moving out' of slum conditions between 2000 and 2010 alone (UN-Habitat, 2010a:33). However, despite the fact that the original benchmark was arguably set too low (at around one-tenth of slum dwellers worldwide), it needs to be remembered that slum improvement sometimes comes at the cost of evictions and displacements (see, e.g., Meth, 2013; Obeng-Odoom and Stilwell, 2013). Progress has also been geographically varied, and although the proportion of urban residents living in slums has dropped in most developing regions, with China and India at the forefront, in absolute terms the number of slum dwellers has continued to rise (UN-Habitat, 2010a:33; see also Figures 1.1 and 1.2).

Current tendencies for absolute growth in numbers of slum dwellers are especially pertinent to women, not only because they often constitute a larger than average share of this group, but because of their typically more ubiquitous and distinctive ties to the 'domestic domain', both normatively and pragmatically. Taken together, these put many urban women on the front line of having to negotiate the injurious implications of challenging living conditions and precarious tenure security (Chant, 2007b, 2012b).

On top of this, and especially pertinent to the intersections we identified in our 'gender–urban–slum interface' in Chapter 2, the UN Special Rapporteur on the

Right to Adequate Housing, Raquel Rolnik stresses how the social and cultural connection of women with domestic space makes women's rights to adequate housing fundamental not just 'to women's day to day life' but also to 'promoting women's autonomy in all spheres of life and for making other human rights effective' (Rolnik, 2012:5). As echoed by Faranak Miraftab (2001:154, 156; see also Larsson, 1989; Quisumbing, 2010; Schlyter, 1989; Schütte, 2014):

> Housing is a key resource for women; it is an asset important to their economic condition and central to their physical and social well-being. It is the site of child-rearing and income generation and a nexus for social networks of support and community-based reliance . . . Housing is a significant economic asset to women that contributes to their independence, economic security, and bargaining power with men in their households and in society at large. Most importantly, it helps women determine their own futures and make the decisions that affect their lives.

Leading on from this, housing is also critical to the identity, dignity and sense of belonging of individuals, especially if their rights are upheld by law (CLEP, 2008). In Dakar, the capital of Senegal, for instance, Ruth Evans (2015:82) asserts that:

> Alongside a regular income, the inheritance and ownership of housing was identified by widows and widowers as a key means of ensuring financial and emotional security in urban areas. Housing was regarded as the main asset that enabled urban households to 'manage/cope' (*se débrouiller*) without having to worry about paying rent.

On a similar note, Bipasha Baruah (2007:2101) found in Ahmedabad, India, that on account of the 'prestige, security, stability, and convenience' offered by property ownership, 'Women . . . indicated that owning well-serviced homes on secure land had significantly influenced their self-image and attitude to the future.'

When women are able to enjoy the stability afforded by access to adequate housing, school attendance among children may increase (UN-Habitat, 2012a:6), which, in turn, is relevant to human capital and capacity-building. Indeed, as documented extensively by Caroline Moser (2006, 2009) in her pioneering longitudinally grounded work on asset-based approaches to poverty reduction, even when people start out in precarious shelter, housing can be an effective pathway out of poverty. This is perhaps especially the case where the poor are able to negotiate ownership, even if this is frequently a protracted process when it comes to slums. Full ownership of land plots and the structures people build on them may take several years to complete in the form of obtaining a legal title deed, and is often contingent on community-wide regularisation as well as personal effort.

While, in principle, as discussed later in this chapter, perceived security among slum dwellers who have yet to formalise their tenure may be just as important as legal property rights (see also later), this is not always the case. Moreover, while, theoretically, access to housing and tenure security could just as readily apply to rental shelter, those excluded from owner occupancy or the prospects thereof frequently prove more vulnerable in practice, with Richard Harris (2015:124) asserting: 'If anything security is even more important for tenants than owners.' Given that less and less land in cities appears to be available for no- or low-cost occupation or purchase due to shrinking amounts in the public domain coupled with tendencies to densification within low-income settlements (Rakodi, 2014:23), the likely rise in the share of rental alternatives, particularly for women, needs urgent consideration (see Kumar, 2010; see also below).

Plate 3.1 Incremental self-build, Comuna 13, Medellín, Colombia
Source: Cathy McIlwaine.

Gender and rights to housing: principles and pronouncements

Gender equality in rights to housing has been established in a number of international treaties and conventions dating back to the Universal Declaration of Human Rights of 1948 (Rolnik, 2012:5), and, pertinent in particular to women, in Article 16 of the Convention on the Elimination of All Forms of Discrimination Against Women (CEDAW) of 1979 (see Hughes and Wickeri, 2011:814–15; UN-Habitat, 2006a; Varley, 2007). Subsequent developments include the reaffirmation in 2007 by Raquel Rolnik at the thirteenth session of the UN's Human Rights Council in New York of 'the human right to adequate housing' as 'the right of every woman, man, youth and child to gain and sustain a safe and secure home and community in which to live in peace and dignity' (UNHRC, 2009:22). Moreover, in 2010, General Recommendation 27 was adopted by the CEDAW Committee, which, in acknowledging discrimination against older women and widows, emphasised older women's rights to adequate housing and protection against forced evictions and homelessness (Begum, 2011:3, 5). The importance of housing for women also features in UN-Habitat's Global Campaign for Secure Tenure (UN-Habitat, 2007a), as well as in the World Urban Campaign (UN-Habitat, 2010b:4). In 2014, the United Nations Human Rights Council also reiterated its commitment to the principle of 'adequate housing as a component of the right to an adequate standard of living', without discrimination of 'any kind', including sex (UN, 2014a).

Notwithstanding these provisions, however, gender continues to be a major axis of discrimination in housing access, and especially ownership, albeit to an apparently lesser degree in urban than in rural areas.

Gender and property ownership in practice: an advantage for urban women?

Accepting Carole Rakodi's (2014) caution that a dearth of good-quality data precludes accurate determination of gender differences in property ownership, UNICEF (2007:Figure 3.4) estimates for a range of Latin American countries that women are seldom more than 25 per cent of landowners. In more recent detailed research on home ownership in eleven countries in the region by Carmen Diana Deere, Gina Alvarado and Jennifer Twyman (2012) it was found that despite women faring rather better in terms of acquisition of land and shelter here than elsewhere in the world, in only two of their case study countries – Nicaragua and Panama – had gender parity been achieved (ibid.:525). For the world more generally, UNFPA (2007:19) conjectures that women's share of land and property ownership is less than 15 per cent of the total.

Notwithstanding that much less research has been carried out on women's land and property in urban as opposed to rural areas (Baruah, 2007), UNFPA (2007:19) asserts that women's long-run prospects of securing property are better in towns and cities than in the countryside, partly because of greater social and economic opportunities, and partly because more land and property is acquired through the market rather than through inheritance. While these points may be valid, it should be noted that it is not necessarily the case that 'modern' markets work in less discriminatory ways than 'traditional' inheritance practices. Moreover, the informality characterising considerable tracts of land acquisition in Global South cities, and which pertains particularly to slums, may not guard against the exercise of social conventions, backed up by (albeit arbitrary) applications of customary and religious law, which tend to favour men (see Rakodi, 2014). Indeed, as Katherine Hughes and Elisabeth Wickeri (2011:839) have argued, women's general disenfranchisement in rural contexts 'reaches deep into urban areas'. One plausible reason for this, as suggested by Rakodi (2014:19), pertains to the relative recency of urbanward migration in a number of developing countries. In instances where people subscribe to conservative, gender-discriminatory mores, practices and religious dictats, these may be more entrenched in the countryside, but do not necessarily disappear on rural–urban movement, and thus continue to impose limits on the exercise of women's rights in cities.

Whatever the case, evidence of continued gender inequality in urban areas is arguably reflected in the fact that only one-third of owner–occupiers were found to be female in data gathered for a UN Gender and Habitat survey in sixteen low-income urban communities in Ghana, Senegal, Tanzania, Uganda, Zambia, Sri Lanka, Colombia and Costa Rica (Miraftab, 2001). Rare exceptions to the general rule of male bias in property ownership include South Africa, where, thanks to the Department of Housing's prioritisation of equal or preferred access to female household heads under the government subsidy programme, female-headed households are no less likely than other households to own their own home or to live in formal shelter (Goebel *et al.*, 2010:578). This also appears to be the case in Chile, where Alejandra Ramm (2014) points out that the expansion of social protection and targeting of vulnerable groups in the wake of post-1990 democratisation have led to unmarried women being far more likely to receive a state housing subsidies than men, especially compared with the authoritarian period of the 1970s and 1980s. Although governmental prioritisation of women may have been based on over-generalised assumptions that female household heads were likely to be poorer and more vulnerable than their male counterparts, the upshot has been to benefit single women to the extent that more women now apply for housing subsidies and are regarded as household heads, even if they have a male partner in the background. Thus, rather than being a sign of growing vulnerability, Ramm (2014:13) talks about a 'strategic' and 'empowering' use of lone motherhood, and deems this significant in helping to account for a virtual doubling in the share of Chilean households headed by women between 1990 (20 per cent) and 2011 (nearly 40 per cent) (see also Box 3.4).

This country-specific experience may help to bear out the findings of another study by Nestor Gandelman (2009), which, in addition to Chile, includes Honduras and Nicaragua. Although Gandelman's research reveals that women are less likely to be owner–occupiers than men in all three countries, it also confirms that female heads of household have a higher probability of possessing land title compared with women in general. By the same token, Gandelman is keen to emphasise that female household headship is not necessarily a precursor to acquiring property, with prior full or even part ownership among women conceivably acting as a catalyst in women's decisions to assume headship in the first place.

The extent to which women in general or female household heads are able to obtain land or property title varies considerably from country to country. In Guayaquil, Ecuador, for instance, female household heads in slum communities may have a slight advantage over their partnered counterparts in this regard, and in the long run may not be especially disadvantaged in terms of income (Moser, 2010), even if female household heads tend to fare less well than male household heads in terms of land and property ownership (Moser and Felton, 2010). In turn, that women in general face property disenfranchisement accords with the more general observation in male-headed units – ownership almost invariably devolves to men (Rakodi, 2010:355; see also Evans, 2015, on Senegal; Hughes and Wickeri, 2011:900, on Tanzania).

There are also cases where potential female heads abandon the quest for ownership in their own right for social reasons. In the Philippines, for example, unmarried mothers often choose not to obtain their own property but instead 'embed' themselves in the households of extended kin to divert attention from their 'unwed' status (Chant and McIlwaine, 1995). Thus, it may not just be that discriminatory owner–occupancy markets and titling procedures disadvantage women, but that prospective female heads of household, especially if single, and socially stigmatised as a result, may be discouraged from setting up on their own.

The intersecting influence of economics on decision-making also need to be taken into account in this equation, with Rakodi (2014:18) summarising that: 'in many parts of the world social disapprobation of women who remain unmarried, combined with economic disadvantage, prevent many women from establishing independent households and, if they do, constrain their ability to afford land and housing construction'.

On top of this, in countries with legacies of conflict or civil war, qualms about safety and security may prompt female heads of household to opt for dwellings annexed to landlord-occupied rental housing rather than establishing themselves as independent owner–occupiers, as noted, inter alia, for slums in Luanda, Angola (Ducados, 2007; see also Chapter 6).

Male bias in inheritance and property rights

Women's comparatively limited access to property ownership is a reflection not just of the socially (and/or economically) minority status of female household heads, but of the fact that inheritance routinely discriminates against women, ranging from situations, as in Swaziland, where women have no right to inherit property (COHRE, 2004:140–1), to those in which they are legally entitled only to lesser shares than men (CPRC, 2010; Hughes and Wickeri, 2011). There are also several instances in which women's statutory rights are compromised by lack of knowledge, plural legal systems and socio-cultural emphasis on the prerogatives

Plate 3.2 Woman and child resisting eviction from an inner-city slum in Buenos Aires, Argentina

Source: UN-Habitat/Pepe Mateos.

of males and their consanguineal kin over land and property (see Cooper, 2010; Hughes and Wickeri, 2011; Ossome, 2014).

Thus while bearing in mind Rakodi's (2014:15) point that 'Few constitutions contain explicit legal obstacles to women's land and property ownership', it is also true that 'legislation related to property rights and registration may discriminate against poor people in general and women in particular, explicitly or in practice'. Indeed, while taking into account caveats in data, it is worth noting that in the Middle East, North Africa and sub-Saharan Africa inheritance remains so glaringly unequal (see Figure 3.1) that even if in principle there appears to be total or substantial equality in property rights, in practice this is far less likely, especially where secular laws coexist with religious and/or customary conventions.

In Dakar, for instance, in-depth research on widows and property by Ruth Evans (2015:80–90) among the Serer (an ethnic group constituting 15 per cent of the national population) has revealed that, although inheritance may be more favourable for women in Senegal compared with other countries in sub-Saharan Africa, and particularly in urban areas, in polygamous marriages competition over shares of the deceased husbands' estates can be fraught and complicated. In this light, local NGOs report that polygamy is 'increasingly incompatible with urban lifestyles' and that jealousies between co-wives have become more evident as urbanisation has continued. In accordance with Islamic law in which daughters and wives are legally entitled to lesser fractions of the patriarchal estate than sons, it is common that co-wives with the largest number of adult sons generally gain

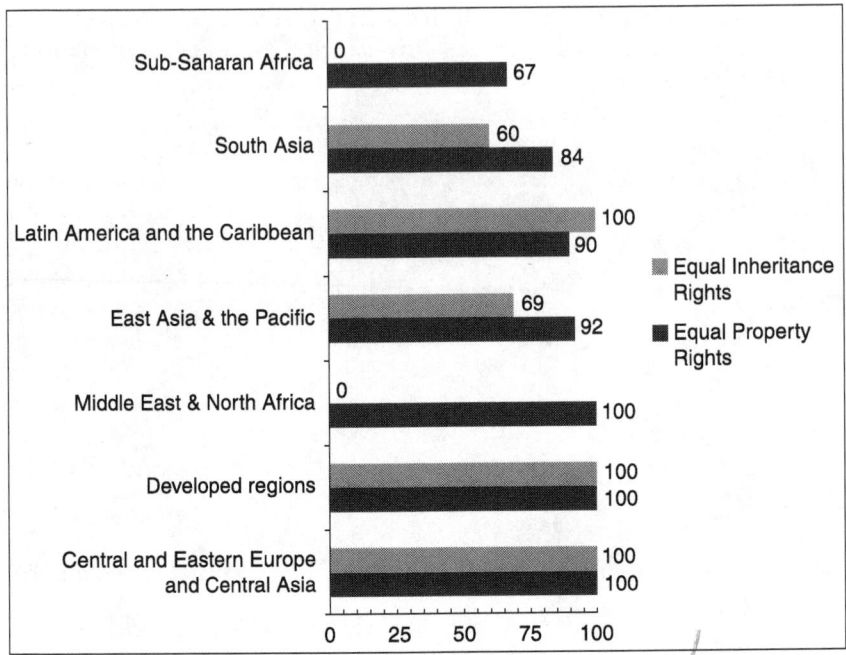

Figure 3.1 Gender equality in property and inheritance rights by world region (percentage)

Source: Adapted from UN-Women 2011a:Figure 1.9, 39.

most from the division of inherited assets, while co-wives with more daughters or fewer or no children 'lose out'. Despite the fact that revisions to statutory law, and particularly to the Senegalese Constitution and Family Code, have exhorted greater rights and entitlements for widows, many people do not speak French, which is the language of secular legislation, and in this context the confusion occasioned by legal pluralism is exacerbated.

Another point is that despite the gender-neutrality of statutory laws in several countries, which may even contain specific provisions promoting women's rights or gender equality, in many instances 'this is not sufficient to ensure that women enjoy equal access to property rights', with the 'relationships in which they are embedded and the norms that govern social interaction' being ultimately just as, if not more, important (Rakodi, 2014:18). Such observations are applicable not only to a number of countries in Africa, but to others in South Asia, where although women nominally have the same legal rights as men to own property, a host of cultural traditions deny them inheritance or even management prerogatives (Baruah, 2007:2100). In the context of a survey of over 100 women in Ahmedabad's slums, for example, Baruah (ibid.:2104) found that fewer than 10 per cent had been the recipients of parental property, and in these cases only because there were no male successors. The vast majority of women abandoned their claims to rightful inheritance because this would potentially weaken their brothers' willingness to support them in times of crisis. Indeed, although some mothers were in favour of granting land to daughters as parts of their dowries (rather than money or jewellery), others worried that this would reduce their ability to make claims on male kin, which in turn would also impact them, given social taboos which prevent parents from seeking help from married daughters (ibid.:2014–15).

In short, male bias in inheritance and property acts as major obstacle to gender equality in urban as well as rural areas, with UN-Habitat (2008b:3) noting that 'in many parts of the world, women start from a disadvantaged position, since their ability to access land and housing frequently depends on their relationship to men'. Male ownership effectively equates with male control over women (Hughes and Wickeri, 2011:850), and, as asserted by COHRE (2008:2; see also Varley, 2013:132): 'When addressing housing as a human right, it is impossible to adopt a gender neutral approach. Women, either by law or by action, are excluded from or discriminated against in virtually every aspect of housing.' Given tenuous, and frequently male-contingent, property rights, women commonly face eviction and/ or homelessness in the event of divorce or desertion. Widowhood may also lead to the same, as evidenced in instances of 'property grabbing' by in-laws in India (Nakray, 2010), and in sub-Saharan Africa (Cooper, 2010; Rakodi, 2010; Sweetman, 2008; World Bank, 2007:109) from women whose spouses have died of HIV/AIDS.

Vulnerabilities and negative outcomes are especially pertinent where women are poor (Hughes and Wickeri, 2011:851), with a study of Malawi conducted by Ngwira (n.d., cited in Rakodi, 2014:18) indicating that poverty is a major risk factor for urban widows who face a far higher rate of dispossession (66 per cent) compared with their male counterparts (26 per cent). Indeed, the only alternatives for widows facing destitution through dispossession may be to subject themselves to various self-sacrificial, and even demeaning, strategies to retain rights to property, such as committing to post-conjugal celibacy or entering into forced unions with their spouses' brothers (Levirate marriage) (see COHRE, 2004, 2008; Kothari, 2005; Nakray, 2010; UN-Habitat, 2007a:8). Moreover, women may be disenfranchised as daughters, regardless of the efforts they have made to support parents and/or brothers economically (see Chant, 2007a:181–3, Box 4.9, on The Gambia; see also CPRC, 2010). In some cases, as noted for India by Cecile Jackson (2003), this is because mothers may favour the inheritance of sons over daughters, given the expectation that the former will provide for them in their old age.

Gender and housing alternatives in slums

Aside from male-biased inheritance practices, and discriminatory housing and regularisation programmes, common explanations for gender disparities in shelter include women's limited access to stable employment and earnings, as well as finance and credit (Benschop, 2004; COHRE, 2004; Hughes and Wickeri, 2011; UNMP/TFEGE, 2005:75). Indeed, even where women may be able to access housing, the spectre of property taxes may discourage them from seeking ownership through regularisation programmes and the like (Khosla, 2009:39). Additional factors dissuading women from pursuing title in their own right, or even opting for joint spousal registration, include deeply entrenched patterns of patriarchy which require women to defer to men's prerogatives in respect of ownership and management of key household assets (Hughes and Wickeri, 2011:847). Indeed, even where women may be de jure owners, this may mean little in respect of their de facto rights over sale, transfer, or daily utilisation (Chant, 2007b; GADN, 2013:45; Holden with Tefera, 2008; Varley, 2007). Another interesting observation, drawn from South Africa by Sophie Mills (2010), is that women may be reluctant to secure individual title and/or use housing finance to upgrade their homes because, in a context of prevailing norms of female altruism, this can put even more pressure on them to help others.

Questions of gender and tenure security in slums

Carole Rakodi's (2014) extensive review of urban women's access to land and housing conducted for the World Bank's *World Development Report 2014* on 'Voice, Agency and Participation' highlights that women value security above all else, which also applies to urban residents in general. However, for poor people living in slums, this is often difficult to achieve. This is not only on account of the fact that many (quasi) owner–occupiers therein have unregularised tenure, but because renters may not have formal contracts, and 'sharers' (persons living in others' property or land plots on a 'courtesy' basis) may be vulnerable to summary eviction. In light of this, Rakodi's point that 'security has perceptual and practical as well as legal dimensions' from the point of view of tenure is well made (ibid.:12; see also Figure 3.2).

In terms of legal dimensions, Rakodi refers to UN-Habitat's (2011b:11) definition that: 'A person or household can be said to have secure tenure when they are protected from involuntary removal from their land or residence, except in exceptional circumstances, and then only by means of a known and agreed legal procedure, which must itself be objective, equally applicable, contestable and independent.'

One of the salient problems here is that 'known and agreed' legal procedures may not be especially comprehensible to poor people, and poor women in particular, especially where they may have limited literacy, inadequate legal knowledge and restricted access to the justice system, whether on grounds of expense, time or lack of experience or confidence (Rakodi, 2014:12; see also Evans, 2015:90). In turn, there is also a question as to whether security, as a 'state of mind', might be better ensured through the provision of infrastructure and services rather than a title deed (Rakodi, 2014:12; see also Gilbert, 2002, 2012; Obeng-Odoom and Stilwell, 2013; Varley, 1987, 2002). This said, Baruah (2007:2099–100) notes that in upgraded slums in Ahmedabad, where the municipality has invested heavily in services and infrastructure, guarantees against eviction have been assured for only a decade, and this, coupled with non-standardised legal ownership documents, means that many women in these settlements are deeply concerned about what will happen when the ten-year

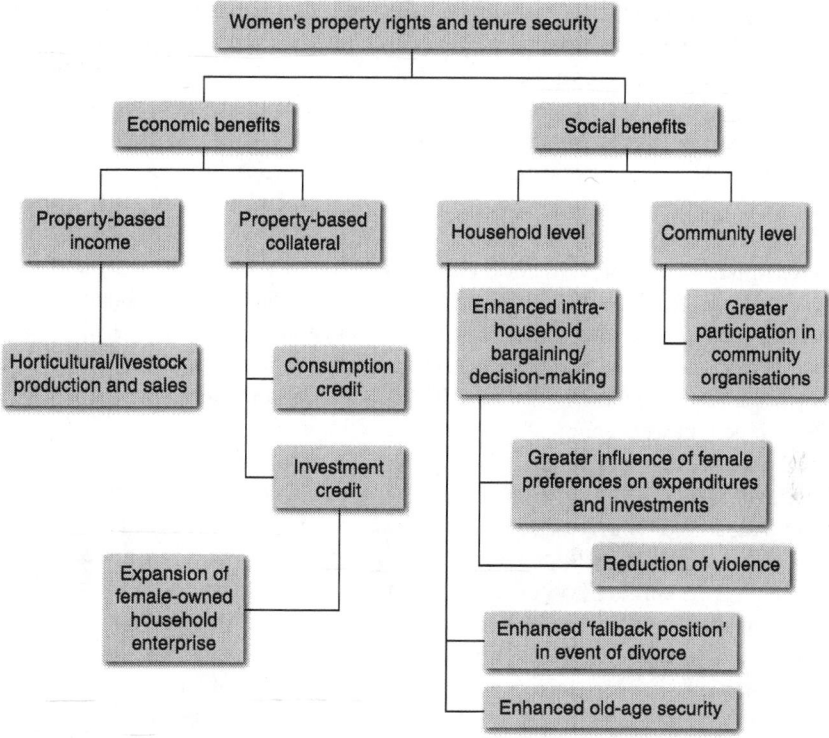

Figure 3.2 Potential social and economic benefits from increasing women's property rights and security in urban areas

Source: Adapted from CPRC, 2010:Annex 3.

deadline expires, especially given the attractiveness of serviced land to more powerful competitors in the market. One of the arguments commonly put forward by government officials interviewed by Baruah in the course of her research was that issuance of formal title deeds (*pattas*) might encourage people to sell to higher-income buyers and thereby exacerbate risks of homelessness among the poor. However, this was dispelled by her finding that 'Women in both upgraded and non-upgraded slums were consistently more interested in secure tenure of landed assets and the opportunity to raise their children in hygienic environments than in financial gains from selling property' (ibid.:2101).

The latter example feeds into perceptual dimensions of security, which, as Rakodi (2014:12) points out, can range from negative aspects such as fear of eviction to more positive elements such as 'a sense of belonging and safety'. In the particular case of poor women, key considerations revolve around assurances that they will not be ousted from their homes by public landowners or private landlords, or indeed by members of their own families in the event of divorce, separation or bereavement.

In respect of practical dimensions of security of tenure, Rakodi (2014:13–14) draws particular attention to the role played by housing (and land) in the livelihood strategies of poor households. This is linked with how control over residential space and independence (benefits which are most likely to be attached to secured ownership) can impact in numerous ways on people's capacity to manage their own lives, and use their dwellings for purposes other than residence per se, such as operating home-based businesses (see also Chant, 2007b; Evans, 2015; Gough and Kellett, 2001; Kellett and Tipple, 2011; Moser, 2009).

Accepting that 'urban women's access to land with secure tenure is influenced by the legal framework, social and familial relations and the opportunities available through various channels of land administration' (Rakodi, 2014:14), it is vital to acknowledge that the alternatives available to many poor women may be parlous in the extreme. UN-Habitat (2012a:7) points out that although more men than women may be technically homeless, and boys are more likely to live on the streets than girls, 'Women are more likely to experience "hidden homelessness" than men.' This refers to women putting up with unsafe or unhealthy living conditions and/or abusive domestic environments because of fears that losing a roof over their heads will lead to further 'poverty and distress', or force them to surrender their children to government officials. One variant on this is noted for Ahmedabad, where kinship networks often play a vital role in providing temporary accommodation for rural–urban, inter-urban or intra-urban female migrants. Those women who are unpartnered or divorced often face such degrading and anxiety-provoking conditions in the homes of their brothers or other male relatives, even where they devote their entire salaries to the 'host' households, that their only perceived exit is though remarriage (Baruah, 2007:2103).

Whether driven by economic constraints, legislative barriers or socio-cultural norms, a scenario obtains in many cities where those who are the main occupiers of housing are often those with the fewest rights. The injustice of this situation is underscored by the fact that women have long made substantial contributions of time, money and labour to creating the housing stock in urban areas of the South, where between 25 per cent and 60 per cent is self-financed and/or built (see Chant, 1987, 1996, 2011a; D'Cruz and Satterthwaite, 2005:9; Gondwe and Ayenagbo, 2013; Harris, 2015; Moser and Peake, 1987).

Rental shelter

Leading on from the above, it is perhaps little surprise that gender discrimination and inequality obstruct women's access not only to owner- or 'quasi' owner-occupied housing, especially in a context of rising land scarcity and unaffordability, but also to rental shelter. Rental housing in general has not only been rather neglected policy-wise (Gilbert, 2003; Kumar, 2010), but even fewer provisions have been developed to protect women in this sub-market (see Miraftab, 2001:149). This is despite the fact that, compared with their male-headed counterparts, female-headed households in many cities are likelier to rent than own accommodation (see Baruah, 2007; Hoa *et al.*, 2013:21; Masika *et al.*,

Plate 3.3 Woman contributing to self-build housing stock, Querétaro, Mexico

Source: Sylvia Chant.

1997:10). Although quite large numbers of small-scale slum landlords are female (see Kumar, 2010; Rakodi, 2013:23–4), the majority are men, and because the systems in which they operate tend to be patriarchal, fair treatment for female tenants may be elusive. For instance, in Tanzania, where the 1984 Rent Restriction Act was amended and subsequently repealed in 2005 on the grounds that it gave tenants too many rights (Hughes and Wickeri, 2011:834), the lack of current government support places renters at serious risk of arbitrary actions by proprietors (ibid.:876–8). In cases where couples in rented accommodation divorce, it is likely to be the men who stay behind (ibid.: 842), and limited access by single women is compounded not only by their perceived lack of regular employment and earnings, but in some cases by stigma against HIV/AIDS (ibid:859–60). In India, too, Baruah (2007:2102–3) notes for Ahmedabad that landlords' concerns about women's economic security can act as a barrier to access, especially where the costs of upgrading are often transferred rapidly by owner–occupiers or quasi-owner–occupiers on to tenants. An additional factor, highlighted by Penny Vera-Sanso (2006) for southern Indian cities is that rental accommodation may be hard to obtain or hold on to in the face of aspersions about the sexual propriety of women without male 'guardians'. In some contexts, such as Quito, Ecuador, discrimination on the basis of sexuality is a further issue, as observed among lesbian women (Benavides Llerena *et al.*, 2007:1.6.12).

In light of the general observation that poor women's restricted access to land and property in cities and slums can hinder their possibilities of establishing micro-enterprises (Valenzuela, 2005:1), those in rental or shared accommodation are likely to be even more prejudicially affected, given that scope for

Plate 3.4 Gender collaboration in self-build, Querétaro, Mexico

Source: Sylvia Chant.

entrepreneurial activities may be limited by landlords, or by the objections of fellow family members or residents in cramped, overcrowded dwellings or multi-occupancy compounds (see Chant 2007b; see also Gondwe and Ayenagbo, 2013: 69). That said, inadequate space for storing and/or protecting produce or machinery can affect owners and tenants alike in slums, not to mention in resettlement programmes. Citing work by Julian Walker, Alexandre Apsan Frediani and Jean-François Tirani (2013) on Mumbai's Slum Rehabilitation Scheme, for example, Cecilia Tacoli (2014:2) notes how, despite the advantages of water and sanitation in the high-rise apartments offered to former slum dwellers, these are often cancelled out by space constraints, along with the loss of neighbourhood networks. On top of this, barriers to entrepreneurship can be compounded by the challenges of poor location and general inadequacy of services and infrastructure common to all informal settlements, as discussed further in Chapters 4, 7 and 8 particularly.

Pro-female property initiatives

Given substantial gaps between international human rights provisions and actual practice, it is no surprise that various efforts have been made to introduce pro-female land and property titling as a means of bolstering women's 'fallback' position and their possibilities for economic as well as social advancement. As articulated by Rakodi (2014:3), 'Evidence is mounting that registration of property rights has positive effects for poor people in general and women in particular' (see also Figure 3.2). Rakodi also notes that: 'Registration/titling of property is likely to enhance women's well-being and property rights if it is gender sensitive, systematic and affordable, especially where households previously had little security' (ibid.:42).

The multi-stakeholder Global Land Tools Network (GLTN), for which UN-Habitat is secretariat, aims to 'promote practical approaches, particularly through recognition of a continuum of land rights' to enhance tenure security (UN-Habitat, 2010b:5). This provides an important means of negotiating women's land rights in contexts where these may fall somewhere on a spectrum between formal and customary law. In terms of practical examples and their spin-offs, regularisation of title for urban squatters in Peru released time for women, as well as for men, to engage in activities other than simple protection of their properties (Morrison *et al.*, 2010:11). In Vietnam, a World Bank land titling programme enhanced women's access to loans, and, in turn, business start-ups and expansion (World Bank, 2011a). In Zambia, Habitat for Humanity's 'Zambia Women Build' resulted in improvements in women's personal safety and security (Habitat for Humanity, 2009). In southern Ethiopia, where land tenure has traditionally been characterised by patrilineal inheritance and virilocal residence, joint certification of freehold titles among husbands and wives has led to growing confidence among the latter (many of whom are in polygamous marriages) that they will not face dispossession in the event of divorce or bereavement (Holden with Tefera, 2008). In Costa Rica, where prior to the passing of the Law Promoting Social Equality for Women in 1990 women abandoned by spouses or live-in partners had few options other than to move in with another man for support, joint (and separate) titling of property in women's names has allowed women to exert much more control over their personal lives, including greater freedom to operate domestic-based businesses, and enhanced powers to negotiate the terms of their relationships, such as opting out of abusive or unsatisfactory unions, or engaging in new partnerships on a non-cohabiting basis (see Chant, 2007a:Box 6.2, 206–7; also Box 3.1, below, on Nepal).

Drawing on work by UN-Habitat (2007a:20–1) on policy surrounding women's land, property and housing rights worldwide, Rakodi (2014:16) points out how the laws pertaining to the property rights of married women may be based on 'community of property', 'separation of property', or a combination of the two. In the former case, all property acquired during the marriage is deemed to be joint, and is nominally divided equally between spouses on divorce, or is passed on to the other spouse when one of them dies. In the case of 'separation of property', by contrast, husbands or wives are entitled to keep property acquired before the marriage, or by gift or inheritance during their union (see also Widman, 2014: 136–7, on Madagascar). In general terms, Rakodi (2014:16) claims that 'community of property' is fairest from a gendered perspective since this inhibits parties from disposing of conjugal property without the consent of their spouse,

---

Box 3.1   The evolution of women's land rights in Nepal

In 2002 Nepal passed the Country Code (11th Amendment Act), nearly ten years after demands by gender equality advocates in the country, which provided for equal inheritance rights for unmarried daughters and sons. However, this measure went only part-way since married women still stood to lose their natal property rights.

In 2006, as Nepal emerged from a decade of conflict, children were able to claim citizenship through their mothers for the first time through the Gender Equality Act, which extended divorce rights as well as further protecting women against domestic and sexual violence. With specific regard to property, married women were granted the right to keep inherited property, and they were entitled to use property without the consent of male family members.

In 2007, the Ministry of Finance introduced gender-responsive budgeting which resulted in an increase of government spending directly responsive to women's needs from 11 to 17 per cent between 2007 and 2010, as well as a 10 per cent tax exemption for land registered in women's names, which aimed to incentivise families to share their property with daughters, sisters and wives. As a result, households reporting some degree of ownership among women more than doubled – from 11 per cent to 35 per cent – between 2001 and 2009.

Source: UN Women, 2011a:22–3.

Box 3.2   Some practical entry points to addressing housing and secure tenure among women

- Access to micro-credit linked to housing.
- Housing projects which address women's rights in context of improving shelter strategies.
- Policy advocacy targeting affordable housing to poor women.
- Ensuring women's access to housing and secure tenure through social housing, government projects and slum-upgrading initiatives.
- Regulation of the rental market to protect vulnerable groups.
- Housing cooperatives.

Source: UN-Habitat, 2008d:12–13.

---

and also provides, at least in principle, for continued rights for women following widowhood or marital dissolution.

Since land rights per se are not the only pathway to enhancing women's access to housing and security of tenure, it also has to be noted that they should ideally be accompanied by complementary mechanisms such as support for housing cooperatives and micro-finance as identified by UN-Habitat (2008d) in the context of a review of best practices in gender mainstreaming in urban authorities (see Box 3.2). *access (financial) to housing*

In respect of the role of micro-credit for housing as a means of strengthening shelter options for poor women, demonstrable successes are indicated, inter alia, by the example of the Kuyasa Fund in Cape Town, South Africa. This was set up by a local urban-based NGO in the early 2000s. Working with a variety of development organisations, Kuyasa has used wholesale loan finance for client disbursements, and has aimed to facilitate access to housing finance for the poor, with particular targeting to women, who form nearly three-quarters of their clients (see Mills, 2010; UN-Habitat, 2008d:61–4).

Support for cooperatives and groups, along with legal aid, also provides possibilities to strengthen poor women's access to urban land and housing (see Box 3.3). Moreover, as exemplified by Ramm's (2014) case study of Chile, housing subsidies to groups of women deemed to be particularly vulnerable can be valuable not merely in improving their access to shelter, but also in enhancing their social status and psychological well-being (see Box 3.4)

Where states (and NGOs) have taken a less proactive role in complying with internationally endorsed rights to adequate housing, or need to be pushed into doing something about women's shelter needs, women themselves have often driven the agenda. For example, a network of women's self-help and community organisations in Kenya, operating under the auspices of GROOTS (Grassroots Women Operating Together in Sisterhood) Kenya, has facilitated the training of community watchdogs in a total of sixteen communities across four regions to act

Box 3.3   Selected recommendations to improve the gender responsiveness of law, policy and practice pertaining to land and housing for poor urban women

- The principle of non-discrimination in international conventions and national constitutions should translate into domestic legislation relating to property rights, inheritance, land administration and marital relations, which

  - acknowledges the right to secure tenure and adequate housing;
  - affirms gender equality regardless of marital status;
  - recognises women's right to own and control separate property; and
  - entitles sons and daughters to equal shares in cases of intestate successions.

- Progressive harmonisation of customary and religious law with statutory laws that uphold the principle of gender equality.
- A gender-sensitive legal framework for regulating landlord–tenant relationships.
- Support to home owners' associations and cooperatives and savings groups.
- Legal aid to low-income women in support of land and property rights.

Source: Adapted from Rakodi, 2014:41–6.

Box 3.4   Housing subsidies and unmarried mothers in Chile

When democracy returned to Chile in 1990, after nearly two decades of dictatorship, the new centre-left coalition government, Concertación, aimed to extend welfare to groups of the population hitherto largely excluded from the reach of social spending. Given the new regime's particular interests in assisting vulnerable people with limited capacity to generate income, households headed by lone parents entered into the frame, with the period between 1990 and 2010 witnessing an unprecedented granting of housing subsidies to unmarried mothers through various programmes. Compared with 1990, when more men and married couples received housing subsidies, by 2000 the bias had switched to women, and by 2006 to single women.

Among the positive outcomes experienced by beneficiaries are the possibilities for independence (for example, not having to live with their parents), increased authority within their homes, enhanced material well-being (even if 50 per cent of households in the poorest quintile are headed by women) and the prospects of passing an asset to their children.

Source: Ramm, 2014.

as community paralegals and linked them to elders, chiefs and councillors to monitor and prevent land-grabbing and asset-stripping (Huairou Commission, 2010b; see also Manda *et al.*, 2011, on Malawi; and Box 3.5, below, on Ecuador).

Box 3.5   Civil society initiatives to assist women's access to land and housing in urban Ecuador

Programa CAVIP

This stands for the Advisory Programme for the Construction and Improvement of Low-income Housing (Programa Nacional de Asesoramiento para la Construcción y Mejoramiento de la Vivienda Popular), which was launched in 1995 by the Ecuadorian Housing Ministry with the support of the German Development Agency (GTZ). With particular priority accorded to female-headed households, the scheme has provided improved housing for 2270 households, and training workshops – in health, construction techniques and social capital building – to 15,000 people.

Colectivo de Mujeres Luchando por la Vida

An organisation consisting of women and women's organisations which has sought to regularise tenure and secure housing finance.

El Grupo África Mía

An organisation of Afro-Ecuadorian women which has sought acquisition of land and self-build opportunities, working collectively in *mingas* at weekends.

Ciudad Programa Paso a Paso

Dating from 2004, and supported by an array of private and public international entities, especially from Spain, this programme works to enhance access to credit for housing and housing improvements through a multiplicity of stakeholders.

Fondo Ecuatoriano Popularum Progressio

An initiative which tackles poverty and housing privations on several fronts, including access to land and property, environmental conservation and management, and family well-being, which has featured special efforts to engage women, for example by introducing women-friendly meeting timetables.

Hogar de Cristo

Based in Guayaquil, Ecuador's largest city, this organisation promotes housing, education, health and faith, with one of its most recent initiatives being the construction of 35,000 dwellings on Ecuador's Pacific coast.

Fundación Mariana de Jesús

A religious organisation which since the early 1990s has attempted to improve access to housing among the urban poor, and which has benefited more than 7000 households.

Source: Benavides Llerena *et al.*, 2007:3.7.

In India, too, female-initiated and female-led neighbourhood savings groups in urban slums have frequently led to major accomplishments, such as improvements to housing and infrastructure, the accumulation of important financial assets, and the development of federations of low-income residents (Patel and Mitlin, 2010). The first women-led federation grew out of savings groups started by female pavement dwellers in Mumbai in 1986 and became known as 'Mahila Milan' (Women Together). This joined forces with a local NGO, the Society for the Promotion of Area Resources (SPARC), and over time recruited the help of various institutions in the city to address their problems. Through making direct contact with government departments, police stations, hospitals and the like, the women obtained better access to healthcare, learned how to complain effectively to officials, and managed to secure ration cards entitling them to subsidised fuel and basic food, which had hitherto been unavailable to pavement dwellers (ibid.:380; see also Doshi, 2013; Patel, 2011:94–5). From these beginnings, men ceded more ground to women in community decision-making, and the women's groups encouraged other women's groups to do the same. Diversification and the scaling up of women's activities into land and housing came when the pavement dwellers were threatened with eviction, and with the help of SPARC entered into a three-way partnership with India's National Slum Dwellers Federation (NSDF), which had been established in 1975.

Over time, the Mahila Milan savings groups have managed to launch several housing and service initiatives, including resident committee-backed police units in slums. These nationally linked federations have also formed an international network – 'Shack/Slum Dwellers International' (SDI) – which extends across sixteen countries and offers not only possibilities for international exchange but greater opportunities for negotiating with international agencies (Patel and Mitlin, 2010:383). Collectively, SDI has succeeded in securing over 100,000 land plots, over 50,000 households and over 600 communal (and community-designed) washing and toilet blocks (ibid.). According to Patel and Mitlin (ibid.:383; see also Box 3.6): 'The constant presence of a critical mass of women leaders increases

---

Box 3.6   Components of building gender-sensitive cultures in SDI federations

- Empathy to the problems of poverty rather than discipline (e.g. avoidance of exclusion for missing loan repayments).
- Incremental affordable development (rather than maximum material consumption).
- Collective rather than individual decisions and actions.
- Flexibility in respect of community need and timing.
- Membership through participation rather than fixed financial dues.
- Recognition that everyone (non-leaders as well as leaders) has a contribution to make.
- Experiential learning rather than making recourse to professional 'experts'.

Source: Patel and Mitlin, 2010:381–2.

---

the capacity of the Federations to secure gains that are gender-sensitive, and the presence of women leaders encourages others to aspire to this role.'

Yet, despite a number of fruitful initiatives, it is equally evident that women's rights to housing in many instances are seriously compromised, falling far short of the seven elements which the UN Special Rapporteur deems constitute an essential package (see Box 3.7). Furthermore, it is important to bear in mind that some interventions aiming to improve women's lives can at times make them unintentionally more vulnerable. In the context of slum upgrading in Cato Manor, Durban, for example, Paula Meth (2014) found that, although women who had moved to upgraded housing felt an enhanced sense of security and pride in their new living conditions, and professed to have experienced less generalised crime

---

Box 3.7   Seven elements of the right to housing

- Security of tenure.
- Habitability.
- Availability of services, infrastructure and public equipment.
- Adequate location.
- Cultural adequacy.
- Accessibility, non-discrimination and prioritisation of vulnerable groups.
- Affordable cost.

Source: Rolnik, 2012:6.

---

and danger, new forms of domestic violence had emerged. This was linked mainly to male family members trying to appropriate home ownership from the women, as well as to the fact that the new, more enclosed houses allowed people to hide domestic abuse more easily than in their previous shelters.

Concluding comments

This chapter has discussed the significance for women in urban areas of gender-unequal access to shelter, with particular reference to land, housing and tenure security. Women's palpable disadvantages not only fly in the face of human rights principles and conventions, but hamper the possibilities of improved livelihoods and prospects of exiting poverty. Yet, while women still face major barriers to gender equality in property acquisition through a range of discriminatory practices, our discussion has highlighted a range of pro-female initiatives that indicate the potential benefits of ensuring their access to land and housing on an equal basis to men's.

That said, improving women's access to land and housing in its own will not bring about major or lasting gender transformations. As the series of criteria presented in Box 3.7 reveals, and in accordance with the tenets of the 'gender–urban–slum interface' outlined in Chapter 2, the right to housing per se is not only intrinsically important but crucial in terms of its relations to the fulfilment of other needs and interests. For example, lack of security of tenure, especially in the shape of a formal deed, can inhibit the installation of services such as water and electricity (Rolnik, 2012:11). Moreover, as summarised by Baruah (2007:2108) in the context of Ahmedabad:

> In addition to property, urban women prioritise access to jobs, water, and basic services, such as clinics, schools, and crèches as the means to secure livelihoods and to improve the conditions of their reproductive labour. Without livelihoods, incomes, and access to basic services, access to land and property will not take women very far. Therefore, pro-urban land policy must be located within a broader urban development framework aimed at raising incomes, optimising livelihood opportunities, educating both women and men about the rights and privileges of property ownership, and providing housing and infrastructure.

The subject of sanitation and water, in particular, forms a core aspect of our discussion on gender in relation to services in cities and slums, and we turn to this in our next chapter.

4 Gender and services in cities and slums

Introduction: access to 'WASH' and related services in the Global South

This chapter concentrates primarily on water, sanitation and hygiene (commonly referred to as 'WASH' services), which are central to the well-being of populations everywhere, particularly in terms of individual and public health gains (see Allen *et al.*, 2006; Jones *et al.*, 2014:12; see also Chapter 5, this volume), but also in respect of human and financial capital. The typical lack or inadequacy of these services in several slums in the Global South can, accordingly, pose serious problems to occupants. Recalling the 'gender–urban–slum interface', WASH services incorporate a key set of physical and natural assets, and, where weak, can undermine livelihoods in several ways. Moreover, in a context in which access to water and sanitation is a basic human right, deprivation of such services constitutes a violation. Here slum-dwelling women and girls are particularly implicated given their major responsibility for providing household members with vital domestic needs (Bapat and Agarwal, 2003; Jarvis *et al.*, 2009). Yet, despite the importance of WASH, there is very little research on the everyday experiences of infrastructural and service provision (or lack thereof), which brings to bear the point that this issue must be conceptualised beyond the frame of technocratic interventions to address specific problems, how it becomes imbued with wider power relations, and how, in turn, provision can become a tool for subjugating or empowering certain groups within cities (see Anand, 2012; Jones *et al.*, 2014; Larkin, 2013:338; Robinson, 2006; Zeiderman, 2013). As summarised by Stephen Graham and Colin McFarlane (2015:2), for example: 'While infrastructure debates have made important contributions to how we understand the "supply-side" dimensions of infrastructure, there has been surprisingly little about how people produce, live with, contest, and are subjugated to or facilitated by infrastructure.'

With the above in mind, this chapter outlines the nature of the challenges facing women and girls from deficient WASH services in urban slums and the ways in which improved access not only stands to enhance their personal well-being and that of their families and communities, but is crucial to realising their rights and advancing gender equality (WaterAid, 2015; see also Chapter 5, this volume). While the bulk of our discussion is devoted to WASH services, we also make brief reference to electricity and solid waste collection. We leave policing and transport to Chapters 6 and 7 (on violence and mobility), respectively.

Access to WASH as human and gendered rights

Drinking water and sanitation were designated as human rights by the Convention on the Elimination of All Forms of Discrimination Against Women (CEDAW) of 1979, and in many countries in the Global South, including South Africa, The Gambia, Ecuador, Bolivia and Uruguay, the 'right to water' is enshrined in their constitutions (Brown, 2010:60). However, it was not until 2010, a decade after the Millennium Declaration, in which MDG7, Target 10 called on the world to 'reduce by half the proportion of the population without sustainable access to safe drinking water and basic sanitation by 2015', that rights of access to water and sanitation were formally endorsed by the UN Human Rights Council. In turn, although by 2012 almost 90 per cent of the world's population was estimated to benefit from improved access to this resource, it is important to note that this does not cover water for bathing, washing and cleaning (Joshi *et al.*, 2011:102; Satterthwaite *et al.*, 2013:15; WHO/UNICEF, 2014:7). Additionally, despite 116 countries supposedly having met the MDG target, recent estimates have suggested that 1.8 billion people globally have to drink water that is faecally contaminated, with a further 1.1 billion consuming water that is of 'moderate risk' (WHO/UNICEF, 2014:42).

Although access to drinking water is generally much better in urban as against rural areas (see Figure 4.1), slum communities usually fare worse than other parts of the city, with lack of public provision typically forcing the poorest to buy water from informal vendors who sell on the streets or from dedicated commercial outlets (ibid.). In Mombasa, Kenya, for example, one-third of better-off residents in informal settlements have access to a piped water supply while the poorest are twice as likely as their wealthier counterparts to use water kiosks (ibid.:29; see also Jones *et al.*, 2014:12). Since informally sold water often costs considerably more than networked supplies (see Chant, 1984; Moser, 1998; see also below), commercially procured water often requires supplementation with other supplies, such as collecting rainwater in jerry cans and other receptacles, including plastic bins.

Advances in sanitation are even less encouraging, with sub-Saharan Africa standing out as a region with particularly notable shortfalls: here, only 41 per cent of the population enjoyed an improved sanitation facility by 2012, compared with an average for developing regions of 64 per cent (see WHO/UNICEF, 2014:7; see also Figure 4.2). Indeed, as noted by David Satterthwaite *et al.* (2013:15), despite sanitation coverage increasing by one-third since 1990, more than 15 per cent of the world's population still has to resort to 'open defecation' (OD). This refers to bodily waste being left exposed, including in uncovered pit latrines. While nearly two-thirds (60 per cent) of affected parties reside in India (see below), there has been general drop from 45 per cent in 1990 to around 20 per cent in 2015 (UNICEF, 2015:46–7), largely accounted for by Asia and Latin America and the Caribbean, there has been an increase in 26 of 44 countries in sub-Saharan Africa (WHO/

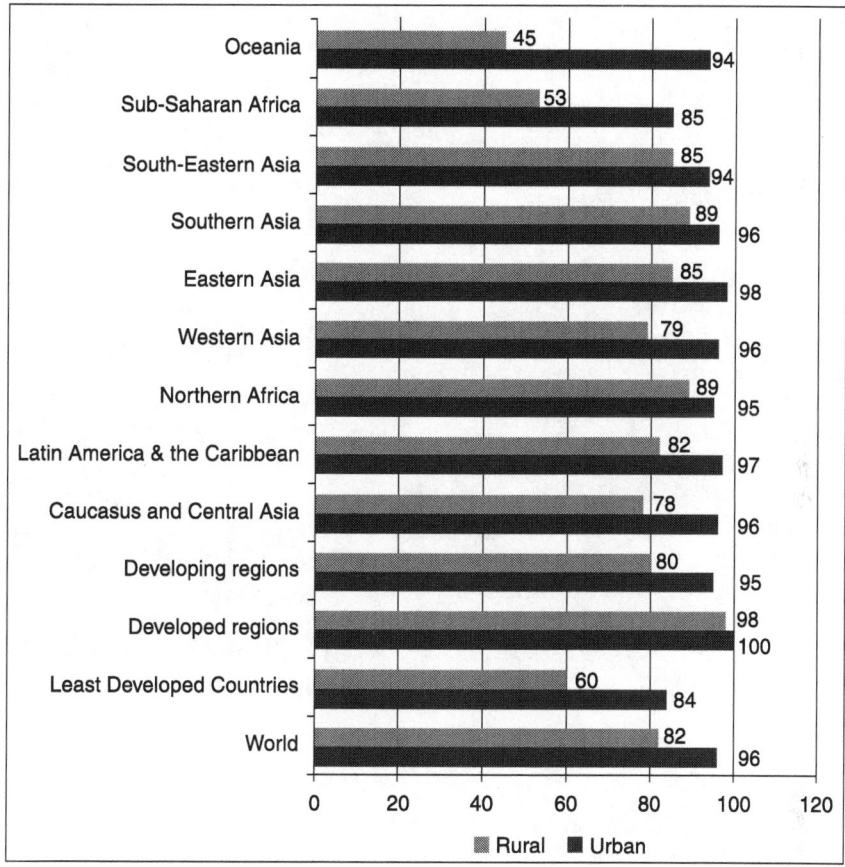

Figure 4.1 Proportion of rural/urban populations using an improved water source by region, 2012 (percentage)

Source: Adapted from WHO/UNICEF, 2014:73.

UNICEF, 2014:21). Notwithstanding that urban populations in general are less deprived than their rural counterparts, with an alleged 21 per cent of people lacking access to improved sanitation facilities in the former compared with 53 per cent in the latter, as of 2010 (Satterthwaite *et al.*, 2013:17; see also Box 4.1), urban slums bear a substantial brunt of deficits (UN, 2010a:61–2). This is partly because improvements in urban sanitation are often cancelled out by demographic growth. In informal settlements in fast-growing Tanzanian cities such as Morogoro and Dar es Salaam, for example, pressure on sanitation facilities is such that several households are forced to share pit latrines. This poses not only extreme discomfort and risks to health but also a major challenge in terms of labour and affordability in relation to convenience and cleaning (Hughes and Wickeri, 2011:892).

In Kenya, too, Hawkins *et al.* (2013:30) point out that less than 1 per cent of the slum-dwelling population has access to private toilets, while in India not even

Plate 4.1 Collecting rainwater during a tropical storm, Fajara, The Gambia

Source: Sylvia Chant.

one-quarter of slum households in Chennai, Delhi, Mumbai and Kolkata has access to improved toilet facilities of any type (Gupta *et al.*, 2009:20; see also Sujatha and Janardhanam, 2010; and Box 4.1). Affordability is also an issue with people increasingly having to pay to use communal toilets (see Subbaraman *et al.*, 2014, on Mumbai; see also below). In light of these constraints, in Delhi, Meerut, Indore and Nagpur, between one-third and one-half of poor households practise open defecation (see Kar with Chambers, 2008), and in Ahmedabad this often entails using very public areas such as rivers and railway tracks (Baruah, 2007:2096). This is not only distressing on a personal level, but has wider public health impacts, given the possibilities of cross-contamination, especially where rivers also provide the main sources of water for drinking and bathing (see Chant, 1984; Patel, 2011:100).

Closely related to water and sanitation are hygiene services, which entail education and training around risk-minimising behaviour with regard to health, and which are also essential rights, but did not receive much attention until the WHO/UNICEF (2014) Joint Monitoring Programme (JMP) for Water Supply and Sanitation started monitoring activities such as hand washing recently. The scarce data available to date touch upon whether there is a dedicated place to wash hands and whether with soap or other local detergents, and reflects very low levels, especially among those residing in poor areas (ibid.).

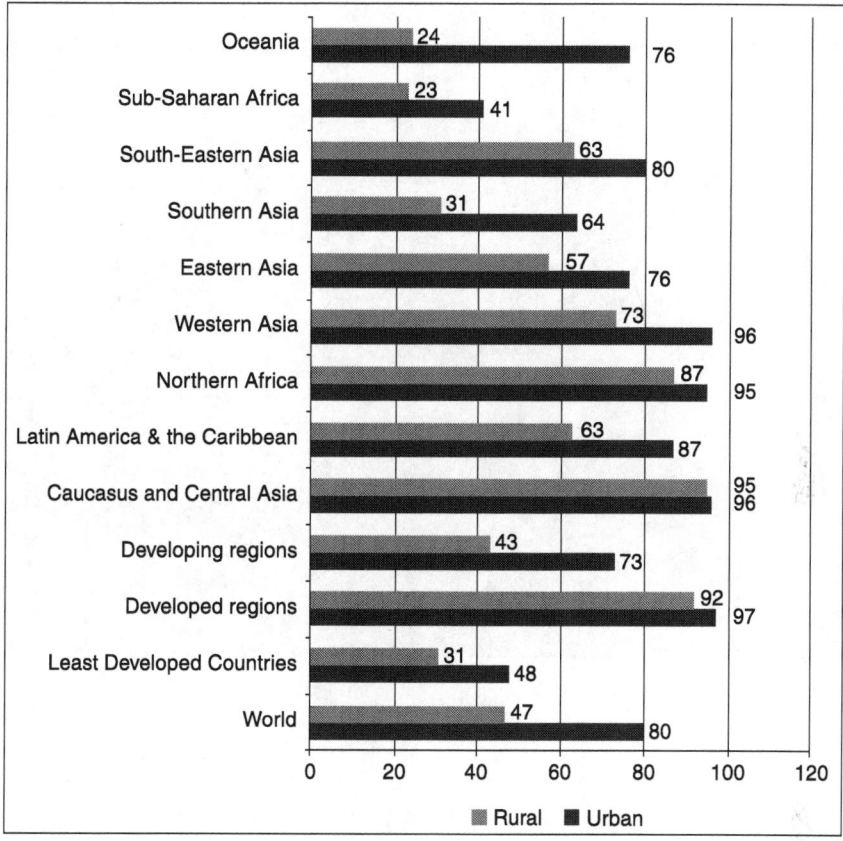

Figure 4.2 Proportion of rural/urban populations using improved sanitation facilities by region, 2012 (percentage)

Source: Adapted from WHO/UNICEF, 2014:72.

As with the deeply gendered impacts on slum-dwelling women and girls of water and sanitation, not least because of their responsibilities for catering to the daily domestic needs of all household members, some aspects relating to hygiene affect them on a very personal basis, and perhaps most notably in respect of menstrual hygiene management (MHM). This has been even more neglected by the WASH sector than hand washing, despite the fact that approximately 26 per cent of the total global female population is of reproductive age and therefore likely to menstruate every month for between two and seven days (House *et al.*, 2012:22). According to Thérèse Mahon and Maria Fernandes (2010:100), this requires:

> clean water for washing cloths used to absorb menstrual blood and having a place to dry them, having somewhere private to change cloths or

Plate 4.2 Pit latrine, Kanifing, The Gambia

Source: Sylvia Chant.

Box 4.1   Typology of improved and unimproved sources of drinking water and sanitation

	Drinking water	*Sanitation*
Improved	Piped water into dwelling/plot Public tap or standpipe Tube well or bore hole Protected spring Protected dug well Rainwater collection	Flush or pour-flush to piped sewer system, septic tank, or pit latrine Ventilated improved pit (VIP) latrine Pit latrine with slab Composting toilet
Unimproved	Unprotected dug well Unprotected spring Cart with small tank or drum Tanker truck Surface water (e.g. river, canal) Bottled water (unimproved if this is from unimproved water source)	Flush or pour-flush to other than piped sewer system, septic tank or pit latrine Uncovered pit latrine/open pit Bucket Hanging toilet or latrine Shared/public facilities No facilities (bush or field)

Source: UNICEF/WHO, 2012:Table 6, 33.

disposable sanitary pads, facilities to dispose of used cloths and pads, and access to information to understand the menstrual cycle and how to manage menstruation hygienically.

In many cases, of course, this is excessively difficult. With commercially produced sanitary pads often far beyond the financial means of poor women and girls, not to mention frequently being regarded as culturally inappropriate, a range of alternatives has long been the default option. At one extreme are natural materials such as mud, cow dung and leaves, but more common are strips of cloth that are reused after washing. While these can be perfectly hygienic if scrubbed with clean water and soap and dried in the sun (which helps to kill bacteria), conditions in many slums preclude this. Indeed, a UNICEF study in Bangladesh (cited in House *et al.*, 2012: 93) reported that one-third of women rinse their menstrual cloths in water alone and hide them in roof beams or thatch in their houses, which prevents them drying properly and can trigger fungal and reproductive-tract infections, as well as lead to greater susceptibility to HIV (ibid.:65; also Prügl, 2015:628n). Even less hygienic is when factory workers substitute conventional/formal sanitary products with textile waste accumulated on factory floors (Prügl, 2015:628n), or sanitary towels recycled from rubbish dumps on the fringes of urban slums (House *et al.*, 2012:93). In order to escape the threats to health imposed by these potentially life-threatening 'options', some women and girls resort to transactional sex in order to purchase 'safe' sanitary products, as in the case of peri-urban settlements in Ghana (see Dolan *et al.*, 2014).

On top of these challenges, costs during menstruation are incurred by needs for extra use of water for personal bathing and sanitation (Sommer *et al.*, 2015). Yet, given their elusiveness, and in a process referred to by House *et al.* (2012:22) as a 'cycle of neglect' (see also Mahon and Fernandes, 2010:102; Tilley *et al.*, 2013), women's and girls' lack of access to sanitary products and facilities, not to mention social and cultural taboos surrounding menstruation, all have negative effects on their education, health, dignity and gender equity (see below).

In light of the above, it is of little surprise that access to WASH is central to the post-2015 agenda, with a proposal that Target 2 of SDG6 should aim to 'achieve access to adequate sanitation and hygiene for all by 2030 with specific attention paid to the needs of women and girls and those in vulnerable situations' (WHO/UNICEF, 2014:25; see also Box 4.2).

Gendered effects of lack of access to WASH services in slums

While access to WASH services is clearly a fundamental right for all women, it is important to outline more specifically why this is the case and how under-provision affects female slum dwellers in particular. Although there is limited dedicated research on the interrelations between service availability and female poverty (Morrison *et al.*, 2010:107), evidence from small-scale qualitative studies suggests that gender-inequitable time burdens resulting from service deficits constrain women's and girls' ability to participate in all spheres of urban life (Chant, 1984,

---

Box 4.2   Access to WASH (water, sanitation and hygiene) services in the post-2015 agenda

The World Health Organisation/United Nations Children's Fund Joint Monitoring Programme for Water Supply and Sanitation commissioned an extensive review for the purposes of informing post-2015 WASH targets and monitoring indicators. This entailed widespread consultation with over 100 experts from more than 60 organisations across the world over a three-year period.

The targets arising from this process build on the existing MDG targets but with non-discrimination and equity as core components. These are, by 2030, to:

- eliminate open defecation;
- achieve universal access to basic drinking water, sanitation and hygiene for households, schools and healthcare facilities;
- halve the proportion of the population without access at home to safely managed drinking water and sanitation services; and
- progressively eliminate inequalities in access.

These targets are a central element of the proposed SDG6, which is to 'Ensure availability and sustainable management of water and sanitation for all'. Importantly, Target 6.2 specifically mentions women and girls: 'By 2030, achieve access to adequate and equitable sanitation and hygiene for all and end open defecation, paying special attention to the needs of women and girls and those in vulnerable situations' (UN Open Working Group, 2014:12).

Sources: WHO/UNICEF, 2014; UN Open Working Group, 2014.

2007b; UNMP/TFEGE, 2005). The heavy 'reproduction tax' (Palmer, 1992) exacted by these burdens reduces women's potential for rest and recreation, not to mention well-remunerated 'decent work', as well as having knock-on effects on human capital formation among younger female generations. For example, where girls are enlisted in reproductive tasks, this can impinge heavily upon their education, training and job experience (see below). Another critical consideration is that lack of services thwarts women's ability to engage in the kinds of small-scale, basic income-generating activities that might be their only options in a situation of limited skills and training, and exiguous start-up capital (Chant, 2007b; Truelove, 2011; see also below and Chapter 8, this volume).

Where decent services do not exist, as is the case in many slums throughout the Global South, women have to engage in several forms of compensating labour. Where dwellings lack domestic mains-supplied water, for instance, this vital resource needs to be collected from public standpipes, wells, bore holes, rivers or storage drums served by private tankers, with WHO data estimating that 72 per cent of this burden falls on women (Birch, 2011:79). Indeed, although men and boys may assist in the process, women and girls, due to their primary domestic roles, are more than twice as likely to undertake the task of water collection as their male counterparts (UN-Habitat, 2012a). Even if journeys are short in terms of distance, they may take long to execute where traversing inhospitable terrain, or queuing at outlets, is involved. At communal sources, for example, women may have to compete with one another, compounding the stress and conflict entailed in performing routine chores (see, e.g., Thompson *et al.*, 2000, on women and public water taps in urban Kenya; also Miraftab, 2001:148; and Box 4.3, below). Indeed, there may even be personal risk of injury or death, whether through accidents caused by delivery vehicles (see Bapat and Agarwal, 2003:86, on Pune, India), or drowning in rivers or canals (see Truelove, 2011, on New Delhi). As affirmed by Charisma Acey (2010:12) on the basis of her ethnographic research with nearly 800 households in southern Nigeria, women report 'spending

---

Box 4.3   Women's everyday struggles in a Bamako slum

In Samé, a squatter settlement in the north-west of Bamako, Mali, the burden of everyday struggles to ensure health through compound maintenance falls disproportionately on women, with additional disadvantages accruing from the fact that women have few opportunities to determine what is actually built on their compounds and which spaces are utilised for different functions.

Among the difficulties facing women where internal domestic space is at a premium is that most household work has to be done in the open air. In cases where male household heads do not invest in compound walls, this means that women's work is carried out with exposure to the elements – making it harder to make or keep things clean, not to mention compromising women's privacy, which may make them personally uncomfortable both physically and socially.

Indeed, given a large number of compounds which comprise extended families or a mixture of owner–occupiers and tenants, women end up 'having to deal with the day-to-day details of sharing space for housekeeping work'. This raises problems in terms of women timing their domestic labour to work around not only their own families' needs, but others', resulting in conflicts over children and animals, as well as the upkeep of communal infrastructure, such as kitchens and toilets. Moreover, given that women are responsible for disposing of rubbish – which is usually dumped in the road – 'Women are identified as culprits for the nuisances associated with piles of garbage.'

Source: Chant, 2007b:Box 6, 25
(based on Simard and De Koninck, 2001).

hours upon precious hour each day searching for water, to meet the daily needs of their households'. In light of this, it is no surprise that Diane Cornman-Levy *et al.* (2011:193) assert that, despite the opportunities for social interaction among women provided by communal services, 'The hard work of living in a slum or squatter settlement does not allow much time for leisure.'

In contexts in which there is inadequate public provision, and especially where privatisation has made the costs of water increasingly unaffordable for the poor (see Bayliss and McKinley, 2007), this has led to particular hardships for women (Anand, 2012; Brown, 2010). Indeed, Vandana Shiva (1998) has noted that water privatisation and commoditisation, which link access to the resource with capital or political power, have effectively created a 'patriarchal water order'.

Since privatisation is often associated with the poor's increased reliance on informal commercial suppliers, this can be extremely inimical since costs can be up to 8–10 times higher than from public sector providers (Chant, 2007b:62; see also Hughes and Wickeri, 2011:897–8; Patel, 2011:103–4; World Bank/IMF, 2013). Indeed, in some extreme cases, such as Nigeria, sales of 'pure water' or 'sachet water' for drinking, which are generally sold by men to female consumers, are traded at around 200 times more per litre than state pipe-borne water (Acey, 2010:13). Yet this does not necessarily provide a guarantee of quality. In Indonesia, for instance, the poor calibre of water purchased from informal operators such as cart vendors or tank operators may exacerbate children's susceptibility to conditions such as diarrhoea (Sverdlik, 2011:127), with obvious ramifications in terms of increasing women's unpaid care burdens (see also IWPR, 2015:16; Patel, 2011:101). In turn, when women have to tend to the sick, they often need additional water, which again impacts their already limited time and budgets (see Brown, 2010, on Tanzania).

Invidious practical and pecuniary challenges to water access in slums may also lead women to engage in ever more risky and potentially illegal or criminal behaviour, as described by Yaffa Truelove (2011) for New Delhi, where practices range from paying local henchmen to access water from tube wells, to bribing tanker drivers to make more regular deliveries, to illegally tapping into water pipes serving middle-class neighbourhoods. The latter, in particular, clearly puts women at risk of apprehension by security guards or police officers (ibid.:148; see also Bapat and Agarwal, 2003).

In respect of sanitation, too, women living in poorly served settlements are characteristically responsible for disposing of faecal matter in their compounds, or accompanying their children to appropriate sites (Chant, 2007b). Furthermore, it is now widely reported in a range of settings that women and girls are at particular risk of attack in and around toilet facilities located some distance from their homes, especially where, for reasons of modesty, they are more likely to use them under cover of darkness (Cornman-Levy *et al.*, 2011; McIlwaine, 2013; Sommer *et al.*, 2015; see also below, and Chapter 6, this volume).

The time burdens occasioned by such service deficits have immensely deleterious ramifications for women's and girls' accumulation of human and financial capital. For example, lack of access to WASH at home has a negative

Plate 4.3 Girls queuing at public water standpipe, Querétaro, Mexico

Source: Sylvia Chant.

impact on girls' education when they have to spend long hours collecting water or finding safe places to defecate or urinate (Truelove, 2011; see also below). These problems are exacerbated within schools themselves, where learning can be affected by a dearth of on-site drinking water and toilet facilities for students and staff (WaterAid 2015; seealso Chant, 2007b).

Poor water supplies, especially where these entail personal collection of water or waiting for infrequent deliveries, can also compromise women's ability to engage in paid employment in general, as noted by Truelove (2011) for New Delhi (see also IWPR, 2015:12). More specifically, lack of water can constrain particular types of home-based income-generating alternatives which might normally be preferred or be the only option for women who lack formal skills and education and have to rely solely on the resources provided by (gendered) socialisation at their disposal (Chant, 2014). For instance, lack of water can affect women's ability to perform laundry work, which can be a major generator of income in areas where male migrant workers are away from their wives for several months at a time (see Chant, 1996, on Costa Rica). Lack of water may further undermine women's ability to run small enterprises selling fruit and vegetables cultivated in urban plots, as noted by Brown (2010) in Dar es Salaam, Tanzania. When water is not only scarce or periodic but contaminated, this clearly has adverse health effects and threatens food security (ibid.; see also WaterAid, 2015). Redoubtable challenges also present themselves with regard to preparing food for sale in unserviced and insanitary conditions (Chant, 1996, 2007b). Proof that decent water provision can eliminate these disadvantages is evidenced in urban Ghana, where the introduction of a reliable resource afforded women potters the opportunity to increase the time they spent on productive activities and to expand their product range, and allowed women more generally to develop new initiatives in cola-nut and palm-oil processing as well as to distil a local alcoholic beverage known as akpeteshie (WSSCC, 2006:20). Sanitation projects also have the potential to provide livelihoods for vulnerable people in urban areas, and to challenge prevailing gender roles and identities via providing skills training in areas traditionally associated with men, such as plumbing (WaterAid, 2014; see also Box 4.4).

WASH, gendered dignity and exclusion

Despite these developments, and as intimated earlier, lack of WASH services not only impacts women's and girls' workloads but can seriously compromise their dignity and self-respect. As described graphically by Catarina de Albuquerque, a UN independent expert on the issue of human rights obligations related to safe drinking water and sanitation:

> Sanitation is not just about health, housing, education, work, gender equality, and the ability to survive. Sanitation, more than many other human rights issues, evokes the concept of human dignity; consider the vulnerability and shame that so many people experience every day when, again, they are forced to defecate in the open, in a bucket or a plastic bag . . . Dignity closely relates to self-respect, which is difficult to maintain when being forced to squat down in the open, with no respect for privacy, not having the opportunity to clean oneself after defecating and facing the constant threat of assault in such a vulnerable moment.
>
> (Extract from a 2009 report cited in Amnesty International, 2010:25)

Although sanitation shortfalls affect everyone, there is little doubt that women suffer most. For reasons of propriety, for example, women often have to restrict the times they visit, or accompany their children to, communal toilets, even when menstruating or pregnant (see, e.g., Amnesty International, 2010; Chant, 2011a; Ivens, 2008; Joshi, 2013; Tilley *et al.*, 2013). While communal facilities may be sex-segregated, as in some Indian slums, and a number of women declare a preference for shared toilets because these allow for some spatial distancing between the functions of cooking, cleaning and waste on hygiene grounds (Patel,

Plate 4.4 Drying laundry outside a tenement housing window in Mandaue City, Philippines
Source: Sylvia Chant.

2011:106), problems of privacy may still obtain. As Khosla (2009:9) points out when discussing toilet provision in India, the benchmark norm is one urinal for every forty men, and one sanitation facility for every twenty women. However, because women take charge of children's sanitation at their outlets, these are almost invariably over-subscribed. On top of this, women and girls may deprive themselves of food and drink in order to minimise the need to urinate or defecate, which carries a host of potential health problems (Patel, 2011:100). In New Delhi, for example, female slum dwellers interviewed by Yaffa Truelove (2011) stressed how they had to 'discipline their bodies' in an attempt to restrict defecation to early morning and late at night. This happens even where women and girls have stomach and bowel problems, such as diarrhoea, because a worse fate awaits them on account of public 'shame, humiliation and embarrassment' (ibid.:148). Adolescent girls are often the most vulnerable in their search for private and safe toilets, fearing damage to family honour if their trips become public knowledge or, worse still, that they will be attacked in the course of using communal sanitation facilities (see also Nallari, 2015, on Bengaluru, India).

Indeed, on account of a combination of cultural or religious norms, together with practical challenges linked with the availability and nature of menstrual management, women and girls are often especially restricted in their movements during menstruation (see Mahon and Fernandez, 2010:103, on Nepal), which flies in the face of their particularly pressing needs for water and sanitation facilities at such times. As Catherine Dolan *et al.* (2014:654) aptly note: 'Menstrual management does not operate in a vacuum; it is implicated by situated cultural processes, including gender and generational power structures.' For girls, non-attendance at school is a major effect, as discussed above, but it is also associated with various types of abuse and harassment from men when they detect that girls have reached puberty, referred to in Ghana as 'Eve-teasing' (ibid.:650; see also Jewitt and Ryley, 2014). For women in general, menstruation can sometimes mean being unable to leave home or participate in normal community life or paid work. While this can sometimes result in temporary relief from time burdens, it ultimately restricts their opportunities and rights in terms of participation in the religious, social and economic life of cities (House *et al.*, 2012).

It is also important to remember that concerns in this area not only relate to sanitation per se, but to lack of water and/or private spaces for bathing and cleaning. Pressures on cleanliness may be particularly pronounced around menstruation (Mahon and Fernandes, 2010; Tilley *et al.*, 2013; see above), but also extend more widely. As described by Deepa Joshi *et al.* (2011:103–5) for India, for instance, being unable to fulfil norms of personal hygiene (a prerequisite for many jobs) or failing to maintain clean dwellings (in accordance with norms of 'good housewifery') prove just as stressful to slum-dwelling women as a lack of sanitary facilities for themselves or visitors (see also Truelove, 2011). Indeed, with notions of 'filth', 'pollution' and 'nuisance' justifying a wave of slum demolitions in Delhi as it aspires to brand itself as a 'world-class city' (see Ghertner, 2008), this point becomes especially pertinent.

Gender and other service deficiencies in slums

While WASH services mainly refer to water, sanitation and hygiene, they also include solid waste management (Mahon and Fernandes, 2010), with deficits in this regard again particularly impacting female inhabitants of slums. Where no municipal rubbish collection is in place, or people cannot afford to pay for private waste contractors, women have to dispose of solid waste, and in cases where there is no domestic sanitation, as noted previously, faecal matter and waste water too (Khosla, 2009). In parts of the world where privatisation has occurred in waste management, as in a number of South African cities, women not only have to spend more time keeping their communities' streets clean, but those formerly employed as municipal waste pickers may lose their jobs, or, if re-engaged by private companies, may be relegated to low-end work (see Samson, 2003). Despite women's primary responsibility for informal solid waste disposal in many low-income communities, in the Amukoko slum in Lagos, Nigeria, Marja Järvelä and Eva-Marita Rinne-Koistinen (2005:382) note that commercial waste collection is a male activity, with the 'mallam men' responsible for gathering detritus from community dumping grounds in pushcarts often harassing women, especially those from Muslim households. As mentioned earlier, one key gender-specific aspect of waste management refers to the disposal of sanitary pads. This can often cause deep distress for women and girls as they attempt covert disposal which does not contravene cultural, religious or social mores (House *et al.*, 2012:95–6).

Plate 4.5 Making the message loud and clear: advising against indiscriminate solid waste dumping in The Gambia in English, French, Arabic and local languages, including Wollof, Mandinka and Fula

Source: Sylvia Chant.

From a more positive perspective, perhaps, informal recycling or waste-picking can provide some livelihood options for women in slums that lack formal solid waste services. In Pune, India, for example, Poornima Chikarmane (2012) describes how a cooperative of informal waste pickers, waste buyers, waste collectors and other urban poor joined forces with the Pune municipality (Pune Municipal Corporation; PMC) to manage solid waste management in the city. Called SWaCH (Solid Waste Collection Handling, but also a word meaning 'clean' in the local language), the cooperative comprises mainly (78 per cent) female members and provides front-end waste management services. SWaCH members make money from user fees and the sale of recyclable materials that they recover. In turn, this has led to an increase in self-respect and well-being among the women: 'The faceless waste picker causing nuisance at the municipal container has become a person who interacts with fellow residents on an equal footing' (ibid.:9; see also Navarrete, 2015; and below).

Less lucrative in its potential to spawn alternative income-generating activities among women is the lack of electricity, which is sometimes pirated from legally connected power lines, but even when slum residents have their own supplies they often have to guard against others stealing power and can also face substantial bills when electricity has been appropriated without their knowledge (Rashid, 2009; Subbaraman *et al.*, 2014). Moreover, having a legal connection may not guarantee protection from 'blackouts' (loss of supply) or 'brownouts' (low

Plate 4.6 Woman in an outdoor kitchen, Fajara, The Gambia

Source: Sylvia Chant.

voltage). Where electricity is not available (or only intermittently so), time has to be spent collecting or buying fuel and making fires to cook and heat water; and, due to lack of refrigeration, to shopping on a daily basis (Chant, 1996). To save money, people may also deny themselves the luxury of lighting after dark, which can clearly impact the operation of home-based businesses, as well as the ability of children and young adults to study (Subbaraman *et al.*, 2014; see also Chapter 8, this volume). Needless to say, caring for children in contexts of limited electricity, as with all the other services discussed in this chapter, adds massively to women's 'time poverty' (Blackden and Wodon, 2006; Chant, 1984, 2007b; Gammage, 2010; IWPR, 2015; Morrison *et al.*, 2010; UNMP/TFEGE, 2005).

The question of amenities is also a major issue. Where people suffer cramped conditions within their dwellings, the (safe) outside space available to them in the vicinity becomes of major significance, not only on account of paid and unpaid labour, but also in respect of relaxation and/or recreation (see Birch, 2011:85, on young and elderly women; also Gondwe and Ayenagbo, 2013). When such areas are potentially contaminated by solid waste, or prone to accidents arising from passing traffic, the risks to, and undermining of, quality of life among women and children in particular are exacerbated (Patel, 2011:102). A further issue relates to the dearth of 'female-only' spaces, such as community-based women's centres which might allow women to converse and interact freely without straying unacceptably far from their homes (see Schütte, 2014).

Pro-women WASH initiatives

On a more positive note, the case of SWaCH in Pune (outlined above) illustrates how women are responding to the challenges of infrastructural deficiencies that undermine their well-being in slums. Indeed, initiatives that revolve around improving WASH services for women, especially those addressing menstrual hygiene management, have now begun to burgeon in many poor neighbourhoods across the Global South both through women's own organising efforts and through interventions from NGOs (Mahon and Fernandes, 2010).

Programmes addressing this hitherto neglected issue include information-sharing, together with challenging taboos and cultures of silence surrounding menstruation, as well as more specific projects to facilitate access to sanitary pads in order to encourage girls to remain in school. For example, Sarah Jewitt and Harriet Ryley (2014:144) discuss Project Mwezi in Kisumu, Kenya, which was initially established by a British student and funded through charitable donations from the UK. This programme provides menstruation-related education for adolescent girls, as well as training on how to sew reusable 'Mwezi towels' using secondhand materials. In the same area, another NGO, the Kisumu Medical and Education Trust (K-MET), has developed machine-made pads. Also in Kenya, ZanaAfrica (ZanaA) has raised awareness of menstrual management through weekly school-based 'Empowerment Clubs', which not only encourage the use of sanitary towels and the development of related sanitary products but simul-taneously equip girls with information technology skills in an effort to reduce school absenteeism (see Box 4.4). Indeed, despite some controversy, there is general agreement that the provision of sanitary products can successfully increase girls' school attendance rates (Jewitt and Ryley, 2014, on Kenya; see also Dolan *et al.*, 2014, on Ghana). In addition to developing projects where women and girls engage in small-scale enterprises to make their own sanitary items, House *et al.* (2012:88) highlight initiatives to improve access to large-scale com-mercial products. These range from 'Makapads' in Uganda, which are fabricated from biodegradable papyrus and paper waste by social enterprises, to 'Bwiza pads' in Rwanda, which are assembled from imported materials and sold by local entrepreneurs. Whatever the specific product, the end result is greater choice for women and girls, which ultimately facilitates greater freedom, as well as acquisition of education and skills, entrepreneurial experience, and the accumulation of financial capital (see Chant, 2016, on the Nike Foundation's 'Girl Effect').

Through these kinds of initiatives, recognition that lack of access to WASH is a cause of gender inequality as well as a symptom of discrimination against women, especially in slum environments, has been reaffirmed.

Indeed, that 'women play a central part in the provision, management and safeguarding of water' was enshrined as one of the four 'Dublin Principles' agreed at the 1992 Conference on Water and the Environment (Harris, 2009:403). Although in practice women remain rather under-represented in the 'water world', and management continues to be dominated by men (UN-Water, 2005:7), the Dublin Principles nominally continue to guide international governance today

Box 4.4 Addressing menstruation, technology and empowerment: ZanaAfrica, EmpowerNet Clubs and making sanitary pads, Kibera, Nairobi, Kenya

In Kenya, 65 per cent of all women and girls cannot afford sanitary pads. Related to this, many women lose valuable hours of paid and unpaid work and 60 per cent of girls (1 million) miss on average six weeks of school per year because of lack of access to sanitary towels and to accessible, safe and private toilet facilities. This can lead to poor educational performance and school dropout, which severely undermine young women's economic opportunities and achievements as well as wider processes of empowerment. Girls who drop out of school also earn less than their peers, have sex and marry earlier, and are four times more likely to contract HIV.

ZanaAfrica (ZanaA) addresses gender inequality by working with women and girls in a range of contexts in order to equip them to be future leaders. In their work in the Kibera slum in Nairobi, they have developed a series of interrelated programmes in schools to address girls' educational attainment and attendance. It was found that one of the most immediate causes of school absenteeism was menstruation and especially lack of access to sanitary pads. As a result, the organisation commenced regular distribution of sanitary products and underwear to girls, which resulted in improved attendance.

ZanaA also took this initiative further by developing weekly 'Empowerment Clubs', which focus on broader psycho-social support in the context of poverty, gender and puberty. While the focus is on girls, they work with over 1000 students in groups of 15–20 young men and women (sex-segregated, where possible) and discuss issues such as peer pressure, drug use, self-esteem, relationships, love, health and diseases. Partnering with the Girl Effect, in 2011 an IT component was added to these clubs which introduced schoolgirls to the internet and social media through the use of laptops, modems, mobile phones and flip cameras in portable computer labs where girls learned basic skills in order to access the outside world using social media in a safe context. Through these 'EmpowerNet Clubs', girls were trained to blog and tweet about a range of subjects which gave them important skills while also allowing them to connect with other girls residing beyond the slum environment. Evaluations showed that the provision of sanitary towels and underwear allowed girls to participate in the initiative, where they not only attained technical training but acquired greater confidence and self-respect.

ZanaA is also working more widely with women in Kenya to make sanitary pads that are affordable, hygienic and environmentally friendly. Unlike expensive, imported sanitary towels, ZanaA's products are made by local women (thus creating employment) using local agricultural resources and sold through other NGOs via door-to-door saleswomen. Some of the profits are used to produce and place educational health inserts in the sanitary pad packages.

Sources: House *et al.*, 2012; Thaker, 2011; www.zanaafrica.org/.

(Harris, 2009:403), and have gained traction through the growing realisation that working with women makes WASH service projects more effective. For instance, the Water Supply and Sanitation Collaboration Council (WSSCC, 2006:8) notes that female involvement makes for better technical design, more sustainable and safe services, and greater potential to 'scale up' by empowering women and women's groups.

Although many women at the grassroots still tend to be engaged only as rank-and-file water users and implementers of projects – rather than consulted or integrated into decision-making processes in programming and policy – in the spirit of recognising that women's disproportionate responsibility for providing WASH services requires making their views more central within international, national and local governance structures, several initiatives are being implemented by relevant organisations. One example is the International Water Association (IWA), whose recent report, *An Avoidable Crisis*, recommends – and has committed resources to – developing specific programmes and vows 'to engage and encourage female participation at the educational level and at the professional level' (IWA, 2014:4). In another case, based in Tanzania, the WSSCC (2006) reports how Acord, a women's NGO, worked in a township to identify water sources and management processes. Finding that the water committees were run by men even though women were responsible for collecting water for household use, Acord helped to establish new committees in which 40 per cent of the members were female. This, in turn, not only assured that women's needs gained more priority but resulted in women demanding training in water management, sanitation and hygiene, and ultimately in improved services (ibid.:17).

At the national level, further welcome developments include an increase in the number of women serving as ministers of water and the environment, with female ministers in South Africa, Lesotho and Uganda implementing affirmative action programmes to train women for water- and sanitation-related careers, including science and engineering (ibid.; see also Panda, 2007). Moreover, in an example of gender mainstreaming at the institutional level, an urban water and sanitation project in Zanzibar funded by the African Development Bank (AfDB, 2012:3) specifically demanded and funded a 'gender review of the water policy and gender sensitisation of ZAWA (Zanzibar Water Authority) staff' as well as the gender-sensitive construction of school water supply and facilities.

Concluding comments

This chapter has examined how the lack of WASH and other services can severely undermine women's well-being in terms of their emotional and physical health as well as their ability to contribute to wider community and urban development in respect of maximising their economic contributions. While access to clean water and adequate sanitation facilities has nominally been integral to the WASH agenda since the Dublin Principles on Water and Sanitation in 1992, hygiene services, and especially menstrual hygiene management, have, until very recently, been routinely ignored. This is disturbing, given the particular pertinence of the latter for women and girls in the face of considerable social and cultural stigma associated with menstruation together with the demanding practicalities of life in slum communities. While Anupama Nallari's (2015:86) comment relates to adolescent girls in Bengaluru, India, it arguably has resonance for young female slum dwellers everywhere:

> Lack of sanitation . . . is not just an inconvenience for adolescent girls. It shapes their very identity and how they experience the world around them. In a sense, the lack of sanitation is a metaphor for their lives – a painful reflection and prediction of their own lack of value.

In light of the broader range of issues covered in this chapter, Bipasha Baruah's (2007:2102; see also IWPR, 2015:15) observations pertaining to slum upgrading in the context of Ahmedabad are arguably more widely applicable, too:

> The physical, mental and spiritual transition from eking out an existence in areas that are perceived as eyesores, and hotbeds of urban crime, disease, and disrepair, to living in low-income housing societies complete with basic amenities, has a strong dignifying effect on slum residents in general, and women in particular.

On a more negative note, Baruah's point about perceptions of unimproved slums being 'hotbeds . . . of disease' is not that far from the truth in many cases, with service deficiencies in WASH playing a major part in gendered health inequalities. As affirmed by the Commonwealth Secretariat (2013:8): 'Shortages of clean water and sanitation can exacerbate both water-borne diseases such as diarrhoea and dysentery and vector-borne diseases such as malaria and dengue.' These health problems are, hardly surprisingly, often at their most pronounced in urban slums, and have particularly injurious implications for women and girls, as explored further in the next chapter.

5 Gender and health

An urban penalty for slum-dwelling women?

Introduction: the gender–health nexus as a development issue in cities

Health is firmly established as a major development issue, manifested in the fact that four of the MDGs relate to health in some way: reduce child mortality; improve maternal health; combat HIV/AIDS, malaria and other diseases; and ensure environmental sustainability (Schweitzer et al., 2012:15). Among these, Target 7c on access to safe water and sanitation is especially pertinent in urban slums, as identified in Chapter 4. Indeed, after being underweight at birth, the second most common health risk in low-income countries, as measured by disability adjusted life years (DALYs), owes to the assemblage of unsafe water, sanitation and hygiene (WHO, 2009a:12). This, in turn, accounts for the fact that diarrhoea remains a leading cause of death among children under the age of five (UNICEF, 2015:46). For these reasons, it is little surprise that there is a proposed SDG dedicated to health, which is to 'ensure healthy lives and promote well-being for all at all ages' (UN Open Working Group, 2014:9).

Although health conditions in cities in general are better than those in rural areas, this is not necessarily the case for the urban poor, and perhaps especially for women (García-Moreno and Chawla, 2011; Jones et al., 2014; Montgomery, 2009). That said, while 'urbanisation creates new issues for health and healthcare for women', many of which are 'hazardous' (Meleis, 2011:2), knowledge of intra-urban differences in health status, whether between women and men or between slum and non-slum settlements, remains sparse (see Mwangangi, 2011:229). By the same token, there is arguably sufficient data to suggest that, 'In most cities, there are large differences in mortality rates and the prevalence of many life- and health-threatening diseases between neighbourhoods or districts with concentrations of low-income groups and those areas with a predominance of middle- and higher-income groups' (Mitlin and Satterthwaite, 2013:92; see also Gulis et al., 2004:226; UN-Habitat/WHO, 2010:xiii). As further echoed by Kate Hawkins et al. (2013:5): 'The evidence consistently shows that poor people living in informal settlements in urban areas face a disproportionate health challenge', in which there are strong gendered dimensions:

residence in low-income urban areas is . . . associated with particular health challenges for women and girls, such as those linked with sexual, reproductive and maternal health; alcohol use; non-communicable diseases related to poor diet, tobacco and sedentary lifestyles; as well as an ongoing high prevalence of infectious diseases such as HIV and TB. There is also concern about the mental health burden arising from the stresses of surviving on the economic margins in large cities characterised by high levels of crime and violence, and more fragmented access to social support.

(Ibid.)

In light of broad acknowledgement globally that gender inequalities are extremely significant in the social determinants of health (Connell, 2012; Cook, 2013; Sen and Ostlin, 2011; WHO, 2009b), and that these are likely to be particularly marked in urban slums of the Global South, this chapter explores the challenges facing women and girls therein. This is highly relevant to our conceptual framework of a 'gender–urban–slum interface' in several ways. Not only does women's right to health, as a 'first-generation' right, directly influence mortality, morbidity, fertility, migration, household dynamics and ageing, but it also intersects with such factors as housing and access to land and WASH services (see Chapters 3 and 4). While disparities in women's access to these services and assets are frequently underpinned by gender inequalities that serve to compound ill-health, it is essential to think through the ways in which poor health *itself* impinges on women's ability to mobilise and accumulate physical, financial and human capital in slum environments. This chapter not only elucidates these two-way relationships but discusses some interventions that can help to alleviate the gendered health effects of slum life within the broader context of the MDGs and proposed SDGs.

Gender and health in cities and slums

Urban health, slum dwelling and multiple disease burdens

While recognising that a significant number of the income poor reside in non-slum areas, slum populations would appear to fare worse than the majority of urban inhabitants in terms of physical and mental ill-being alike. In the arena of physical ill-health, communicable disease is often the most prominent, especially in deprived and densely populated slum areas (see Unger and Riley, 2007; see also below). In a context in which nine-tenths of child diarrhoea globally, and 4–8 per cent of the overall burden of disease is caused by poor-quality water, sanitation and hygiene (Harpham, 2009:110), it is perhaps no surprise that almost half of the urban residents in Africa, Asia and Latin America have one or more communicable diseases, such as diarrhoea or worm infections (Sclar *et al.*, 2005:901). Non-existent or deficient sanitation also increases the risks of malaria, dengue and yellow fever because the relevant vectors breed in pools of standing water, latrines and septic tanks (ibid.; Harpham, 2009). Moreover, as evidenced by the outbreak of Ebola in the West African countries of Guinea, Liberia and Sierra Leone in

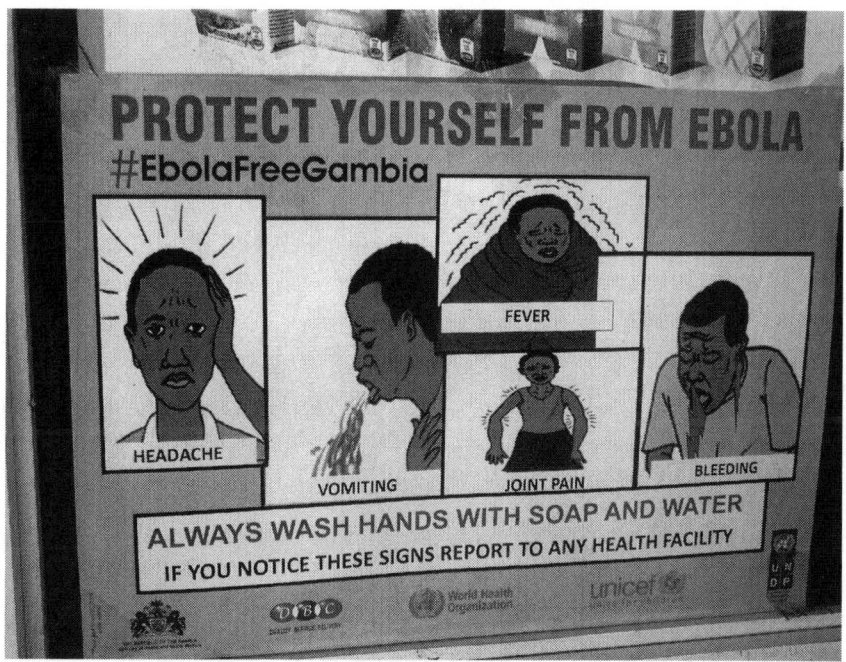

Plate 5.1 Public information campaign against Ebola, The Gambia, January 2015

Source: Sylvia Chant.

2014, there was not only an unprecedented 'urbanisation' of the virus but a situation in which poor sanitary conditions in slums, together with overcrowding, led to disproportionate levels of infection and death among lower-income residents in cities such as Freetown and Monrovia (see World Bank, 2015). More generally, high levels of overcrowding in slums makes contracting tuberculosis, respiratory infections and meningitis more likely, especially where this is compounded by malnutrition. Similarly, when populations are inadequately vaccinated, over-crowding means that diseases such as diphtheria, whooping cough and measles are transmitted much more easily. Attention has also been drawn to the global interconnectedness of networks and 'global cities' in spreading transmissible disease (see, e.g., Ali and Keil, 2012).

However, beyond communicable 'diseases of poverty', it is important to recognise that degenerative conditions such as cardio-vascular disease, diabetes and cancer are also on the rise (Agyei-Mensah *et al.*, 2015; Levine, 2011:32), not only in urban areas in general, but specifically in slums. The latter phenomenon appears to be especially marked among women, possibly due to female bias in demographic ageing (see Chapter 1), with breast and cervical cancer increasingly prevalent causes of female mortality in developing countries (Frenk and Gómez-Dantés, 2011:17, 20; Mwangangi, 2011:237). Clearly this poses a threatening situation to people facing inadequate public healthcare and problems of spatial inaccessibility which prevent early diagnosis and treatment, as well as by their inability to afford costly private alternatives (see Moser, 2011; Mwangangi, 2011). While there is much talk about most developing countries now facing a 'double disease burden' of non-communicable and communicable diseases (Mitra and Rodriguez-Fernandez, 2010; Sverdlik, 2011), this could well be interpreted as a 'triple burden', according to Julio Frenk and Octavio Gómez-Dantés (2011:16), who assert:

> the developing world simultaneously faces a triple burden of ill-health: first the unfinished agenda of common infections, malnutrition, and reproductive health problems; second, the emerging challenge represented by noncommunicable diseases, mental disorders, and the growing scourge of injury and violence; and third, the health risks associated with globalisation, including the threat of pandemics like AIDS and influenza, the trade in harmful products like tobacco, the health consequences of climate change, and the dissemination of harmful lifestyles leading to the epidemic of obesity.

Similarly, and in particular relation to urban areas, UN-Habitat/WHO (2010:xii) identify a 'triple threat of urban diseases and health conditions' comprising infectious diseases such as HIV, tuberculosis, pneumonia and diarrhoea, non-communicable diseases such as heart disease, cancers and diabetes, and a range of injuries (especially traffic accidents) and violence. As further noted by Frenk and Gómez-Dantés (2011:16): 'This protracted health transition is compressed in urban environments, especially in slums,' which makes understanding the gender dimensions of health imperative (see Frye *et al.*, 2008; Hawkins *et al.*, 2013; and see below).

Despite a general paucity of data on intra-urban differentials in health, most slum/non-slum comparisons to date have focused on communicable diseases, with research based on India's 2005–6 National Family Health Survey (NFHS-3) in the context of eight large Indian cities – Chennai, Delhi, Hyderabad, Indore, Meerut, Mumbai and Nagpur – revealing that slum dwellers suffer a disproportionate risk of transmissible illnesses such as tuberculosis, which, after HIV/AIDS, is the second-biggest cause of death by a single infectious agent worldwide, and mainly concentrated in the Global South (Mitlin and Satterthwaite, 2013:111). In Kenya, data from the African Population and Health Research Centre compiled in 2002 indicate that the prevalence of diarrhoea containing blood in children under three years old, in two weeks prior to interview, was nearly 12 per cent in Nairobi's informal settlements, as against just under 4 per cent in Nairobi as a whole (ibid.:53, Figure 3.2). This is accompanied by vulnerability to health conditions linked with inadequate healthcare and diet, such as anaemia, with women and young children particularly affected (Gupta *et al.*, 2009: 43ff.). Indeed, again in Nairobi, infant and child mortality rates, as expressed in deaths per 1000 live births, are both around 50 in the city as a whole, but in informal settlements infant mortality rates are about twice this level, and child mortality as high as 150. In the city's largest slums, such as Kibera and Embakasi, rates are higher still, with as many as 250 under-five deaths for every 1000 live

births in the latter settlement (Mitlin and Satterthwaite, 2013:92; see also Figure 5.1 and below).

Indeed, even if, on balance, health conditions are generally better than in rural areas, Demographic and Health Surveys (DHSs) conducted in forty-seven low- and middle-income countries have demonstrated that, after controlling for wealth, education and other socio-economic indicators, the 'urban advantage' for children in respect of lower mortality rates and nutritional status largely disappears (Sverdlik, 2011:141). Even in comparatively wealthy developing countries, such as Brazil, Colombia, the Dominican Republic and Paraguay, rates of infant and child mortality are actually *higher* among urban populations when compared with their rural counterparts (ibid.:142).

Malnutrition and food insecurity

Accepting that nutritional status remains a major factor influencing in health in cities (Hawkins *et al.*, 2013; McNicoll, 2013; Mitlin and Satterthwaite, 2013), Cecilia Tacoli, Budoor Bukhari and Susannah Fisher (2013:iv) point out that there are often huge disparities between wealthy and poor residents, and that 'low and irregular incomes are the root cause of urban food insecurity, but inadequate housing and basic infrastructure and limited access to services contribute to levels of malnutrition and food insecurity that are often as high, if not higher than in rural areas'.

In light of this, it is no surprise that the prevalence of malnutrition in India and Bangladesh is more than twice as high in slums than in non-slum areas, at 54 per cent versus 21 per cent, and 51.4 per cent versus 24 per cent, respectively (UN-Habitat, 2010d:1). In the Democratic Republic of Congo, too, 41 per cent of children are malnourished in slums, compared with 16 per cent of their non-slum counterparts (ibid.). A detailed study of 11–18-year-olds in Dhaka, Bangladesh, conducted by Takashi Izutsu *et al.* (2006) corroborates these patterns, with another study of Bangladesh, based on Urban Health Survey data for six cities, discovering a considerably higher incidence of smoking (of both cigarettes and *bidis* – hand-rolled cigarettes which have greater concentrations of tar and nicotine) among men in slums (59.6 per cent) than in non-slum areas (46.4 per cent) (Khan *et al.*, 2009; see also Gulis *et al.*, 2004:225). Tobacco consumption is widely associated with risks of premature death not only among smokers themselves, but, as Khan *et al.* (2009:7–8) note, within their households too, with the 'devastating effects' arguably worst for people living in poverty. This is partly because tobacco use can divert income from food expenditure (ibid.). However, another issue is its role in exacerbating the risks of respiratory disease commonly associated with overcrowded and poorly ventilated slum dwellings (see below).

Women and health in slums: a gendered 'urban (slum) penalty'?

Health conditions in slums in general often compare so unfavourably with other parts of cities that the notion of an 'urban penalty' in health has been widely debated (e.g. Harpham, 2009; Hawkins *et al.*, 2013; Montgomery *et al.*, 2004; Satterthwaite, 2011; Sverdlik, 2011). That this is likely to be gendered has been pointed up, inter alia, by Allison Goebel, Belinda Dodson and Trevor Hill (2010:579) in the context of Msunduzi Municipality (formerly Pietermaritzberg) in South Africa. Goebel *et al.* allege that female-headed households are at above-average risk of exposure to an 'urban penalty' in health.

For women in slums, the risks to physical and mental well-being are exacerbated by a range of 'stressors' attached to their inputs to household reproduction in straitened circumstances (see Chant, 2007b; Ekblad, 1993; WHO, 2009b). For example, cooking with solid fuels such as biomass (wood and crop residues), coal and charcoal is far more harmful to both the environment (through deforestation) and individuals (through lung and atmosphere-polluting hydrocarbons and carcinogens) than 'cleaner' but more expensive alternatives, such as kerosene, liquid petroleum, gas and electricity. This is especially the case in cramped, poorly ventilated spaces, such that 'indoor air pollution' has been termed a 'quiet and neglected killer' of poor women and children (UN-Habitat, 2008a; see also Agyei-Mensah *et al.*, 2015; García-Moreno and Chawla, 2011:59; Gupta *et al.*, 2009:39; Gulis *et al.*, 2004: 226; Galea and Vlahov, 2005:346; Hawkins *et al.*, 2013; Rolnik, 2012:13; Sverdlik, 2011:128). Indeed, although cigarette smoking remains a predominantly male preserve, the risks to women caused by exposure to indoor smoke mean that chronic obstructive pulmonary disorder (COPD) is over 50 per cent higher among women than men at a global level (WHO, 2009b:10). In one

Plate 5.2 Woman on a trip to collect water in a peri-urban slum, Pushkar City, India

Source: Danielle Da Silva.

survey in Accra, Ghana, nearly 30 per cent of poor women reported respiratory problems in the two weeks prior to interview – more than twice the rate among women of middling income, and ten times that reported by wealthy women (Sverdlik, 2011:129). On top of this, cramped and unsafe housing conditions may account for a disproportionate number of fire-related fatalities among poor young women (García-Moreno and Chawla, 2011:59). In situations where piped domestic water supplies are unavailable, severe fatigue, strain on joints and so on can arise from carrying heavy vessels over long distances, often over hills on rough footpaths, or through ditches and open sewers (see Chant, 1996; IWPR, 2015:17).

Plate 5.3 Women returning home with laundry washed in River Cuale, Puerto Vallarta, Mexico

Source: Sylvia Chant.

Mental health conditions, as previously intimated, constitute an important aspect of the health panorama for poor and slum-dwelling women. At a global level, depression has been found to affect women and the poor disproportionately (see Patel, 2001; Spitzer, 2005), and for developing regions more particularly it is a leading cause of disability among urban women (Montgomery, 2009; see also Correa-de-Araujo, 2011:110). As summarised by García-Moreno and Chawla (2011:56), the nexus between gender and poverty leads to a situation where poor mental health is particularly biased towards women in low-income neighbourhoods.

Despite rather patchy data on this topic for cities in developing countries, evidence from São Paulo, Brazil, reveals that common mental disorders (CMDs), such as fatigue, anxiety and depression, are highest (at 21 per cent) in its poorest socio-economic district, and lowest (12 per cent) in its wealthiest (Blue, 1996:95). This resonates with recent evidence from Cape Town, South Africa, which demonstrates a higher prevalence of CMDs in peri-urban slums (35 per cent) compared with rural areas (27 per cent), and that gender (being female), unemployment and substance abuse are the most common correlates (Harpham, 2009:112). Critical factors affecting low-income women, aside from the exigencies of their dwelling environments, include unemployment and job precarity, and the insecurities attached to migrant status (Harpham, 2009; Hawkins *et al.*, 2013:17). This is notwithstanding some variations on a gendered front. For example, Izutsu *et al.*'s (2006) aforementioned study in Dhaka found that CMDs such as anxiety and depression were, perhaps rather unusually, more marked in non-slum communities among young women and men alike. The only exception was 'conduct' problems – associated with antisocial behaviour, substance abuse and crime – which were most pronounced among adolescent slum-dwelling males. None the less, and in more general terms, as summarised by Julio Frenk and Oscar Gómez-Dantés (2011:17): 'The rifts in the social fabric, particularly frequent in excluded urban populations . . . create fertile soil for the development of mental problems.'

Despite this scenario, when it comes to healthcare, many countries in the Global South lack public provision for mental and behavioural disorders, and chronic depression among women has been 'particularly neglected' (Pinn and Corry, 2011:177). In relation to Ghana, for example, Victoria de Menil *et al.* (2012) point out that although an estimated 9 per cent of the national disease burden is accounted for by mental illness, people have traditionally been reluctant to seek help for CMDs due to stigma, likelihood of misdiagnosis and poor treatment in psychiatric hospitals. Moreover, in the Ghanaian case, there is a serious dearth of specialist personnel, with only four psychiatrists and 500 psychiatric nurses for a population of 22 million, although this is apparently set to change given the introduction of a progressive new national mental health law (ibid.). More generally, and on the basis of data from WHO World Mental Health Surveys, it appears that fewer than 15 per cent of women in developing countries who suffer from moderate to severe mental disorders, including depression, are treated for their condition (Frenk and Gómez-Dantés, 2011:21).

It should also be noted that mental disorders and other disabilities, such as blindness, impaired hearing and restricted physical mobility, may make women

Plate 5.4 Private mental healthcare facility, Bakau New Town, The Gambia

Source: Sylvia Chant.

more prone than men to stigma and social exclusion, which, coupled with inadequate access to health services, may render them especially vulnerable to deprivation in urban areas (Correa-de-Araujo, 2011).

Gendered health, life-course and rights

Also central to understanding women's experiences of health compared with those of men is the intersectionality of gender with the life-course which highlights important differences among women. For example, the causes of death and disability among women and girls tend to shift from communicable illness during childhood and youth (diarrhoeal and respiratory diseases), to HIV/AIDS, maternal and perinatal conditions among young women and those into their thirties and forties, to stroke, cancers and heart disease among older women (Correa-de-Araujo, 2011:4). On top of this, elderly women are more likely to be affected by mental health disorders, such as dementia (IWPR, 2015:14). The World Health Organisation (2009b:xi) claims that an approach sensitive to life-course changes is essential for understanding how health status in childhood, throughout adolescence and into the reproductive years affects not only women in later life but also subsequent generations. It also notes that such a perspective facilitates recognition that women's health is influenced by both biological and social factors, and especially gender inequalities (see also Cook, 2013; Sen and Ostlin,

2011). As Rebecca Cook (2013:48) has emphasised: 'Women's poor physical and psychological health may represent a metaphor for the poor health of women's rights.' This highlights the need not just to move beyond a focus on health risks associated with women alone, such as cervical cancer, pregnancy and childbirth, but to situate women's health needs alongside wider gendered rights (WHO, 2009b:xi).

In the context of slum communities, as we have seen, these rights are often severely compromised, especially among older women. Notwithstanding poor healthcare coverage in general, girls and women of reproductive age are often given the lion's share of attention, even though the disproportionate ageing of urban populations by gender is likely to make elderly women particularly vulnerable. The vulnerability of older female cohorts not only owes to their greater susceptibility to chronic illnesses, but to the limited social and economic resources available to them, including access to support networks and formal healthcare (Meleis, 2011:7). In the health MDGs, however, they were not identified as a priority group; instead, the focus was on younger generations.

Urban health, gender and the Millennium Development Goals

Despite this major caveat, with 'successful "development" . . . so intimately related to health' (Satterthwaite, 2011:5), it is no wonder that at least the latter featured explicitly in three of the Millennium Development Goals, notably MDG4 (reduce child mortality), MDG5 (improve maternal health) and MDG6 (combat HIV/ AIDS, malaria and other diseases), and that these have galvanised considerable, albeit uneven, advances. As argued by Julian Schweitzer *et al.* (2012:2):

> the available evidence suggests that the health MDGs have been effective in accelerating progress on target indicators, in stimulating global political support in the creation of significant global institutions dedicated to helping countries achieve the MDGs and in stimulating research and debate on systemic approaches to improving health outcomes.

Child mortality

Some progress has been made in MDG4's objective of reducing by two-thirds the under-five mortality rate between 1990 and 2015, with a drop of 28 per cent in developing countries since 1990 and an accelerated rate of decline from 2000 onwards (UN, 2010a:26–7). None the less, in only two regions of the Global South – East Asia and Latin America – has the target been fully achieved (UNICEF, 2015:26–7), and in many poor countries, especially in sub-Saharan Africa, preventable child mortality remains excessively high (UN, 2010a:26–7; see also Figure 5.1). One in seven children in rural areas and urban slums in the poorest countries of the world do not have access to essential health services (Save the Children, 2011a:17–23). This disproportionately affects girls, particularly in parts of East Asia, South Asia and North Africa, where 'son preference' contributes to a neglect of girls' health needs, most notably where healthcare costs are borne by families themselves (Hesketh and Xing, 2006; also World Bank, 2011c:124). On top of this, as previously noted, under-five mortality is particularly rife in poor areas of cities (UN-Habitat/WHO, 2010:xiii). In urban Africa, for example, there are approximately 135 deaths per 1000 live births among the poorest 20 per cent of the urban population compared with around 95 per 1000 in cities overall (ibid.:xiv). While this owes in large part to poor water and sanitation provision in slums, limited access to maternal health services, including skilled birth attendance, is also significant (ibid.:xiii).

The latter, which refers to professional care around birth, reduces the likelihood of mortality and disability among infants, children and mothers alike. Yet, in the Global South, it has been noted that coverage is much lower among the most deprived urban residents. Indeed, as of 2010, UN-Habitat/WHO (2010:65) projected that in 38 per cent of countries in Africa, Asia and the Americas fewer

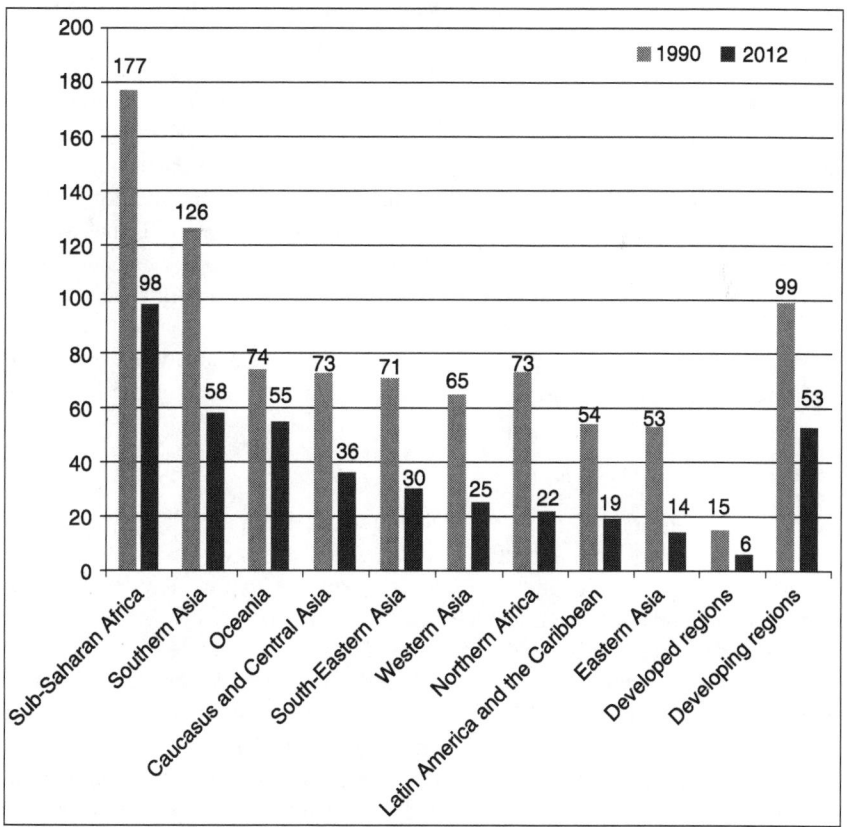

Figure 5.1 Under-five mortality rate by region, 1990–2012 (per 1000 live births)

Source: Adapted from UN, 2014b:24.

than half of the poorest women in urban areas would be served by skilled birth attendants by 2015. According to UNICEF (2015:32–3), the dismal situation whereby women in the poorest quintile are only one-third as likely to have professionally assisted births as their counterparts in the top quintile has not changed in fifteen years. As a more specific example, in Bangladesh, only 6 per cent of the poorest fifth of the urban population has access to skilled birth attendance, compared with 75 per cent among the wealthiest cohort (UN-Habitat/ WHO, 2010:65).

Shortages of trained midwives are partly responsible for the fact that many women fail to receive recommended levels of care during their pregnancies in both urban and rural areas (Save the Children, 2011b:16–20), and in slums, as noted above, this is particularly marked. In major Indian cities, for example, indicators of delivery and post-natal care are consistently poorer than in non-slum areas, and disproportionately affect women on low incomes (Gupta *et al.*, 2009:43–4). In Kenya, too, low (or delayed) take-up of antenatal care in Nairobi slums reduces the proportion of deliveries attended by skilled personnel (Ochako *et al.*, 2011; see also Ziraba *et al.*, 2009). Although antenatal care is free in Kenya, the charging of fees for births or complications in hospitals, as well as the stigmatisation of mothers without possession of antenatal cards, act as particular deterrents to poor women (Essendi *et al.*, 2010). Indeed, it is important to bear in mind that 'adverse maternal outcomes' are functions of a lack not only of affordable care but of appropriate care, for example in terms of the respect paid to poor women by healthcare personnel (ibid.; see also Izugbara and Ngilangwa, 2010). Another critical, but perhaps less widely recognised, factor is that women in poverty often undertake heavy and physically hard workloads, especially in the run-up to childbirth, which places them at risk of miscarriage or other complications. This is compounded by the fact that intimate partner violence often increases when women are pregnant, particularly where husbands are jobless or under severe economic pressure (ibid.; see also Chapter 6, this volume).

Maternal health and mortality

For the above reasons, MDG5 (on reducing maternal mortality by three-quarters worldwide between 1990 and 2015) is one of the most 'off-track' of the eight Millennium Development Goals. Despite a 34 per cent drop in maternal deaths in developing regions, the mean annual rate of decline (2.3 per cent) is far short of the target 5.5 per cent (UN, 2010a:30–1). As David Satterthwaite *et al.* (2013:15) point out: 'no region has managed to meet the target of reducing maternal deaths by three-quarters'. Indeed, with such uneven and hesitant progress, Albrecht Jahn *et al.* (2013:109) assert that 'increased attention and resources' will be needed to address maternal mortality beyond 2015 (see also Commonwealth Secretariat, 2013:4). This is especially likely to be the case in sub-Saharan Africa, which has the highest maternal mortality levels, at 640 maternal deaths per 100,000 live births in urban areas (and 870 in rural areas), as against developing region averages of 290 and 450, respectively (UN, 2010a:32–4; 2010b:1).

Maternal mortality is widely regarded as a 'litmus test' of women's status (Graham, 2004:6), since although most maternal deaths are avoidable, and increasing numbers of women now receive antenatal care, this is compromised by poverty and early and frequent pregnancies, which often stem from male control over female sexuality (Fraser, A., 2005; UNDP, 2005:33; WHO, 2005a).

HIV/AIDS, malaria and other diseases

Rather better progress has been made in MDG6's aim to combat the spread of HIV/AIDS, malaria and other diseases by 2015. HIV infection rates seem to have peaked in 1999, and they have declined significantly since 2002, thanks largely to a massive scaling up in anti-retroviral therapy (ART). That said, in absolute terms the number of people living with HIV is still rising, partly because they are living longer with the condition (UNAIDS, 2010:7–8), but also because treatment is still short of universal, and public information campaigns are not always effective (UN, 2010a:45). Although substantial progress has been made in tackling malaria, the disease remains responsible for over 850,000 deaths each year, of which 90 per cent occur in Africa (ibid.:46). In turn, tuberculosis remains the second-highest communicable cause of death after HIV/AIDS, with only marginal improvements witnessed in recent years (ibid.:51).

While women are just over 50 per cent of HIV-affected persons worldwide, this figure is nearly 60 per cent in sub-Saharan Africa, the traditional heartland of the pandemic, and globally HIV/AIDS is still the leading cause of death among women aged 15–49 years (UNICEF, 2015:38). Women aged 15–24 years are at least twice as likely to contract the disease than their male counterparts (UNAIDS, 2010), which helps to account for the fact that young women currently comprise two-thirds of newly infected persons (UNICEF, 2015:39). Urban residence also seems to put women at particular risk, with HIV prevalence among women in towns and cities in sub-Saharan Africa 1.5 times higher than the figure for their male counterparts, and 1.8 times higher than that for women in rural areas (UN-Habitat/WHO, 2010:54). As Debbie Budlender and Francine Lund (2011:932) comment: 'As is common in heterosexually-driven AIDS epidemics, such as that of South Africa, women are more likely than men to be infected, for both biological and social reasons.'

Slums again feature prominently, with recent research in Korogocho, Nairobi, finding that HIV prevalence was nearly three times the national average of 6.1 per cent (Sverdlik, 2011:131). This is corroborated by another major survey of Nairobi slums (Korogocho and Viwandani), based on primary and secondary data, which found that HIV prevalence was 12 per cent among slum residents compared with 5 per cent among non-slum urban dwellers, and 6 per cent among the rural population, with women disproportionately affected, especially where their first sexual experience had been prior to the age of fifteen years (Madise *et al.*, 2012). Women in this group were 62 per cent more likely to be HIV-positive compared with those who had not had their first sexual encounter until after the age of nineteen (ibid.). Other studies from Kenya and South Africa indicate similar threats to poor urban women (see Hawkins *et al.*, 2013:24).

Young women's greater susceptibility to HIV infection is in part due to their greater physiological vulnerability, but also to socio-cultural factors, such as first intercourse with sexually experienced older men. This frequently intersects with poverty insofar as poor urban women's and girls' dependence on cash income and limited livelihood opportunities increase the possibility of unsafe 'transactional sex' (see Chant and Evans, 2010; Holmqvist, 2009; Hughes and Wickeri, 2011). In the case of Gaborone, Botswana, for example, McIlwaine and Datta (2004:500) discuss how the construction of sexualities among the young women in their research in two schools (one of which was a state school whose pupils were from slum communities) were dominated by fear of HIV/AIDS and teenage pregnancy directly related to transactional sexual relations with older men or 'sugar daddies', or through coercive sex. These processes were underpinned by 'asymmetrical power relations driven by age and gender inequalities', where young women were aware that 'men who rape do not use condoms, and so the chances of contracting HIV and/or becoming pregnant were heightened' (ibid.; see also Jewkes, *et al.*, 2001, on South Africa). However, despite a range of 'behavioural' factors deemed to be associated with urban environments – such as greater opportunities for sexual networking, migration and youthful urban age structures, which have led to interpretations such as that by Nyovani Madise *et al.* (2012:1145), who highlight that 'Ample evidence exists . . . of risky sexual practices among slum residents' – other factors relating to poverty and slum life are also significant. For example, slum-dwelling girls face a greater likelihood of early sexual debut associated with lack of privacy, insecurity and gender-based violence. According to UNAIDS, for example, intimate partner violence (IPV) increases women's risk of contracting HIV by as much as 50 per cent (see García-Moreno and Chawla, 2011:57; Musuya, 2011:242; and Chapter 6, this volume).

On top of this, people may already have weak immune systems resulting from poor nutrition and other communicable diseases, with heavy 'viral loads' increasing their susceptibility to infection and accelerated progression from HIV to AIDS. In turn, HIV-affected individuals are more contagious when co-infected with other diseases, such as bilharzia (up to three times) and malaria (up to seven times). Last but not least, poor urban populations often have limited access to health facilities or preventive healthcare in the form of decent services, and communities riven by HIV/AIDs are less likely to be socially cohesive and/or able to cope with the fallout of the pandemic (see Ambert *et al.*, 2007; Bähre, 2007; Hawkins *et al.*, 2013:25; Madise *et al.*, 2012:1145; Patel, 2011:102–3; UN-Habitat, 2010b:18; Van Donk, 2006; see also Chapter 4, this volume).

HIV/AIDS is clearly not the only infectious condition which affects female and male residents in urban slums, and, as we know, demographic ageing has raised the chances of even low-income slum dwellers contracting the kinds of degenerative mental and physical conditions which have traditionally been more associated with elite groups and populations in wealthier economies. However, even if the epidemic is brought further under control, the prospective threats to health from many other communicable diseases in developing world cities, especially those situated in coastal areas and on floodplains, are likely to become more pronounced in the wake of climate change (see Banks *et al.*, 2011; IWPR, 2015:18–19; Kovats *et al.*, 2014; Levine, 2011:33; Moser and Stein, 2011; Satterthwaite, 2009; Satterthwaite *et al.*, 2007; Sverdlik, 2011:145–7; UN-Habitat, 2010b:24ff.; UNICEF, 2015:6). As summarised by Diana Mitlin and David Satterthwaite (2013:145):

> Most urban centres in low- and middle-income nations have very large deficits in the infrastructure and services needed to limit the direct and indirect impacts of climate change, and local governance structures that lack the capacity and funding – and often the willingness – to address this.

Climate-change-related disasters and their aftermath can also exert a heavy toll on people's mental health, and in the particular case of women may intensify their subjection to various forms of gender-based violence (see Bradshaw, 2013a), as discussed further in the next chapter. Given the likelihood that urban poor populations will be unduly affected, the need to generate more data which is appropriately disaggregated at the intra-urban level is paramount (Montgomery, 2009).

The post-2015 Sustainable Development Goal (SDG) agenda for health

As noted in the introduction to this chapter, the proposed SDGs include a dedicated health goal to 'ensure healthy lives and promote well-being for all at all ages' (UN Open Working Group, 2014:9). A series of targets are included within this goal relating to maternal mortality, infant and child mortality, and AIDS, as well as non-communicable diseases and mental health and well-being. Although there is no explicit gender component here, under the proposed SDG5 (on the empowerment of women and girls) women's health is identified in relation to ensuring women's universal access to sexual and reproductive health and rights (ibid.:11). This is especially significant given that it was neglected in the MDGs despite being called for, inter alia, following the Fourth International Conference on Population and Development (ICPD) in Cairo in 1994 (Glasier *et al.*, 2006) and the Beijing Platform for Action of 1995, and by the UN Taskforce on Education and Gender Equality commissioned by former UN Secretary General Kofi Annan (UNMP/TFEGE, 2005)

While women in urban areas in developing countries tend to have better sexual and reproductive health outcomes than those residing in rural areas, those living in slums tend to fare worse than both their wealthier urban counterparts and women in rural areas (Sclar *et al.*, 2005:902). More specifically, and as highlighted in some detail in Chapter 2, fertility levels are higher among urban poor women than female city residents in general, linked, inter alia, with lower levels of contraceptive use and lack of appropriate reproductive and sexual health-related information.

Although there have been important shifts globally and especially in the Global South towards recognising women's reproductive and sexual rights as basic human rights, which entails ensuring that women have control over their own bodies (Corrêa, 2008), women in slums do not always have this 'luxury'. Indeed, the WHO (2009b:xii) notes that the most important risk factors for mortality for women of reproductive age in low- and middle-income countries are lack of contraception and unsafe sex. While use of 'modern' contraception among women (or their partners) in the Global South increased from 8 per cent in the 1960s to 62 per cent in 2009 (ibid.:43; UN-DESA, 2011), young women, especially those who are unmarried and poor, often face difficulties in relation to access, as well as acceptance on the part of their menfolk (see Chant and Evans, 2010; Chant and Touray, 2012, on The Gambia). Indeed, research in Nairobi, Kenya, by Msiyaphazi Zulu *et al.* (2002) highlights how female slum residents are more likely to have their sexual debut at earlier ages than other urban dwellers, to have more sexual partners and to be privy to less sexual health information. Not surprisingly, they also have higher levels of HIV/AIDS and other sexually transmitted infections, with obvious effects on health outcomes and wider well-being.

Limited access to contraception means that many women facing unwanted pregnancies have to resort to unsafe abortion, especially where legal provision is unavailable. Indeed, globally, the proportion of unsafe abortions increased from 44 per cent in 1995 to 49 per cent in 2008 (Sedgh *et al.*, 2012:625), and typically poorer women are at greatest risk (IWPR, 2015:14). Research in two of Nairobi's slum communities, for example, has revealed that, along with eclampsia, haemorrhage, sepsis and uterine rupture, one of the leading causes of maternal mortality is attributable to abortion complications (Ziraba *et al.*, 2009:8). Even if unsafe abortions do not lead to death, they invariably cause health problems. In the case of Colombia, for example, an estimated one-third of all women nationally having a clandestine abortion develop complications that require treatment in a health facility, which is not always available (Prada *et al.*, 2011:7).

Interventions to improve women's health and well-being in slums

Moving beyond reproductive and sexual health and rights, it is imperative to consider how provision of health services in general in slums tends to be sorely limited, is almost invariably of poor quality, and is frequently complicated by a diverse array of providers, including many that are off-limits to the poorest residents. As Sclar *et al.* (2005:902; see also Jones *et al.*, 2014:27) have emphasised:

> Urban health services can be characterised as a patchwork of various types of providers – such as public hospitals and clinics, private physicians and nurses in private hospitals and clinics, as well as non-profit or faith-based nongovern-mental organisation clinics. User fees, which are frequently charged by public and private health providers, are often unaffordable to slum dwellers.

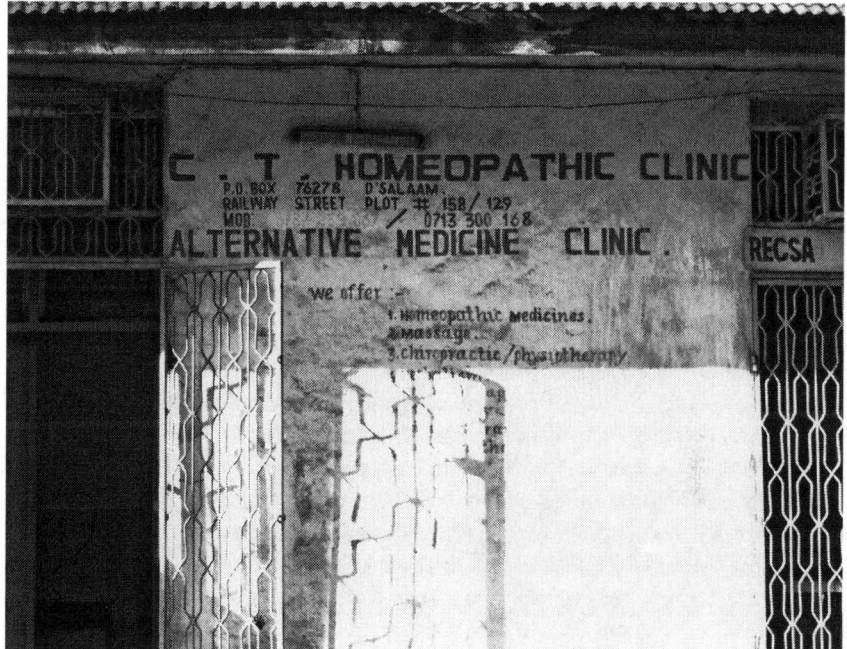

Plate 5.5 Alternative medicine in Dar es Salaam, Tanzania

Source: Sylvia Chant.

Although 'traditional healthcare' – which involves low-cost 'natural' (non-pharmaceutical/allopathic) medicine and an accessible network of community-based healers, and often enjoys wider support from low-income groups – was endorsed by the World Health Organisation as far back as the Alma Ata Declaration of 1978, in most instances this has been only weakly followed through by nation states in terms of public backing, and at particular detriment perhaps to women, who are often the most excluded from formal health services and as such are more likely to embrace alternative medical options (see ARI, 2014; Jennings, 2005; Moret, 2008).

As the main users of health services for themselves or their family members, women invariably bear the brunt of poor health service provision, especially as they are the ones who typically have to assume the care burden of sick household members, and in the process stand greater risks of becoming infected themselves (Browner, 1989; Chant with Craske, 2003:chapter 5). Alongside female bias in the nursing profession, this is one possible reason why the Ebola epidemic in West Africa in 2014–15 disproportionately affected the female populace, with an alleged 60–70 per cent of cases of infection and fatalities occurring among women.

Whatever the case, it is now widely established that strategies and interventions to improve women's health must take into account the underlying determinants of health, and especially gender inequalities. The specific socio-economic and cultural barriers that hamper women's efforts to protect and improve their health must also be addressed through appropriate interventions (WHO, 2009b: 73). For female slum dwellers, an arguably fruitful starting point is the basic upgrading of slums. Indeed, recognising the importance of holistic approaches to health, which focus on social and environmental aspects as well as on specific

---

Box 5.1   The multiple health-related impacts of slum upgrading on women in Agra, India

In the city of Agra, a tourism-based urban economy which is home to the internationally renowned spectacles of the Taj Mahal and Agra Fort, an initiative called the Crosscutting Agra Programme (CAP) has been working to improve sanitation in low-income communities and to enhance livelihoods among young women and men in participatory and inclusive ways. CAP is supported by the Agra Municipal Corporation (Agra Nagar Nigam) and USAID, and enlists the help of an urban development NGO, CURE (Centre for Urban and Regional Excellence), in community mobilisation, organisation and planning.

Recognising that women are most affected by poor sanitation, their participation was sought in the design, location and construction of household and community toilets, with women themselves contributing 50 per cent of the costs of construction, providing labour, and overseeing the building process. A women's Toilet Savings Group was established to help women to attain the funds necessary for personal toilets, with loans also provided from a community credit facility (CCF). In one of the communities covered by the project, Yamuna Bridge, critical design inputs proposed by women for toilets and bathing areas included ledges for soap and hooks for clothes, more open and visible toilets for children, and the organisation of washing areas which would aid the building of social capital and enhance the safety and security of young women and children.

In line with 'slum upgrading plus' principles, CAP has also assisted women in forming enterprise groups that help them to benefit from the prosperity generated by Agra's tourism value chain, not only providing space for livelihood activities and training in finance management and client engagement but setting up an alliance with the private sector for the development of tourism-based products. As a result of this initiative, women's daily incomes have grown up to tenfold and their livelihoods have become more sustainable, with over 100 days of work a year.

The CAP settlements in Agra have been better mainstreamed not only into the city economy but into the city system as a whole, thereby increasing residents' access to a range of municipal services.

Source: Khosla, 2009:46–7.

health initiatives (Hawkins *et al.*, 2013:6), it is no surprise that slum upgrading can have major positive effects on women's general health and other aspects of well-being. Notwithstanding some valid criticisms, including the reinforcement of prejudicial and essentialising gender stereotypes (Joshi, 2013; also Gruffydd Jones, 2012), in practical terms there are often considerable gains for women, as evidenced, inter alia, in the award-winning multi-stakeholder Ahmedabad Slum Networking Programme in India (see AMC, 2005; Bhatt 2003; Dutta, 2000; Khosla, 2009:46–7; Tripathi, 1999; see also Box 5.1).

Service improvements such as electrification and water access are not only likely to improve health outcomes in immediate ways but also to alleviate the psychological, physical and economic burdens attached to longer-term consequences of ill-health such as coping with the loss of household earners, caring for the sick and dealing with death.

Also vital here are holistic health interventions which pay due attention to demand-side factors, such as the impact of personal, household and community influences on people's health (as well as people's perceived benefits of healthcare systems), alongside supply-side factors, such the nature of health services per se and the multisectorality of comprehensive health protection and provision (Mwangangi, 2011:229). As noted by Sheela Patel (2011:93):

> If a woman is given a prescription for medicine to alleviate her cough yet continues to spend much of her day in a tiny shack inhaling fumes from her cooking stove and from vehicles speeding past outside, she will continue to have respiratory trouble. If she is instructed on how to cook healthy meals for her family yet cannot afford to buy enough food, her children will continue to suffer from malnourishment. If she is educated about the importance of sanitation but has no access to clean water, her family will continue to contract gastrointestinal disease.

Recognition of these challenges, and the need for healthier cities, is now under way, with the World Health Organisation on World Health Day 2010 recommending five main actions:

- improving living conditions;
- ensuring participatory urban governance;
- promoting urban planning for health behaviours and safety;
- building urban resilience to emergencies and disasters; and
- fostering inclusive cities which are accessible and age-friendly (Mwangangi, 2011:239).

Many of these principles are endorsed in other sets of recommendations for enhancing the health of women in developing countries, such as the 'four-pillar' package advocated by Julio Frenk and Octavio Gómez-Dantés (2011:16). The latter is built around health promotion and disease prevention, universal access to healthcare services which address the 'triple burden' of disease, innovations in the delivery of healthcare services which make use of ICT (such as mobile phones) and other technological developments, and, perhaps most importantly, 'the endorsement and enforcement of human rights related to women's health' (ibid.).

Funding is likely to be a perennial problem in cash-strapped developing societies, but public social insurance which has recently been introduced in Mexico under the auspices of 'Seguro Popular' is open to enrolment by poor Mexican households, and nominally 'assures legislated access to a comprehensive package of health services' (Frenk and Gómez-Dantés, 2011:25; see also Gideon, 2014, on Plan AUGE in Chile). Given that the only alternative might be to charge user fees, which are frequently 'regressive and inequitable' (Mwangangi, 2011:235), and likely particularly to disadvantage women who may have less access to cash and fewer opportunities for disbursing scant household funds for the purposes of their own or their children's health, this is undoubtedly an important pathway to access.

The World Health Organisation (2009b:76) points out that the demand for health services that meet women's needs is often galvanised by organisations working at the community level. It is also at this level, and especially in urban slum communities, where many innovative interventions are being developed. One such example is found in the community-based and community-run pharmacies in poor urban neighbourhoods in Manila, the Philippines. Known as 'Botika Binhis' (literally 'seed pharmacies' in Tagalog), these not only improve women's access to healthcare but provide jobs for the women involved, and relieve them of the burden of having to use dangerous, inefficient and potentially unaffordable transport to travel to pharmacies outside their communities (see Box 5.2).

In relation to HIV/AIDS, the Huairou Commission has pioneered the development of female-dominated networks of home-based caregivers through 'Home-Based Care Alliances' that have been established throughout Africa following their introduction in Kenya (via GROOTS Kenya and GROOTS International) and Uganda. Acting as community development agents, the women involved provide primary healthcare, sanitation and counselling for people living with HIV and other chronic conditions, and proffer services in patients' homes, supplementing the work of the formal healthcare system. Over time, and in the wake of increasing access to ART, women have adapted their activities from caring for the bedridden to ensuring that affected parties receive appropriate management of their condition through linking to clinical services, regular check-ups and providing nutritional support (Hayes for the Huairou Commission, 2010). Caregivers also work to improve the situation of the most vulnerable women in their communities beyond their health needs. In Kenya, for instance, community watchdog groups have been founded by home-based caregivers to prevent evictions of widows and children (see Chapter 3, this volume). GROOTS Kenya has also facilitated the training of community watchdogs to act as community paralegals and linked them to elders, chiefs and councillors to monitor and prevent land-grabbing and asset-stripping. The watchdog groups have been replicated in sixteen communities across four regions of Kenya (Huairou Commission, 2011).

Finally, many interventions to improve women's health relate to their reproductive and sexual rights. While these entail a wide variety of initiatives,

---

Box 5.2   Botika Binhis community pharmacies in Manila, Philippines

Botika Binhis are community-based and community-run pharmacies operated mainly by female residents of poor urban neighbourhoods which provide cheap medicine and healthcare to slum dwellers. The first pharmacy was established in 2003 with support from DAMPA (Damayan ng Maralitang Pilipinong Api), a grassroots organisation focusing specifically on issues relating to women, children and the elderly.

DAMPA's Botika Binhi community pharmacy programme focuses not just on cheap medicine, but also on diagnostics and medical services, and community organisation to increase the number of women members in neighbourhood-based pharmacies. Each pharmacy is typically used by more than 500 clients in the neighbourhood, with members paying dues of five to ten Philippine pesos (less than one US dollar) and engaging in monthly community meetings about management issues.

The pharmacies are open twenty-four hours a day, seven days a week, with at least two women on each staff rota. This often comprises a woman who has extended her domestic space to sell pharmaceutical products, and another who has been a regular visitor or user, although, significantly perhaps, neither is paid a stipend for her 'voluntary' work.

In 2010, there were 36 community pharmacy outlets in the Metro Manila region, used by an estimated 50,000 households, with plans to expand to 95 outlets.

The main challenge for the Botika Binhis, aside from their reliance on unpaid female labour, is the high cost of drugs, which means that DAMPA is constantly looking for donors to pay for medicine (although they are in the process of becoming a pharmaceutical distributor to allow groups to buy and sell generic drugs at wholesale prices). In addition, most of the outlets are built on land with no secure tenure which means that structures are vulnerable to constant threat of demolition and/or resettlement.

Source: Yonder and Tamaki for the Huairou Commission, 2010.

---

many revolve around women's access to contraception, safe abortion and various types of training and education in their rights and gender inequalities (see Box 5.3). Although most work directly with women, increasingly there are efforts to work with men, and especially young men, as a means of addressing the deep-rooted causes of gender inequalities that affect women's experiences of ill-health in the first place.

Concluding comments

This chapter has explored the health challenges faced by women residing in cities of the Global South and specifically in urban slums. It has outlined how the

Box 5.3   Defending women's reproductive and sexual rights in Cali, Colombia: the role of Fundación Sí Mujer

Sí Mujer was founded by a psychologist, María Ladi Londoño Echeverry, in 1984 in Cali, Colombia, with the aim of defending women's rights. Since its establishment it has provided integrated health services for women in relation to sexual and reproductive rights. These services include support for victims of sexual violence, treatment for incomplete abortions, contraceptive advice, psychological counselling, medical consultations and legal abortions.

Despite the decriminalisation of abortion in Colombia in 2006 in three circumstances – 'when pregnancy threatens a woman's life or health, in cases of severe foetal malformations incompatible with life, and in cases of rape, incest or unwanted insemination' (Díaz Amado, 2010:119) – access remains limited. This is because women are unaware of this partial legalisation, because mainstream health providers refuse to provide abortion services, or they are too afraid to approach any form of service provider (ibid.).

Lamentably, Fundación Sí Mujer has been at the centre of widespread controversy nationally around its provision of legal abortions. The organisation has had to battle the state authorities, including interventions from the police trying to prevent women from entering the premises, as well as continued negative press coverage. Although women from all walks of life use the services of Sí Mujer, those from slums comprise a significant proportion of its clientele because the services are provided free of charge (interview with Alexandra Lamb Guevara, 8 September 2014).

Fundación Sí Mujer is also committed to the prevention of unwanted pregnancies through training and education programmes on reproductive and sexual rights, with a particular focus on promoting gender equality. This is especially important given that, between 2010 and 2012, 17,578 child pregnancies were registered in the city of Cali, with the majority among children from the lowest income groups, living in the most marginalised *barrios* of the city. In 2014, Sí Mujer implemented an innovative child-friendly healthcare service designed, implemented and run with the active participation and leadership of children and young people themselves called the 'Servicio Amigable en Salud y Derechos Sexuales y Reproductivos para Niñas, Niños, Adolescentes y Jóvenes' (Friendly Service in Health, Sexual and Reproductive Rights for Girls, Boys, Adolescents and Youth), funded by a British NGO, Children of the Andes (COTA). This runs training programmes using music, drama and street art workshops and cine-forums as well as peer training provided by youth leaders. All the work is with young men as well as women, with the aim of destigmatising sexual and reproductive health and rights. While many of these activities take place at the organisation, a mobile version also travels directly into the most marginalised urban neighbourhoods.

Sources: Díaz Amado, 2010; http://fundacionsimujer.org/wp/.

Plate 5.6 Fundación Sí Mujer women's organisation, Cali, Colombia

Source: Cathy McIlwaine.

inadequacy of housing together with limited access to WASH services not only place particular burdens on women but endanger their health status, related to their disproportionate responsibilities for daily social reproduction. While Sclar *et al.* (2005:902) point to the 'health debt' that will accrue if the environmental and urban causes of the growing health burden on the urban poor continue to be neglected, it is important to emphasise that this is a *gendered* health debt, with women and girls most severely affected. Indeed, in addition to the health effects associated with residing in slums, women's health is further undermined by gender inequalities which, for those of reproductive age in particular, impact upon their ability to exercise their sexual and reproductive rights. In many slum communities across the Global South, women are unable to access contraception, safe abortions to deal with unwanted pregnancies, or assisted childbirth, which results not only in health complications but, in extreme cases, death.

Yet, while it is clear that the health challenges faced by women affect their ability to contribute to the functioning of their households and communities, this chapter has also shown that grassroots women in particular, often in partnership with national or international NGOs, are developing innovative interventions to ameliorate the worst effects of these processes and work towards prevention through engaging with young men alongside women. Provided there is gender balance in such initiatives, there is potential to shift from a situation in which women and girls are disproportionately charged with responsibilities for safeguarding community health, as presaged, inter alia, in the UN's Global Strategy for Women's and Children's Health of 2010 (see Gideon, 2014:13).

The importance of male engagement is perhaps particularly pertinent in the context of gender-based violence, which is now recognised as a major public health issue for women globally, and especially for those residing in cities and slums, as we discuss in the next chapter.

6   Gender-based violence
in cities and slums

Introduction: gender-based violence and the
Global South city

Although gender-based violence (GBV), and more specifically violence against women (VAW), was absent from the Millennium Development Agenda, it is now acknowledged as one of world's greatest contemporary challenges. This is reflected, inter alia, in the specific inclusion of 'freedom from violence against women and girls' in the proposed fifth Sustainable Development Goal on gender equality (see Chapter 1, this volume). Moreover, in the context of GBV and VAW constituting a 'new dominant global agenda' (Moser and McIlwaine, 2014:337), cities in the Global South are a significant priority (McIlwaine, 2013; Moser, 2012). Rates of urban violence are escalating everywhere, especially in developing regions, as part of wider processes of increasing poverty, inequality, drug use, access to firearms and other weaponry, and political and civil conflict. Within this scenario the prevalence of GBV has risen concomitantly (Moser, 2004; Winton, 2004).

Acknowledging that VAW is routinely under-reported, and assumes multiple forms, ranging from physical to sexual to psychological (IWPR, 2015:14; see also below), within a global context in which an estimated 35 per cent of women have experienced either physical or sexual violence at the hands of intimate male partners or other men (WHO, 2013:12), they are twice as likely to experience violence in cities especially in developing regions (UN-Habitat, 2007a). A high proportion of this violence is fatal, with 39 per cent of all murders of women committed by intimate partners (WHO, 2013:2), but even when non-fatal VAW (not to mention the fear of it) can seriously undermine women's and girls' health and well-being, their engagement in wider economic, social and political activities, and their ability to move freely around urban space.

While the underlying causes of GBV and VAW are rooted in deep-seated patriarchal structures and gender asymmetries, a number of features of urban life act as important triggers in their perpetration in cities and especially in slums where levels of violence against women and girls are typically at their most marked, both within their own homes and in their communities at large (McIlwaine, 2013, 2015). This reinforces the need for a multi-spatial and multi-dimensional analytical perspective as encapsulated within our 'gender–urban–slum interface'.

essential!

Within the 'gender–urban–slum interface', GBV is a core cross-cutting issue that intersects with all the other main components, such as how women's reproductive and sexual rights are exercised, how their labour force participation is shaped, and how much access they enjoy to human, social, financial and other capitals and assets. As noted above, GBV also compromises women's spatial mobility and freedoms. In totality, gendered power relations are crucial in understanding how and why VAW occurs (Moser and McIlwaine, 2006), and since VAW represents an extreme case of the assertion of patriarchal power over women (McIlwaine, 2014a:493), it is no surprise that it has been widely regarded as 'the worst manifestation of gender discrimination' (Sweet and Ortiz Escalante, 2010:2130).

The World Health Organisation's (2014:2) definition of violence is:

> the intentional use of physical force or power, threatened or actual, against oneself or another person, or against a group or community, that either results in or has a high likelihood of resulting in injury, death, psychological harm, maldevelopment or deprivation.

Acknowledging that 'definitions of violence often overlap with conflict and crime', as in 'violent crime', for example (WHO, 2002, cited in Moser, 2004:4), as identified above, the importance of addressing violence in urban areas is now widely recognised at city, national and international levels, especially in terms of women's safety (Moser, 2012:435). With this in mind, our discussion traces the rather complex anatomy of violence in cities and slums, with particular reference to its gendered dimensions in different urban spaces, and in relation to some of the key implications for female slum dwellers.

The complex anatomy of gender-based violence in cities and slums

Crime and violence in urban areas

In recent years it has been estimated that between 25 and 30 per cent of urban crime is due to violence (UN-Habitat, 2006b), a figure which is all the more disturbing considering that around 60 per cent of urban dwellers in developing regions have been victims of crime, and as many as 70 per cent in parts of Latin America and Africa (UN-Habitat, 2007b). Indeed, as flagged up by Orlando Pérez (2013:217): 'The Latin American region has the dubious distinction of having the highest rates of crime and violence in the world,' with rates about five times higher than elsewhere. In the cities and slums of Latin America, and beyond, fear of crime acts as a major deterrent to numerous activities, from walking to school, to using public transport, to working (especially at night), to launching business ventures (see UN-Habitat, 2012b:101–2; see also McIlwaine and Moser, 2007; Moser and McIlwaine, 2004). As Caroline Moser (2004:3) points out, this can seriously erode the assets of the poor and undermine their livelihoods and well-being, in addition to which she highlights that:

Although accelerating rates of violence and crime are by no means an urban-specific problem, they are particularly problematic in urban areas. The sheer scale of violence in poor areas or slums means that, in many contexts, it has become 'routinised' or 'normalised' into the functional reality of daily life.

(Moser, 2004:6)

As further observed by Claudia García-Moreno and Manupreet Chawla (2011:58) in the context of a discussion on how poverty and inequality intersect with violence against women:

A woman in a poor urban slum is more likely than women elsewhere in the city to have to cross unsafe parts of town, walk through badly lit streets, and wait for transportation in unsafe places. Poverty and inequality also isolate women, and may prevent them from forming and utilising social support networks when violence occurs.

Female and male aspects of gender-based violence in urban environments

GBV takes on a diverse range of forms, but most generic definitions are rooted in the 1993 UN Declaration of the Elimination of Violence Against Women. In this, Article 1 defines GBV as:

Any act of gender-based violence that results in, or is likely to result in, physical, sexual or psychological harm or suffering to women, including threats of such acts, coercion or arbitrary deprivations of liberty, whether occurring in public or in private life.

Here, families, communities, public space, markets and institutions are variously implicated (McIlwaine, 2014a:493–4). In a small minority of cases men suffer GBV, sometimes at the hands of women, but usually from other men, but the bulk of GBV comprises VAW (ibid.; see also below). Due to high levels of impunity surrounding VAW, it is no surprise that Victor Uribe-Urán (2013:50) contends on the basis of arguments advanced by the United Nations Fund for Population Activities (2005) that it is 'perhaps the most widespread and socially tolerated of human rights violations'. This opinion is echoed by Mo Hume (2004:63), who notes for El Salvador (but with more general applicability) that a high threshold for tolerating violence means that gender violence is 'normalised' as a central element in gender relations, and receives insufficient attention in policy discourse.

One of the main reasons why data on GBV remains sparse and uneven (OECD, 2013) is under-reporting, with Tia Palermo, Jennifer Bleck and Amber Peterman (2013:1) suggesting that only 7 per cent of women globally report GBV to a formal source such as the police or some other judicial entity. That said, there seems to be slightly greater reporting in towns and cities than in rural environments, conceivably because women are more sensitised to violence as an issue of gender equality, or because, pragmatically, filing a complaint is easier. Indeed, in rural areas of Zambia, 43.3 per cent of households live more than 16 kilometres from a police post, compared with only 23.3 per cent of urban households (see Evans, 2013b:8–9). Similarly, in research on Bangladesh by Ruchira Tabassum Naved *et al.* (2006), which examined help-seeking behaviour among abused women, it was found that while 66 per cent of women in general remained silent about their abuse due to stigma and fear of experiencing even more harm, women in urban areas were more likely to seek and receive help (60 per cent) compared with their rural counterparts (51 per cent), even if only 2 per cent of this help was institutional. The issue of tolerance is important here, as noted by McIlwaine (2013:77) who asserts that: 'Urbanisation is generally associated with the loosening of patriarchal restrictions which can mean that women as individuals and as urban dwellers are less likely to tolerate gender-based violence.' This situation has been referred to as the 'sanctions and sanctuary framework' (Krug *et al.*, 2002:99), whereby levels of partner violence are assumed to be lower where community sanctions (formal or informal) are stronger and where women have access to shelter or family assistance. On top of this, there is evidence that support for women survivors of VAW is more likely to be available in cities than in rural areas (McIlwaine, 2013).

In conjunction with one another, the factors identified above could help to explain why VAW by male partners tends to be less prevalent in cities than in rural areas, even if violence by non-partners tends to be higher in the former, and especially in slums (ibid.), and when domestic violence is added to the mix women overall are twice as likely to suffer acts of violent aggression as their male counterparts (UN-Habitat, 2006b).

Exemplifying differential exposure to risks of particular types of GBV in rural and urban contexts, in Brazil 37 per cent of women in rural areas have experienced intimate partner violence, compared with 29 per cent of urban women residents, while 40 per cent of urban women have been the target of non-partner violence as against 23 per cent in the countryside (WHO, 2005b, cited in McIlwaine, 2013:67). Lower levels of urban domestic violence, as intimated above, could partly be due to the fact that urban women are less likely than their rural counterparts to accept violence as a 'normal' sanction for objectively trivial issues such as burning food, arguments, going out without informing spouses or refusing to have sex (see Table 6.1).

Yet prevailing patterns must be situated within the context of alarmingly high rates of violence in urban areas more generally. Although the spectre of under-reporting is never far away, in a study of nine low-income urban *barrios* in Guatemala, an average of forty-one types of so-called 'everyday violence' were identified by community members, while in Colombia the comparable average was twenty-five. However, in one community in Bogotá, sixty different types of violence were distinguished, with many of them gender-based (Moser and McIlwaine, 2006:92).

Leading on from this, there is increasing, if somewhat belated, recognition of the disturbing extent of GBV, and specifically VAW, in cities and slums across

Table 6.1 Women's attitudes towards and justification for VAW by their partner/husband
(percentage of women who agree)

Country	Burning food		Conjugal arguments		Leaving house without informing husband		Denial of sexual relations	
	Rural	Urban	Rural	Urban	Rural	Urban	Rural	Urban
Cameroon 2004	25.8	13.8	33.3	21.1	40	28.2	27.1	14.8
Ethiopia 2005	67.5	30.8	63.9	34.6	69.1	41.5	49.6	19.8
Ghana 2003	18.5	8.9	34.3	24.3	39.2	28.4	24.1	15.5
Kenya 2003	17.7	12.3	50	33.5	41.9	31.6	31.8	22.1
Nigeria 2003	35	22.7	47.8	35.4	58.4	42.2	42.5	28.1
Senegal 2005	27.4	19.1	58.1	38.7	60.8	38	55.4	34
Egypt 2005	25	10.4	47	23.8	49.4	27.4	43	20.1
Nepal 2001	5.1	3.9	8.8	8	12.1	13.2	3.1	2.7
Philippines 2003	4.3	2.2	7.1	3.7	12.6	6	4.5	2.4
Bolivia 2003	9.2	3.6	9.9	4.9	12.9	7.2	4.5	1.9
Dominican Republic 2002	3.6	1.8	1.7	0.8	5	2.3	1.3	0.6
Haiti 2000	14.4	6.6	14	6.4	34.4	23.4	16.9	10.2
Nicaragua 2001	7.9	2.6	7.5	2.6	9.9	3.4	4.8	1.7

Source: Adapted from McIlwaine, 2013:68 (using data from www.measuredhs.com).

the Global South. In major Indian cities, for instance, the estimated rate of physical and/or sexual violence against ever-married women aged 15–49 ranges from 15 per cent in Delhi to 41 per cent in Chennai, with levels commonly twice as high in slums as in non-slum areas, and highest among the poorest quartile of the population (Gupta *et al.*, 2009:62). In research conducted in 2008 in two areas of low-income settlement in Kampala, Uganda (Rubaga and Makindye divisions), nearly 50 per cent of women who were currently married reported physical and/or sexual violence from a partner, with as many 30 per cent having experienced an assault of this nature within the last year (Musuya, 2011:240). Indeed, a global study conducted by the Centre on Housing Rights and Evictions (COHRE, 2008:14) concluded that: 'Violence against women in . . . slums is rampant . . . and emerges as perhaps the strongest cross-cutting theme.' Risks appear to be particularly pronounced where women lack ownership or entitlement to property, partly because they have few alternative avenues for independence (ibid.; see also Hughes and Wickeri, 2011:853; Khosla, 2009:16; Kothari, 2005). As summarised by Raquel Rolnik (2012:11): 'For women who are victims of domestic violence, lack of security of tenure may be fatal: many cannot end a relationship with the aggressor as they cannot see a viable housing option for themselves and their children.' As additionally noted by the Chronic Poverty Research Centre (CPRC, 2010:71): 'poverty can be a cause of physical insecurity [and] physical insecurity also further perpetuates chronic poverty'. In turn, the heavy costs of GBV are borne not only by women themselves but by societies as a whole (see ECLAC, 2004:26). GBV generates costs at community and city levels as it pressurises healthcare facilities, which are often oversubscribed in slums as it is (Duvvury *et al.*, 2013:9; Chapter 5, this volume), stretches judicial and social infrastructure (Morrison *et al.*, 2007), and compromises people's development of human and social capital (McIlwaine, 2015; Moser and McIlwaine, 2004). Indeed, Caroline Moser (2004:3) observes how an increase in violence in a low-income community in Guayaquil, Ecuador, between the late 1970s and early 1990s not only forced residents to improve their domestic security but particularly impacted women, who were often the targets of violent crime and robbery on buses, and whose fear for their personal safety, especially after dark, meant that they dropped out of night school in increasing numbers (see also McIlwaine and Moser, 2007, on urban Colombia and Guatemala).

Of course, violence in cities also affects young men, and they are perhaps just as vulnerable as women and girls, especially in slums, where becoming part of a youth gang is frequently the only livelihood option (see, e.g., ECLAC, 2004; Kruijt and Koonings, 2009; Jones and Rodgers, 2009; McIlwaine and Moser, 2000), or the sole strategy to forge a social identity and ensure protection in the neighbourhood (Pérez, 2013:225). Gang violence has been described by Orlando Pérez (ibid.:217) as 'one of the most serious problems of crime in Central America'. Membership of gangs linked to drugs and street violence is often associated with the premature mortality of men (Rodgers *et al.*, 2011), with three out of every four young people dying from violence in Latin America being male (Figueroa Perea, 1998). Citing data from a seven-city Pan American Health Organisation study, Moser (2004:7) also observes not only that young men are 'most likely to be the victims and perpetrators' of violence, but that homicide rates among 15–24-year-olds in countries such as Brazil and Puerto Rico are more than ten times higher among males than females. Moser (ibid.:7) is advisedly careful to point out that using homicide and mortality rates as proxies for violence is inadequate, not least because the former can often include unintentional deaths, such as from car accidents, and tends also to marginalise non-fatal violence. In relation to GBV, this is also part of a wider process of rendering GBV invisible in the face of more sensational urban violence often associated with gangs, as noted by Wilding (2010) in Rio de Janeiro, or with political conflict, as in the case of Kabul, Afghanistan (Esser, 2014; see also Moser and McIlwaine, 2014). As Polly Wilding and Ruth Pearson (2013:165) remind us in the context of Rio de Janeiro, the extent to which urban violence affects women has arguably been somewhat sidelined in the literature on cities, given the 'predominance and visibility of male-on-male violence and consequent masculine homicide and incarceration statistics' (see also Kern and Mullings (2013:36ff.) on 'garrison communities' in Kingston, Jamaica, which they describe as 'ghettoised spaces of poverty and violent political sectarian control').

Although gangs are most likely to be the domains of young men, young women are also involved as members or as girlfriends of members. In Santa Cruz del Quiché in Guatemala, for instance, a minority of gangs, such as '*Las Chicas*' (The Girls), are female only, but in a rival gang, '*Las Chicas Big*' (The Big Girls), female membership mainly comprises the girlfriends of young men (Moser and McIlwaine, 2004). Wilding and Pearson (2013:165) recount a similar situation in relation to slum-based gangs in Rio de Janeiro, where

> many women are also actively engaged in these environments – as carriers, informants, honey traps and instigators, variously mitigating the impacts of violence, hiding guns and suffering violations or indignities in the name of discipline and punishment which gang members inflict on those they wish to control and intimidate.

Wilding and Pearson further note that the impacts of gangs extend far more widely than their directly involved male (and female) constituents in slum communities: 'gang members do not operate in male-only spaces so the impact of gang activity (and corresponding police interventions) is felt not just by men and boys, but also by the women and girls who live in these areas' (ibid.).

Pursuant to the above, women also suffer from 'street violence' in urban areas more generally, as evidenced in alarmingly high rates of abduction, rape and/or murder in cities such as Ciudad Juárez on Mexico's border with the United States, where precipitating factors appear to have been rising levels of female employment in export industries and, more recently, rivalry between drug cartels (see Jarvis *et al.*, 2009:112; see also Prieto-Carrón *et al.*, 2007; Sweet and Ortiz Escalante, 2010; Wright, 2013; and Box 6.1). Although the aetiology of urban street violence is complex and geographically varied, in a generic sense it appears that inequality, rather than poverty per se, is a major precipitating cause of both violence and crime (see Moser, 2004:8). Yet this is not to deny poverty is also associated with many service deficiencies that can exacerbate threats to citizen security, with risks in many cities aggravated by lack of simple infrastructure, such as adequate streetlighting (Anderson and Panzio, 1986; see also below). As summarised by Moser (2004:10):

> Cities – and their peripheries – where many of the urban poor reside – often contain unsafe spaces that reflect poor infrastructure and design, and where rape, robbery and violent crime exist. Unsafe spaces also include public transport, and isolated or unlit areas such as dark paths and lanes, isolated bus stops or public latrines. The need to commute long distances, and to work early in the morning or late at night – needs largely relating to the urban poor – exacerbate these spatial dangers.

In light of the above, it is perhaps no surprise that in some instances:

> women's collective fear of public spaces is resulting in the abandonment in parts of cities, and such widespread desertion of public space makes cities even more unfriendly, and an environment to be feared not just by women, but by all citizens.

(Tankel, 2011:353)

Box 6.1   Urban femicide in Ciudad Juárez, Mexico

'Femicide' is defined as 'a form of gender violence' which involves 'the systematic killing of women, with relation to the fact that they are women' (Sweet and Ortiz Escalante, 2010:2138). In the context of Ciudad Juárez in the state of Chihuahua on Mexico's border with the United States, the term has been appropriated by women's groups in this city of around 1.5 million inhabitants to reframe women's disproportionate subjection to a 'rash of murders and disappearances as a human/women's rights/gender-violence issue, not simply murders' (ibid.:2140).

Indeed, the instances of brutality and 'extraordinary physical violence' perpetrated against women in Ciudad Juárez are legion, often involving excessive sexual humiliation (including gang rape), torture and bodily mutilation, such as branding, and the excision of breasts and nipples (Livingston, 2004; Staudt, 2008).

It is difficult to explain the number and brutality of killings in Ciudad Juárez since the early 1990s, purportedly now in the region of 1000 women. This is partly because of lack of investigation on the part of the police, partly because of the destruction of official records, and partly because of the popular notion that the victims bring extremes of gender violence upon themselves. In terms of the latter, they do this by transgressing the boundaries of 'acceptable womanhood', not only by involvement in prostitution, but also by occupying about half of the positions in multinational export-processing factories (*maquiladoras*). The latter not only signals female economic independence, but an unwelcome incursion into male-dominated breadwinning opportunities, and neglect of women's stereotypically familial domestic duties (Sweet and Ortiz Escalante, 2010:2138–40). On top of this, in an 'anarchic environment' in which many labour and environmental laws are not implemented (ibid.:2139), the fact that women are selling their labour power to their historic enemy (the United States) conceivably makes them more 'disposable' in the eyes of the main perpetrators of violence (Livingston, 2004).

Sources: Livingston, 2004; Prieto-Carrón *et al.*, 2007; Staudt, 2008; Sweet and Ortiz Escalante, 2010.

Even if 'public space' is often uppermost in discourses of 'safe cities' for women, it is paramount to acknowledge that there are 'connections and continuums between the public and private, and how they are socially constructed and habitually entwined' (Tankel, 2011:353). Taking on board the exhortation that 'A gendered analysis of urban violence has to explore the two-way links between the private and public sphere and spaces' (Wilding and Pearson, 2013:159; see also Hume, 2004; McIlwaine, 2014a), it is crucial to stress that women are often as much at risk of violence in their own homes and neighbourhoods as they are in cities at large. This is especially the case where they have to venture out of their dwellings to collect water or use communal sanitation facilities (as discussed in Chapter 4), and where basic infrastructure, such as adequate streetlighting and effective policing, are lacking (ActionAid, 2011; Chant and McIlwaine, 2013a, 2013b; Hughes and Wickeri, 2011:884; Khosla, 2009; Moser and McIlwaine, 2004; see also Box 6.2, and below).

Urban violence against women in particular relation to slum residence

Leading on from the above, it is increasingly acknowledged that certain aspects of living in cities, and especially in slum neighbourhoods, make the perpetration of VAW more likely (McIlwaine, 2013).

Box 6.2   Women's concerns about urban security and safety in Cape Town, South Africa

In April 2011, at the Western Cape Anti-Eviction Campaign's monthly residential meeting in the Symphony Way Temporary Relocation Area, informally referred to as 'Blikkiesdorp' (Tin Can Town in Afrikaans), residents voluntarily gathered to discuss their personal security concerns within the community. Among the routine discussions of endemic crime and the regular break-ins, which mean residents enjoy little personal security over their possessions, a comment surfaced from Nadia, a resident who had years ago been evicted from her home closer to Cape Town's city centre. Raising her voice above the noise drifting over from the adjacent shacks, she expressed in front of her fellow residents, both male and female, her deep concern over the lack of municipal repair of the streetlights lining the dirt road that leads to the main highway. The non-functioning of the streetlights was posing particular problems for women, rendering them vulnerable to harassment, theft, physical abuse and sexual violence. In the early hours of the morning, when many of the area's women began their long commutes towards the city centre, often involving a protracted walk followed by multiple minibus trips, the functioning presence of streetlights was known to deter crime and allow for residents' safe passage through an otherwise-unsecured area.

Nadia's complaint illustrates one of the many ways in which women's safety can be compromised by the simple lack of municipal service delivery in informal settlements. On the other hand, installing and maintaining streetlights in low-income housing areas throughout the Global South would vastly improve the safety and well-being of the poor, particularly women, in a way that the residents themselves have shown to be both productive and desired.

Source: Fleming, 2011.

Plate 6.1 'Blikkiesdorp' (Tin Can Town), Cape Town, South Africa

Source: Andrew Fleming.

Many issues enter the picture here, not least poverty, which, as previously mentioned, has been cited as an important 'aggravating factor' in VAW (ibid.:70). In Lima, Peru, for example, the proportion of poor women experiencing domestic violence, especially of a physical nature, is considerably higher than is the case for their middle-class counterparts (Gonzales de Olarte and Gavilano Llosa, 1999:42). It is also important to bear in mind here that the intersectionality of gender with age, conjugal status and so on may expose some women to different forms of 'public' as well as 'private' abuse. For example, young women appear to be the key targets of sexual abuse in slums, including gang rape. However, frail and elderly women may also be vulnerable to attack, along with women who 'transgress' heteronormative boundaries, such as those who, in one form or another, live 'independently'. This category includes lone women and lone mothers, who, as revealed by evidence gathered in slums in Chittagong and Dhaka in Bangladesh, Hyderabad in India, and Nairobi, Kenya, are often so insecure about living without men that they opt to stay in abusive relationships with 'real or make-do "husbands"' (Joshi *et al.*, 2011:100). Sexuality is another issue, with a reported 90 per cent of lesbian women in Quito, Ecuador, having suffered abuse in their neighbourhoods on account of 'lesbophobia' (Benavides Llerena *et al.*, 2007:1.6.12; see also Bell and Valentine, 1995; Oswin, 2012).

In turn, it is important to note that certain types of occupation in which urban poor and/or slum-dwelling women are engaged may put them at heightened risk of violence. Perhaps the most obvious is sex work, which tends to be concentrated in cities and which is associated with high levels of gender-based abuse. In a survey of 540 female sex workers in Dhaka, Bangladesh, cited by Watts and Zimmerman (2002:1236), for example, 49 per cent had been raped and 59 per cent had been beaten by police in the previous year. While sex work is clearly a particularly 'risky' occupation, as indicated by the case study in Box 6.1 on 'femicide' in Ciudad Juárez, women's higher levels of labour force participation in urban areas may also lead to a male backlash, especially where large numbers of men are unemployed and resort to violence as they attempt to assert control over their lives and those of their womenfolk (Chant with Craske, 2003; Chant and McIlwaine, 1995). It should also be noted that women working in low-paid jobs are more likely than their professional counterparts to experience GBV (Krug *et al.*, 2002).

As indicated in the case of Blikkiesdorp in Box 6.2, service and infrastructural deficiencies also have a major part to play in explaining particular forms and concentrations of GBV in slums. For example, lack of power and lighting inside low-income communities is often very injurious to women and girls, especially where they have to use shared toilets and washblocks, and where each and every trip, particularly after dark, is likely to be circumscribed by fear of violence en route to or at the destination (Bapat and Agarwal, 2003, on Pune, India; see also Chapter 4, this volume). As described by Amnesty International (2010) with respect to Nairobi's largest slum, Kibera, shared sanitary facilities are a major factor, along with flimsy housing, poor lighting, inadequate/corrupt policing and weakly enforced legislation, in explaining vulnerability to attacks from strangers as well as from intimate partners (see also Hughes and Wickeri, 2011:884; Khosla, 2009:16; UNFPA, 2007:24; and Table 6.2).

Housing is another major consideration in accounting for women's propensity to suffer violence in slum communities. Where dwellings are flimsy and there are no security patrols, women and girls may be vulnerable to break-ins, theft and rape (Hughes and Wickeri, 2011:884). The frequent anonymity and social isolation of female urban dwellers, especially recent migrants, may not only make them more vulnerable to attack from strangers but also deprive them of neighbourhood-based and institutional help when encountering intimate partner abuse (see COHRE, 2008:24; UNFPA, 2007:23). The precipitous rise in sexual violence in Port-au-Prince's 'tent cities' in the aftermath of the January 2010 Haitian earthquake presents an extreme case where insecure housing and lack of domestic services placed women and girls at serious risk of sexual violence (see Arend, 2012). Such conditions create 'stress-induced violence' (McIlwaine, 2013:70), which may not explain the deep-rooted causes of GBV, but does at least assist in accounting for why it proliferates in some cities and in particular spaces therein.

There seems to be a particularly strong association with GBV in areas or establishments (in slums and beyond) where alcohol is sold, with the latter long identified as a major risk factor in the perpetration of VAW (Heise *et al.*, 2002; Morrison *et al.*, 2007). In urban Colombia and Guatemala, for example, research by Moser and McIlwaine (2004:134) found that the high levels of GBV associated

Table 6.2 Reducing VAW through urban upgrading: the Khayelitsha project

Spatial manifestation	Types of VAW	Spatial and non-spatial VAW prevention or reduction interventions
Domestic spaces	• Assault • Rape • Emotional abuse	• Houses of refuge; counselling and conflict resolution facilities • Equipping of police stations with trauma facilities and female officers • Police training in handling domestic and VAW violence cases • Awareness-raising campaigns on domestic rights
Open public space (open fields, narrow lanes, empty stalls)	• Rape • Assault • Murder	• Improvement of street lighting, visibility and telephone systems • Rape-relief centres and self-defence training • Safe walkways and lockable vegetable stalls • 24-hour internal public transportation systems • More visible police patrolling and neighbourhood watches
Sanitary facilities	• Rape at facility or near by	• Sewers installation and phasing out of outside toilets • Supervised communal sanitary facilities
Shebeens (places where alcohol is sold)	• Assault • Rape • Drug/alcohol violence	• Relocation of shebeens to areas of efficient social and police control • Alternative socialising opportunities where alcohol is controlled • Adoption of business code of conduct by shebeen owners' association
Schools	• Physical violence • Group rape	• Protection of schools against theft and guns through better fences, metal detectors and guard dogs • Doubling up of guarded schools as safe after-hours playgrounds
Roads and transport	• Assault • Sexual harassment and assault by drivers	• Making stations gun-free zones via metal detectors • Moving jobs and services closer to residents to reduce transport needs • Police-patrolled trains

Source: Adapted from Moser, Winton and Moser, 2005:152–3.

with bars and cantinas meant that women typically avoided them as much as possible, with an additional issue being to safeguard their social reputations. In other contexts, such as South Africa, neighbourhood bars or 'shebeens' are widely linked with the notion that they are frequented only by women who sell 'survival sex' or more formally by commercial sex workers (Wojcicki, 2002; also Table 6.2, and below).

Beyond this, open spaces and wasteland within and on the fringes of slum communities are also usually feared by women, and deservedly so. In poor townships in South Africa, these places are often sites for 'jackrolling', whereby gangs of young men cruise around in cars with the intention of attacking and raping women (Wojcicki, 2002). In urban Colombia and Guatemala, secluded river banks, basketball courts and parks are frequently perceived to be areas where gangs congregate to sell drugs, and where GBV is a serious threat (Moser and McIlwaine, 2004). More generally, women's fear of public spaces in cities may result in serious restrictions on movement. In Mumbia, India, for example, a study of headcounts of people in public places revealed that only 28 per cent were female (Phadke, 2007, cited in Whitzman *et al.*, 2013: 41).

Given the multiple adverse consequences of GBV for women and girls, it is little surprise, as noted previously, that this has become recognised by international agencies as a major health and human rights issue (see WHO, 2009b; Uribe-Urán, 2013:76). While GBV is a major public health concern in terms of its immediate physiological and psychological health effects, such as injuries, miscarriage and post-traumatic stress disorders (PTSDs), it can also be linked with greater susceptibility to HIV and STIs as well as alcohol and drug abuse, depression and suicide (WHO, 2013:21–2). Moreover, other direct and indirect implications relate to women's inability to participate in the labour market (Krug *et al.*, 2002:102–3), or to their enforced confinement on the lower rungs of the occupational ladder (Duvvery *et al.*, 2013). Women's social capital can also be affected through their experience of shame, stigma and rejection, which may, in turn, cause suffering to their children (Heise *et al.*, 2002). These violence-related risks compound several other factors covered in previous chapters in this volume which compromise women's potential to engage fully in urban life (see Agarwal, 2011; World Bank, 2006a). However, women are not passive in the face of GBV: there is widespread evidence of formal and informal interventions and strategies being developed to address the problem.

Strategies to address gender-based violence in cities

Since the 1990s there has been something of a sea-change in attitudes towards VAW, as evidenced, inter alia, in a spate of new laws and initiatives against domestic violence, especially in Latin America (Uribe-Urán, 2013:71ff.). As summarised by Jerker Edström (2014:28):

> After well over a decade of feminist and sexual rights mobilisation framed around human rights in the nineties and into the noughties, issues of sexual and gender-based violence (SGBV) and violence against women (VAW) have become increasingly visible and highlighted in international policy and discourse on gender and development.

Over and above the fact that over 125 countries have outlawed domestic violence (UN Women, 2011b:1), among various strategies to reduce GBV in cities specifically are to make criminal justice systems more gender-responsive, to develop women's networks and partnerships, and to conduct women's safety audits (see García-Moreno and Chawla, 2011:63; McIlwaine, 2013; Moser, 2012).

Indeed, 'strengthening formal criminal justice systems and policing from a gender perspective in cities' is one of the core policy approaches identified by UN-Habitat (2007a), which, in response to campaigning by women's movements, focuses on legal reform and legislative change.

A possible flagship example here is Brazil's 2006 Law of Domestic and Family Violence (or the 'Maria da Penha Law', named after a pioneering feminist who was left paraplegic by her abusive husband), introduced on the back of active campaigning by women's movements throughout the country. This explicitly criminalised domestic violence and introduced a penalty of detention of between six and twelve months for committing such an offence (CEPLAES, 2010). More recently, in March 2015, and again in response to pressure from feminist groups, the Penal Code was redefined to include femicide as any crime that involves domestic violence, discrimination or contempt for women that results in their death. The new legislation imposes harsher sentences of between twelve and thirty years' imprisonment for crimes committed against pregnant women, girls under fourteen years of age and women over sixty, as well as women and girls with disabilities (UN Women, 2015b).

'Safe' design also comes into the picture, which, depending on context, may include streetlighting, parks or neighbourhood layout (see Malaza *et al.*, 2009; see also Table 6.2). Such initiatives, referred to under the rubric of 'Crime Prevention Through Environmental Design' (CPTED) by UN-Habitat (2007a), use spatial and design perspectives, including upgrading or changing urban infrastructure and the physical fabric of the city. These overlap with another strategy that focuses on community-based approaches to enhance urban safety and security and reduce risk factors from a gender perspective (McIlwaine, 2013:75). A major aspect of both types of initiative comprises women's safety audits. Developed initially in 1989 by the Metropolitan Action Committee on Public Violence against Women and Children (METRAC), based in Toronto, Canada, women's safety audits facilitate the identification of actual and perceived safe and unsafe public spaces, with a focus on interventions to reduce potential risk. Participatory methodologies, usually based on transect walks and mapping exercises as well as interviews with service providers, are deployed, working with women in their own neighbourhoods with due regard to acknowledging their 'expert status' and facilitating their agency (Whitzman *et al.*, 2009). In one example of such an audit, slum-dwelling women who had been evicted from eastern Delhi to Bawana, on the outskirts of the city, revealed the relationships between safety and inadequate services. Consonant with our earlier discussions in this Chapter and in Chapter 4, the women highlighted physical and sexual violence and intimidation while accessing sanitation and water. Among various problems, they reported how girls in particular were followed by men and boys when they had to walk to neighbouring areas to collect water, and were sometimes pushed while they filled their buckets. Widespread sexual harassment in toilet blocks was also noted, with the women mentioning that boys and men often invaded the women's wing of the complex (JAGORI in collaboration with Women in Cities International, 2010:11). In principle, the findings from such audits are used to design initiatives to ensure public safety for women in cities and slums and for advocacy work with the state to mainstream women's inputs in urban planning, design and interventions.

Given that most cities have not been designed with women's safety in mind (Meleis, 2011:2), in such instances cash-strapped municipal governments might benefit from public–private partnerships, such as the 'Adopt a Light' company initiative in Nairobi, which, since its launch in 2002 by a businesswoman, Esther Passaris, has illuminated key thoroughfares in and around the capital's major slums. Revenue for the scheme has been generated through selling advertising space on the lamp-posts (see UN-Habitat, 2010b:13; 2012a:38).

Over and above a plethora of local and city-level initiatives, a substantial worldwide development came in 2009 with UN-Habitat's launch of the Global Programme on Safe Cities Free from Violence Against Women in conjunction with UNIFEM (now subsumed under UN Women) (UN-Habitat, 2010b:13; see also ActionAid, 2011). This followed on the heels of UN-Habitat's Safer Cities Programme, which has supported local authorities in developing countries to prevent crime and violence through city-wide advocacy and training (UN-Habitat, 2008c). As noted by Yardena Tankel (2011:352; see also Pain, 2001):

> A key tenet to safe city for women approaches is an exploration into women's insecurities in cities and recognition of the immobilising effects of individual and collective fears of violence which impact women's capacity as active citizens and their right to enjoy city life to the fullest.

One notable example of a city which has introduced a host of initiatives to reduce violence against women is Cebu in the Philippines, which distinguished itself by being the first city in the country to introduce a 'Gender Code' and in 2004 earned the UN-Habitat award of 'Women Friendly City'. Among its major innovations was the NGO-instigated multi-stakeholder 'Bantay Banay' scheme (see Box 6.3), which has since been replicated in most other Filipino cities.

Following the Philippines' opening of women's and children's desks at police stations around the country from the mid-1990s onwards, 2008 saw the opening of the first women-only police station in Manila. Similar initiatives have been introduced in Argentina, Peru and Brazil (Uribe-Urán, 2013:73), and in the latter there are now 450 women's police stations around the country, as well as 147 Special Courts for Domestic and Family Violence against Women (UN Women, 2011a:Box 2.4, 58). In Tanzania, too, the formation of the Tanzania Police Female Network (TPFNet) has led to the opening of gender desks in police stations (Hughes and Wickeri, 2011:856). However, although there is a generally positive correlation between the representation of women in the police force and the reporting of sexual assault (UN Women, 2011a:59), formal denunciations of domestic violence in Tanzania remain rare, and nationally there is only one temporary shelter for women seeking refuge from violent partners – the 'House of Peace', which opened in Dar Es Salaam in 2002 (see Hughes and Wickeri,

---

Box 6.3   Addressing domestic violence in Cebu City, Philippines – the 'Bantay Banay' programme

Located in the Western Visayas, Cebu City forms part of Metro Cebu, the second-largest urban settlement in the Philippines after the capital, Metro Manila.

Cebu is not only renowned as a hub of export industry in the country, and for its major contributions to national prosperity, but also for its record on promoting gender equality and empowering women. Here, the locally based NGO Lihok Pilipina, on the basis of research with hospitals, the police and *barangay* (neighbourhood) officials, launched a flagship programme against domestic violence in the early 1990s known as 'Bantay Banay' (Family Watch in Cebuano). The programme aims to transform domestic violence from a 'private' to a 'public' issue, and to make everyone responsive to, and responsible for, addressing violence against women by sensitising key stakeholders such as women and men in communities, *barangay* officials, local doctors, health workers and police officers to the need to identify and eliminate GBV. This entails becoming familiar with the signs and symptoms of domestic violence, and raising levels of reporting. In some neighbourhoods of the city, Bantay Banay has been so successful that battering by husbands now affects 20 per cent of the female population, whereas previously the figure stood at 60 per cent.

Sources: Chant, 2007a:198; UN-Habitat, 2012b:68–72.

2011:855–8). In other countries, such as South Africa, there is greater institutional support, including in the form of the Thuthuzela Care Centres, although these still cater for only approximately 20 per cent of the women who need assistance (see UN Women, 2011a:Box 2.3, 57). In light of this, one very positive development in Uganda – entailing the support of an internationally funded NGO, CEDOVIP (Centre for Domestic Violence Prevention) in collaboration with ActionAid Uganda, the National Association of Women's Organisations in Uganda (NAWOU) and the Kampala-based NGO 'Raising Voices' – has been to introduce the initiative SASA! Similar to the Bantay Banay programme in the Philippines, SASA! attempts to mobilise communities against violence against women (see Box 6.4).

The importance of working with men, and especially young men, in community-based and public initiatives to address GBV cannot be overemphasised. In the lead-up to the International Day to Eliminate Violence against Women of November 2012, the UNiTE to End Violence against Women Campaign saw UN Women and other in-country UN agencies organising a T-shirt design competition to raise awareness of VAW, with particular targeting of young men aged between eighteen and twenty-five. The winning design was from Colombia and comprised a heart made of band-aid plasters with the caption: 'Violence against women is

---

Box 6.4   Mobilising communities to prevent violence against women and HIV in Kampala, Uganda – SASA!

SASA! (Swahili for 'Now!', but also serves as an acronym for a four-phased approach to community mobilisation to prevent VAW and HIV – 'Start, Awareness, Support and Action') began life in the densely populated and predominantly impoverished Rubaga and Makindye divisions of Kampala, the capital of Uganda, in the early 2000s. Using community activists (CAs) recruited by the NGO CEDOVIP, the initiative draws on a variety of tools, including the SASA! Activist Kit, which was developed by the collaborating partner Raising Voices to sensitise urban poor residents to awareness of violence against women and then address it.

The means used are many and varied, including community drama performances, 'community conversations' (whereby CEDOVIP provides CAs with a set of pictures which enables them to promote small-group discussions in neighbourhood churches, sports centres and so on), audio soap operas, 'quick chats', and the SASA! film, which tells the stories of two women who have experienced violence and HIV infection, and which is available for individual viewing at home or in more public spaces, such as churches, canteens and hair salons. Among other communication materials and strategies are posters and comic strips, card games and media exposure.

Engaging men in the process is regarded as critical, because VAW is a community problem that can occur only where communities tolerate it. While change rarely happens overnight, the general results so far appear to be positive in a context in which 'the belief in men's use of power over women as natural is widespread', and where 'balancing power' between heterosexual couples is gradually gaining traction.

Source: Musuya, 2011:242ff.

---

not in my vocabulary'. The shirt was then worn ostensibly in all cities in the country during the 2012 celebrations (McIlwaine, 2013:76).

Even where reducing gender-based violence may not be the explicit aim of urban initiatives, the general transformation of cities into more pro-poor and resident-friendly spaces can have important effects in this regard. A case in point is Medellín, Colombia, a major industrial city but also a former focal point for Pablo Escobar's drug cartel, which from the late 1990s onwards and particularly under the 'Plan for Medellín 2007–2013' introduced by Mayor Sergio Fajardo included a host of initiatives such as transport and infrastructure projects to address exclusion, investment in poorer areas of the city, increased connectedness of peri-urban communities to the centre, the creation of public parks and spaces, and community involvement in policy, including women's groups and NGOs. Such initiatives can play major roles in reducing seemingly engrained cultures of violence (Maclean, 2014), and indeed the 'Medellín Miracle' in 'social urbanism' is widely credited with prompting a dramatic reduction in the city's homicide rate (from 381 murders per 100,000 of the urban population in the early 1990s to only 31.4 per 100,000 in 2011; ibid.:5; see also Moser and McIlwaine, 2004; and Chapter 7, this volume).

A final policy approach to VAW interventions, worth outlining here because of its multi-dimensional and multi-sectoral perspective, which corresponds with the wider conceptual framing of the 'gender–urban–slum interface', and also focuses attention on the most appropriate scale for institutional action (Moser and McIlwaine, 2014: 340), is Carolyn Whitzman *et al.*'s (2014) 'partnership framework'. This deploys the metaphor of 'four legs for a good table' to explain the importance of linking four categories of actors at different scales in the quest to reduce VAW. These include:

> elected officials who function as 'champions'; public servants who can be valued as 'enablers' (sometimes referred to in this context as 'femocrats' or feminist bureaucrats); community-based groups who perform the role of 'advocates'; and, finally, researchers who serve as 'information brokers'.
>
> (Ibid.:444)

Concluding comments

This chapter has explored the nature of GBV, and specifically VAW, and their particular parameters in cities in the Global South where there are notable concentrations. We have highlighted how the endemic nature of VAW influences women's and girls' well-being, with concomitant ramifications for the health of households and communities. We have also shown how VAW is especially pertinent to slums in general, and to particular spaces therein, with women's limited access to decent housing and adequate services exposing them to heightened threats of attack and abuse. Even though weak services, infrastructure and job markets are not the underlying reasons why VAW occurs in the first place, they certainly appear to compound the phenomenon. In turn, while innovative interventions to address VAW are being developed in cities across the Global South, for the moment it remains one of the most glaring aspects of gender inequality in urban environments. With the multiple disadvantages and adversities entailed in its wake, and in accordance with the tenets of our 'gender–urban–slum interface', VAW needs to be considered as a core cross-cutting issue in understanding women's and girls' experiences of cities and slums, not only because it impacts their contributions to the functioning of urban environments, but also because it denies them fundamental rights to the benefits nominally linked with contemporary urbanisation.

While many aspects of VAW are at their most intense in slums themselves, as identified earlier in this chapter and in Chapter 2, VAW also acts as a major deterrent to women's and girls' ability to move in urban space more generally, with serious consequences for their economic and social rights and freedoms. Lack of spatial mobility among women and girls in cities of the Global South,

Plate 6.2 External escalators surrounding a community centre in the showpiece renovated barrio Comuna 13 (formerly one of the city's most violent neighbourhoods), Medellín, Colombia

Source: Cathy McIlwaine.

with due regard for the need to consider the ways in which different intra-urban spaces interlock and influence one another, forms the bulk of our discussion in the next chapter.

7 Gender, mobility and connectivity

Introduction: gender, space and mobilities

As identified when introducing our 'gender–urban–slum interface' in Chapter 2, connectivities and intersectionalities between spaces of different types and scales are of vital significance in understanding gendered experiences and rights within cities, and perhaps nowhere is this more pertinent than in questions of mobility. When women's and girls' freedoms are curtailed at the micro-level of their persons or domestic space, for example, this often impacts, as well as is impacted by, gendered restrictions or exclusions in more macro-level arenas, such as neighbourhoods and urban areas as a whole. Accordingly, a complex array of overlaps between 'private' and 'public' barriers to female movement presents itself. As outlined in the preceding chapter, women and girls often face heavy constraints on their spatial mobility due to the fears and insecurities associated with gender-based violence. However in the context of movements around cities (and slums), a host of other factors – ranging from socialised hegemonic gender divisions and identities to gender-blind (or gender-prejudicial) urban planning – comes into the frame.

Because of the fundamental role played by transport in connecting women to many forms of urban infrastructure, and its more general impacts on influencing gendered mobility, this topic receives particular attention in the first part of this chapter following a brief discussion of gendered dimensions of intra-urban movement. Thereafter, we turn to information and communications technology (ICT), which, in an increasingly digital age, now plays an immensely important part in shaping the 'gender–urban–slum interface', especially in relation to social networks, livelihoods, and personal protection and safety.

Gender and intra-urban movement

Women's and girls' prospects for moving around cities and being connected with others within them (and beyond) are typically circumscribed by gender-insensitive planning coupled with gendered norms and modes of conduct and propriety, as well as trepidations linked with their perceived and actual vulnerabilities (Speak, 2012). Kamran Asdar Ali (2012:595) has described these diverse constraints on female mobilities as comprising a cocktail of 'public harassment, private censure and self-policing'.

While women's intra-urban movements are limited by moralised sexualities, domestic responsibilities, fear, and the idea that they will somehow disrupt public space (Ali, 2012:598; see also Bondi, 2005; Schütte, 2014; Valentine, 1989; Wilson, 2001), men, by contrast, 'experience the city with a far greater sense of security and freedom . . . They traverse the public sphere without the same kind of bodily discipline and emotional restraint that women have to endure' (Ali, 2012:598). Ali also points out, with reference to the work of Ananya Roy (2003:101–2) on Kolkata, India, that men can enjoy the experience initially framed by Baudelaire, as 'bathing in the crowds of the city'.

In some circumstances, women and girls may manoeuvre in public urban spaces only by being chaperoned or accompanied by a male relative or a female peer or adult, or by adopting dress codes that signal invisibility, anonymity and personal restraint. The latter is discussed, inter alia, by Hanaa Hamdan-Saliba and Tovi Fenster (2012; see also Fenster and Hamdan-Saliba 2013) in the context of Palestinian women in Tel Aviv, where spaces of belonging – and exclusion – are marked by ethnic and cultural divisions, as well as by gendered cleavages (see Box 7.1). By the same token, this should not detract from the fact that Palestinian women's practice of crossing Israeli borders on 'leisure trips' is not only an act of resistance to occupation but also a means of challenging patriarchal restrictions on their movements at family and community levels (Richter-Devroe, 2011; see also Secor, 2004).

Box 7.1   The multiple meanings of women's veiling in urban space

Building on the work on 'tactics' developed by Michel de Certeau (1994), which describes reactions to the power practices of individuals and institutions, and which can change the manner in which spaces are managed and ordered, Hamdan-Saliba and Fenster's (2012) discussion of the wearing of the veil (*hijab*) in Arab societies reveals that 'covering the head' embodies a variety of meanings and purposes in its overall role as a 'tactic to cope with Arab gendered and cultural strategies of power'. Generally speaking, the wearing of the *hijab* (and other forms of modest attire) is a 'prerequisite for spatial mobility in public spaces' (ibid.:205), protecting women from sexual harassment in the street and workplace, allaying their fears, and guarding their privacy. Moreover, while the veil is often regarded as a 'symbol and indicator' of the inferior status and subjugation of Arab Muslim women', it can also serve as a marker of women's identities, can confirm spaces of belonging in the city, and can signify 'opposition to Western colonialism and ideology' (ibid.).

Source: Hamdan-Saliba and Fenster, 2012.

Plate 7.1 Veiled mothers with children traversing Djemaa el-Fnaa Square, Marrakech, Morocco

Source: Sylvia Chant.

As might be anticipated the intersectionality of age with gender has a huge bearing on women's and girls' experiences of intra-urban mobility. For example, elderly and differently abled women may be particularly hampered in their movements by lack of pavements or weak mass transportation systems. Women with babies and young children may also find it extremely difficult to negotiate public transport if they have no one with whom to leave their infants. While young women and girls may be physically more able to traverse urban space, for social reasons they can frequently find their freedom of movement comes to an abrupt halt when they reach adolescence, especially if they inhabit dangerous and violent urban neighbourhoods (see Box 7.2).

Box 7.2   The impacts of restrictions on young women's mobility in a Hyderabad slum

In the course of an intervention forming part of ActionAid's Young Urban Women (YUW) programmme in a long-established slum of Hyderabad, India, with a majority Muslim population it was found that young women's mobility became extremely constrained once they reached puberty for a range of religious and cultural reasons. This posed numerous obstacles to women's ability to move around the city, as well as to undertake livelihood activities, at least on their own behalf. Although many of the young women had developed home-based handicraft enterprises making such items as embroidered cloth, bangles and incense sticks, the limitations they faced in interacting with the public meant that they had to rely on a male family member such as an older brother to act as an intermediary when negotiating prices with raw material suppliers and shops. This left the young women in the invidious position of conceding power and decision-making control to male relatives, and facing further vulnerabilities if their familial 'middlemen' proved dishonest or moved away.

Following analysis of the young women's situation, the YUW programme, which has also been introduced in Mumbai and Chennai, and focuses simultaneously on economic independence, livelihoods and sexual and reproductive health and rights, has embarked upon supporting female empowerment and fostering its acceptance among young women's families and wider communities. As part of this process, YUW organises young women into groups of between twenty-five and thirty who attend training sessions and develop solidarity campaigns. One outcome of these sessions in Hyderabad has been to increase neighbourhood police patrols and effectiveness.

Source: Chatterjee, 2015.

Plate 7.2 Women taking a rare moment of group rest and reflection on the steps leading down to the Holy Lake in Pushkar, India

Source: Danielle Da Silva.

Gender and public transport

As noted by one of the foremost international experts on gender and transport, Caren Levy (2013b:25): 'Transport accessibility to urban opportunities relates not only to time/distance, but also to cost, safety and comfort. Transport accessibility also has an integrative dimension in people's lives, enabling them to balance or orchestrate activities on a daily basis.' The particular constraints to movement faced by women and girls in this regard can seriously jeopardise their lives and livelihoods by resulting in lower literacy rates through non-attendance at school (Weiss, 1994; see also World Bank 2011c:169) and restricting their labour force participation (Kantor, 2002; Lessinger, 1990; Vera-Sanso, 1995). Following on from Baishali Chatterjee's (2015) example of young girls in Hyderabad (Box 7.2), in the context of slum neighbourhoods in and around the Orangi Town area of Karachi, Pakistan, Kamran Asdar Ali (2012:594) highlights how general social disapproval of women working is compounded by the harassment they experience en route to work or other daily activities, whether this is in the context of people watching their comings and goings from home (rendering the streets under 'permanent informal surveillance'), or the general baiting to which they are subjected in markets and bus stations. Aside from social and cultural constraints on women's movements, and the fact that women may be the last in households to claim use of any form of vehicle, including bicycles, gender-blind transport planning can

Plate 7.3 Competing for space on the pedestrian-unfriendly streets of Pune, India

Source: UN-Habitat/Carlosfelipe Pardo.

accordingly act to the serious detriment of the well-being and livelihoods of women in towns and cities (García-Moreno and Chawla, 2011; Jarvis *et al.*, 2009; Kunieda and Gauthier, 2007; Peters, 2001; Walker and Vajjhala, 2009).

The design of public transportation systems, which, significantly, are often largely or exclusively managed and operated by men, often assumes male labour patterns, prioritising travel to and from peri-urban areas to city centres during 'peak hours'. This neglects women's engagement in domestic, informal, part-time work in non-centralised zones, non-peak journeys, and disproportionate household and care burdens that require 'trip chaining' – multi-purpose, multi-stop excursions (Boulin, 2007; Kunieda and Gauthier, 2007; Levy, 2013a, 2013b; Schmink, 1986; Titcombe, 2014; UN-Habitat, 2009: 126). Low-income women in cities across the world also face particular challenges regarding transportation costs and time burdens (Hamilton, 2001; IWPR, 2015; Levy, 1992; Tran and Schlyter, 2010), with obstacles compounded for elderly and disabled women and women in sex-segregated societies (Jarvis *et al.*, 2009; Kunieda and Gauthier, 2007). As Ali (2012:596) reports for Karachi: 'Poor women brave urban public transport systems without the social protections that class bestows on elite women.' Barriers and difficulties include buses and minivans failing to stop for women, or favouring men for rush-hour seating. Moreover, women (and men) who are informally employed and have to carry their produce and equipment with them are heavily constrained by poor public transport facilities in many cities. In such instances the unafford-ability and/or unreliability of public transport may confine women to working inside their communities rather than venturing outside of them (UN-Habitat, 2012a:11).

Plate 7.4 'Taking a break': male driver of local urban 'bush taxi', Kanifing, The Gambia

Source: Sylvia Chant.

Another major problem regarding women's use of public transport is personal safety and security. Where transport connections are situated in isolated or poorly lit areas, or bus and train carriages are heavily overcrowded and/or inadequately or ineffectively staffed, women and girls face verbal, sexual and physical harassment and even assault, resulting in physical harm, psychological anxiety and fear of moving around the city (Anderson and Panzio, 1986; Burgess, 2008; Fernando and Porter, 2002; Hamilton, 2001; Jarvis *et al.*, 2009:178–9; Kunieda and Gauthier, 2007; Peters, 2001; see also below). As argued by Levy (2013b: 27), given considerations of safety which so often affect women's choice of intra-urban travel, 'interventions need to be sought which promote the planning and design of transport hubs, routes, and modes as defensible, comfortable and welcoming spaces'.

By addressing concerns about safety and sexual harassment, transport and associated infrastructure can arguably be made more gender responsive and inclusive. One alternative, introduced in cities as diverse as Mexico City, Cairo, Jakarta, Mumbai, New Delhi, Rio de Janeiro and Moscow is to provide women-only buses and/or train carriages (see Malhotra, 2011; Valenti, 2007; Vaswani, 2010; UN-Habitat, 2012a:38). However, although such initiatives might provide immediate solutions to some of the harassment and danger to which women are exposed on intra-urban journeys, they are hardly likely to play a transformative role in gender relations. Conforming, as they do, to stereotypical images of women as vulnerable and in need of protection, and men as aggressors, underlying gendered power dynamics and behaviour patterns may persist largely unchanged (Chant, 2011b:85). As summarised by Claudia García-Moreno and Manupreet Chawla (2011:62):

> it is important to note that such programmes – although they create awareness – perpetuate gender norms and behaviours that discriminate against women and so should be in place only temporarily. Rather than segregating women and girls, the goal should be to create cities where women can travel and enjoy the city independently and at any time of day.

Part of creating such cities that are friendlier to people in general, and women in particular, might involve prioritising pedestrian mobility, rather than cars, as it is critical to recognise that city streets do not need to be home to traffic, especially private motorised vehicles, which are usually owned by men and pose threats of injury and contamination (see Hughes and Wickeri, 2011; Khosla, 2009:17). Although sometimes the introduction of simple low-cost improvements, such as pavement widening or pedestrianisation, can make a huge difference to women's movement around urban space, especially as they often comprise a disproportionate number of the people who have to journey on foot (Levy, 2013b:25), broader initiatives, consisting of several complementary interventions, are required to ensure gender-equitable intra-urban mobility. Creating dedicated cycle paths and introducing affordable, women-friendly mass transit systems might help here, not only by permitting greater female mobility and greater access for women into 'public' areas, but also by encouraging the adoption of healthier lifestyles (see Birch, 2011:89; García-Moreno and Chawla, 2011).

Plate 7.5 The freedom of the street! A young girl playing in a sandy urban thoroughfare where one advantage of the absence of tarmacking is its inhibition of fast-moving vehicular traffic, Greater Banjul, The Gambia

Source: Sylvia Chant.

Showcase examples arguably include the recent major regenerations that have taken place in a range of Colombian cities under the auspices of powerful and popular mayors, such as Enrique Peñalosa in Bogotá and Sergio Fajardo in Medellín (see Castro and Echeverri, 2011; Cornman-Levy *et al.*, 2011:195ff.; Maclean, 2014; see also Box 7.3). In relation to the 'Medellín Miracle' (see Chapter 6), the renowned Metrocables cable-car mass transport system that opened in the city in 2004 was, by linking poor urban peripheral neighbourhoods with the overground Metro system, the first in the world explicitly to address the stigma of poverty, violence and territorial control by illegal militias and gangs (Dávila, 2013). Although the Metrocables project and its various companion initiatives – such as 'Cultura Metro', a behavioural code imposed on transport users with the support of signposting and vigilance – were not explicitly designed with a primary focus on gender, and while women still suffer harassment on the new transport system, they do report feeling safer and say that it is easier for them to balance their work–life commitments more effectively (Levy, 2013b:27).

Gender, virtual space and digital technology

Virtual space is arguably a new and complementary form of public space for women, facilitated by new technology and especially, although not exclusively, the internet, which provides numerous sources of information – for example, on

Plate 7.6 Metrocable cable-car mass public transport system, Medellín, Colombia

Source: Cathy McIlwaine.

Box 7.3   Gender dimensions of improved connectivity in cities: the Bogotá experience under Mayor Enrique Peñalosa

One of most important priorities advanced during Bogotá Mayor Enrique Peñalosa's time in office (1998–2001) was the 'de-marginalisation' and/or 'inclusion of low-income and informal workers and residents' in the country's capital (Montezuma, 2005:4). Policies were pursued to dismantle the barriers preventing poorer citizens from accessing the benefits of urban life by 'equalising' city residents before the state. Providing services to traditionally marginalised groups created stronger social cohesion by ending preferential public treatment for the more affluent (ibid.: 5). During his relatively brief administration, Peñalosa extended access to water to all Bogotá homes and implemented radical reforms in transport, infrastructure and the use of urban space (Walljasper, 2005). He sought to maximise popular mobility through prioritising walkway and bicycle-lane projects over cars, which provided healthy, low-cost, non-polluting travel options. He also actively promoted Bogotá's 'Sunday Ciclovía' tradition, a weekly car-free event which since the 1970s has closed 120 kilometres of city roads to all but pedestrians and those using non-motorised vehicles, such as bicycles and roller-skates (see Castro and Echeverri, 2011).

When cities are 'designed for people, not cars', spaces are opened up for recreation and socialising which are often scant in slum settlements. Pedestrian- and people-friendly projects can also lessen the social inequality that comes with a stratified transport system which favours richer motorists over poorer mass transit users (Kunieda and Gauthier, 2007:7; Walljasper, 2004). The high-quality TransMilenio bus rapid transit system introduced by Peñalosa is now eighty-four kilometres in length and offers safe, affordable and reliable public transport that is accessible to the residents of Bogotá's slums. Serving an average of 1.7 million passengers every day, the system provides universal access to all stations and buses in trunk lines which cater to the needs of women, the disabled and the elderly. Indeed, through TransMilenio, Peñalosa addressed a major obstacle to income-earning by poor women who previously had to source employment within walking distance of their homes to avoid paying hefty transport fares (Kunieda and Gauthier, 2007:4). Women who can access numerous quality and flexible transportation options benefit from such investments because their trips are often for multiple purposes (ibid.:7), although an integrated ticketing system enabling trip-chaining by women would improve matters further. Gender-sensitive investments which reduce the risks and constraints attached to 'dangerous and unreliable mass transit' can also benefit men, of course (ibid.:17).

Building on the legacy of Antanas Mockus, who was very keen to recruit women in all processes, and to enlist more female police officers, Peñalosa sought process-related reforms as well. Project teams engaged a number of young professional women and men (Montezuma, 2005:2), increasing efficiency and avoiding the corruption-related pitfalls that plague many infrastructure initiatives run by seasoned bureaucrats. Cities that enable women to fulfil their potential of playing important roles at all stages of local governance – from strategic planning to urban crisis response – are clearly able to access a greater pool of talent (Lind and Farmelo, 1996).

Bogotá's transformation demonstrates how improved access to urban infrastructure can contribute to increasing gender-inclusive prosperity in its widest sense.

Sources: Castro and Echeverri, 2011; Kunieda and Gauthier, 2007; Lind and Farmelo, 1996; Montezuma, 2005; Walljasper, 2004.

education and employment, novel lines of communication, and potential female mobilisation and organisation (see, e.g., Fenster and Hamdan-Saliba, 2013). In the context of women in Palestine, for example, 'Using . . . virtual space . . . enables the expansion and flexibility of the spatial practices of Palestinian women' (Hamdan-Saliba and Fenster, 2012:207).

Given the importance of the digital revolution to growth, and the likely continued significance of the 'knowledge economy', particularly in urban areas

Plate 7.7 Women cyclists enjoy the Sunday Ciclovía in Bogotá, Colombia

Source: UN-Habitat/Carlosfelipe Pardo.

(see Aker and Mbiti, 2010), it is no surprise that ICT access featured in the MDGs, with MDG8's Target 8F being to increase telephone lines, cellular subscribers and internet users (UN, 2010a). ICT also appears in the proposed SDGs, with SDG9 (on the need to 'build resilient infrastructure, promote inclusive and sustainable industrialisation and foster innovation') specifically referring to the desire 'significantly [to] increase access to ICT and strive to provide universal and affordable access to internet in LDCs by 2020' (UNSDN, 2015:53).

In light of progressively lower entry and maintenance costs (Plan International, 2010:105), the spread of everyday accessible technologies has been especially rapid. Such is the case with mobile telephony, which is based for the most part on 'pre-paid' contracts where there is no billing or credit-checking (Oestmann, 2007:3). Africa now has the fastest-growing mobile telephony market worldwide (de Bruijn *et al.*, 2009), with an average of 30 per cent new mobile phone connections a year since 2001 leading to 60 per cent of the population being connected by 2011 (UN-Habitat, 2012b:55). The same continent has also seen mobile phone access and provision frequently outstripping – and indeed leapfrogging – fixed landline coverage (Oestmann, 2007:6; Scott *et al.*, 2004:1; see also Table 7.1, below). Indeed, a recent study comprising Ghana, Kenya, Nigeria, Senegal, South Africa, Tanzania and Uganda revealed huge increases in mobile phone ownership between 2002 and 2014, with levels in Ghana escalating from 10 per cent to 83 per cent during this period (Pew Research Center, 2015:2). There has also been an increase in smartphone use (ibid.:4), not only in Africa but beyond, with one report suggesting that in 2014 1.76 billion people globally owned a smartphone, representing a mammoth increase of 25 per cent from just the previous year (Viswanath and Basu, 2015:49). Although men still form the majority of mobile and smartphone owners (see below), such growth has several implications for developing livelihood and public safety initiatives for women and girls in cities of the Global South.

The potential for urban women and girls of new digital technologies

Following on from exhortations at the Fourth World Women's Conference at Beijing in 1995 for greater female participation in the digital sector (ESCAP,

Table 7.1 Global variations in percentages of mobile telephone subscribers and internet users, 2002–2007

	2002		2007	
	Mobile subscribers	*Internet users*	*Mobile subscribers*	*Internet users*
Africa	4	1	28	5
Americas	30	28	72	43
Asia	12	6	38	14
Europe	51	26	111	44
Oceania	49	44	79	53
World total	19	11	50	21

Source: Adapted from ITU, 2009:4.

2002:12), former UN Secretary General Kofi Annan deemed ICT an essential tool for realising MDG3's objective of 'empowering women and promoting gender equality'. In the proposed SDGs, ICT is even more prominent in relation to women. For example, within SDG5, on achieving gender equality and empowerment for all women and girls, Target 5B refers to the need to 'enhance the use of enabling technologies, in particular ICT, to promote women's empowerment' (UNSDN, 2015:48). ICT has the potential not only to improve women's lives by enhancing their access to information but also to increase their productivity through expanding their skill sets and opening up opportunities for wage employment and 'techno-preneurship' in the fields of e-commerce and computerised small and medium-sized enterprises, as well as affording the opportunity for 'remote working' (see Buskens and Webb, 2009; Kleine, 2013; Ng and Mitter, 2005). Malaysia, for example, is especially interested in developing ICT capacity among women as part of a drive to create teleworking jobs (ESCAP, 2002; see also Chapter 8, this volume). Another spin-off is increasing the potential for greater female participation in urban 'e-governance' (see Khosla, 2009:40, on India).

Even basic or entry-level technology, such as mobile telephony, can improve social interaction and serve as a time-saving communication device (Scott *et al.*, 2004:2). Enhanced access to information, for example, reduces uncertainty and transaction costs, enabling traders to secure better deals, lessening their reliance on intermediaries, and widening access to a broader range of buyers (Chen, 2004; Moodley, 2005; Overå, 2008; World Bank, 2003a), including in global markets (Evans, 2013a; Gurumurthy, 2004:28–9). Evidence from Africa reveals that usage is predominantly for financial arrangements, such as the transfer of money for agricultural produce (Scott *et al.*, 2004:8), and for the trade of perishable goods (Molony, 2009:93), but, impacting women in particular, it can also increase the speed and efficiency of rural–urban remittance transfers (Oestmann, 2007:4; Scott *et al.*, 2004:7). In addition, several women in countries such as The Gambia and the Philippines now make livings from selling mobile phone and dongle credit, whether as dedicated roadside vendors or as employees of home-based stores.

The growth of cities not only increases opportunities for women in the information economy but is also likely to boost national IT capacity, reduce poverty, and increase urban (and national) prosperity. In light of the multiple potential benefits of gender-sensitive investments in this sector, a number of global and national-level policy initiatives have attempted to improve women's digital literacy and access to information technologies in recent years (see Sarikakis and Shade, 2011:71–81; see also Box 7.4).

ICTs and protection from gender-based violence

Another very innovative use by women of digital technology, which crosses over into questions of physical mobility in urban areas, is to map spaces in the city where women are particularly vulnerable to sexual harassment or abuse (provided by reports via texts and emails, as well as community mobilisation). One of the earliest examples of such an initiative is the Blank Noise project in India, started

Plate 7.8 Female roadside phone credit seller, Kanifing, The Gambia

Source: Sylvia Chant.

Box 7.4   Women in Liberia and the Trade at Hand – Business Opportunities for Your Cell Phone project

Liberia's Trade at Hand programme, developed by the International Trade Centre (ITC) in collaboration with Liberia's Ministry of Commerce and Industry (MCIL) and launched in 2009, aims to 'empower' women economically and to enhance productivity more generally – both of which are primary objectives of incumbent President Ellen Johnson-Sirleaf's government (now in her second term of office) – through ICT. Initially linking fifty women traders in Monrovia with fifty women farmers through a mobile phone software system, the programme provides information on products, quantities, prices, location and transport via SMS, allows exchanges of offers, and matches sale and purchase demands. In order to include illiterate women, the system uses readily recognisable symbols.

As a result of the programme, market women save money and time, no longer making multiple phone calls to sellers as they can view many offers simultaneously, and secure competitive prices and high-quality goods. At the same time farmers can offload their produce and thereby minimise wastage. Liberia's national economic development benefits from increased efficiency of food flow into towns, for consumption and export, aiding infrastructural and economic revival in the aftermath of its fourteen-year civil war, and allowing women to play a critical role. Trade at Hand has also been successfully implemented in Senegal, Mali and Burkina Faso.

Recognising Liberia's high unemployment rate (85 per cent) and low ICT development and trade infrastructure, programmes such as Trade at Hand may be most successful when accompanied by interventions to combat social and economic exclusion.

Sources: Gakuru *et al.*, 2009; ITC, 2009; ITC/MCIL, 2009; Liberian Observer, 2009; MFFF, 2011; USDS, 2011; World Bank, 2010.

---

in 2003 in Bangalore, which has now spread to other Indian cities, as described by García-Moreno and Chawla (2011:62; see also www.stopstreetharassment.org/tag/blank-noise/page/4/). Another is the Harass Map, launched by volunteers in Egypt in 2010, which showed an alarming increase in gender-based violence during the uprisings of 2011, especially in Cairo. Incidents of abuse ranged from catcalls, comments and 'ogling', to stalking and following, to touching, to rape and other sexual assaults. The purpose is not just to alert women in spaces where they are most likely to encounter abuse but to raise public awareness of harassment as a crime. The reports are followed up by a Community Outreach Unit that works on a voluntary basis one day a month and uses the information collated to train local leaders and 'community captains' to organise their neighbourhoods so as to minimise the risk of further harassment (http://harassmap.org/en/what-we-do/the-map/).

Plate 7.9 Mobilising Africa, Dar es Salaam, Tanzania

Source: Sylvia Chant.

An additional recent example using similar technologies is the SafetiPin initiative, launched in 2013 in India in the wake of the brutal gang rape and murder of a young female student ('Nirbhaya') on a Delhi bus in December 2012. SafetiPin is a mobile app designed to gather information through crowd-sourcing about safety and dangers in cities as well as to raise awareness about challenging sexual harassment in the street. Drawing inspiration from the women's safety audits discussed in Chapter 6 (see also Whitzman *et al.*, 2014), SafetiPin maps a safety audit score of a location via a pin in a map (green for safer areas, orange for less safe areas, and red for unsafe areas) in Delhi itself and five other Indian cities – Guwahati, Chennai, Kerala, Pune and Bangalore. While the name partly derives from the safety audit, it also recalls how in the days before such mobile app technology women used safety pins as a form of defence against street harassment in crowded places. Moreover, of course, they symbolise holding fabric together. As the co-founders of the organisation, Kalpana Viswanath and Ashish Basu (2015:47) point out: 'Our hope is that our SafetiPin can play that role with the fabric of our society.'

The data from the app, which permit analysis of the profiles of greatest at-risk persons, are uploaded to the website of the SafetiPin organisation, which works in partnerships with NGOs, local government and private companies. In its aims to share information as widely as possible, a particular objective is to pressurise city authorities into addressing gendered safety issues in public spaces more effectively. Significantly, SafetiPin has developed initiatives specifically in slum areas as well as in the city as a whole. For example, in Delhi, it has partnered with the feminist NGO Jagori to establish 'safety centres' in slum communities so that people without mobile phones can participate and have their concerns mapped onto the online platform on their behalf. The centres also promote activism and mobilisation through encouraging community members to initiate and develop campaigns and lobby stakeholders around issues such as streetlighting (ibid.; see also http://safetipin.com/). While this integrated version of SafetiPin is very much an Indian venture, the app has also been used in Jakarta, Indonesia, and a Spanish version has been launched in Bogotá, Colombia.

Yet, despite the strides made by and for women in ICT, it is important to acknowledge the persistence of a gendered 'digital divide' (Perrons, 2004:chapter 6). This is evident in even the most basic of technologies, such as mobile phones, with the sub-Saharan African study referred to earlier showing that men are more likely than women to possess a mobile in six of the seven countries included in the survey, with the level of male ownership in Uganda standing at 77 per cent, as against only 54 per cent among women (Pew Research Center, 2015:4). However, the gaps tend to widen when it comes to access to more sophisticated new technologies, such as computer hardware and the internet (Buskens and Webb, 2009; Perrons, 2004:chapter 6; ESCAP, 2002:5). With 'virtual space' or 'cyberspace' being what we might describe as a non-material facet of public space, women in general, and poor women in particular, are less likely than men to gain computer skills. This is partly a function of greater illiteracy among women (see Khosla, 2009:40, on India), and partly due to the fact that girls may miss out on school-based IT training, which is not normally taught until secondary and tertiary levels (Evans, 2013a, on Zambia). Beyond this, women are less likely to enjoy the mobility, social licence and funds necessary to access public internet facilities (World Bank, 2011c:272). In Indonesia, for example, girls aged 15–24 are only half as likely as boys and young men to use the internet (Plan International, 2010:19), with parental restrictions on girls' use of public space disfavouring their access to internet cafés. The gap is even greater in Ghana, where only 6.6 per cent of female youth frequent internet cafés, compared with 16.5 per cent of their male counterparts (ibid.:114).

It has also been noted that when women do use the internet their pathways of navigation predominantly follow portals of communication such as social networking sites, while their male counterparts seem more interested in how computers and the internet work, and accordingly spend more time researching links on technology and downloading new software (Plan International, 2010:111). However, with competition and declining costs of ICT, and an increase over the past decade of self-named 'gURLs' – a term originating in the United States which refers to 'technologically savvy young women' – there is an increasing female presence in cyberspace via websites and weblogs (commonly known as 'blogs') (Polak, 2006, cited in Plan International, 2010:111). None the less, like the city itself, ICT presents risks as well as opportunities (Plan International, 2010:9). Women, especially adolescent girls, are more vulnerable to cyber-abuse, such as misguided contact with traffickers and perpetrators of sexual assault (ibid.:10).

Plate 7.10 Expanding mobile phone services, The Gambia

Source: Sylvia Chant.

Cyberspace does not lend itself readily to regulation or control. Indeed on internet-facilitated mobile phones in The Gambia, where competition between providers has doubled in the past few years, and internet connectivity has massively expanded since the ACE (African Coast to Europe) submarine cable was activated in December 2012, it is possible to download pornography freely from a wide range of international websites, much of which portrays women in humiliating and degrading states. However, governments can make efforts to regulate age-restricted sites, as well as redesign online content to 'design out' crime, much as has been attempted in the physical realms of public space (Jacobs, 1996; Newman, 1972; Pain, 2000). In Chile, Dorothea Kleine (2013:209) also notes that while cyber-cafés have been 'coded' largely as spaces for young males, often with an interest in online pornography, government-backed 'infocentros' set up to provide people with access to the internet and computing skills have facilitated greater access among women in part by branding them as spaces of learning, and also by offering child-friendly facilities and late opening hours.

On a final note, given that poor urban residents, especially women, are often disadvantaged in their access to digital technology, optimism around the recent meteoric rise in use of ICTs, and its developmental impacts, should not be unreserved. For one, just as mobile telephony and other forms of digital technology do not always eliminate intermediaries – as in Nigeria's hand-loomed ('*ase-oke*') cloth-making sector, where it can even act as a 'technology of inequality' (Jagun *et al.*, 2007) – ICT can also reinforce divisions not only between women and men, but among women themselves (see also Chapter 8, this volume). Second, current aspirations for one laptop per child (OLPC) seem out of reach for the poorest nations of the world, with even middle-income countries struggling to make the requisite complementary large-scale investments in teacher training, curriculum development and reforms in academic assessment. As such, ICT may not necessarily be a 'magic bullet', with Warschauer and Ames (2010:46) asserting that 'there is no magic laptop that can solve the educational problems of the world's poor'.

Concluding comments

This chapter has highlighted how women and girls lack equal rights to the city in terms of spatial mobility for a range of pragmatic, ideological and socio-cultural reasons, most of which are underpinned by prevailing gender inequalities and asymmetries. Indeed, women face numerous restrictions in their intra-urban movements both indirectly, through gender-blind planning initiatives, especially revolving around transport infrastructure, as well as directly through fear of the dangers of gender-based violence and harassment. In conjunction, these varied constraints severely undermine women's and girls' abilities to participate fully in the social and economic life of cities, with female slum dwellers typically the most compromised.

While by no means a panacea, our discussion has raised the possibility that various forms of digital technology can help women to overcome – or at the very least challenge – some of the constraints they face on a daily basis. Yet, with a note of caution, technology in itself is unlikely to eliminate the perpetration of violence against women and girls, and indeed in some cases may exacerbate it, especially when the portrayal of women on the internet and social media platforms is frequently sexist, demeaning and privileges a hyper-masculine 'gaze' and power. In turn, even if ICT can provide some jobs for women and improve the cost-efficiency of micro-enterprises, it may not eliminate large-scale urban unemployment in the context of neoliberal restructuring and the aftermath of the recent global financial crisis. In light of this, other investments in informal individual and home-based business support, as well as job creation, may be equally, if not more, fruitful priorities if gender-equitable urban growth and development are to be achieved and sustained. This is explored further in our next chapter.

8 Gender and urban productivity

Education, employment and entrepreneurship

We have already seen how housing, services and infrastructure (physical and digital) exert a major brake on women's possibilities of gaining from urbanisation within the context of prevailing gender divisions of labour, notions of female 'propriety', and gender-differentiated access to public spaces in the Global South. These issues are deeply implicated in the sphere of urban productivity, the topic of this chapter, with women's multiple and intersecting disadvantages across domestic, community and city-wide spaces, and especially in slums, frequently compromising the possibilities nominally afforded by urban environments for the acquisition of education, vocational skills and training, and access to employment and other income-generating activities.

This chapter focuses in detail on two elements of the 'gender–urban–slum interface' – gender disparities in human capital and gender divisions of labour in the urban economy – both of which are crucial in affording opportunities for women, and especially female slum dwellers, to participate in the economic life of the city, as well as to realise their human rights.

Although discernible progress has been made in narrowing gender gaps in education in developing regions, especially in urban areas, this does not always translate into gender equality in employment. As identified by UN Women (2015c:14): 'Despite women's increasing levels of education, gender stereotypes in households and labour markets continue to structure the kinds of work that women and men do, the conditions under which they work and their rewards from work.' This is immensely important not only from the point of view of how women contribute to (and benefit from) 'urban prosperity', but also in terms of how employment might actually 'empower' them, personally and/or collectively (Chant and McIlwaine, 2013a; see also Kabeer, 2008a, 2008b). As this chapter illustrates, the relationship between female labour force participation and empowerment is by no means clear cut; rather, it is heavily mediated by a complex confluence of women's household and family circumstances, the employment and income-generating options available to them, and a host of social, financial and physical assets that they may (or may not) have at their disposal (see Chant and Datu, 2015; Chant and McIlwaine, 2013a, 2013b). For women and girls residing in urban slums, access to human capital, decent work and entrepreneurial opportunities is often particularly constrained, even if there are several examples which indicate how the mobilisation and organisation of women at the grassroots, and beyond, are effecting, and stand to effect, positive change in their working lives.

Gender in relation to education, vocational training and human capital formation

Education, human capital development and a skilled workforce are all foundational to people's livelihoods in cities. Education provides people with opportunities to develop their capacities to enhance participation across the wide spectrum of economic, social, cultural and political spheres of urban life. Educated women, on average, delay marriage and childbirth, are less vulnerable to HIV/AIDS, enjoy more power in their homes and in public arenas, and have fewer children, who themselves tend to be healthier and better educated (Grown, 2005; Lloyd, 2009; Murphy *et al.*, 2011; Plan International, 2009, 2010; Tembon and Fort, 2008; UNMP/TFEGE, 2005).

A major attempt to harness this latent potential, as well as to redress the pernicious effects of historical legacies of male bias in literacy and education, is embodied in MDG2 (to achieve universal primary education by 2015) and MDG3 (to promote gender equality and empower women), with Target 3A being to eliminate gender disparity in primary and secondary education, preferably by 2005, and in all levels of education no later than 2015. Education remains a priority into the proposed SDGs, with SDG4 calling to ensure 'inclusive and

Plate 8.1 Pupils leaving their morning shift at a co-educational junior school, Liberia, Costa Rica

Source: Sylvia Chant.

equitable quality education' and the 'promotion of lifelong learning opportunities for all', with Target 4.1 urging that all girls and boys should enjoy 'complete free, equitable and quality primary and secondary education leading to relevant and effective learning outcomes' by 2030 (UN Open Working Group, 2014:10).

In respect of MDG2, there has been substantial progress towards universal primary education in several countries, although not enough to meet the goal everywhere by 2015 (see UN, 2010a:16). While the primary school completion rate by 2010 had reached 90 per cent for all those entering school, in sub-Saharan Africa as many as one-quarter of children are still out of education, and more generally 120 million young people are illiterate (Satterthwaite *et al.*, 2013:15).

In order to measure progress in education, the UN now uses the 'gender parity index', which is calculated by girls' gross school enrolment ratio divided by the corresponding ratio for boys (UN, 2014b:21). Gender parity is nominally achieved when the ratio is between 0.97 and 1.03. As indicated in Figure 8.1, considerable advances were made at primary level between 1990 and 2012, especially in Southern Asia, which has now met the goal despite having one of the lowest starting points (0.72) at the beginning of the period (ibid.:21). The lowest recorded current score is currently in sub-Saharan Africa, where despite major post-1990 achievements, especially in Benin, Burkina Faso, Chad, Guinea, Mauritania, Senegal and Sierra Leone, parity at a regional level is only 0.92 (ibid.). However, it should be remembered that enrolment does not equate with attendance (or completion) and that girls and boys from poorer echelons of society may be especially disadvantaged. Indeed, where intra-urban comparative data and analysis exist, evidence points to school attendance being lower in slum than in non-slum areas. In Delhi, for instance, which harbours one of the largest disparities in urban India, slum children aged 6–17 years are 19 per cent less likely to attend school than their non-slum counterparts (Gupta *et al.*, 2009:30), and in Nigeria this is as low as 35 per cent (UN-Habitat, 2010d:2). Part of the problem owes to frequent under-provision of state schools in slums, with increasing numbers of households in Kibera, Nairobi, Kenya, now resorting to private alternatives, albeit in the community itself, and offering low fees to local children (see Yorgancioglu, 2014).

While by 2009 adolescent girls enjoyed a mean of six years of education in their lifetime (up from four years in 1990), thus placing them in a position to proceed to secondary education, at this level gender gaps begin to widen (UN-DESA, 2010:43). However, this is not always to the detriment of girls, with Latin America and the Caribbean back in 1990 enjoying not only gender parity but a female bias, and East and Southeast Asia now also in a situation where secondary enrolment favours girls (see Figure 8.2).

In tertiary education, gender gaps tend to be more pronounced, but again unevenly across regions. Although there is significant bias towards male enrolment in sub-Saharan Africa and to a lesser extent in Southern and Western Asia, in all other regions the opposite situation prevails (UN, 2014b:21; see also Figure 8.3). That said, in many instances women remain poorly represented in traditionally 'masculine' fields such as science and engineering (UN-DESA, 2010:43; see also Chant with Craske, 2003).

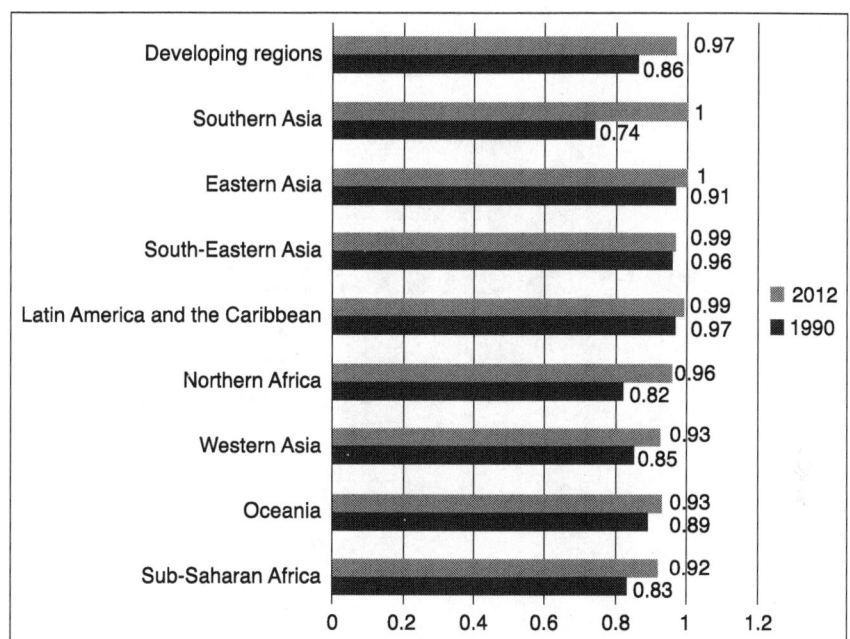

Figure 8.1 Gender parity index for gross enrolment ratios in primary education, 1990–2012

Source: Adapted from UN, 2014b:20.

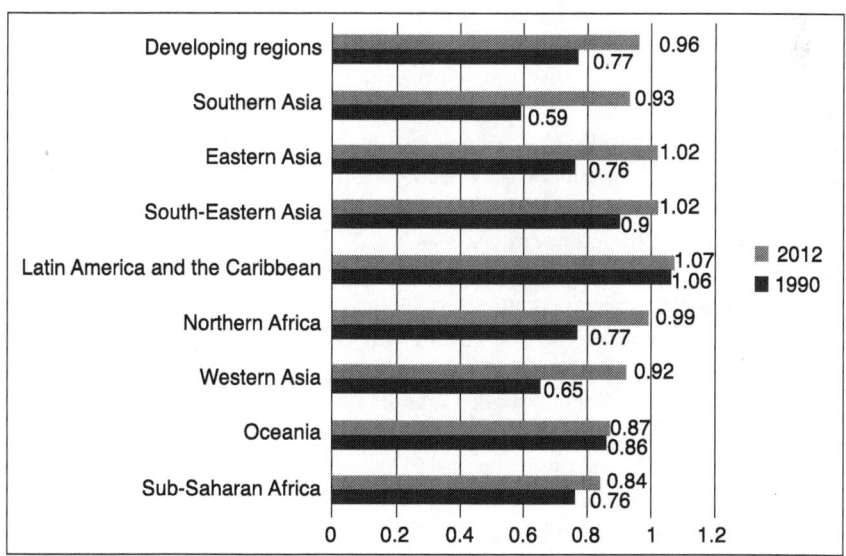

Figure 8.2 Gender parity index for gross enrolment ratios in secondary education, 1990–2012

Source: Adapted from UN, 2014b:20.

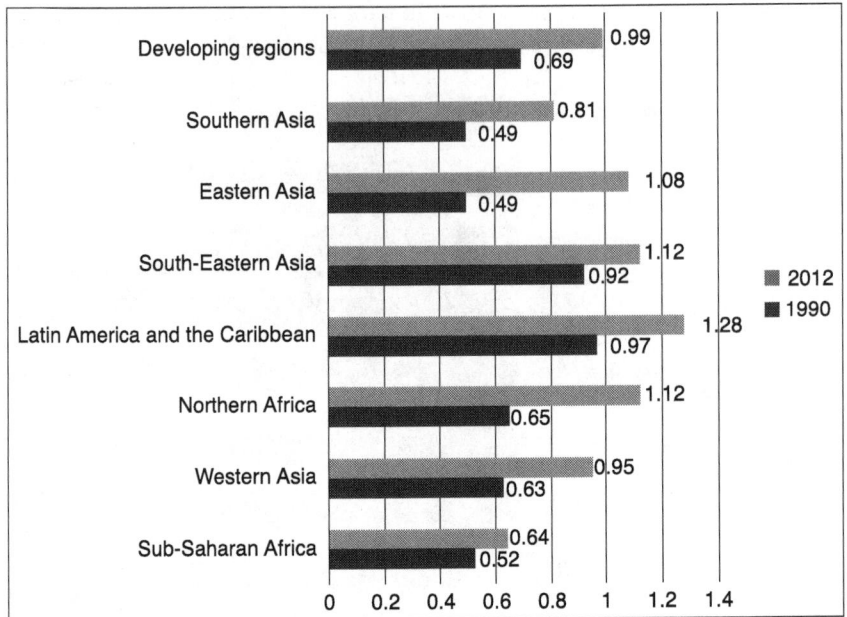

Figure 8.3 Gender parity index for gross enrolment ratios in tertiary education, 1990–2012

Source: Adapted from UN, 2014b:20.

Notwithstanding the major strides made in some regions discussed above, in global terms women still constitute approximately two-thirds of 774 million adult illiterates, a proportion which has seen little change in recent decades (UN-DESA, 2010:43). Although this is partly due to the historical legacy of gender gaps coupled with female-biased demographic ageing, even among contemporary generations of girls completion of education (especially at secondary and tertiary levels) is often disproportionately low (Lloyd, 2009; Morrison *et al.*, 2010; Tembon and Fort, 2008; Satterthwaite *et al.*, 2013; Yadav and Srivastava, 2006; UN, 2010a). This is not to deny that urban girls tend to be somewhat more advantaged than their rural counterparts, however. For example, drawing on data from the 2007 Demographic and Health Survey of Zambia (CSO *et al.*, 2009: 36–8), Alice Evans (2013b:5) points out not only that literacy rates are higher in urban than rural areas, but that gender gaps are narrower. While in rural areas only 51 per cent of women are able to read and write (as against 75 per cent of men), in urban areas female and male rates are 81 per cent and 90 per cent, respectively. In turn, while median years of completed schooling among rural women are 4.9 (as against 6.2 for men), in urban areas the corresponding figures are 8 and 8.7 years. In developing countries more generally, school attendance among girls aged 10–14 years is 18 per cent higher in urban than rural areas, and 37 per cent higher among the 15–19 years age cohort (Plan International, 2010). However, socio-economic disparities also enter the equation, and it is important to point out that urban averages can conceal important intra-city differences, as noted earlier in relation to school dropout rates among slum-dwelling girls (Plan International, 2012; see also Figure 2.3, this volume). In major Indian cities such as Delhi the proportion of women with no education or less than five years of schooling is 57 per cent in slums, compared with 28 per cent in non-slum areas, and in Kolkata the respective levels are 51 per cent and 28 per cent (Gupta *et al.*, 2009:Figure 2.11, 32).

In relation to gender and wealth patterns more broadly, UN Women (2015c:46) points out that attendance at secondary school in twenty-three developing countries is significantly lower for those in the poorest quintile compared with the most privileged fifth of the population. On the basis of 2011 data from Mozambique, for instance, girls from the poorest quintile were twenty-seven times less likely to attend secondary school than their wealthiest counterparts, notwithstanding that the disparity had been as high as forty-eight times in 2003. Moreover, as previously noted, even if enrolments are high, this does not guarantee attendance or completion; besides which, the quality of education is not always appropriate or 'empowering' (ibid.:47; see also Evans, 2013a, 2013b; Jeffery and Jeffery, 1998).

The multiple barriers to girls' education – ranging from economic to practical to social and symbolic – not only affect women and their families but also impede the well-being of all (Klasen, 2002; Tjon-A-Ten *et al.*, 2011). For example, poor and/or slum-dwelling girls may be hampered from private study by lack of space, light, tranquillity or basic infrastructure, or because during their time out of school they are required to perform domestic chores, which, as we documented in Chapter 4, can be extremely onerous in un- or semi-serviced neighbourhoods (see Chant and Touray, 2012, 2013; Hughes and Wickeri, 2011:889). Several young women may also be withdrawn from school (if they have enrolled in the first place) if their parents or guardians do not regard girls' education as important, or because their labour is needed from a young age to contribute to household finances, even if there is considerable evidence that young people can and do combine work and schooling (see, e.g., De Vreyer *et al.*, 2013; Jones and Chant, 2009). Another notable factor, and especially pertinent to pubescent girls who lack adequate sanitation in their homes as well as in school environments, is that fears about the possible exposure to sexual intercourse on the part of parents, and concerns about the shame and ridicule around menstruation among girls themselves, can radically reduce their school attendance and educational achievement, as observed, inter alia, in the context of Tanzania, Ethiopia and India by Varina Tjon-A-Ten *et al.* (2011; see also Chapter 4, this volume).

Interventions to redress these problems accordingly need to be holistic, which is not to deny the committed and often ambitious efforts made by governments to progress gender equality in education (GCE, 2005). For example, in The Gambia, a 'Girl Friendly' schools initiative was formally launched in 2001 with the support of UNICEF. This led to the establishment of a dedicated Girls' Education Unit (known since 2004 as the Gender Education Unit) within the Department of State for Education, and the waiving of 'upper basic' (junior secondary) school fees for girls. The step of constructing female-only toilet blocks has been instrumental in

Plate 8.2 Young 'gypsy' dancers who make their living entertaining tourists on the outskirts of New Delhi, India

Source: Danielle Da Silva.

encouraging more parents to let their daughters attend school (Chant and Touray, 2013; see also Khosla *et al.*, 2004). Related strategies to improve female enrolment and completion rates have included the training of more female teachers, the establishment of school-linked mothers' clubs, subsidies for the purchase of uniforms and educational materials, scholarship schemes, and workshops to encourage girls to study traditionally 'male' subjects, such as the sciences, mathematics and technology (which fall under the rubric of 'STEM'). None the less, only younger generations of Gambians have benefited from recent advances in educational provision, with less than half (46 per cent) of the population being literate at a national level, and the average female literacy rate (37 per cent) still far lower than that for men (60 per cent). Moreover, even now girls are disproportionately represented among the 15 per cent of Gambian youth educated in madrassas (traditional Islamic schools), which have only belatedly begun to incorporate non-traditional, secular and vocational subjects into their curricula (see Chant and Touray, 2012, 2013; Martin, 2003).

Education-to-work transitions

Although, as noted earlier, the acquisition of education can lead to a wide range of positive outcomes for women and girls, such as strengthening their decision-making power, raising awareness of rights, and delaying (unwanted) pregnancy

Plate 8.3 Madrassa schoolgirls watch an athletics training event at the National Stadium, Bakau, The Gambia

Source: Sylvia Chant.

and marriage, the relationship between female education and employment is not clear cut (UN Women, 2015c:80). While education is commonly associated with higher rates of employment and better wages (Dollar and Gatti, 1999; Lloyd, 2009; Tembon and Fort, 2008), for example, 'decent work' in the second decade of the twenty-first century appears to be increasingly elusive for young people in general, and for young women in particular (ILO, 2006, 2008b:19; see also Box 8.1). Indeed, it has been widely observed that young people now have less access to decent employment than earlier generations, which undoubtedly owes in part to the recent global financial crisis. For example, in 2013, the world youth unemployment rate was 12.6 per cent, with higher levels in developing regions, where 90 per cent of the global youth population resides (UN Women, 2015c:26; see also Chant, forthcoming; Stavropoulou and Jones, 2013).

In 2008 a target was added to MDG1 to 'achieve full and productive employment and decent work for all, including women and young people'. This has arguably been accorded greater priority in the proposed SDGs, with SDG8 exhorting the promotion of 'sustained, inclusive and sustainable economic growth, full and productive employment and decent work for all', and, within this, Target 8.5 specifying that by 2030 there should be 'full and productive employment and decent work for all women and men, including for young people and persons with disabilities, and equal pay for work of equal value' (United Nations Open Working Group, 2014:14). Moreover, in light of notable gender gaps in labour markets to date (see Kantor, 2010; also Chen, 2010a), it is timely

---

Box 8.1   Strategic objectives of the ILO's 'Decent Work' agenda

1. *Employment.* This refers to job creation through sound and sustainable investment and growth, access to the benefits of the global economy, supportive public policies and an enabling environment for entrepreneurship.
2. *Standards and fundamental principles and rights at work.* Following on from the ILO Declaration on Fundamental Principles and Rights at Work of 1998, this objective calls for the creation of work that does not involve forced labour, exploitation, discrimination and/or denial of association (e.g. prohibition on the formation of trade unions).
3. *Social protection.* This principle is concerned with ensuring that workers have formal protection for old age, invalidity, sickness and health care, and with creating safe and dignified working conditions.
4. *Social dialogue.* This advocates the opening of channels of communication between different stakeholders in the economy, and particularly giving workers in the informal economy more of a voice and representation.

Sources: ILO, 2001, 2003.

---

that calls for 'decent work' – the priority theme of the fifty-fifth session of the Commission on Status of Women (CSW) in 2011 – have been reinforced by appeals to promote increased female enrolment in education, to facilitate women's transition to decent work through training and networking, to develop public awareness campaigns to encourage women's entry into non-traditional sectors, and to engage men, employers and the state to recognise and alleviate women's reproductive work (UNCSW, 2011; see also Box 8.1, above). Given the contemporary scenario in developing regions, however, imminent achievements may be somewhat elusive.

While young women in towns and cities may enjoy a wider range of employment opportunities than their rural counterparts, they are often channelled by parents and/or teachers into low-paid, 'feminised' occupations, which can be to the detriment of girls' long-term earnings and career mobility (ILO, 2008a:6). For example, in Ghana and The Gambia, the vocational training and apprenticeships in which poor young urban women tend to enrol are usually in sex-segregated areas such as hairdressing, beauty therapy, dressmaking and cloth-dyeing, rather than more remunerative, traditionally 'masculine' trades, such as metalwork, plumbing and carpentry, or newer ones such as IT (see Jones and Chant, 2009; see also below). Investing in vocational training which is both gender sensitive and responsive to the demands of the labour market can help facilitate poor women's (and men's) entry into work (ILO, 2008b). In Botswana, for instance, the Women's Affairs Department within the Ministry for Labour and Home Affairs has drafted a National Policy for Mainstreaming Gender into Vocational Training and Workplace Learning, which aims to:

- increase women's access to vocational education and training;
- promote gender training of educators and make curricular more gender inclusive, so as to reduce gender stereotyping;
- raise awareness, encourage reporting and develop response mechanisms to sexual harassment; and
- collect sex-disaggregated data on men and women's training needs, so as to address occupational segregation (ibid.:40).

Recognising that gender-sensitive policy drafting might constitute an important first step, however, stated objectives should not be taken as outcomes. Many measures to improve girls' access to education and skills appear promising but are largely unproven (Lloyd, 2009:59). Even if gender mainstreamed, vocational institutions in Africa often deliver low-quality training that is inaccessible to the poorest members of society (AU, 2007). Moreover, young women, like their male counterparts, may remain jobless if there is low aggregate demand (ibid.; see also Evans, 2013a). Globally, one in three youths is unable to find work, has given up the job hunt, or is working but still living below the US$2.50 a day poverty line (Chant, forthcoming; see also above).

Gender and employment in towns and cities

Presently, women are an estimated 40 per cent of the global labour force (World Bank, 2011c:236). This share has been increasing over time not only because of marginally declining disparities in rates of male and female labour force participation, with the gap between the two falling from 28 per cent to 26 per cent between 1992 and 2012 (UN Women, 2015c:74), but also on account of urbanisation. Indeed, in rapidly urbanising countries, such as Bangladesh, the labour force participation of women aged 20–24 years grew by nearly 250 per cent between 1995 and 2000 alone (World Bank, 2011c:60). More generally, it is widely observed that women typically have more and better opportunities for employment in urban than in rural labour markets (see, e.g., Ali, 2012:587; Bradshaw, 2013a; Malaza *et al.*, 2009). Indeed, even if in some countries, such as Zambia, data from the Living Conditions Monitoring Survey Report (CSO, 2011, cited by Evans, 2013b:5) indicates that a higher proportion of rural than urban women are in the labour force (66 per cent as against 47 per cent), over half (56.3 per cent) of rural female workers are unpaid family workers, compared with only 12.5 per cent of their urban counterparts.

Rising female labour force participation in Global South cities has been driven by a panoply of negative as well as positive forces. As summarised by Cecilia Tacoli (2014:4) for example: 'in many cases, women's work is not so much a choice as lack of choice'. On one hand, urban women's access to employment, which has often been promoted by international and national agencies, has come

Plate 8.4 Multi-tasking: Gambian hairdresser with her six-month-old daughter in tow

Source: Sylvia Chant.

about through opportunities and aspirations, galvanised, inter alia, by rising levels of education and falling fertility rates. On the other hand, women's remunerated work seems to have been prompted by what UN Women (2015c:76) refers to as the 'distress sale of labour', whereby poverty and lack of social protection increasingly make additional incomes, including those of women, essential to household survival. This certainly seems to have been the case in several countries in Latin America and sub-Saharan Africa, with massive rises in female labour force participation provoked initially by the 1980s 'lost decade' of debt crisis, recession and structural adjustment programmes (SAPs) which saw declining wages, rising prices and job losses among men, and subsequently sustained through 'open-door' trade regimes and increased offshoring of labour (see Ansell *et al.*, 2015; Chant with Craske, 2003; Elson, 2013; González de la Rocha, 1994; Kabeer, 2013; Willis, 2002). A somewhat ironic twist in this tale, as asserted by Alexandra Kelbert and Naomi Hossain (2014:23), is that: 'some neoliberal policies have been a friend to feminism, particularly by pushing open the doors to labour markets previously closed to women'. On top of this, growing numbers of households headed by women have driven supply-side dynamics (see Bradshaw, 1995; Chant, 1997, 2007a; Safa, 1995).

Although the past decade has seen a modest upward trend in employment in most parts of the developing world, large numbers of workers remain in what the ILO (2011:21) describes as 'vulnerable employment', comprising own-account and unpaid family workers. Broadly equating with what has traditionally been more commonly referred to as 'informal employment', which also comprises subcontracted outworkers, 'vulnerable employment' is generally characterised by low pay and poor working conditions (UN, 2010a:8–11), despite its considerable contributions to GDP (see Jütting *et al.*, 2008; Khosla, 2009:13; Williams and Lansky, 2013).

Women are over-represented in both informal and vulnerable employment (see Figure 8.4), and they are more likely to be under-employed, as well as unemployed, as youth and adults (UN-DESA, 2010:76–80; see also ILO, 2009, 2010b; UN-Habitat, 2012a:4). In sub-Saharan Africa, for instance, 36.4 per cent of women were unemployed in 2006, as against 25.3 per cent of men, with figures for South Africa suggesting respective levels of 30.7 per cent and 21.2 per cent (Budlender and Lund, 2011:935). In turn, as UN Women (2015c:79) points out, and as discussed in greater detail below, 75 per cent of women's employment is informal and not covered by social protection in many parts of the developing world.

This is not to deny that some women in developing world cities are involved in higher-tier occupations in industry, services and the public sector, thereby reaping not only economic but social and status spin-offs of 'urban prosperity' (see, e.g., Werner, 2012, on the increase of female engineers in the Dominican Republic; and Evans, 2013a, on the same trend in Zambia). However, as revealed by the World Economic Forum's Corporate Gender Gap Report, which surveyed 600 of the world's largest employers across sixteen different industries in twenty major OECD economies to gauge 'the current representation of female employees' (Zahidi and Ibarra, 2010:3), women are generally clustered in entry- or mid-level positions. As noted by the World Bank (2011c:204), female representation on the boards of large firms in Europe stands at only 12 per cent, while in the Americas it is 10 per cent, in Asia and the Pacific 7 per cent, and in the Middle East and Africa a mere 3 per cent. This is despite compelling evidence produced in a recent review of 215 Fortune 500 companies over twenty-eight years, which found that firms with larger numbers of female executives enjoyed profits of between 18 and

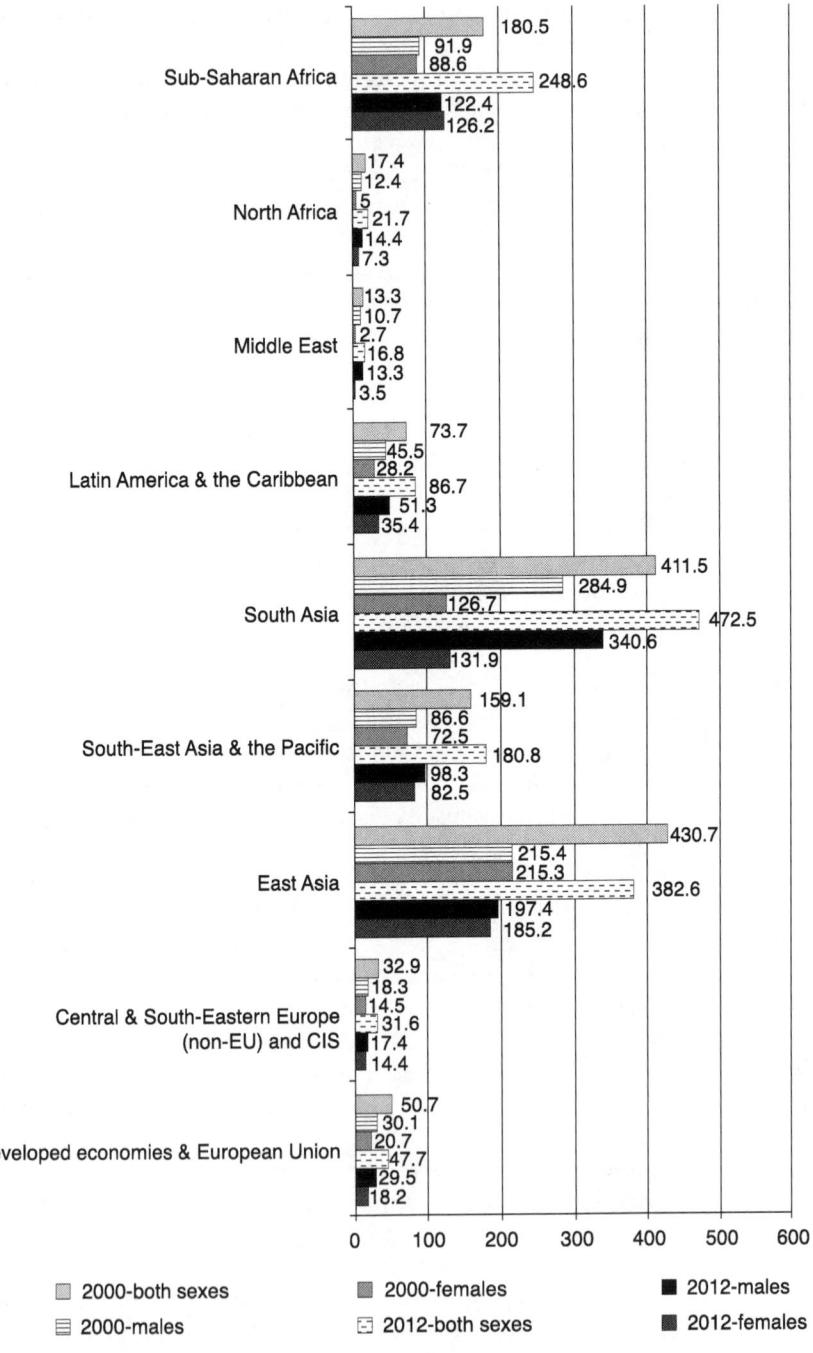

Figure 8.4 Vulnerable employment by gender and region, 2000–2012 (millions)

Source: Compiled from ILO, 2014:Table A13, 99.

69 per cent higher than the norm in respect of revenue, assets and stockholder equity (Puri, 2013:90).

The above-mentioned World Economic Forum study found that the two greatest barriers to professional women's ascent to positions of senior leadership are: first, general social norms and cultural practices; and, second, masculine/patriarchal corporate culture. While challenging deep-seated gender biases is likely to be complex, a useful and rather basic starting point would be for companies to track pay differences between women and men. To date, however, this is only undertaken by a fraction of firms (around one-quarter in the World Economic Forum survey; see Zahidi and Ibarra, 2010:8; see also below).

Urban employment: opportunities for poor and slum-dwelling women?

Urbanisation has been accompanied, as well as driven, by sectoral economic shifts where the vast bulk of national wealth is progressively generated by secondary, and especially tertiary, activities (Chant and McIlwaine, 2009: chapter 5). Although sub-Saharan Africa stands out as the only region where more than half (59 per cent) of the labour force remains in agriculture, the proportion was as much as 79 per cent in 1965. As of 2012, shares of the labour force in industry and services were 8.9 per cent and 30 per cent, respectively – considerably lower than in other regions (see Figures 8.5 and 8.6).

Although women constitute a greater proportion of the world's agricultural labour force than its total labour force (43 per cent versus 40 per cent; World

Plate 8.5 Female bread-sellers on the central plaza in Quinché, Ecuador

Source: Sylvia Chant.

Plate 8.6 Women shoe-traders in Gaborone, Botswana

Source: UN-Habitat/Cathy McIlwaine.

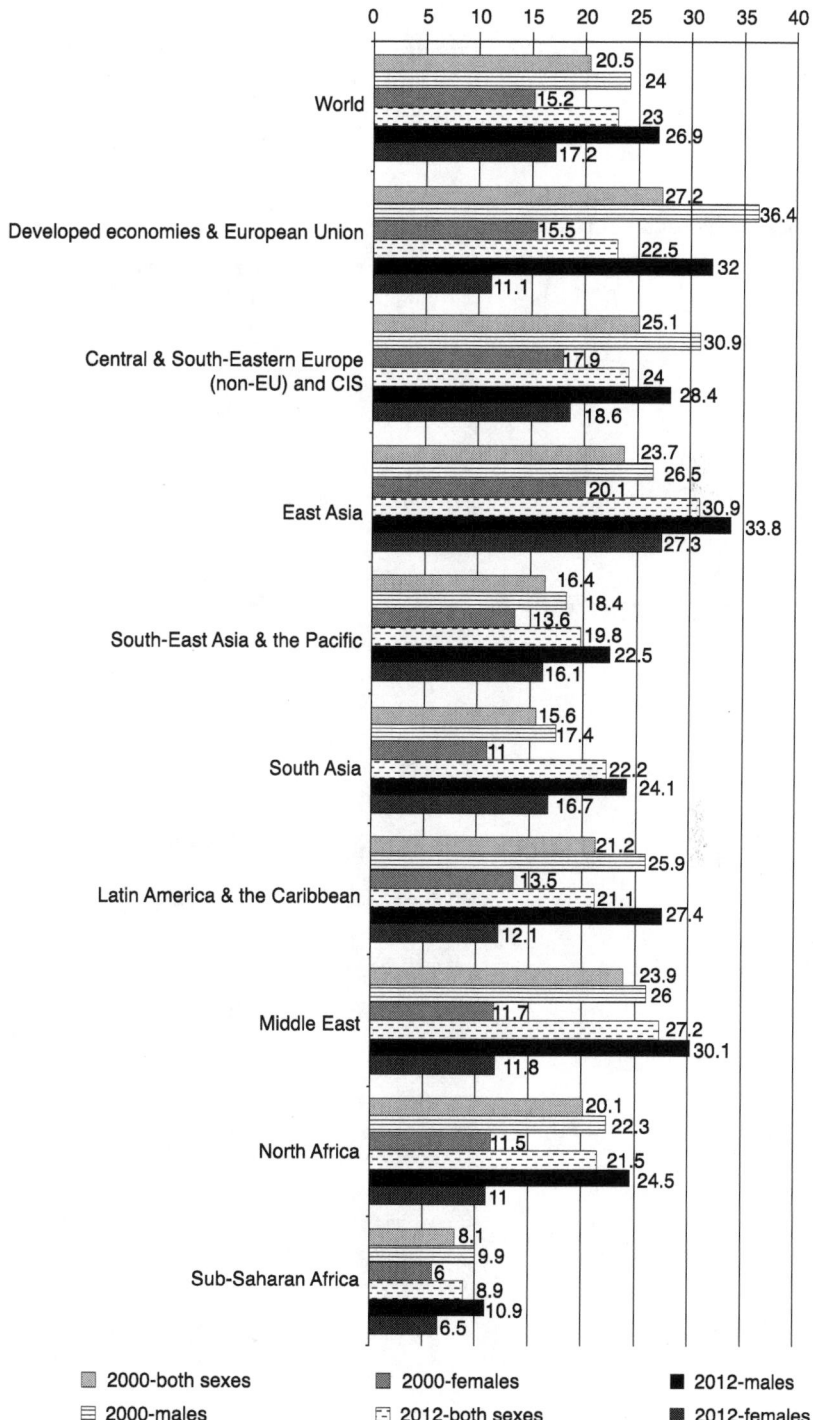

Figure 8.5 Industrial employment shares by gender and region, 2000–2012 (percentage)

Source: Compiled from ILO, 2014:Table A10, 96.

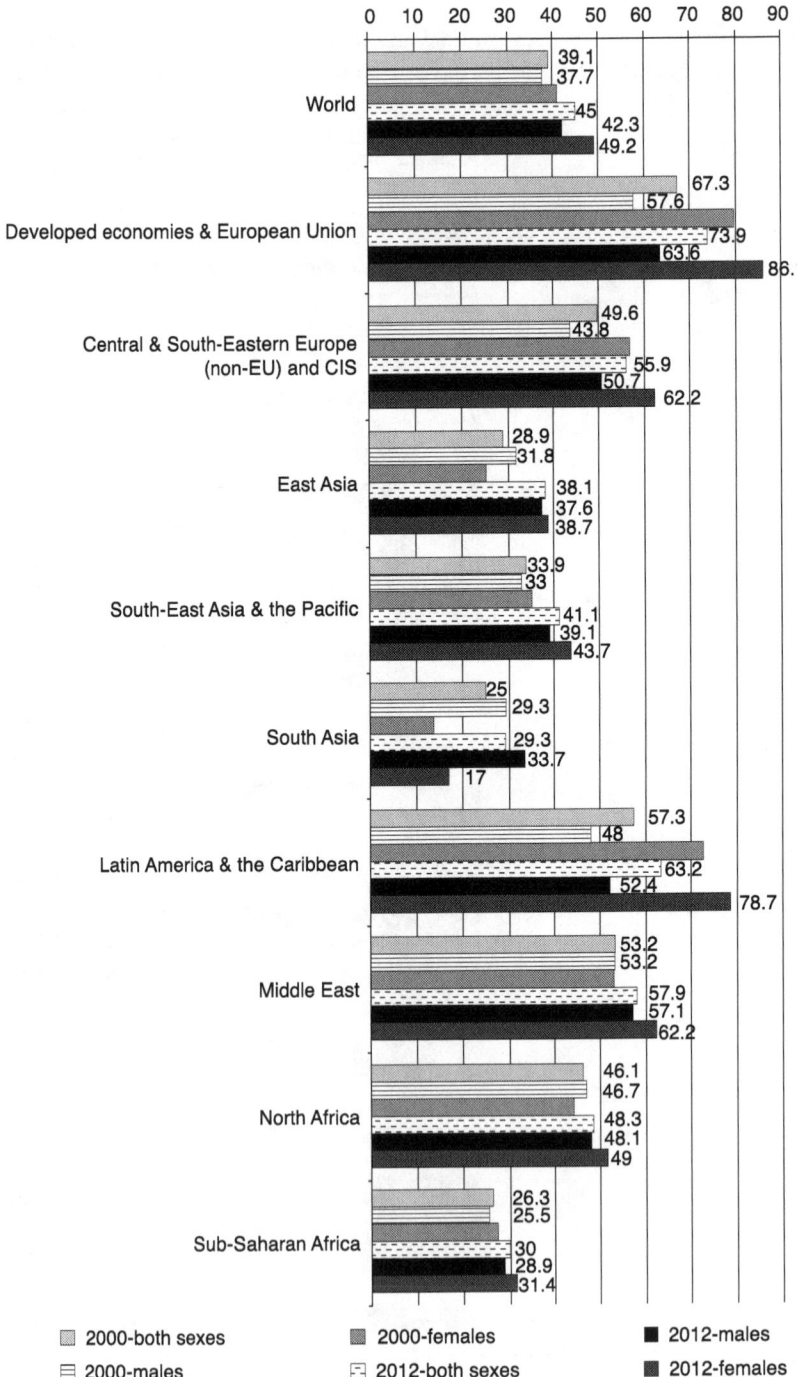

Figure 8.6 Service sector employment shares by gender and region, 2000–2012 (percentage)

Source: Compiled from ILO, 2014:Table A10, 96.

Bank, 2011c:236), the expansion of predominantly urban-based economic sectors has generated new opportunities for female employment and income generation, particularly in commerce and services (see Figure 8.6). The latter includes domestic service, which in a range of developing economies employs between 4 and 10 per cent of the labour force, and in which between 74 and 94 per cent of workers are women (UN Women, 2011a:35). Although Martha Chen and Caroline Skinner (2014:222) warn against tendencies to under-enumeration, detailed studies suggest that domestic work represents 5 per cent of urban informal employment in India, 9 per cent in Brazil, and as much as 35 per cent in South Africa. Meanwhile, in India, the sector has become markedly feminised in recent decades, moving from a situation whereby only 37 per cent of domestic workers were female in 1971 to 72 per cent in 2004–5 (Rao, 2011:762). In South Africa, the 8 per cent of workers in domestic service are predominantly female (Budlender and Lund, 2011:935), while in Lagos, Nigeria, Zahrah Nesbitt-Ahmed (2014) points out that there remain decidedly 'masculine' niches in domestic employment, particularly in respect of gardening, security and chauffering, but it is women for the most part who are involved in house cleaning and nannying. Although wages vary according to whether domestic workers live out or live in (and thus receive part of their payment 'in kind', in the form of board and lodging), length of time in the job and so on, on average women are paid less than men in the same sector, and only occasionally surpass the monthly minimum wage of 18,000 naira (approximately US$113). Indeed, more generally, domestic service tends to be one of the most exploitative occupations in respect of earnings and living conditions, with Latin American workers in this sector, which has long been decidedly 'feminised', reportedly earning less than 40 per cent of the average urban wage (Tacoli, 2012:19, cited in McIlwaine, 2012:9; see also below).

Leading on from this, and from a more general perspective, the increasing feminisation of labour associated with urbanisation has also been accompanied by a notable *informalisation* of labour across developing regions, particularly since the debt crisis of the 1980s and the neoliberal economic reforms that have followed in its wake (see Pearson, 2013). These parallel processes have generated considerable discussion as to whether informalisation and feminisation are mutually causal, especially given that the phrase 'feminisation of labour' not only refers to the increased presence of women in the ranks of remunerated workers but also to the fact that increasing shares of work in the global economy have come to be marked by attributes typically associated with women's activities, most of which are poorly paid and informal in nature, and lack social protection and benefits (see Chen *et al.*, 2004; Chen and Skinner, 2014; Kabeer, 2008b; ILO, 2010c; Moghadam, 1995; UN-DESA/UNDAW, 2009; UNRISD, 2010a:107). Moreover, evidence of the fallout of the recent global financial crisis suggests that this is impacting heavily on the poorest workers in the informal economy, who are disproportionately female (see Floro *et al.*, 2010; Horn, 2010; Tacoli, 2012). For various parts of Asia, for instance, Maria Stavropoulou and Nicola Jones (2013:28) report that low-skilled, low-salaried women are often most vulnerable to losing their jobs, and sometimes have to turn to sex work in order to survive. Despite the fact that the glut of informal employment makes it difficult to estimate wage gaps between women and men, it is claimed that women worldwide earn 10 per cent to 30 per cent less than men for comparable work (Puri, 2013:91; see also Barker, 2014:85–6), with UN Women (2015c:71) noting that the general discrepancy is in the order of 24 per cent. Although gender pay gaps are often wider in rural areas, they can be greater in cities where there are wider ranges of formal and informal jobs and income-generating activities that are more differentiated in terms of remuneration. Such is the case in South Asia, where UN Women (2015c:97) reports that urban women earn an estimated 42 per cent less than men, compared with a figure of 28 per cent among their rural counterparts.

In light of the above, while it is generally assumed that rising levels of engagement in economic activity are 'good' for women, it is important to acknowledge that upward trends may not entail increases in recognition, rewards and/or quality of work (ILO, 2010a), nor, indeed, a commensurate stepping up of assistance in the domestic sphere on the part of men or boys, or public bodies (e.g. Chant, 2007a; Kabeer, 2013:69; McDowell *et al.*, 2006; Pearson, 2000:225; World Bank, 2011c:173).

Obstacles to gender equality in urban employment and entrepreneurship

Stemming to a large degree from women's 'reproduction tax' (Palmer, 1992), or what ILO refers to as the 'motherhood penalty', and to other discriminatory

Plate 8.7 Henna ladies offer hand and foot painting on Djemaa el-Fnaa Square, Marrakech, Morocco

Source: Sylvia Chant.

Plate 8.8 'Men are more mobile': ambulant trading in car accessories, The Gambia
Source: Sylvia Chant.

practices in the home as well as in the labour market and society at large, gender gaps remain significant in terms of where women and men are engaged in urban economies (for example, in industry and services), and on what basis, notably 'formal' or 'informal' (Chen *et al.*, 2004; Heintz, 2006; Kabeer, 2008a, 2008b). In Latin America and the Caribbean, for example, Chen and Skinner (2014:220) report that 54 per cent of women's non-agricultural employment is informal verus 48 per cent of men's, and in sub-Saharan Africa the respective figures are as high as 74 per cent versus 61 per cent. Detailed case studies of particular cities conducted by Herrera *et al.* (2012) reveal gaps of even greater magnitude, such as in Abidjan, the capital of the Ivory Coast, where 89.7 per cent of women in non-agricultural employment are informally employed, as against 69 per cent of men, and in the Togolese capital, Lomé, where 90.3 per cent of women are informally employed, compared with 75.1 per cent of their male counterparts (cited in Chen and Skinner, 2014:Table 20.1, 221).

With respect to gender divisions in formal industrial employment, women tend to feature prominently only in multinational export-processing branch plants (producing garments, textiles and electronics), where female-biased recruitment derives from assumptions about them being a docile but reliable workforce who can be paid lower wages than men yet achieve higher rates of efficiency (Elson and Pearson, 1981; see also UN Women, 2011a:35). Even then, a notable 'masculinisation' of some sectors of export processing has occurred as firms have upgraded their products and introduced higher levels of technology (see, e.g., Chen *et al.*, 2004; Popli, 2013:296; Werner, 2012). As the globalisation of production has gathered pace in recent decades, women's engagement in export processing in many places has been progressively less in factories and more in other spaces, such as the home, through subcontracting arrangements, contributing to the aforementioned trend to an 'informalisation' of labour (Pearson, 2013:23).

Leading on from the above, gaps between poor women and men are equally, if not more, marked in the informal economy (Chant and McIlwaine, 2009:chapter 6; Chant and Pedwell, 2008; Chen, 2010a; Meagher, 2010; see also Figure 8.7). This is due to several factors, including women's restricted use of space, their lower levels of skills and job experience, limited access to start-up capital, and secondary role in 'family businesses' (Chen *et al.*, 2004; Lessinger, 1990). Given constraints on women's spatial mobility arising from moral and social norms (as discussed in Chapter 7) and due to the demands associated with female-skewed reproductive ties, women's informal economic activities are commonly domestically based. As Sarah Bibler and Elaine Zuckerman (2013:6) point out, while the *World Development Report 2013: Jobs* asserts that women prefer home-based work so that they can reconcile these with their childcare duties (World Bank, 2012:54), it ignores 'the gendered division of labour and absence of affordable childcare necessitating this "preference"' (Bibler and Zuckerman, 2013:6). In urban Pakistan, for example, although poor women are increasingly forced into work through economic pressures, and may engage in garment factory work, domestic service or street-sweeping, a large number are also confined through the demands of multi-tasking to their own homes, fabricating goods which are then sold on to middlemen (see Ali, 2012:587; see also Chapter 7, this volume). One exception here is presented for the case of the western Afghanistan city of Heart, where in some neighbourhoods wealthy and poor people live cheek by jowl, and this spatial proximity allows low-income women to provide domestic services to more affluent households without threatening constraints on Afghan women's culturally proscribed daily movements (see Schütte, 2014).

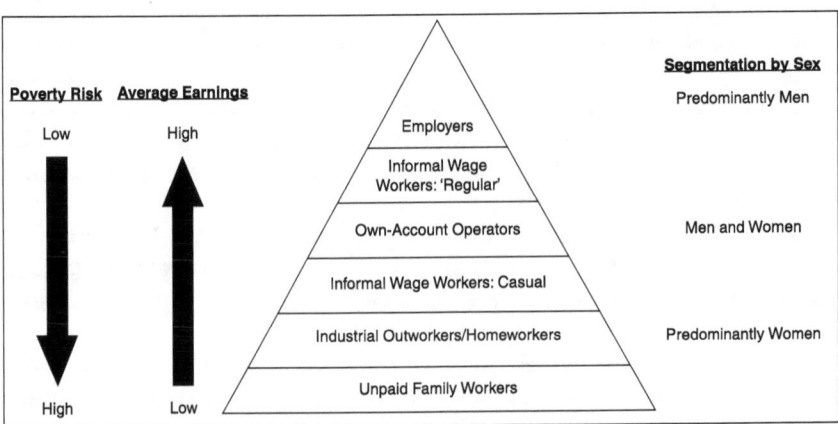

Figure 8.7 Segmentation by sex within the informal economy

Source: Chen, 2010a:Figure 7.1, 468.

Another exception to this trend lies in cases where women have very little option other than to engage in precarious or even potentially life-threatening occupations, such as sex work (see, e.g., Chant and McIlwaine, 1995; García-Moreno and Chawla, 2011:56). That said, where they attach themselves to men for livelihood support in the context of casual and not overtly commercial relationships ('sexual exchange'), as historically observed by Nici Nelson (1997) in the slums of Nairobi, then, again, they may not venture very far from their immediate environs (see also Chant and Evans, 2010, on The Gambia; Kamndaya *et al.*, 2015, on Blantyre, Malawi; and Cole and Thomas, 2009, for broader discussion and references; also Chapter 6, this volume).

In practical terms, domestic-based income-generating options are clearly limited for female slum dwellers on account of their frequently peripheral locations which preclude access to remunerative markets, and on account of their heavy reproductive time burdens (Chant and McIlwaine, 2013a, 2013b; Speak, 2012). A further issue is that competition among women in similar situations who may only have scope to engage in a narrow range of under-capitalised activities, coupled with the constraints of space, infrastructural deficiencies and limited local markets (Gondwe and Ayenagbo, 2013; Gough and Yankson, 2011), can lead to a 'discouraged labour effect' provoking workforce dropout (Standing, 1999). On top of this, and as highlighted in Chapter 4, profits from home-based businesses are compromised by the non-existence or poor and erratic nature of power and water supplies (Chant, 2007b, 2014: Chen and Skinner, 2014:225; Gough and Kellett, 2001). As documented by Bipasha Baruah (2007:2096) for slums in Ahmedabad, India, the prohibitive costs of kerosene, which many people have to use in the absence of electricity, means many residents can work only in daylight hours. Leading on from this, it is perhaps no surprise that while gender wage gaps remain pronounced in general (ITUC, 2009:11–25), disparities in remuneration tend to be greater in the informal than in the formal economy (see, e.g., Chant and Pedwell, 2008; Chen *et al.*, 2004; Heintz, 2010; Popli, 2013).

By the same token, own-account business ventures are often perceived as positive by women, and, in a situation of marginal opportunities for salaried employment, can tap into global as well as local pathways to status and financial well-being (Gough, 2010; Kinyanjui, 2014; Langevang and Gough, 2012). Yet, notwithstanding that informal businesses are likely to be under-represented in the statistics, it appears that business ownership (referring to ventures in which more than one person is employed) among women is fractional compared to men, with only 1–3 per cent of employed women in developing regions being 'employers', as against double this proportion among their male counterparts, with the greatest disparity in North Africa, where only 2 per cent of employed women employ others, compared with 13 per cent of men (UN Women, 2012). On the whole, therefore, women's own-account businesses are solo ventures, small-scale and under-capitalised. They also routinely revolve around food, and other domestic activities which dovetail closely with women's reproductive roles, symbolically as well as pragmatically (see Chant, 2014; Chant with Craske, 2003). In The Gambia, for instance, low-income women's 'doorside' enterprises typically comprise the selling of fruits, snacks or breakfast delicacies such as *akara* (fried bean balls accompanied by palm oil sauce) or *bullet* (a mixture of fish and spaghetti) in *tapalapa* bread (a local form of freshly baked baguette). In Costa Rican slums, women prepare fruit juice ices and *empanadas* (filled pastries), and take in washing or sewing. In the Philippines, where a higher level of diversification in informal work may be accounted for by the substantial existence of export-processing factories, many women engage in subcontracted assembly work for pyrotechnics (fireworks), footwear or fashion accessory firms. In addition, women not only operate small *sari-sari* (grocery) stores and run home-based eateries (*carinderias*) but may also branch out into establishing domestic-based mahjong parlours (where card-games, dominoes and so on are also played), and even 'neighbourhood cinemas', where DVDs are projected onto bare walls or improvised screens made out of bed-sheets (see Chant, 2007a). In the slums of Ahmedabad, Baruah (2007:2099) also documents a wide range of home-based trades and occupations performed by women (sometimes on a subcontracted basis), such as the making or elaboration of clothes, footwear, toys, handicrafts, *bidis* (hand-rolled cigarettes), *agarbatti* (incense) and *papads* (gram flour wafers). Yet, despite the ingenuity of such enterprises, and the fact that the kinds of work women do may be more significant in terms of 'empowerment' than labour force involvement per se (see Kabeer *et al.*, 2011, on Bangladesh), profits are often as sparse as they are volatile, even if they do provide critical, if modest, inputs to household finances.

New horizons for women through digital technology, 'green economy' work and grassroots initiatives

As noted in Chapter 7, the development of ICT has the potential to provide a 'gender-neutral', or at least more level, playing field for male and female workers in urban economies. To date, however, and partly as a consequence of the gendered 'digital divide', women's employment in ICT tends to be confined to low-level routine tasks such as data entry rather than more creative and strategic roles in software design and management (see Lugo and Sampson, 2008; Mitter and Rowbotham, 1997). With the possibility that teleworking may bring more 'remote' work for women within the home, there are also questions as to how liberating this is likely to be (see Chant with Craske, 2003: 224–5; ESCAP, 2002:6–7). While not denying that some women have been able to secure niches in comparatively well-paid work in the digital sector, such as in call centres in urban India (see Patel, 2010), UNRISD (2010a:119) cautions:

> The boom of information technology services and of the off-shoring of office work by multinational companies have opened-up career opportunities in formal skill-intensive employment for educated, English-speaking women from the urban middle classes. While women make up a large share of the workforce in this emerging sector, segmentation and discrimination along the lines of gender, caste and class are widespread, and women tend to be concentrated in low-end occupations.

Plate 8.9 African breakfast: a roadside vendor prepares freshly cooked 'akara', Kanifing, The Gambia

Source: Sylvia Chant.

Another gender-neutral area, with potentially more benefits for poor women, arguably arises with efforts to promote a green economy in urban areas (see Box 8.2). Yet, in many respects this builds on what several women already do insofar as they recycle and/or elaborate a range of products from discarded

Plate 8.10 Mother constrained in her mobility due to childhood polio minding small-scale, home-based retail outlet and her children, Puerto Vallarta, Mexico

Source: Sylvia Chant.

waste, such as tin cans, paper, glassware and clothing. Moreover, notwithstanding some potential spin-offs from opening up apparently 'non-traditional' jobs for women, and clear benefits for the environment, the scope for significant increases in women's access to urban employment and income remains tenuous. For example, female and child waste pickers are more likely than their male counterparts to concentrate in the primary gathering of waste, while men tend to do the sorting and selling (see Beall, 1997; Navarrete, 2015). Indeed, in another green economy initiative launched in Ouagadougou, the capital of Burkina Faso (which has admittedly created jobs for 1200 women in the form of a 'Green Brigade' of street cleaning in the city), women's roles under this government programme are to remove waste and litter from the streets (see UN-Habitat, 2012a:Box 20, 39). In turn, despite the often fundamental role played by waste pickers in environmental sustainability, the introduction of so-called 'sustainable waste management systems' in various South African cities has often led to restricted access for waste pickers to municipal dumps or the ability to bid for solid waste management contracts, provoking serious losses in livelihoods and incomes (Samson, 2009a). Waste pickers are also frequently squeezed out or penalised when municipal governments embark upon public–private partnerships for landfill recycling (Samson, 2009b), with women workers most affected by exclusion from collective bargaining agreements (Samson, 2003).

Notwithstanding commonly observed gender disparities in participation and leadership in trade unions and other labour associations, the power of organising

Plate 8.11 Recycling tin cans to make into cooking pots, Greater Banjul, The Gambia

Source: Sylvia Chant.

Box 8.2   Women and the 'green economy': organising waste pickers in Pune, India

India's National Action Plan for Climate Change (2000) and National Environmental Policy (2006) recognise the major contribution of waste pickers to carbon reduction and environmental protection and also their rights to collect and recycle waste. This is massively important to the lives and livelihoods of informal urban workers throughout India, including many women.

In the city of Pune, for example, women constitute 90 per cent of the approximately 9500 waste collectors in the city, who fall into three main groups: those who collect waste from public bins and the street; those who work in landfill sites; and those who work on a door-to-door basis with trolleys buying waste that people do not deposit in bins because it is of some value, such as paper and empty beer bottles.

Two-thirds of waste workers belong to the waste collectors' union, KKPKP, which, in partnership with local authorities, has promoted a socially and ecologically innovative model of waste recovery. The new model emerged out of a study conducted in 2007 on the composition of waste collected from public bins by about ninety trucks in Pune and taken to the city's dumps. On finding that 90 per cent of this waste was biodegradable, the KKPKP proposed dropping all but ten of the ninety trucks, and encouraged households to separate their waste at source. This allowed biodegradable waste to be composted in situ, leaving the waste workers to collect from the residents' homes only non-biodegradable rubbish for the dumps. In addition, a sorting shed has been provided by the municipality that allows pickers to sort their waste in one another's company, rather than at home.

This initiative saves money and also has considerable environmental, social and gender benefits, such as raising women's incomes and situating them at the centre of green economic activities.

One woman, Suman, who started her waste collection activities at the age of thirteen, when she picked up recyclable material from the roadside and public bins, has found union membership and the transition to door-to-door collection extremely positive for her life and livelihood. She not only works fewer hours and collects better-quality waste but enjoys social interaction with her clients. An additional spin-off of KKPKP membership has been that two of her four children have received scholarships from the union, with one currently studying for a Master's degree in journalism, and another working as manager of one of the union's scrap shops.

Sources: Chen, 2011; Shekar, 2009; Stevens, 2009:Box 9, 16.

among women in urban areas, even among the poor and marginalised, has revealed some extremely positive impacts, as in the case of the Self-Employed Women's Association (SEWA) in India (see Box 8.3, below) and the Red de Mujeres (Women's Network) of street vendors in Peru (see Box 8.4).

Box 8.3   The Self-Employed Women's Association (SEWA), India

Over 90 per cent of working women in India are engaged in the informal economy, or more precisely are 'self-employed'. Until the creation of SEWA women's needs for fair credit, maternity protection, fair wages, skills training, continual work and legal help were largely unmet. SEWA (*sewa* means 'to serve' in most Indian languages) was recognised as a union in 1972 through the lobbying and perseverance of a young female lawyer, Elaben Bhatt, who established the association in Gujarat as part of the larger Textile Labour Union (TLA). The association has since grown substantially, absorbing ever more trades, and grounding itself in the reality of poor self-employed women. In 2006, it had a membership in India of nearly a million spread across nine states. The main goals of the organisation are to organise women workers to gain access to security in work, food and social protection. SEWA aims for self-reliance, in that women should be autonomous and self-reliant, individually and collectively, both economically and in terms of their decision-making ability. Its ideals are rooted in Gandhian ideals of non-violence, truth and uniting people of all faiths. It does this through establishing other unions and cooperatives. The bulk of its twenty-six-member Executive Committee consists of the women it aims to represent and includes agricultural labourers, *bidi* makers, paper pickers and embroiderers. SEWA currently runs the following programmes:

- SEWA Bank: extends credit to its members and offers women the opportunity improve their economic situation by supplying them with services that they would not find at a traditional bank, as well as more traditional services, such as insurance, pensions and so on. In 2005–6, the bank had 44,909 members and 2,91,535 accounts.
- Healthcare: run by members. The approach emphasises health education as well as curative care. It also involves coordination and collaboration with government health services. SEWA has established several midwife and healthcare cooperatives.
- Childcare: via cooperatives and local organisations, in 1999 SEWA provided a total of 117 childcare centres catering to nearly 6000 children.
- Insurance: this scheme has demonstrated that insurance for the poor can be run in a self-reliant and financially viable way. Members are protected against the various crises that threaten their lives and work (widowhood, fire and natural hazards).

- Legal help: SEWA provides legal education and support to its members, fighting such issues as harassment, unfair dismissal and the non-payment of wages.
- SEWA Academy: a centre for workers' education and capacity-building. The academy stresses the self-development of each worker, and it is the means by which SEWA unites its members through a common ideology, thus building the broader movement. It works through training, literacy, research and policy action, and communication through print and electronic media.
- Gujarat Mahila Housing SEWA Trust: set up in 1994, this focuses on housing and infrastructure upgrading and finance, as well as earthquake reconstruction and developing women's homes as workplaces.

SEWA members are also involved in mass mobilisation through campaigns around issues affecting them, which strengthens the SEWA movement and also highlights their own issues. In addition, through the creation of national-level federations, self-employed women are linked, through their primary organisations, to larger economic structures. SEWA has helped to form membership-based organisations of informal workers both nationally and internationally, such as the National Association of Street Vendors of India (NASVI) and HomeNet South Asia (a regional association of organisations of female home-based producers). SEWA is also a founding member of Women in Informal Employment: Globalising and Organising (WIEGO), an international research and advocacy organisation. Benefits have included rising remuneration for garment piecework, skills acquisition and equipment, all of which will prospectively be enhanced by the recently launched Inclusive Cities project involving partners such as HomeNet South Asia and WIEGO. Major recognition of SEWA occurred in 2006 when the International Confederation of Free Trade Unions (ICFTU) granted the organisation full membership.

Sources: Chant and McIlwaine, 2009:Box 11.2, 299–300;
Chen, 2005, 2006; ICP, 2009; www.sewa.org/;
www.sewabank.com/; www.sewahousing.org.

Another interesting example is provided by the efforts to expand women's livelihood options on the part of the Women's Construction Collective (WCC) of Kingston, Jamaica. This is a non-profit organisation which trains and supports low-income women in construction techniques relating mainly to carpentry, masonry and repair and maintenance. The organisation aims to empower women economically in a sustainable way while also breaking down reactive gender-stereotyped assumptions about the inappropriateness of 'male jobs' for women. By 2010, WCC had trained over 500 women in a range of different construction trades, created a space where women could meet to discuss the issues they

---

Box 8.4 Street vendors organising in Lima, Peru

Street vendors number more than 210,000 in the Peruvian capital, Lima, with two-thirds of them women. Although street-vending organisations have a long history in Lima, women have traditionally been under-represented in the leadership of both organisations and federations. To redress this situation the Women's Network of Street and Market Vendors of Lima, Peru (Red de Mujeres Trabajadores Ambulantes y Comerciantes de Mercados de Lima, Perú) was launched in 2004 by street vendor (and former formal sector worker) Gloria Solórzano to encourage women into leadership roles within existing street vendor organisations, and to help them better defend their economic, social and cultural rights. With support from a Peruvian NGO, Alternativa, and Intermón Oxfam, the network has fostered greater solidarity among male and female street vendors, while simultaneously tackling male bias in representation and leadership. It also aims to build alliances with local and global public and private institutions. Among the various activities promoted by the network to these ends are 'empowerment workshops', leadership capacity-building, cultural events and training in income-generating skills in new areas, such as chocolate-making. One plan for the future is a 'Women's House' (Casa de la Mujer), which will provide affordable childcare during working hours, with an after-school component for school-age children.

Source: Roever and Aliaga Linares, 2011.

---

experienced through their work, provided technical support to the construction industry more widely and promoted women in the industry through membership of the Incorporated Masterbuilders Association of Jamaica (Yonder and Tamaki for Huairou Commission, 2010).

Alongside grassroots and NGO-partnered initiatives, public bodies at urban and national levels can also play major roles in promoting gender-transformative employment. For example, in Senegal, the government has supported an all-women taxi fleet (Hinshaw, 2010), and in Vietnam, as part of the gender-mainstreamed infrastructural programme in the Ho Chi Minh City Mass Rapid Transit Programme, 20 per cent of all construction jobs are now reserved for women (ADB, 2011:3). Other examples relate to legislative interventions. In a number of countries, for example, minimum wage legislation has been applied to informal work, where women are disproportionately concentrated, which has led to both an increase in earnings and a narrowing of the gender pay gap (UN Women, 2015c:100). One such case is Brazil, where the doubling of the minimum wage in the 1990s closed the differential in male–female earnings from 38 per cent to 29 per cent between 1995 and 2007 (ibid.: 73). A major step towards rectifying persistent gendered inequalities in the Brazilian labour market has also been taken recently with the country's domestic labour law of 2014 (see Box 8.5).

Box 8.5   Landmark legislation for Brazilian domestic workers

Preceded by the ILO's adoption of the Domestic Workers Convention of 2011, which called for domestic workers to enjoy the same rights as other workers, including working hours, rest periods and limits on payments in kind (e.g. bed and board), in 2014 a new law was passed in Brazil to strengthen the rights of around 7 million domestic workers in the country.

Key stipulations include the following:

* employers must register domestic workers;
* employers should comply with the Brazilian Labour Code (e.g. minimum wage, lunch break, holiday pay, overtime pay, social security and severance pay) or face fines; and
* regulation of domestic workers' hours to an 8-hour day/44-hour week.

Source: www.mdgfund.org/story/
winning-rights-brazil-s-domestic-workers.

Plate 8.12 Women workers file past a drain under construction on the outskirts of Delhi, India

Source: Belinda Fleischmann.

Concluding comments

This chapter has outlined the educational and economic challenges for women living in cities and slums. While there have been improvements in the provision of education for girls, especially (although not exclusively) at lower levels of the hierarchy, parity remains elusive in some regions, especially among poor and slum-dwelling populations. Moreover, young women who do manage to accumulate human capital face real challenges in translating this into decent work. In general terms, this is due to a complex assemblage of factors, including widespread gender discrimination and stereotyping which restrict the types of jobs open to women in the formal sector and/or channel women into the lower echelons of the informal economy where earnings are lowest and conditions far below ILO standards of 'decent work'. Women's economic opportunities are further constrained by their caring responsibilities for children, the elderly and other family members. While these affect all women, in urban slums the challenges are often greatest as women also have to juggle the demands deriving from lack of access to property and other physical and financial assets in their own right or under their own control, adequate urban services and infrastructure, safe and affordable means of public transport, and guarantees of personal security.

However, towards the end of this chapter we also identified that low-income urban women, on their own account, or in conjunction with civil society or governmental authorities, have improved their employment conditions and prospects in myriad innovative ways. Leading on from this, the next chapter turns to a more dedicated discussion of the ways in which gender inequalities can be addressed through grassroots informal as well as formal political means.

9   Gender, urban politics
and governance

Female engagement in urban politics and governance is not just a fundamental right, but an integral and potentially major route to gender equality in urban environments. Accordingly, the importance of active involvement by women in civic participation has been stressed, inter alia, by UN-Habitat in its Gender Equality Action Plan (UN-Habitat, 2008b; see also UN-Habitat, 2010b). Given that the hub of national politics and protest is usually urban-based (see Beall and Fox, 2009; Beall et al., 2010; Dyson, 2010; Mitlin and Satterthwaite, 2013), the fact that women's parliamentary representation featured as one of the three main indicators in MDG3 – to 'promote gender equality and empower women' – was arguably a step in the right direction. Moreover, that there is a suggested expanded indicator within the proposed SDG5 which calls for increasing the 'percentage of seats held by women and minorities in national parliament and/or sub-national elected office according to their respective share of the population' (UNSDN, 2015:27) signifies a gratifying strengthening of commitment in this domain.

Gendered disparities in power and rights, relating to formal and informal political participation, and community and civic representation and governance, constitute a key component of our 'gender–urban–slum interface'. Accepting that it is difficult to advance women's and girls' empowerment and agency without ensuring their equal rights (UN Women, 2015c:27), enhanced participation in urban politics and governance conceivably plays a crucial part in helping to securing women's and girls' access to the legal, material and social resources vital to closing most, if not all, of the prejudicial gender gaps we have covered in the volume thus far. Various forms of mobilising and organising among women, particularly in slums and among the urban poor, sometimes orchestrated by women themselves, and sometimes in conjunction with NGOs, state actors and international development bodies, have managed to accomplish significant achievements in such realms as services, safety, housing and livelihood activities. In this chapter we attempt to provide a more integrated discussion on female political participation and representation in towns and cities, and the potential for transforming gender through activism, advocacy and policy at slum and city-wide scales.

Gender equality in legislation and national politics

Although there are many countries in the Global South where gender discrimination is embedded in legislation which impacts several dimensions of women's lives, quite significant progress has been made at the global level, much of which owes to dedicated pressure from, and campaigning by, women's movements in local, national and international arenas. In relation to legal reform, for example, 143 countries now have explicit commitments to gender equality enshrined in their constitutions, and 132 have equalised the minimum age of marriage (without parental consent) at eighteen years or older. In addition, 119 countries have passed legislation on domestic violence, with a further 125 introducing legislation pertaining to equality in the workplace, and women's safety in public spaces (UN Women, 2015c:28). Significantly, from the point of view of this chapter, and in relation to MDG3, there have also been some important advances in women holding seats in national parliaments (UN, 2010a:25), albeit often driven by the introduction of quotas – a controversial, but arguably essential, measure to augment the presence of women in political arenas (see Chant with Craske, 2003:chapter 2). Compared with the situation before the end of the UN Decade for Women, for example, when only four countries globally had female quotas, around a hundred do today. However, this is not to deny that under-representation remains persistent in developed and developing countries alike. In only forty-six countries of the world, for example, do women comprise over 30 per cent of members in national parliament; in developing countries the average is just 21 per cent (UN, 2014b; see also Figure 9.1). The global mean female representation in elected assemblies in 2014 was only 22 per cent, and even if this constitutes an improvement from 2000, when it was a mere 14 per cent (UN Women, 2015c:52), if progress continues at the sluggish pace that has characterised the past fifteen years, then it might be 2055 before parity is achieved (UN, 2012). Indeed, even in world-record-setting countries such as Rwanda, where women gained 56 per cent of the seats in the 2008 election, it has to be borne in mind that in that country's post-genocide context, this was still less than the proportion of women in the population (60 per cent) at the time (see UN-Habitat, 2008d:14, 21). None the less, the structures set in place in Rwanda to ensure women's participation at all levels of governance (see Box 9.1) seem to have had some bearing on subsequent victories. This includes the fact that by 2014 as many as 64 per cent of Rwanda's parliamentary members were female, as well as half of the country's fourteen supreme court justices (Hunt, 2014:151).

In light of the somewhat mixed assemblage of successes and shortcomings described above, it is perhaps no surprise that in most countries gender gaps are even greater at ministerial level (UNIFEM, 2008:26; see also Figure 9.2). Taking into account local councillors as well as parliamentarians, only one-fifth are female in a diverse range of contexts (UN-Habitat, 2008b:3; see also Patel and Mitlin, 2010). Moreover, recent research shows that female politicians often endure only single terms in office due to unrealistic expectations in respect of time commitments (given their disproportionate share of domestic responsibilities and

---

Box 9.1   Rwanda: increasing female participation at all levels of national governance

In 2001 Rwanda introduced a 'triple balloting system' to ensure the election of women to district-level councils. Triple balloting involves initial engagement by voters in three ballots: one general, one for women, and one for youth. Thereafter an indirect election takes place in which seats are allocated to all those elected in the general ballot, and one-third of elected candidates alike on the women and youth ballots. One of the positive dimensions of this system is that it provides space for women who do not feel comfortable about challenging male political rivals.

Another electoral innovation introduced in Rwanda is a parallel system of women councils and women-only elections, which further guarantees that women will be represented on all elected bodies. The ten-member councils play an important advocacy role, ensuring that women are aware of their rights, and in turn feed through to locally elected bodies female constituents' views on such sectors as education, health and security.

In 2003, 39 women were elected to the 80-member Chamber of Deputies through the tiered electoral system outlined above. As part of the effort to widen women's participation in politics, a Ministry of Gender was also created, and progressive legislation on gender-based violence was introduced.

However, while this is laudable, it has also been noted, somewhat paradoxically, that there has also been an increasing trend towards authoritarianism. In the short term, this has undermined women's ability to influence policy-making, although in the longer run it is argued that the expanded participation of women in the electoral system will have lasting benefits for gender equality.

Sources: Burnet, 2008; Hunt, 2014 ;
UN-Habitat, 2008d:21–2; UN Women, 2011b.

---

unpaid carework), because they are expected to enact gender-friendly measures, and because they suffer disproportionate criticism and discrimination (Pedwell and Perrons, 2007). Irrespective of whether this will prove to be the case in the many Latin America countries (such as Argentina, Brazil and Costa Rica) where female presidents have recently been elected for the first time, affirmative action measures – such as quota systems – are arguably critical to increasing female political representation, as already highlighted for Rwanda. In Nepal, too, a new quota seems to have played a major role in bringing women's representation in the Constituent Assembly to an unprecedented 33 per cent in the 2008 elections (UN Women, 2011a:23; see also Chant with Craske, 2003:chapter 2; UN, 2010a:25; World Bank, 2011c:308).

Plate 9.1 Interesting symbolism in 2015 poster on women's empowerment on a major traffic artery, Greater Banjul, The Gambia

Source: Sylvia Chant.

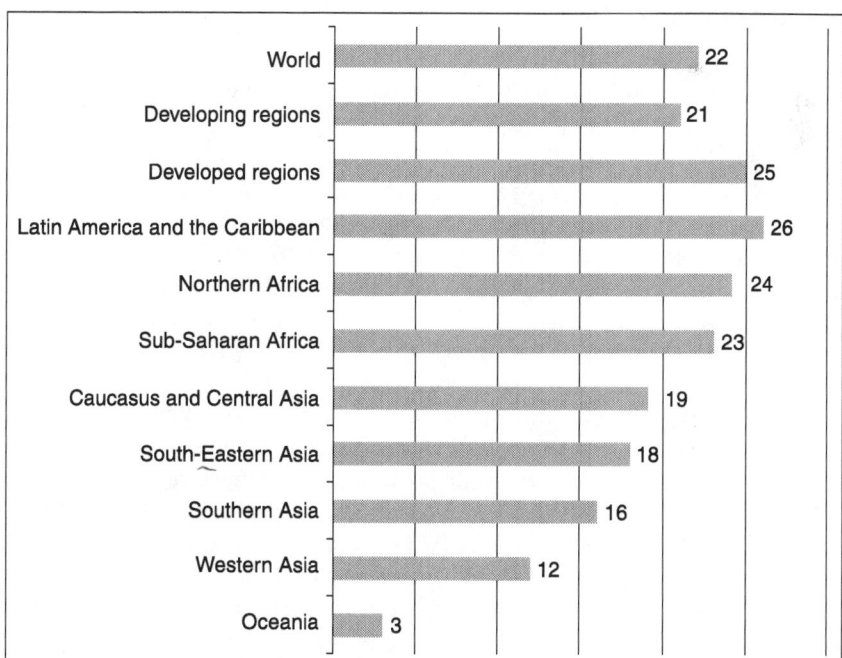

Figure 9.1 Proportion of seats in lower or single house of parliament held by women, 2014 (percentage)

Source: Adapted from UN, 2014b:23.

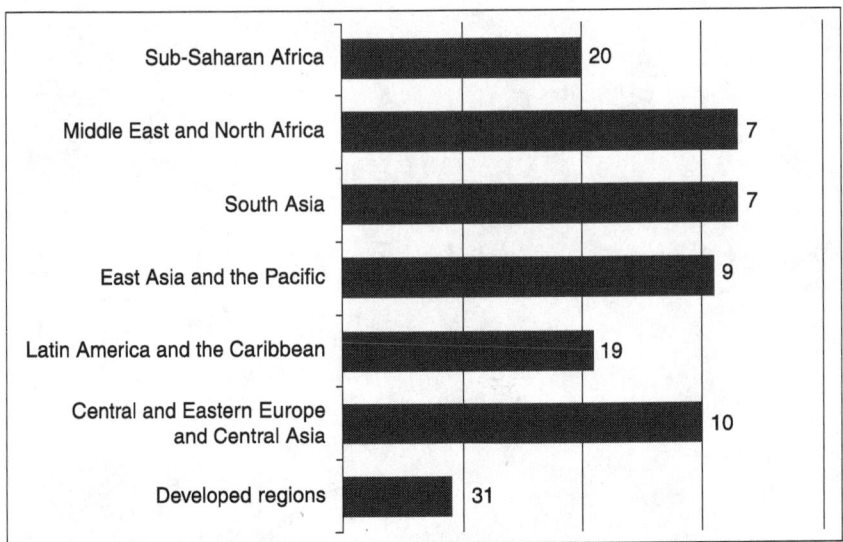

Figure 9.2 Women in ministerial positions by region, 2010 (average percentage per country)

Source: Compiled from UN Women, 2011a:Annex 1, 122–5.

Women in urban politics and governance

At the urban level, the Institute for Women's Policy Research (2015:19) notes: 'The same social norms and gender stereotypes that restrict women's opportunities and rights pose challenges for their ability to participate in social and political processes.' However, in reality, and building on a long legacy of women engaging in collective struggle in towns and cities around the world for basic services and infrastructure, housing, healthcare and rights to use public urban space for informal economic activity (see, e.g., Benjamin, 2007; Patel and Mitlin, 2004, 2010; Rai, 2009:chapter 2), there has been a mounting female presence and visibility in recognised structures of governance. In Latin America, for example, the unprecedented mobilisation of poor urban women in defence of household and neighbourhood survival which took place during the 1980s era of recession and structural adjustment, and an increasingly vocal and demanding women's movement more generally, coincided with, as well as fuelled, a wave of demo-cratisation and decentralisation within, as well as beyond, the region (see Chant with Craske, 2003:chapters 2 and 3). Coupled with the general spread of 'rights-based' and 'multi-stakeholder' agendas in local-level governance, these tendencies have been key to opening up new political spaces for urban women. In Brazil, for instance, women have been the majority of participants in budgetary assemblies in Porto Alegre, which has been a pioneer in inclusive urban governance (see Jarvis *et al.*, 2009: 240–1). In India, too, the 73rd and 74th Constitutional Amend-ment Acts, introduced in 1992, required 30 per cent of seats on local councils (or assemblies – locally termed *panchayati raj*) to be occupied by women (Khosla,

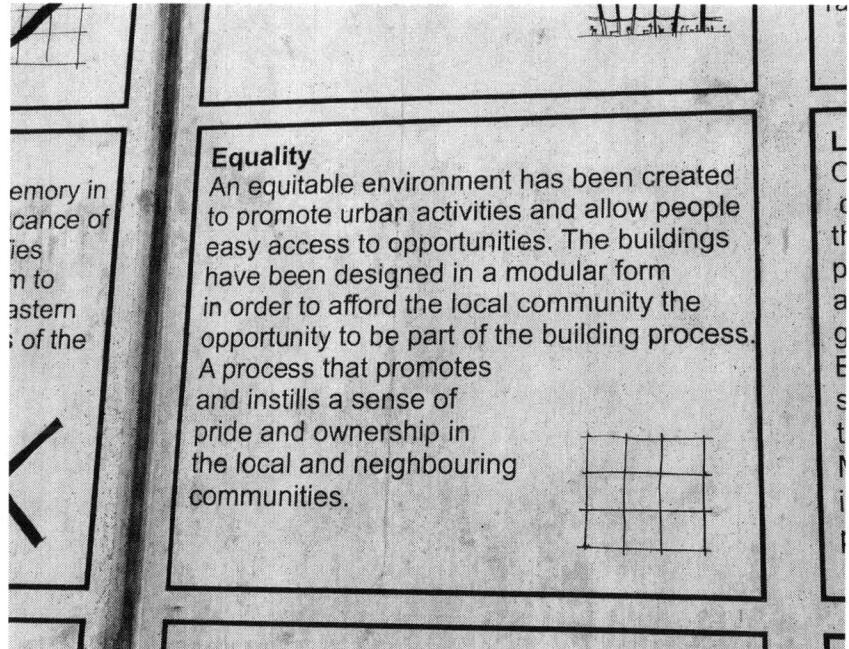

Plate 9.2 Equality in urban planning: 'Freedom Charter' memorialisation forming part of post-apartheid reconstruction, Walter Sisulu Square, Kliptown, Soweto, South Africa

Source: Michael Keith.

2009; see also below). In Naga City, the Philippines, the instigation of an 'empowerment ordinance' in 1995 which was designed to encourage participation and partnerships between municipal officialdom and citizens, and sought ways to engage women as well as men, paved the way through e-governance and media for a number of pro-gender equality initiatives, including the Women's Development Code in 2003, the creation of a Women's Council to provide gendered feedback on policy and planning, and a Labour–Management Cooperation Ordinance requiring that at least one in three employer representatives is female (UN-Habitat, 2008d, cited in UN-Habitat, 2012a:Box 10, 28). In Belén, in the province of Heredia, Costa Rica, a gender-mainstreaming project launched in the municipality in 2004 permitted women's groups to determine how far gender issues were being addressed in municipal planning (ibid.:Box 13, 31).

In order to convert aims into accomplishments, however, the Huairou Commission (2010a) stresses the importance of women becoming active and equal partners with local government in order for decentralisation to work to their advantage, which regrettably is not always the case. Nor is it always the case that the gap is bridged between women elected to public office and grassroots women's groups (Huairou Commission, 2010b; see also IWPR, 2015). None the less, various initiatives are already in place to ensure that grassroots women are able to

Plate 9.3 Women in Buenos Aires, Argentina, made homeless by fire in their slum
    settlement, demand a response from the municipal authorities

Source: UN-Habitat/Pepe Mateos.

make their voices heard. For example, inspired by Indian non-governmental
organisations such as SPARC (Society for the Promotion of Area Resource
Centres) and Mahila Mandal, a 'Local to Local Dialogue' was pioneered by the
Huairou Commission in conjunction with UN-Habitat to develop 'locally designed
strategies whereby grassroots women's groups initiate and engage in ongoing
dialogue with local authorities to negotiate a range of issues and priorities to
influence policies, plans and programmes in ways that address women's priorities'
(Huairou Commission, 2004:12). This encompasses tools to build collective
action and alliances, as well as women's capacity and female leadership.

India, along with South Africa (where due to active campaigning the share of
female councillors rose from 19 per cent to 28 per cent between 1995 and 2000;
see Beall, 2010:634), has experienced one of the highest increases in women's
representation in local government across the developing world. This has not been
without problems and setbacks in both countries, however. In the case of India, for
instance, as noted, amendments to the Constitution in 1992 esnured that 30 per
cent of seats in the *panchayati raj* would be occupied by women, and this was
increased to 50 per cent in 2009, yet it has often been claimed that women's
enforced and perhaps rather arbitrary recruitment into local governance has led to
them becoming proxies for male household members (*parshad patis*) (Khosla,
2009:10). In turn, and perhaps unsurprisingly, this has not always led to discernible
declines in gender discrimination. In July 2012, for example, one Uttar Pradesh
panchayat banned the use of cell phones among women, ordered the covering of

women's heads in public, and outlawed 'love marriages' (see Sandler and Rao, 2012:548). In South Africa, meanwhile, there have been accusations that women's unprecedented entry into parliament 'has meant little for poor black women still oppressed by a patriarchal state'. The critics suggest that these poorer women have not been defended by their elite 'sisters', with the latter complicit in the cutting of child support and other welfare provisions (Benjamin, 2007:198). Yet, despite these caveats, Jo Beall (2010) argues that the mounting female presence in upper-tier decision-making bodies has played a critical role in helping to prioritise matters of fundamental importance in women's daily lives, such as basic infrastructure and services (see also IWPR, 2015:19–20; UN Women, 2011a:23). Even then, though, unqualified optimism about the rising participation of women in urban politics and governance is inadvisable, first because this may do little to detach women from responsibility for traditionally 'female' concerns; second, because of the rather insidious way that 'female empowerment' often comes at the cost of taking on greater obligations in the unpaid sphere; and, third, because local government entities are frequently resource-constrained, and as such arguably offer rather limited bases for power, influence and transformation. As Beall (2010:636) cautions:

> it is important that the pursuit of decentralisation and women's rights does not become a vehicle for putting a human face of neoliberal preoccupations with privatisation, deregulation and cost recovery at the expense of poor women. For decentralisation and women's rights to be positively correlated they both need to be part of wider democratic processes in which women are represented politically at all levels of governance. Rather women's political gains through participation in local governance need to permeate upwards and articulate with national-level politics and policy.

Beall's concerns are echoed by others working in South Africa (e.g. Miraftab, 2010), as well as further afield. For example, in Ecuador and Venezuela, under transitions to more left-wing governments over the past two decades, in which rising female political participation has featured prominently, the maternalist framing of women as 'problem-solvers' for poverty in their communities has changed little. If anything, what Amy Lind (2010) refers to as the 'institutionalisation of women's struggles' has mainly served to compensate for weak welfare states (see also Lind, 2002). A related problem is that women's engagement in movements and programmes around basic services and poverty reduction tend to feminise responsibility in ways that burden women even more, sideline men further, and neglect strategic gender interests in favour of practical gender needs (Molyneux, 1984, 2001; also Moser, 1989, 1993).

For example, as observed by Sheela Patel (2011:105) in the context of India, poor urban women who are denied access to many 'traditional avenues of power' have to adopt a position as 'eternal supplicants' by pleading with those in power for aid and assistance, which is often only overcome by utilising the power of association. In turn, Sapana Doshi (2013:853, 857) highlights the case of the

SPARC Alliance in Mumbai, a model of 'participatory development and non-confrontational negotiation', in which 'slum subjectivities' have been constructed through gendered discourses that have 'elevated women's participation both as a development solution and as a benefit to the poor', with the 'feminisation of participation' characterised by 'an inherently divided subjectivity' which 'has privileged women's domestic social-reproductive roles as "housewives" to the exclusion of those with working lives outside of the home'. Indeed, citing views aired by the Gender and Water Alliance (GWA), Saskia Ivens (2008:64) affirms that, 'For many organisations, the effectiveness and efficiency of programmes and projects is currently the most important reason to incorporate a gender perspective.' Such 'efficiency' rationales can also be found in the justifications for 'involving women' in several other cases (see also Chant, 2008, 2016; Moser, 2014, on instrumentalising gender). For example, in a World Bank-funded slum-upgrading project in the Venezuelan capital, Carácas, gender did not explicitly feature in the original design of the project, but it was introduced once the initiative had got under way, mainly on account of the cost savings generated by women's 'voluntaristic' contributions (see Box 9.2, below).

Box 9.2   Instrumentalising gender in a slum-upgrading project, Carácas, Venezuela

The Carácas Slum Upgrading Project (CAMEBA) was launched in 2000 as a community driven development (CDD) initiative oriented to improving the conditions of selected slum neighbourhoods in the metropolitan area of Carácas and covering around 15 per cent of the overall slum population. Gender was not an explicit goal in the project's design phase but an early change of management in FUNDACOMUN, the decentralised government agency responsible for funding CAMEBA, helped to raise women's profile. More specifically, women became active participants in community consultations and training, and played major roles as 'neighbour inspectors' (remunerated community representatives responsible for supervising construction works), construction workers and project staff. The World Bank undertook a review of this project as part of a study of 'good gender practices' in Latin America and the Caribbean, and determined that the involvement of women in CAMEBA had been resoundingly positive on account of their 'commitment to solve community problems and their constant presence in slums', concluding: 'women's gender roles make them central stakeholders in improving the physical infrastructure in poor urban communities'.

While it is arguably difficult to see how such a project could transform gender relations when it relies heavily on women's existing roles, female participants were offered training workshops which covered, inter alia, gender identity, self-esteem, violence and children's rights and citizenship. Moreover, many women have been taken on board as remunerated project staff, which has helped to improve financial security for themselves and their households. Other alleged benefits for women have been a 'heightened sense of empowerment', a greater ability to solve problems and deal with crises, and positive shifts in gender role models for girls.

The question of 'who benefits' most, however, is pertinent here, with evidence that the 'returns' of women's participation to the project are substantial. For example, women have played an important role in facilitating project staff's interaction with their communities, in attending meetings, in improving the quality of civil works, and in guaranteeing their maintenance. One important advantage from the project perspective is that women have exhibited better use of materials and staff time than men, generating cost savings. This has led the World Bank to pronounce that 'Women's participation in CAMEBA has resulted in more *efficient* and *sustainable* project operations' (emphasis in original), and that 'the returns of a gender focus in CDD projects are extremely high given that investing in the participation of women represents no significant additional cost to the fixed costs of investing in communities'. (Apparently some of the workshops for women would have been run for all community members anyway.)

The World Bank's overall conclusions and 'lessons learned' (presented verbatim) were:

- Women's constant presence in the slums makes them direct project interlocutors and crucial agents during project implementation.
- Women's commitment to solving the problems of their communities makes them an indispensable ally for projects aimed at improving community services.
- In the case of CAMEBA, women's engagement in the project has translated into better-quality civil works, improved work maintenance, smoother project–community relations and higher project impact.
- At the same time, their participation has benefited women, their families and communities by means of improving households' well-being and strengthening community institutional capacity.

Source: World Bank, 2003a, cited in Chant, 2007b:Box 8, 64.

Criticisms of a utilitarian approach to gender, even where 'rights' and 'empowerment' might be professed aims, abound in a range of broader initiatives around poverty reduction which may not be specifically urban, but, by the very nature of rising urban populations, affect legions of women in towns and cities in developing countries. Harnessing women's 'empowerment' to poverty reduction not only tends to blur the distinctions between poverty and gendered privation (see Jackson, 1996) but also frequently involves using women as a 'conduit of policy' (Molyneux, 2006, 2007), in a manner which capitalises on, and often 're-traditionalises', their altruistic and maternal roles (ibid.; also Bradshaw, 2008; Chant, 2008; Cornwall and Anyidoho, 2010; Tabbush, 2010). This has been the case in the context of poverty reduction strategy policies (PRSPs) (Bradshaw and Linneker, 2010), in micro-finance schemes (see Maclean, 2010; Mayoux, 2006; Roy, 2002, 2010; Sweetman, 2010), and in conditional cash transfer programmes (CCTs) (Bradshaw, 2008; Oxfam GB and Concern Worldwide, 2011; Unterhalter, 2009:18–19), and appears to do little to bring about change in the gendered status quo. Moreover, although there may be some benefits for some women resulting from pan-national anti-poverty interventions, this may be not only group- but place-contingent, as revealed by contrasting outcomes for indigenous women in different parts of Mexico from the Progresa/Oportunidades (now Prospera) CCT (see González de la Rocha, 2010; Hernández-Pérez, 2010, 2012).

Indeed, regardless of whether women's civic participation remains more 'bottom-up' than formal in nature, and bearing in mind Andrea Cornwall's (2002) caution that when new participatory spaces are created they are hardly immune to existing relations of power and can reproduce rather than challenge entrenched hierarchies and inequalities, it is critical to recall the point made by Doshi (2013), among others, that identification with, and reinforcement of, 'traditional roles' may be deployed by women themselves in convincing others about the legitimacy of their concerns. As Shahra Razavi (2007:26) observes, demands made by women on the state can prove successful, often by 'harnessing their maternal roles to political claims making and advocacy for justice and for better conditions and social support for their families and communities' (see also Chant with Craske, 2003:chapters 2 and 3). Not only is a 'feminisation of responsibility' (Chant, 2007a, 2008) implied in the political process itself here, but the outcomes, as we have seen, can be equally pernicious.

Gender-responsive budgeting

To work around these problems, and to ensure that gender equality goals remain uppermost, part of the answer might be to strengthen gender-responsive budgeting (GRB), which has been introduced in several cities in the Global South, and can potentially correct 'planning and investment decisions within government spending' (Khosla, 2009:29) as well as assist in increasing public awareness of gender, and accountability to stakeholders.

In urban areas, Rena Khosla (2009:30) argues that full-fledged GRB should help to achieve three main aims: first, the balancing of gender needs; second, guarantees of pro-female urban expenditures in areas such as water supply, sanitation and infrastructure; and third, women-specific urban spending in the arenas of housing, markets, public transport and recreational centres. In some cases the introduction of gender budgeting has scored some successes, not least in Brazil, where even though by 2003 women were already very active (constituting 56.4 per cent of participants in Porto Alegre; Jarvis *et al.*, 2009:241; see also above), in the same year the Women's Coordination Group (Coordenadoria da Mulher) attempted to increase women's presence in budgeting meetings through the creation of play areas for children, gender-sensitive dissemination of information, and meetings between government officials and women's groups (UN-Habitat, 2012a:24; see also Box 3.1, this volume, on Nepal). By the same token in many contexts, obstacles include fractional amounts of overall budgets, lack of capacity in gender awareness, and lukewarm political will (see Elson, 1998; Elson and Sharp, 2010; NCRFW, 2004).

To maximise efficacy, as iterated earlier, and as evidenced in several examples in our preceding chapters, these types of approaches need to be combined with efforts which involve urban poor and slum-dwelling women and girls. As a further instance, in the context of the Huairou Commission's collaborations with grass-roots women's organisations to develop practical and sustainable solutions to meet basic needs while simultaneously building female capacity at the local level to engage in inclusive governance partnerships, GROOTS Kenya has established resource centres oriented to providing paralegal support to disinherited women and children (Huairou Commission, 2011). That said, constituent groups are rarely equal partners, with one of the key challenges being recognising, legitimising and formally resourcing female participants' unpaid 'voluntary' work.

Concluding comments

Despite some undoubted spin-offs for women from formal and informal modes of civic and political participation, one major concern is how the general instru-mentalism of state (and NGO) initiatives which court women's engagement plays out in terms of their well-being and rights. Although women's efforts in urban political, governance and policy terrains can undoubtedly help to reduce income poverty and other types of hardship which are associated with the multiple gendered deprivations common to cities and slums in developing regions, one also has to ask about the cost of this. If women's engagement is prioritised only in the interests of creating wealth for all, then one of the biggest questions is where they stand in relation to others in the queue for benefits. If 'trickle-down' was not automatic in the early years of urbanisation's massive take-off in the developing world in the mid-twentieth century, then is it any more likely to happen in the twenty-first century, with inequality in general greater than ever, and the spectre of global financial crisis threatening major losses of employment and state-funded social support? In the short term, and possibly in the longer term too, to entrap women in the largely unpaid, and fundamentally altruistic, work of building better cities arguably goes against the grain of transforming gender, or creating a more equal share of urban wealth and well-being among women and men. By the same token, as asserted by Khosla (2009:10), without women's involvement – especially in decision-making positions – there is little likelihood of granting gender issues a seat at the political and policy table. As she articulates in the context of gender mainstreaming in India's urban renewal mission (JNNURM):

> Gender blending at a city level will demand a thorough and comprehensive analysis of gender-based inequalities in the local context, together with their

causes and effects; and the designing of strategic interventions, estimation of costs and benefits, development of monitoring frameworks to ensure accountability, and creation of capacity and commitment for engendering urban development. A massive gender shift in urban planning can only be manoeuvred from those who drive urban development at the very helm.

(Khosla, 2009:10)

How progress might be made towards more gender-equitable cities, with particular reference to the needs and interests of low-income, slum-dwelling women, forms the primary component of our concluding reflections in Chapter 10.

10 Conclusion

Creating more gender-equitable cities

Despite sanguine predictions of an urban age in which the dividends of increased wealth, reduced poverty and more democratic governance nominally beckon for all, it is vital to remember that the vast majority of cities remain contested, unequal and conflictive spaces, in which poor people, regardless of gender, migrant origin, age, ethnicity and so on face enormous challenges to security, full citizenship and rights (Chant, 2013; Chant and Datu, 2015; Tacoli and Chant, 2014). We recognise, accordingly, the importance of acknowledging the many and intersecting axes of gendered social and economic difference which impact upon urban residents in the Global South, and especially those who reside in slums. Yet, while we clearly accept that women are not the only constituency to be disadvantaged in urban environments, we do feel that a gender agenda has to be in the front line of attempts to make cities more equitable. This is partly because we view the gap between women's investments in building better cities in their everyday lives and the relative dearth of benefits they derive not only as an injustice in and of itself but also as a brake on the advances in gender equality which urbanisation could potentially help to generate.

In view of the above, we not only have to consider gender-differentiated *outcomes* of urban life, but also gender-differentiated *inputs*, in terms of housing, service provision, productivity and so on, and at different intersecting scales, extending from the home, through neighbourhood/community, to city and nation, as emphasised throughout this book with recourse to the 'gender–urban–slum interface' formulated in Chapter 2. Tackling gender relations is a sine qua non in the process of evening out inputs and outcomes, especially since the frequently targeted and instrumental use of women in policy interventions – where their *condition*, rather than their *position*, is the main focus (Johnson, 2005:57) – frequently proves inadequate in destabilising gendered hierarchies except in marginal ways. It is thus patently crucial to address not only the 'practical gender needs' of women in urban environments but their 'strategic gender interests', as Caroline Moser (1989, 1993) exhorted more than two decades ago on the basis of Maxine Molyneux's (1984) seminal theoretical formulation (see also Chapter 2, this volume).

In the more specific recommendations which follow, it is important to recall that our 'gender–urban–slum interface' comprises a broad and interconnected spectrum of issues including, inter alia, urban demographics, gender divisions in the urban economy, gender gaps in assets of varying kinds, matters of space, mobility and connectivity, and urban governance and politics. Some of these issues (for example, selected aspects of urban demographics, such as migrant selectivity and ageing) are rather long term and contextual in nature (although arguably still amenable to change), whereas others are potentially more immediately and directly responsive to policy interventions. Recognising the iterative momentum generated by initiatives and processes in different spheres, akin to the gendered 'web of institutionalisation' outlined by Caren Levy (1996; see Chapter 2, this volume), but also the desirability of fomenting change where it is prospectively most feasible, we collect our thoughts on priorities for policy under three major headings: 'unpaid work, quality of life and infrastructure', 'productivity' and 'equity in power and rights'.

Priorities for policy

Unpaid work, quality of life and infrastructure

Gender equality in cities demands not only support for women's participation in paid employment (in the ways suggested in Chapter 8, and addressed further below), but that the value of unpaid reproductive work is fully acknowledged. To date, the latter has often been conspicuous by its absence from development projects. Indeed, as noted in a recent in-depth review by Sarah Bibler and Elaine Zuckerman (2013:3) of World Bank employment-related projects approved between 2008 and 2012 in four sub-Saharan African countries (Malawi, Mali, Niger and Rwanda), in only three out of thirty-six projects was women's care-related time poverty identified, signalling a persistent undervaluation of women's essential unpaid contributions. That the balancing of paid work and unpaid carework is one of the major challenges for urban women, and especially for those residing in slums, has been stressed consistently throughout this volume (see also Tacoli and Chant, 2014). In light of this, it is gratifying that the proposals of the UN Open Working Group (2014) for SDG5 ('achieve gender equality and empower all women and girls') comprise, inter alia, a target to promote shared responsibility in the household as well as greater public provision of services and infrastructure to support unpaid domestic labour, with potential requirements for data on the 'average number of hours spent on paid and unpaid work combined (total work burden), by sex' (UNSDN, 2015:32). This reflects the OECD's prior call for two indicators in this area: the female-to-male ratio of average time devoted to household chores (unpaid care); and the female-to-male ratio of total workload (both paid and unpaid work) (Harper *et al.*, 2014:7).

Unpaid reproductive work, in general, and in cities and slums in particular, needs much greater valorisation and support, given its critical role in ensuring the daily regeneration of the labour force, the functioning of cities, and gender-differentiated contributions to 'urban prosperity'. This labour needs to be recognised not only in and of itself, but on grounds that it constrains women's participation in paid employment, as well as in social, political and cultural realms, inhibits the development of capabilities among girls who may have to 'carry the can' for the expanded burdens of mothers and other female kin, and can also seriously disadvantage children of both sexes, especially in light of the recent global financial crisis (see Ansell *et al.*, 2015; Esplen *et al.*, 2010; González de la Rocha, 1994, 2007; Moser, 1992; Pearson, 2010:422). As asserted by Shahra Razavi (2007:26), 'Ultimately, it is only when all persons are conceived from the start as interdependent – that is as persons who need, give and receive care – that gender equality can be reached.'

Following a workshop on 'Bringing Unpaid Care into Global Policy Spaces', held in London in September 2012, discussion revolved around the need to take on board Nancy Fraser's (1995, 2005) seminal work on the 'three Rs' of 'recognition', 'remuneration' and 'redistribution'. As articulated by Caroline Sweetman (2012:618, 619) in her summary of the proceedings, 'recognition' is about 'noting the critical nature of carework, and its worth to society'; 'remuneration' relates to how to reward carers adequately; and 'redistribution' entails 'shifting half the responsibility for care to men'.

Women's efforts can clearly be supported in a number of ways, and benefits may well ensue from a multi-pronged approach. One is to measure women's unpaid work more effectively and widely – an issue which dates back at least three decades in respect of discourse, and which, as reported by UN Women's Deputy Executive Director Lakshmi Puri (2013:91), is something which is being strongly advocated by the organisation, as is now evinced in SDG5. In the context of cities where many slum-dwelling women suffer excessive disadvantages, not only on account of lack of services and shelter deficits, which have knock-on effects on health and well-being but in respect of care policies per se, such developments are paramount.

Notwithstanding a dearth of explicit care policies in several Global South countries, since 'Unpaid carework is the bedrock of social provisioning and underpins economic growth and social development' (UNRISD, 2010a:186), direct attention to the burdens of childcare along with other types of unpaid carework typically performed by women can include paid community-based options, workplace nurseries and care homes, state parental or carer support transfers, and dedicated private and/or public facilities. While women's care burdens might be alleviated in part through cash transfers, as noted by Razavi (2007:25), the provision of public services for care-related needs is generally regarded as more favourable, not least because it goes some way to arresting the persistent identification of women with reproductive labour, and its dubious status as a 'private' responsibility. Where such services exist they should be subsidised and affordable, and within easy reach of people's homes, as has been attempted, inter alia, through Costa Rica's 'Hogares Comunitarios' (Community Households) programme, which provides subsidised childcare in poor neighbourhoods via the training of local women as 'community mothers' (see Sancho Montero, 1995; see also Gough and Kellett, 2001; Moser and McIlwaine, 2004, on a similar – and identically named – initiative in Colombia). However, given that it is women who feature as the paid carers of children, and very frequently mothers who deliver and collect their offspring, this still implies gender-differentiated investments in children and does little to shake off the primary female identification with care. That said, it is also important to acknowledge that women may not wish to abandon care roles in their entirety, but simply to have them more valorised – as is eloquently summarised by Razavi (2007:25–6): 'it is not just men and patriarchs who have seen care as part of a female ethical world, which is characterised by interpersonal connections, compassion and care' (see below).

Following on from this, and in the context of discussion around pre-school programmes in Argentina and Mexico, Razavi (2013:126) underlines a historical tendency for care-related initiatives to rely 'heavily on low-cost services and community work'. It is therefore perhaps only when the 'private' work that women perform in their homes and communities is made 'public', and duly enforced as a collective social responsibility, that greater realisation of gender inequities (and their inefficiencies as well as injustices) will dawn. This may require a major overhaul in thinking through macro-economic policy, as argued, inter alia, by Diane Elson (2013:207) in her review of economic crises and gender between the 1980s and 2010s:

> Securing a sustainable crisis-free gender-equitable global economy requires a fundamental reorganisation of the relations between . . . three spheres, so that finance and production serve the needs of reproduction, the sphere in which the care essential to human well-being is provided.

As Elson (ibid.:208) further urges, we need to

> rethink what goods and services we want to produce and consume, and what criteria we are going to use to judge economic success. Measures to end crisis will not be sustainable if they simply seek to restore growth and greed.

Elson's views are echoed by several individuals, including Gary Barker, a world-renowned campaigner in the relatively new field of promoting transformations in hegemonic masculinity, who warns against the dangers of becoming a 'care-less' rather than a 'caring' society (Barker, 2014:89; see also below). Gender equality advocates and researchers Sarah Bibler and Elaine Zuckerman (2013:3) further affirm that:

> The challenge is to recognise the foundational value of caregiving and ensure that greater resources, such as government expenditure and natural resource rents from oil, mineral, and gas extraction, are devoted to delivering quality care services. This would free up women's time and strengthen human capacity, thus contributing substantially to poverty reduction and economic growth.

Leading on from this, and one element in cultivating greater public sensitisation to the societal value of care, an important strategy to lighten women's and girls' typically enforced load of unrecognised work is purposively to engage men and boys, as now explicitly emphasised in the new SDG for gender (see also Chant, 2007a; Khosla *et al.*, 2004; Parpart, 2015; UNCSW, 2009). In order for the spirit of SDG5 to translate into practice, policies and programmes might conceivably provide incentives for men to share in carework, as in paternity leave, and changes in 'paid work cultures' that comprise shorter and more flexible working days (see Razavi, 2007:26–7). A further potential requirement could be that, in order to qualify for use of public care facilities, men ought to assist in the delivery and collection of care receivers. In relation to his call for a 'radical agenda for men's caregiving', for instance, Barker (2014:89) stresses that key initiatives should ideally include demands for equal, non-transferable, paid parental leave, state- or workplace-supported child and family care, and national policies to increase men's participation in reproductive and sexual health such that '50 per cent of contraceptive use happens via male bodies'. In turn, and as further noted by Barker (ibid.: 88), the more equitable sharing of unpaid carework between women and men, and girls and boys, has the potential not only for rendering this labour more valued, but also for promoting more gender-equitable attitudes in societies at large:

> valuing the care economy and taking it to be as serious as any other joint human endeavour would both acknowledge and empower the women and girls who at present provide most of it, and it would encourage men and boys to carry out more of it – with benefits for all of us. It would provide more of the gender equality dividend.

Plate 10.1 Paternal childcare, The Gambia

Source: Sylvia Chant.

Greater public investment in services would also undoubtedly help to reduce women's reproductive labour burdens, with the planning, design, use and management of these services ideally involving the joint participation of women and men (see, e.g., AMC, 2005; Ivens, 2008; Joshi *et al.*, 2011; Kar with Chambers, 2008; Khosla, 2009; Khosla *et al.*, 2004; Malaza *et al.*, 2009). Indeed, the unpaid work that women perform in their homes and neighbourhoods relates not only to care in a direct sense – for example, feeding children or attending to sick or elderly individuals – but also to a more extended remit of activities that impact on quality of life in slum settlements, or are pertinent to people living in poverty, such as saving household resources by shopping around, preparing nutritious meals on low incomes, and conserving water and power for environmental as well as practical and pecuniary ends (Chant, 1984, 2007b). The fact that the burden of responsibility for these activities is almost always assigned to women, who, on account of gender socialisation, typically experience guilt when they cannot comply and/or self-sacrifice by denying themselves food, clothing, rest and recreation, is a phenomenon which poses immeasurable challenges. It is unlikely to change as long as unequal gender divisions of labour and power persist. Moreover, where laws are not in place to safeguard women and girls from domestic violence, and/or are inadequately monitored and enforced, women may face punitive and even life-threatening treatment at the hands of partners or fathers through failure to live up to normative gendered expectations, as we detailed particularly in Chapter 6. In Tanzania, for example, lack of legislation that criminalises domestic violence and marital rape, a Law of Marriage Act which requires attempts at reconciliation before couples are allowed to divorce, and threats of homelessness affecting women who desire independence cumulatively endanger women's lives on a daily basis (see Hughes and Wickeri, 2011:840–2; see also below). Without major attempts to change patriarchal attitudes and behaviours even the best-intentioned and most gender-equitable laws are likely to languish as principle rather than practice (see Chant and Gutmann, 2000; also Chant and Touray, 2012).

Leading on from this, another eminently important element in strengthening women's control of their environment, and themselves as persons, is to increase their access to, and security in, shelter. While urbanisation offers unprecedented potential to do away with deep-seated patriarchal power structures, as Hughes and Wickeri (2011:839) exhort: 'urban growth must be managed in a way that ensures women's full realisation of their right to adequate housing'. This should extend to all women, including the particularly marginalised constituencies of elderly women, widows, lone mothers, lesbians and women suffering from sickness or disability. As discussed particularly in Chapter 3, closer compliance with the provisions of CEDAW and other relevant international human rights instruments can be approached in multiple ways, including through state, NGO and private sector support of the numerous initiatives generated by women themselves in the form of group savings and collective land acquisition and building schemes (see also Baptist and Patel, 2011; Benavides Llerena *et al.*, 2007; D'Cruz and Satterthwaite, 2005).

Partnerships can take the form of gender-responsive housing finance, assistance in obtaining tenure security, subsidised materials, and training in construction techniques (see, e.g., Chant, 1996; Mills, 2010; Moser and Peake, 1987; Patel and Mitlin, 2010). An integral role should also be played by concerted efforts to increase pro-female housing rights initiatives, such as in statutory joint or individual titling, or mechanisms to ensure that women are fully represented on committees which decide on land rights in communities that observe customary law (Chant, 2007b; Cooper, 2010; CPRC, 2020; Rakodi, 2014; Rolnik, 2012; Varley, 2007).

Support for paralegal services which assist women in their ability to realise their land and shelter entitlements is also crucial (UNMP/TGEFE, 2005:84), as is revealed in the example of GROOTS Kenya's efforts to provide paralegal services for disinherited women, as discussed in Chapter 2 (see also Huairou Commission, 2011), and in the context of Nigeria where the Women's Aid Collective (WACOL) works to help widows to defend their inheritance rights (COHRE, 2004:77–8). Recalling the significance of rental accommodation for urban women, interventions to promote their access to, and security in, this sector need to be part of the picture (Miraftab, 2001:156).

In turn, for women in rental and owner- or quasi-owner-occupied housing alike, greater media exposure of abuses in respect of tenure security, shelter adequacy and personal safety could also raise visibility and public accountability. Although, as noted by Hughes and Wickeri (2011:844), women's lack of knowledge of their rights, and societal awareness of instances when those rights are violated, whether within or outside the justice system, tend to be more compromised in rural than in urban areas, media dissemination and campaigns can undoubtedly be effective, and could be strengthened further by increasing poor women's access to ICT not only within but beyond towns and cities. As asserted by Alice Evans (2013b: 13–14) in relation to research on the possibilities presented by TV and social media for changing gender in the Global South (e.g. Chong and La Ferrara, 2009, on Brazil; Jensen and Oster, 2009, on Tamil Nadu, India), a range of new beliefs and behaviours – for example, around divorce, fertility, gender-based violence and so on – may be set in motion by role models in popular culture which even out the nominal advantages women gain through 'physical association in urban contexts' (Evans, 2013b:14).

Productivity

Ensuring women's rights to adequate housing, services and infrastructure, along with education, training and work, is also likely to play a major part in enhancing poor and slum-dwelling urban women's access to, and benefits from, productivity.

While various MDG targets have been important in increasing female gains in education and employment, much more needs to be done to cater to the needs of women workers in cities, who, along with rising numbers of their male counterparts, are likely to remain predominantly engaged in the informal economy (Williams and Lansky, 2013). Indeed, further informalisation is on the cards as some cities de-industrialise or formal manufacturing plants are reduced in favour of offloading jobs into the homeworking sector, and public sector employment is scaled down in the interests of cost-cutting (see Chen and Skinner, 2014). As was highlighted in the context of a recent workshop on 'Inclusive Cities' in New Delhi, since 80 per cent of Indian urban workers are informally employed, and like many other developing nations India's economy is a 'hybrid' of 'modern–traditional' and 'formal–informal' activities, economic diversity and informal businesses should be promoted rather than penalised (Chen, 2011; SEWA-IIHS, 2011).

Urban policies relating to land and land use are vital here, with restrictions on home-based enterprise, slum clearance, the gating of middle-income and elite residential neighbourhoods, and constrained access by informal entrepreneurs to public spaces often exacting huge tolls on people's – and especially women's – capacity to avoid poverty and marginalisation (Chen and Skinner, 2014; Kinyanjui, 2014; Speak, 2012). Aside from recognising the rights of informal workers in the city through land channels, and acknowledging that 'there is no single solution for the problem of labour informality, given the heterogeneity of informal work' (UNRISD, 2010a:125), a variety of mechanisms for supporting small businesses and the self-employed – at the same time as promoting 'decent work' – might be taken into the equation. These include better provision of vocational educational and training with a view to enhancing the diversification of often competitive informal activities, easier access to loans on favourable terms, assistance in promoting greater health and safety at work, and the reduction and/or phasing of costs of formalisation (see Chant and McIlwaine, 2009:chapter 6; see also Navarrete, 2015, for discussion and references).

Greater and more spatially even investments in physical infrastructure, such as public transport, constitute a further integral element in this scenario, with sex-disaggregated data noted as being a sine qua non to the gender-sensitivity of transport planning (Fernando and Porter, 2002; Levy, 2013a, 2013b; Peters, 2001; Titcombe, 2014). Yet, as highlighted in Chapter 7, single-issue interventions in transport, or the creation of nominally gender-friendly public spaces and amenities, may not benefit women unless complementary measures are also put in place, not least in terms of other hard infrastructure such as streetlighting. Similarly, training women in, and facilitating their access to, virtual spaces and connectivity through digital technology are insufficient when the physical spaces they inhabit remain subject to erratic or unaffordable power supplies, where women's earnings are too low to purchase the necessary equipment, or where social conventions inhibit their engagement in the 'modern' economy.

In light of this, encouraging and supporting associations of female informal entrepreneurs is critical in strengthening their routinely marginalised position and activities (Chen and Skinner, 2014; Kinyanjui, 2014). The power of organisation is indicated by the examples of very successful women workers' organisations discussed in Chapter 8 in the context of India and Peru, and also features in Chen's (2010a) '3V' framework for the working poor, which, in comprising the imperatives of 'voice', 'visibility' and 'validity', serves as another

---

Box 10.1 The '3V' framework

To ensure that economic policies are (re)oriented towards creating more and better employment, the working poor, and especially women, need to be empowered to hold policy-makers accountable.

This requires three *enabling conditions*:

- *Visibility* requires that the working poor, especially women, in the informal economy are visible in labour force statistics. More countries need to collect statistics on informal employment, broadly defined, and countries that already do so need to improve the quality of the statistics that they collect. Also, all forms of informal employment need to be integrated into economic models of labour markets. Since existing models focus on the supply and demand of wage labour, the self-employed tend to be excluded. A second area of neglect pertains to insufficient delineation between different types of waged workers. A third problem is that the extent of under-employment is not taken into account, despite its role in providing a more accurate measure of the 'employment problem' in developing countries than open unemployment.
- *Voice*: the working poor, especially women, in the informal economy need a representative – and stronger – voice in the processes and institutions that determine economic policies and formulate the 'rules of the (economic) game'. This requires building and supporting organisations of informal workers and extending the coverage of existing trade unions, cooperatives and other workers' organisations to include informal workers. This also requires making rule-setting and policy-making institutions more inclusive and helping representatives of the working poor to gain 'a seat at the (policy) table'.
- *Validity* refers to recognition and validation. The working poor, especially women, in the informal economy need legal identity and validity as workers and economic agents, and also need to be recognised as legitimate targets of employment policy.

Source: Chen, 2010a.

---

potentially fruitful tool to promote greater gender equality in urban environments (see Box 10.1; see also Grimshaw and Rubery, 2007; Perrons, 2010).

Bearing in mind that not all women are informally employed, general questions pertaining to gender-differentiated productivity also need to be tackled, such as the abiding lower value accorded to women's labour, often irrespective of the work itself (Perrons, 2010; Perrons and Plomien, 2010), and the fact that without due attention to unpaid carework any affirmative actions to ensure non-discrimination against women in workforce recruitment are likely to come to nothing. 'Smart management' for gender-aware and fair economic growth requires not only the growth of female employment, asset ownership and incomes (Sanders and Porterfield, 2010) as well as better job conditions and protection (Arbache *et al.*, 2010; Besley and Cord, 2007; Cueto, 2005; Kabeer, 2008b; Lucas, 2007; UN-Habitat, 2008b), but also an 'enabling' social, economic and political environment for genuine transformations in gender roles and relations to take place.

Equity in power and rights

So, too, gender-equitable cities need to promote women's and men's participation in civic engagement and urban governance and politics, while avoiding the all-too-frequent situation whereby high levels of women's activism at the grassroots does not translate into high-profile representation in formal municipal or national political arenas.

Imperative in efforts to support such engagement is recognition of state–society synergies, and that progressive policy reform rarely happens through social mobilisation or state action alone but through collaborative efforts of civil society and governments (Citizenship DRC, 2011:26, 46; Gaventa and McGee, 2010; Khosla, 2009),

Also critical is a long-term focus since major transformations seldom occur overnight. For example, there is mounting evidence of the limitations of gender mainstreaming, ad hoc workshops and women's invitations to decision-making fora – where their participation is often token and muted (Evans, 2013a; Goetz and Hassim, 2003; Parpart, 2009, 2014). As such, building women's capacity for 'good governance' is indispensable (UN-Habitat, 2010b:28ff.). While some initiatives instigated by both NGOs and governments have shown promise in enhancing female civic activism and participation (see Abers, 2003, on Brazil; Kabeer *et al.*, 2010, on Bangladesh), another strategy might be to work through existing educational structures wherein younger generations of women and men are encouraged to develop interest in, and are equipped with the practical tools to engage with, civic issues, thereby enhancing dialogue and sustainable participation from the bottom up (Evans, 2013a).

Part and parcel of designing gender-responsive *pro-prosperity* measures is also to correct the common dilemma posed for women by involving them predominantly or exclusively in *anti-poverty* programmes where they usually end up with more unpaid work on their shoulders (Concern Worldwide and Oxfam, 2011; Molyneux, 2006, 2007). In order to counter the 'feminisation of responsibility' (Chant, 2008) or adverse effects of the 'feminisation of policy' (Roy, 2002, 2010) which such neglect implies, it is vital for poverty reduction programmes whether centred on employment, entrepreneurship, micro-finance or cash transfers, to recognise the burdens women currently bear, and to seek to alleviate these through greater public provision of care facilities and/or via promoting more engagement on the part of men and boys (Chant, 2007a, 2007b; Chant and Gutmann, 2000; Chant and Sweetman, 2012; Cornwall *et al.*, 2011; Parpart, 2015).

Leading on from this, while 'smart economics' thinking seems to have encroached into the urban development agenda, with concepts of 'smarter cities' and the like, it is important to acknowledge that although mobilising investments in women can have huge impacts on the generation of wealth, there is also a serious danger of instrumentalising gender (under the auspices of promoting 'gender equality') to meet these ends, as well as missing the vital point of evening out women's and men's inputs and rewards in urban environments (Chant, 2012a, 2016; Moser, 2014). It is accordingly paramount that principles of gender rights and justice remain uppermost in urban policy and planning. At the bottom line this will involve attempts to ensure equality of opportunity through effective monitoring and enforcement, and to enjoin (and ensure) not only female but also male participation in all institutions at all scales, from the micro-level to the macro (see, e.g., Masika *et al.*, 1997:15; Patel, 2011). As articulated by UN Women (2011b:5): 'engaging men is critical to transformative social change; it is a "positive-sum" game', not least because if men's greater social, economic and political weight is brought to bear in the process, change is likely to be more rapid and enduring.

Mainstreaming gender effectively at all levels of policy dialogue and engagement may well, in the long run, obviate the need for separate treatment of women in the flagship publications of international agencies, including those of UN-Habitat. While we applaud the initiative UN-Habitat undertook in respect of commissioning and publishing the first *State of Women in Cities* in 2013, and there was arguably a need for a dedicated document given that UN-Habitat's two-yearly *State of the World's Cities* reports have historically paid little attention to gender, there is scope within a 'twin-track' approach used by many international agencies for gender to be more meaningfully mainstreamed and for a 'gender lens' (Davids and Van Driel, 2010) to be applied to the more general treatment of urban matters (Chant, 2013). This was disappointingly not the case with *State of the World's Cities 2012/2013*, however, with a meagre ten mentions of 'women' and only four of 'gender quality' in its 150 pages.

Essential to effective mainstreaming, and to finessing strategies to ensure that cities become more gender equitable, will be to address baseline information deficits. While recognising that slums and poverty are not synonymous, there is a good deal of overlap, and as is no doubt obvious by now, we believe that location in the city *does* matter in terms of gendered shares of urban wealth and well-being, broadly defined. As iterated at several junctures in this volume, poor women living in far-flung peri-urban slums lacking safe, affordable transport, and the power and resources to connect digitally as well as physically, seem to be at disproportionate risk of multiple privations. To improve knowledge, and to take appropriate action, we need not only better sex-disaggregated data (see CPRC, 2010:ix) but much more in the way of spatially disaggregated data and analysis at national, urban and intra-urban levels (see also Chant and Datu, 2015).

Finally, the built environment of the city can oppress women, often on account of the fact that urban forms have evolved through historically successive actions intended to secure and/or advance male primacy in economic, social and political spheres (see Burgess, 2008; Massey, 1994; Jarvis *et al.*, 2009; McDowell, 1983, 1999). As Jarvis *et al.* (2009:113) contend: 'The urban landscape reproduces masculine and feminine identities in numerous ways, both visible and more subtle.' As such, tinkering with physical aspects of the urban fabric itself is unlikely to effect transformative change, notwithstanding that simple general design principles such as mixed land use, gender-friendly affordable transportation, the provision of open space, decent housing, and due regard for the different needs of women across the lifecourse can constitute positive first steps (Birch, 2011:91). However, only by recognising the intersections of cities with patriarchal relations, and by eliminating male bias in the institutions which give rise to gender inequality, will fairer shares of urban well-being become a right and a reality for women in cities everywhere. As emphasised, inter alia, by UN-Habitat (2012a:47):

> Urban design is not only about making places look good and aesthetically pleasing; it is also about functionality and making sure things work well for everyone. Failure to take into account the different needs of women and men in built environments has created built environments that may look good but often fail to meet the everyday needs of users. Sense of place, character, vibrancy and attractive physical environments are all appropriate goals for urban environments, although if these goals are not considered from a gender perspective they may not be met.

Plate 10.2 Putting women in the public domain: female police officers in Johannesburg, South Africa

Source: Michael Keith.

Looking forward: what role for the Sustainable Development Goals in advancing gender equality in cities and slums?

To conclude our discussion, we feel it is important to raise questions about the potential that the new post-2015 Sustainable Development Goals Agenda may have for improving women's lives in cities, and especially in slums in the Global South.

Acknowledging that this agenda, in the words of Mayra Moro-Coco and Natalie Raaber (2012:4), 'comes at a time when the failures of the current, predominant patriarchal and neoliberal model of growth and development are widely acknowledged and visible' and that '[n]o dimension of development is gender-neutral, therefore any post-2015 development framework must integrate a systematic gender perspective and strong political commitment to women's rights and gender equality', it is encouraging that the SDGs have been formulated on the basis of widespread international stakeholder participation in which there is considerable commitment to ensure that these yield 'lasting change for women's rights, empowerment and equality' (Puri, 2013:91; see also UN Women, 2014). Indeed, and from the perspective of a major constituency in these discussions, the Post-2015 Women's Coalition (2014) insisted not only that gender equality, women's human rights and women's empowerment should be core, but that 'The post-2015 development framework cannot be a continuation of the MDG framework, just tweaked through a few improvements to the formulation of goals, targets and indicators' (Elson and Balakrishnan, 2013:2).

Despite justified criticisms that gender was somewhat 'ghettoised' in the MDGs (see Antrobus, 2004, 2005; Chant, 2007b; Saith, 2006; Sweetman, 2005; UNMP/TFEGE, 2005), UN Women, like many other organisations, has been strongly in favour of a 'twin-track' approach which involves retaining a 'stand-alone' goal. Although this might, on the surface, seem retrogressive, it is vital to acknowledge that the new gender SDG is much more consistent with the radical principles enshrined in the Beijing Platform for Action of 1995 in prioritising ending violence against women and girls, universal sexual and reproductive health and rights (SRHRs), women's equal participation in decision-making from the household through to the highest echelons of governance, and the achievement of equal opportunities in respect of women's economic empowerment. The latter not only comprises equality in education, access to land and credit, decent work and equal pay, but, as indicated earlier in this chapter, the very important promotion of gender-equitable sharing of domestic work and caregiving (see CWGL, 2013; GADN, 2013; Harper *et al.*, 2014; Puri, 2013:91; UN Women, 2014, 2015c:234; see also Fraser, N., 2005; Sweetman, 2012).

The other, and major, achievement in this twin-track scenario is the inclusion of gender targets, if not explicitly, then implicitly, by use of the word 'all' in several other goals relating to poverty, education, health, employment, services and sustainable inclusive urbanisation, many of which are extremely pertinent to urban women and girls, including those residing in slums. Indeed, the UK-based Gender and Development Network has insisted, inter alia, not only that targets in all SDGs should be 'specifically designed to transform power relations between women and men' (GADN, 2013:2; see also Boxes 1.3 and 1.4, this volume), but that particular attention should be accorded to income-poor and otherwise marginalised women, with due regard for better data and analysis on differences among women and intersectionality on grounds of age, 'race', sexuality and so on.

Bearing in mind that the devil is usually in the detail, critical in ensuring that prescriptions become practice is to think about how the SDGs will be implemented, which, in the case of the MDGs, was insufficiently elaborated (see Satterthwaite *et al.*, 2013:1). At the bottom line, and with due regard for urban contexts, this should involve local authorities which are adequately financed for purpose and are accountable to their stakeholders, not least grassroots women (ibid.:1–2)

Feminised urban futures are not just about women being the majority in number, but also, and ideally, entail changes in the *nature* of towns and cities, such that women are able to shed the minority status to which they have been subjected over centuries in numerous dimensions of their lives. Here it is worth recalling the point we made in Chapter 1: women and girls need to be at the heart of urbanisation's 'transformative powers', and not merely for instrumental reasons. Rather, gender inequalities need to be addressed and women's rights ensured in order for them to participate in, and benefit from, the current and sustained wave of urban growth in the Global South. In particular, slum-dwelling women and girls, who frequently comprise the bulk of urban residents, must be able to meet their own needs, extend their choices and access opportunities. While throughout the book we have outlined a range of ways in which female populations at the grassroots in developing regions have already attempted to organise and generate positive change, there must also be wider structural shifts – economically, socially and culturally – to establish the enabling environment for this to happen, in which gender transformations are not only prioritised as ends, but as means as well. In this vein, we hope that our proposed 'gender–urban–slum interface', and the review we have provided of its key components, will serve as an empirical, methodological and conceptual contribution to the process.

Bibliography

Abers, Rebecca (2003) 'Reflections on What Makes Empowered Participatory Governance Happen', in Archon Fung and Erik Wright (eds) *Deepening Democracy: Institutional Innovations in Empowered Participatory Governance* (London: Verso), 200–7. (www. ssc.wisc.edu/~wright/Deepening.pdf).

Aboderin, Isabella (2010) 'Poverty in Old Age in Sub-Saharan Africa: Examining the Impacts of Gender with Particular Reference to Ghana', in Sylvia Chant (ed.) *The International Handbook of Gender and Poverty: Concepts, Research, Policy* (Cheltenham: Edward Elgar), 215–19.

Acey, Charisma (2010) 'Gender and Community Mobilisation for Urban Water Infrastructure Investment in Southern Nigeria', *Gender and Development*, 18:1, 11–26.

ActionAid (2011) *Women and the City: Examining the Gender Impact of Violence and Urbanisation: A Comparative Study of Brazil, Cambodia, Ethiopia, Liberia and Nepal* (Johannesburg: ActionAid). (www.actionaid.org/sites/files/actionaid/actionaid_2011_ women_and_the_city.pdf).

Adepoju, Aderanti and Mbugua, Wariara (1997) 'The African Family: An Overview of Changing Forms', in Aderanti Adepoju (ed.) *Family, Population and Development in Africa* (London: Zed), 41–59.

Africa Research Institute (ARI) (2014) *Modern African Remedies: Herbal Medicine and Community Development in Nigeria*, Policy Voice Series (London: ARI).

African Development Bank (AfDB) (2012) *Zanzibar Urban Water and Sanitation Project Appraisal Report* (Abijan: AfDB). (www.afdb.org/fileadmin/uploads/afdb/Documents/ Project-and-Operations/Tanzania_-_Zanzibar_Urban_Water_and_Sanitation_Project__ Appraisal_Report.pdf).

African Union (AU) (2007) 'Strategy to Revitalise Technical and Vocational Education and Training in Africa', Meeting of the Bureau of the Conference of Ministers of Education of the African Union (COMEDAF II+), 29–31 May, Addis Ababa, Ethiopia. (http://info.worldbank.org/etools/docs/library/243614/TVET%20Strategy%20in%20 Africa.pdf).

Agarwal, Siddarth (2011) 'The State of Urban Health in India: Comparing the Poorest Quartile to the Rest of the Urban Population in Selected States and Cities', *Environment and Urbanization*, 23:1, 13–28.

Agesa, Richard (2003) 'Gender Differences in the Urban to Rural Wage Gap and the Prevalence of the Male Migrant', *Journal of Developing Areas*, 37:1, 13–34.

Agyei-Mensah, Samuel, Owusu, George and Wrigley-Asante, Charlotte (2015) 'Urban Health in Africa: Looking Beyond the MDGs', *International Development Planning Review*, 37:1, 53–60.

Ahmedabad Municipal Corporation (AMC) (2005) *Ahmedabad Slum Networking Programme: A Partnership Programme of Infrastructure and Social Development in Slums of Ahmedabad City: The Dubai International Award for Best Practices to Improve the Living Environment* (Ahmedabad: AMC). (www.egovamc.com/snp/snp.pdf).

Aker, Jenny C. and Mbiti, Isaac, M. (2010) 'Mobile Phones and Economic Development in Africa', *Journal of Economic Perspectives*, 24:3, 207–232.

Alber, Gotelind (2011) *Gender, Cities and Climate Change*, Thematic Report prepared for Cities and Climate Change Global Report on Human Settlements. (http://mirror.un Habitat.org/downloads/docs/GRHS2011/GRHS2011ThematicStudyGender.pdf).

Ali, Harris and Keil, Roger (2012) 'Global Cities and Infectious Disease', in Ben Derudder, Michael Hoyler, Peter J.Taylor and Frank Witlox (eds) *International Handbook of Globalisation and World Cities* (Cheltenham: Edward Elgar), 347–57.

Ali, Kamran Asdar (2012) 'Women, Work and Public Spaces: Conflict and Coexistence in Karachi's Poor Neighbourhoods', *International Journal of Urban and Regional Research*, 36:3, 585–605.

Allen, Adriana, Dávila, Julio and Hoffman, Pascale (2006) *Governance of Water and Sanitation Services for the Peri-urban Poor: A Framework for Understanding and Action in Metropolitan Regions* (London: University College London, Development Planning Unit).

Ambert, Cecile, Jassey, Katja and Thomas, Liz (2007) 'HIV, AIDS and Urban Development Issues in Sub-Saharan Africa: Beyond Sex and Medicines: Why Getting the Basics Right is Part of the Response', Report prepared for Division for Urban Development, Swedish International Development Agency, Stockholm. (www.sida.se/sida/jsp/sida.jsp?d=118&a=30644&searchWords=hiv/aids%20urban%20development).

Amnesty International (2010) *Insecurity and Indignity: Women's Experiences in the Slums of Nairobi, Kenya* (London: Amnesty International). (www.amnesty.org/en/library/asset/AFR32/002/2010/en/12a9d334-0b62-40e1-ae4a-e5333752d68c/afr320022010en.pdf).

Anand, Nikhil (2012) 'Municipal Disconnect: On Abject Water and its Urban Infrastructures', *Ethnography*, 13:4, 487–509.

Anderson, Jeanine and Panzio, Nelson (1986) 'Transportation and Public Safety: Services that Make Service Use Possible', in Judith Bruce and Marilyn Köhn (eds) *Learning about Women and Urban Services in Latin America and the Caribbean* (New York: Population Council), 246–60.

Angotti, Tom (2006) 'Review Essay: Apocalyptic Anti-urbanism: Mike Davis and his Planet of Slums', *International Journal of Urban and Regional Research Volume*, 30:4, 961–7.

Ansell, Nicola, Tsoeu, Seroala and Hadju, Flora (2015) 'Women's Changing Responsibilities in Neoliberal Africa: A Relational Time–Space Analysis of Lesotho's Garment Industry', *Gender, Place and Culture*, 22:3, 363–82.

Antrobus, Peggy (2004) 'MDGs – the Most Distracting Gimmick', in Women's International Coalition for Economic Justice (ed.) *Seeking Accountability on Women's Human Rights: Women Debate the UN Millennium Development Goals* (New York: WICEJ), 14–16.

Antrobus, Peggy (2005) 'Critiquing the MDGs from a Caribbean Perspective', in Caroline Sweetman (ed.) *Gender and the Millennium Development Goals* (Oxford: Oxfam), 94–104.

Appadurai, Arjun (2002) 'Deep Democracy: Urban Governmentality and the Horizon of Politics', *Environment and Urbanization*, 13:2, 23–43.

Arabindoo, Pushpa (2011) 'Beyond the Return of the "Slum"', *City: Analysis of Urban Trends, Culture, Theory, Policy, Action*, 15:6, 631–5.

Arbache, Jorge Saba, Kolev, Alexandre and Filipiak, Ewa (2010) *Gender Disparities in Africa's Labor Market* (Washington, DC: World Bank).

Arend, Elizabeth (2012) *IFIs and Gender Based Violence: Case Study Haiti* (Washington, DC: Gender Action).

Arimah, Ben (2007) 'The Face of Urban Poverty: Explaining the Prevalence of Slums in Developing Countries', Paper presented at UNU-WIDER Workshop: 'Beyond the Tipping Point: Development in an Urban World', LSE, London, 18–20 October.

Asian Development Bank (ADB) (2011) 'Gender and Development', *In Focus*, Asian Development Bank, Manila. (www.asiandevbank.org/Documents/Brochures/InFocus/infocus-gender.pdf).

Bähre, Erik (2007) 'Reluctant Solidarity: Death, Urban Poverty and Neighbourly Assistance in South Africa', *Ethnography*, 8:1, 33–59.

Banks, Nicola, Roy, Manaj and Hulme, David (2011) 'Neglecting the Urban Poor in Bangladesh: Research, Policy and Action in the Context of Climate Change', *Environment and Urbanisation*, 23:2, 487–502.

Bapat, Meera (2009) *Poverty Lines and Lives of the Poor: Underestimation of Urban Poverty – the Case of India*, Poverty Reduction in Urban Areas Series Working Paper 20 (London: International Institute for Environment and Development).

Bapat, Meera and Agarwal, Indu (2003) 'Our Needs, Our Priorities: Women and Men from the Slums in Mumbai and Pune Talk about Their Needs for Water and Sanitation', *Environment and Urbanization*, 15:2, 71–86.

Baptist, Carrie and Patel, Sheela (2011) 'Information is Power: Community and Policy Effects of Participatory Enumerations', Paper presented at 'The City in Urban Poverty' workshop, Development Planning Unit, University College London, 10–11 November.

Barker, Gary (2014) 'A Radical Agenda for Men's Caregiving', *IDS Bulletin*, 45:1, 85–90.

Barker, Gary, Nascimento, Marcos, Ricardo, Christine, Olinger, Marianna and Segundo, Marcio (2011) 'Masculinities, Social Exclusion and Prospects for Change: Reflections from Promundo's Work in Rio de Janeiro, Brazil', in Andrea Cornwall, Jerker Edström and Alan Greig (eds) *Men and Development: Politicising Masculinities* (London: Zed), 170–84.

Baruah, Bipasha (2007) 'Gendered Realities: Exploring Property Ownership and Tenancy Agreements in Urban India', *World Development*, 35:12, 2096–109.

Bastia, Tanja and Busse, Erika (2011) 'Transnational Migration and Changing Gender Relations in Peruvian and Bolivian Cities', *Diversities*, 13:1, 19–33.

Bayliss, Kate and McKinley, Terry (2007) *Privatising Basic Utilities in Sub-Saharan Africa: The MDG Impact*, Policy Research Brief No. 3 (Brasilia: International Poverty Centre).

Beall, Jo (1996) *Urban Governance: Why Gender Matters*, Gender in Development Monograph Series No. 1 (New York: UNDP). (www.ucl.ac.uk/dpu-projects/drivers_urb_change/urb_society/pdf_gender/UNDP_Beall_gender_matters.pdf).

Beall, Jo (1997) 'Thoughts on Poverty from a South Asian Rubbish Dump: Gender, Inequality and Household Waste', *IDS Bulletin*, 28:3, 73–90.

Beall, Jo (2010) 'Decentralisation, Women's Rights and Poverty: Learning From India and South Africa', in Sylvia Chant (ed.) *The International Handbook of Gender and Poverty: Concepts, Research, Policy* (Cheltenham: Edward Elgar), 633–7.

Beall, Jo and Fox, Sean (2009) *Cities and Development* (London: Routledge).

Beall, Jo, Guha-Khasnobis, Basudeb and Kanbur, Ravi (2010) 'Beyond the Tipping Point: A Multidisciplinary Perspective on Urbanisation and Development', in Jo Beall, Basudeb Guha-Khasnobis and Ravi Kanbur (eds) *Urbanisation and Development: Multidisciplinary Perspectives* (Oxford: Oxford University Press), 3–16.

Begum, Ferdous Ara (2011) 'Effective Protection of the Human Rights of Older Women through the CEDAW Convention and the General Recommendation Number 27', Paper presented at the First Substantive Session of the Open Ended Working Group on Strengthening the Human Rights of Older People, United Nations, New York, 18–21 April. (http://social.un.org/ageing-working-group/documents/Ferdous%20Begum%20CEDAW%20GR27%20revised.pdf).

Bell, David and Valentine, Gill (1995) *Mapping Desire: Geographies of Sexualities* (London: Routledge).

Benavides Llerena, Gina, Sánchez Pinto, Silvana, Chávez Nuñez, Gardenia, Solesdipa Toro, Azucena and Sol Paredes, María (2007) *Diagnóstico de la Situación del Derecho de las Mujeres a la Vivienda Adecuada desde una Perspectiva de Género en Ecuador* (Quito: Comité de América Latina y El Caribe Para la Defensa de los Derechos de la Mujer).

Benjamin, Saranel (2007) 'The Feminisation of Poverty in Post-apartheid South Africa: A Story Told by the Women of Bayview, Chatsworth', *Journal of Developing Societies*, 23, 175–296.

Benschop, Marjolein (2004) *Progress Report: On Removing Discrimination against Women in Respect of Property and Inheritance Rights* (Nairobi: UN-Habitat).

Berry, Kim (2011) 'Disowning Dependence: Single Women's Collective Struggle for Independence and Land Rights in Northwestern India', *Feminist Review*, 98, 136–52.

Besley, Timothy and Cord, Louise (2007) *Delivering on the Promise of Pro-poor Growth: Insights and Lessons from Country Experiences* (Basingstoke/New York: Palgrave Macmillan).

Bhan, Gautam (2009) '"This is No Longer the City I Once Knew": Evictions, the Urban Poor and the Right to the City in Millennial Delhi', *Environment and Urbanisation*, 21:1, 127–42.

Bhatt, Mihir (2003) 'The Case of Ahmedabad, India', Case Study Report for the UN Global Report on Human Settlements 2003, Development Planning Unit, University College London.

Bibler, Sandra and Zuckerman, Elaine (2013) *The Care Connection: The World Bank and Women's Unpaid Carework in Select Sub-Saharan African Countries*, WIDER Working Paper 2013/131, Helsinki-UNU-WIDER. (www.genderaction.org/carereport.pdf).

Biles, James (2008) 'Informal Work and Livelihoods in Mexico: Getting by or Getting ahead?', *Professional Geographer*, 60:4, 541–55.

Birch, Eugenie L. (2011) 'Design of Healthy Cities for Women', in Afaf Ibrahim Meleis, Eugenie L. Birch and Susan F. Wachter (eds) *Women's Health and the World's Cities* (Philadelphia: University of Pennsylvania Press), 73–92.

Bird, Kate, Higgins, Kate and McKay, Andy (2010) 'Conflict, Education and the Intergenerational Transmission of Poverty in Northern Uganda', *Journal of International Development*, 22, 1183–96.

Blackden, Mark and Wodon, Quentin (eds) (2006) *Gender, Time Use and Poverty in Sub-Saharan Africa*, World Bank Working Paper No. 73 (Washington, DC: World Bank).

Blue, Ilona (1996) 'Urban Inequalities in Mental Health: The Case of São Paulo', *Environment and Urbanisation*, 8:2, 91–9.

Bondi, Liz (2005) *Gender and the Reality of Cities: Embodies Identities, Social Relations and Performativities*, Institute of Geography Online Paper Series, University of Edinburgh. (www.era.lib.ed.ac.uk/handle/1842/822).

Boulin, Jean-Yves (2007) 'Local Time Policies in Europe', in Diane Perrons, Colette Fagan, Linda McDowell, Kath Ray and Kevin Ward (eds) *Gender Divisions and Working Time in the New Economy* (Cheltenham: Edward Elgar), 193–206.

Bradshaw, Sarah (1995) 'Female-headed Households in Honduras: Perspectives on Rural–Urban Differences', *Third World Planning Review*, 17:2, 117–31.

Bradshaw, Sarah (2008) 'From Structural Adjustment to Social Adjustment: A Gendered Analysis of Conditional Cash Transfer Programmes in Mexico and Nicaragua', *Global Social Policy*, 8:2,188–207.

Bradshaw, Sarah (2013a) *Gender, Development and Disasters* (Cheltenham: Edward Elgar).

Bradshaw, Sarah (2013b) 'Women's Decision-Making in Rural and Urban Households in Nicaragua: The Influence of Income and Ideology', *Environment and Urbanization*, 25:1, 81–94.

Bradshaw, Sarah and Linneker, Brian (2010) 'Poverty Alleviation in a Changing Policy and Political Context: The Case of PRSPs with Particular Reference to Nicaragua', in Sylvia Chant (ed.) *The International Handbook of Gender and Poverty: Concepts, Research, Policy* (Cheltenham: Edward Elgar), 516–21.

Bradshaw, Sarah and Linneker, Brian (2014) *Gender and Environmental Change in the Developing World*, Working Paper, International Institute of Environment and Development, London (http://pubs.iied.org/pdfs/10716IIED.pdf).

Brouder, Alan and Sweetman, Caroline (2015) 'Introduction: Working on Gender Equality in Urban Areas', *Gender and Development*, 23:1, 1–12.

Brown, Rebecca (2010) 'Unequal Burden: Water Privatisation and Women's Human Rights in Tanzania', *Gender and Development*, 18:1, 59–67.

Browner, Carole H. (1989) 'Women, Households and Health in Latin America', *Social Science and Medicine*, 28, 461–73.

Bruce, Judith and Köhn, Marilyn (eds) (1986) *Learning about Women and Urban Services in Latin America and the Caribbean* (New York: Population Council).

Bryceson, Deborah Fahy, Gough, Katherine, Rigg, Jonathan and Agergaard, Jytte (2009) 'Critical Commentary: The World Development Report 2009', *Urban Studies*, 46:4, 723–38.

Budlender, Debbie (2004) *Why Should we Care about Unpaid Care Work?* (New York: UNIFEM).

Budlender, Debbie (2008) *The Statistical Evidence on Care and Non-Care Work across Six Countries*, Programme Paper No. 4 (Geneva: UNRISD).

Budlender, Debbie (ed.) (2010) *Time Use Studies and Unpaid Care Work* (New York: Routledge).

Budlender, Debbie and Lund, Francine (2011) 'South Africa: A Legacy of Family Disruption', *Development and Change*, 42:45, 925–46.

Burgess, Gemma (2008) 'Planning and the Gender Equality Duty: Why Does Gender Matter?', *People, Place and Policy Online*, 2/3, 112–21.

Burnet, Jennie E. (2008) 'Gender Balance and the Meanings of Women in Governance in Post-genocide Rwanda', *African Affairs*, 107:428, 361–86.

Buskens, Ineke and Webb, Anne (eds) (2009) *African Women and ICTS: Investigating Technology, Gender and Empowerment* (London: Zed Books).

Buvinic, Mayra and King, Elizabeth M. (2007) 'Smart Economics: More Needs to be Done to Promote the Economic Power of Women', *Finance and Development*, 44:2. (www.imf.org/external/pubs/ft/fandd/2007/06/king.htm).

Campbell, Perri (2006) 'Iraq's Democratisation: Communicating Women's Rights and Social change in Cyberspace', *Proceedings Social Change in the 21st Century Conference 2006* (Brisbane: Queensland University of Technology), 1–13. (http://eprints.qut.edu.au/6081/).

Campesi, Giuseppe (2010) 'Policing, Urban Poverty and Insecurity in Latin America: The Case of Mexico City and Buenos Aires', *Theoretical Criminology*, 14, 447–72.

Castells, Manuel (1978) *City, Class and Power* (London: Macmillan).

Castro, Lorenzo and Echeverri, Alejandro (2011) 'Bogotá and Medellín: Architecture and Politics', *Architectural Design*, 81:3, 96–103.

Central Statistical Office (CSO) (2011) *Living Conditions Monitoring Survey Report 2006 and 2010* (Lusaka: CSO).

Central Statistical Office (CSO), Ministry of Health, Tropical Diseases Research Centre, University of Zambia and Macro International Inc. (2009) *Zambia: Demographic and Health Survey, 2007* (Lusaka/Calverton: CSO/ORC Macro).

Centre for Women's Global Leadership (CWGL) (2013) *The Integration of Gender and Human Rights into the Post-2015 Development Framework* (New Brunswick, NJ: Rutgers University, CWGL).

Centre on Housing Rights and Evictions (COHRE) (2004) *Bringing Equality Home: Promoting and Protecting the Inheritance Rights of Women: A Survey of Law and Practice in Sub-Saharan Africa* (Geneva: COHRE).

Centre on Housing Rights and Evictions (COHRE) (2008) *Women, Slums and Urbanisation: Examining the Causes and Consequences* (Geneva: COHRE).

Centro de Planificación y Estudios Sociales (CEPLAES) (2010) *Women's Police Stations in Latin America* (Quito: CEPLAES).

Chandrasekhar, S. and Mukhopadhyay, Abhiroop (2008) *Poverty, Gender, and Youth. Multiple Dimensions of Urban Well-Being: Evidence from India*, Working Paper No. 11 (New York: Population Council). (www.popcouncil.org/pdfs/wp/pgy/011.pdf).

Chant, Sylvia (1984) 'Household Labour and Self-help Housing in Querétaro, Mexico', *Boletín de Estudios Latinoamericanos y del Caribe*, 37, 45–68.

Chant, Sylvia (1987) 'Domestic Labour, Decision-making and Dwelling Construction: The Experience of Women in Querétaro, Mexico', in Caroline Moser and Linda Peake (eds) *Women, Human Settlements and Housing* (London: Tavistock), 33–54.

Chant, Sylvia (1996) *Gender, Urban Development and Housing* (New York: UNDP).

Chant, Sylvia (1997) *Women-headed Households: Diversity and Dynamics in the Developing World* (Basingstoke: Macmillan).

Chant, Sylvia (1998) 'Households, Gender and Rural–Urban Migration: Reflections on Linkages and Considerations for Policy', *Environment and Urbanisation*, 10:1, 5–21.

Chant, Sylvia (2002) 'Men, Women and Household Diversity', in Cathy McIlwaine and Katie Willis (eds) *Challenge and Change in Middle America and the Caribbean* (Harlow: Pearson Education), 26–60.

Chant, Sylvia (2006) *Re-visiting the 'Feminisation of Poverty' and the UNDP Gender Indices: What Case for a Gendered Poverty Index?*, LSE Gender Institute, New Working Paper Series No. 18. (www.lse.ac.uk/collections/GenderInstitute).

Chant, Sylvia (2007a) *Gender, Generation and Poverty: Exploring the 'Feminisation of Poverty' in Africa, Asia and Latin America* (Cheltenham: Edward Elgar).

Chant, Sylvia (2007b) *Gender, Cities and the Millennium Development Goals in the Global South*, LSE Gender Institute, New Series Working Paper No. 21. (www.lse.ac.uk/collections/genderInstitute/pdf/CHANT%20GI.pdf).

Chant, Sylvia (2008) 'The "Feminisation of Poverty" and the "Feminisation" of Anti-Poverty Programmes: Room for Revision?', *Journal of Development Studies*, 44:2, 165–97.

Chant, Sylvia (ed.) (2010) *The International Handbook of Gender and Poverty: Concepts, Research, Policy* (Cheltenham: Edward Elgar).

Chant, Sylvia (2011a) 'Gender and the City', *LSE Research Magazine* (Spring), 26–27. (www2.lse.ac.uk/researchAndExpertise/LSEResearchMagazine/home.aspx).

Chant, Sylvia (2011b) 'Gender and the Prosperity of Cities', Final draft of lead chapter prepared for UN-Habitat, *State of Women in Cities 2012/13*, November (Nairobi: UN-Habitat).

Chant, Sylvia (2012a) 'The Disappearing of "Smart Economics"? The World Development Report 2012 on Gender Equality: Some Concerns about the Preparatory Process and the Prospects for Paradigm Change', *Global Social Policy*, 12:2, 198–218.

Chant, Sylvia (2012b) 'Gender and Urban Housing in the Global South', in Susan J. Smith, Marja Elsinga, Lorna Fox O'Mahoney, Ong Seow Eng, Susan Wachter and Peter Ward (eds) *International Encyclopedia of Housing and Home*, Vol. 2 (Oxford: Elsevier), 255–63.

Chant, Sylvia (2013) 'Cities through a "Gender Lens": A Golden "Urban Age" for Women in the Global South?', *Environment and Urbanization*, 25:1, 9–29.

Chant, Sylvia (2014) 'Exploring the "Feminisation of Poverty" in Relation to Women's Work and Home-based Enterprise in Slums of the Global South', *International Journal of Gender and Entrepreneurship*, 6:3, 296–316.

Chant, Sylvia (2015) 'Female Household Headship as an Asset? Interrogating the Intersections of Urbanisation, Gender and Domestic Transformations', in Caroline Moser (ed.) *Gender, Asset Accumulation and Just Cities: Pathways to Transformation* (London: Routledge), 21–39.

Chant, Sylvia (2016) 'Women, Girls and World Poverty: Empowerment, Equality or Essentialism?', *International Development Planning Review*, 38:1, tbc.

Chant, Sylvia (forthcoming) 'Youth and Employment', in Gareth Jones, Katherine Brickell, Sylvia Chant and Sarah Thomas de Benítez (eds) *Bringing Youth into Development* (London: Zed Books).

Chant, Sylvia and Brickell, Katherine (2013) 'Domesticating (and De-patriarchalising) the Development Agenda: A Need for Greater Household (and Family) Engagement in Gender-related Policy Interventions?', in Shirin Rai and Georgina Waylen (eds) *New Frontiers in Feminist Political Economy* (London: Routledge), 85–113.

Chant, Sylvia with Craske, Nikki (2003) *Gender in Latin America* (London: Latin America Bureau).

Chant, Sylvia and Datu, Kerwin (2011a) 'Urban Prosperity Doesn't Automatically Mean Gender Equality', *Global Urbanist*, September. (http://globalurbanist.com/2011/09/27/urban-prosperity-doesnt-automatically-mean-gender-equality).

Chant, Sylvia and Datu, Kerwin (2011b) 'Women in Cities: Prosperity or Poverty? A Need for Multidimensional and Multi-Spatial Analysis', Paper presented at 'The City in Urban Poverty' workshop, University College London, 10–11 November.

Chant, Sylvia and Datu, Kerwin (2015) 'Women in Cities: Prosperity or Poverty? The Importance of Multidimensional and Multi-Spatial Analysis', in Charlotte Lemanski and Colin Marx (eds) *The City in Urban Poverty* (Basingstoke: Palgrave Macmillan), 39–63.

Chant, Sylvia and Evans, Alice (2010) 'Looking for the One(s): Young Love and Urban Poverty in the Gambia', *Environment and Urbanization*, 22:2, 353–69.

Chant, Sylvia and Gutmann, Matthew (2000) *Mainstreaming Men into Gender and Development: Debates, Reflections and Experiences* (Oxford: Oxfam).

Chant, Sylvia and McIlwaine, Cathy (1995) *Women of a Lesser Cost: Female Labour, Foreign Exchange and Philippine Development* (London: Zed).

Chant, Sylvia and McIlwaine, Cathy (2009) *Geographies of Development in the 21st Century: An Introduction to the Global South* (Cheltenham: Edward Elgar).

Chant, Sylvia and McIlwaine, Cathy (2013a) 'Gendered Urban Prosperity and Women's Empowerment in 21st Century Cities', *La Camera Blu*, 7, 87–115.

Chant, Sylvia and McIlwaine, Cathy (2013b) 'Gender, Urban Development and the Politics of Space', *e-International Relations*. (www.e-ir.info/2013/06/04/gender-urban-development-and-the-politics-of-space/).

Chant, Sylvia and Pedwell, Carolyn (2008) *Women, Gender and the Informal Economy: An Assessment of ILO Research, and Suggested Ways Forward* (Geneva: International Labour Organisation). (www.ilo.org/wcmsp5/groups/public/---dgreports/---dcomm/documents/publication/wcms_091228.pdf).

Chant, Sylvia and Sweetman, Caroline (2012) 'Fixing Women or Fixing the World? "Smart Economics", Efficiency Approaches and Gender Equality in Development', *Gender and Development*, 20:3, 517–29.

Chant, Sylvia and Touray, Isatou (2012) *Gender in the Gambia in Retrospect and Prospect*, GAMCOTRAP Working Paper No. 1 (Kanifing: GAMCOTRAP).

Chant, Sylvia and Touray, Isatou (2013) 'Women and Gender in the Gambia: Problems, Progress and Prospects', in Abdoulaye Saine, Ebrima Ceesay and Ebrima Sall (eds) *State and Society in the Gambia since Independence* (Trenton, NJ: Africa World Press), 417–70.

Chaplin, Susan E. (2011) 'Indian Cities, Sanitation and the State: The Politics of the Failure to Provide', *Environment and Urbanisation*, 23:1, 57–70.

Chatterjee, Baishali (2015) 'ActionAid's Young Urban Women Programme in Urban India: Taking an Intersectional Approach to Decent Work, Unpaid Care, and Sexual and Reproductive Health and Rights', *Gender and Development*, 23:1, 127–43.

Chatterjee, Partha (2004) *The Politics of the Governed* (New York: Columbia University Press).

Chen, Derek H. C. (2004) *Gender Equality and Economic Development: The Role for Information and Communication Technologies*, World Bank Policy Research Working Paper No. 3285 (Washington, DC: World Bank). (http://info.worldbank.org/etools/docs/library/117321/35079_wps3285.pdf).

Chen, Martha A. (2005) *Towards Economic Freedom: The Impact of SEWA* (Ahmedabad: SEWA).

Chen, Martha A. (2006) *Self-employed Women: A Profile of SEWA's Membership* (Ahmedabad: SEWA).

Chen, Martha A. (2010a) 'Informality, Poverty, and Gender: Evidence from the Global South', in Sylvia Chant (ed.) *The International Handbook of Gender and Poverty: Concepts, Research, Policy* (Cheltenham: Edward Elgar), 463–71.

Chen, Martha A. (2010b) 'Supporting Urban Livelihoods, Reducing Urban Poverty', WIEGO. (http://wiego.org/resources/supporting-urban-livelihoods-reducing-urban-poverty).

Chen, Martha A. (2010c) 'Women's Economic Empowerment: WIEGO Position and Approach', WIEGO. (http://wiego.org/sites/wiego.org/files/resources/files/Chen_Economic%20Empowerment_WIEGO_Position.pdf).

Chen, Martha A. (2011) 'Urban Employment in India: Trends and Trajectories', Powerpoint Presentation prepared for 'Inclusive Cities in India' workshop, New Delhi, 7–8 June. (www.iihs.co.in/wp-content/themes/education/resources/Inclusivecities/Day%20 1.3%20-%20Martha%20Chen%20-%20Urban%20Employment.pdf).

Chen, Martha A., Carr, Marilyn and Vanek, Joann (2004) *Mainstreaming Informal Employment and Gender in Poverty Reduction: A Handbook for Policymakers and Other Stakeholders* (London: Commonwealth Secretariat).

Chen, Martha and Skinner, Caroline (2014) 'The Urban Informal Economy: Enhanced Knowledge, Appropriate Policies and Effective Organisation', in Susan Parnell and Sophie Oldfield (eds) *The Routledge Handbook on Cities of the Global South* (London: Routledge), 219–35.

Chen, Shaohua and Ravallion, Martin (2007) 'Absolute Poverty Measures for the Developing World, 1981–2004', *Proceedings of the National Academy of Sciences USA*, 104, 16757–62.

Chikarmane, Poornima (2012) *Integrating Waste Pickers into Municipal Solid Waste Management in Pune, India*, WIEGO Policy Brief (Urban Policies) No. 8 (Manchester and Cambridge, MA: WIEGO). (www.swachcoop.com/pdf/Chikarmane_WIEGO_PB8. pdf).

Chong, Alberto and La Ferrara, Eliana (2009) 'Television and Divorce: Evidence from Brazilian Favelas', *Journal of the European Economic Association*, 7:2–3, 458–68.

Chronic Poverty Research Centre (CPRC) (2010) *Stemming Girls' Chronic Poverty* (London: ODI). (www.chronicpoverty.org/publications/details/stemming-girls-chronic-poverty).

Citizenship DRC (2011) *Blurring the Boundaries: Citizen Action across States and Societies* (Brighton: Citizenship DRC). (www.drc-citizenship.org/system/ assets/1052734700/original/1052734700-cdrc.2011-blurring.pdf).

Cole, Jennifer and Thomas, Lynn M. (eds) (2009) *Love in Africa* (Chicago: University of Chicago Press).

Comisión Económica Para América Latina y el Caribe (CEPAL) (2001) *Social Panorama of Latin America 2000–2001* (Santiago de Chile: CEPAL).

Comisión Económica Para América Latina y el Caribe (CEPAL) (2010) *Statistical Yearbook for Latin America and the Caribbean* (Santiago de Chile: CEPAL).

Comisión Económica Para América Latina y el Caribe (CEPAL) (2013) *Statistical Yearbook for Latin America and the Caribbean* (Santiago de Chile: CEPAL).

Comisión Económica Para América Latina y el Caribe (CEPAL) (2014) *Statistical Yearbook for Latin America and the Caribbean* (Santiago de Chile: CEPAL).

Commission on Legal Empowerment of the Poor (CLEP) (2008) *Making the Law Work for Everyone* (New York: Commission on Legal Empowerment of the Poor and UNDP). (www.undp.org/legalempowerment/report/).

Commonwealth Secretariat (2013) *MDGs Progress and Post-MDGs Priorities in the Commonwealth*, Discussion Paper No. 16 (London: Commonwealth Secretariat) (www. secretariat.thecommonwealth.org/files/257435/FileName/DP16MDGsProgressandPost-MDGsPriorities.pdf).

Concern Worldwide and Oxfam GB (2011) *Walking the Talk: Cash Transfers and Gender Dynamics* (Oxford: Concern Worldwide and Oxfam GB). (www.cashlearning.org/files/ Walking%20theTalk%20CT&GD_lorez.pdf).

Connell, Raewyn (2012) 'Gender, Health and Theory: Conceptualizing the Issue, in Local and World Perspective', *Social Science and Medicine*, 74, 1675–83.

Cook, Rebecca J. (2013) 'Gender, Health and Human Rights', in Michael Grodin, Daniel Tarantola, George Annas and Sofia Gruskin (eds) *Health and Human Rights in a Changing World* (London: Routledge), 341–51.

Cooper, Elizabeth (2010) *Safeguarding Inheritance: Challenges and Opportunities in African Societies* (London: Chronic Poverty Research Centre, ODI). (www.dfid.gov.uk/r4d/PDF/Outputs/ChronicPoverty_RC/PB19.pdf).

Cornman-Levy, Diane, Dyrness, Grace R., Golden, Jane, Gouverneur, David and Grisso, Jeane Ann (2011) 'Transforming Urban Environments', in Afaf Ibrahim Meleis, Eugenie L. Birch and Susan F. Wachter (eds) *Women's Health and the World's Cities* (Philadelphia: University of Pennsylvania Press),188–208.

Cornwall, Andrea (2002) *Making Spaces, Changing Places: Situating Participation in Development*, IDS Working Paper No. 173 (Falmer: University of Sussex).

Cornwall, Andrea (2004) 'Spaces for Transformation? Reflections on Issues of Power and Difference in Participation in Development', in Samuel Hickey and Giles Mohan (eds) *Participation: From Tyranny to Transformation? Exploring New Approaches to Participation in Development* (London: Zed Books), 75–91.

Cornwall, Andrea (2014) 'Taking off International Development's Straight-Jacket of Gender', *Brown Journal of World Affairs*, 21:1,127–39.

Cornwall, Andrea and Anyidoho, Nana Akua (2010) 'Women's Empowerment: Contentions and Contestations', *Development*, 53:2, 144–9.

Cornwall, Andrea, Corrêa, Sonia and Jolly, Susie (eds) (2008) *Development with a Body: Sexualities, Human Rights and Development* (London: Zed).

Cornwall, Andrea, Edström, Jerker and Greig, Alan (eds) (2011) *Men in Development: Politicising Masculinities* (London: Zed).

Cornwall, Andrea and Molyneux, Maxine (2006) 'The Politics of Rights: Dilemmas for Feminist Praxis: An Introduction', *Third World Quarterly*, 27:1, 1175–91.

Cornwall, Andrea and Molyneux, Maxine (eds) (2008) *The Politics of Rights: Dilemmas for Feminist Praxis* (London: Routledge).

Corrêa, Sonia (2008) 'Sexual and Reproductive Rights', in Vandana Desai and Robert Potter (eds) *The Companion to Development Studies*, 2nd edn (London: Hodder Arnold), 385–90.

Correa-de-Araujo, Rosaly (2011) 'Women with Disabilities and Cities', in Afaf Ibrahim Meleis, Eugenie L. Birch and Susan F. Wachter (eds) *Women's Health and the World's Cities* (Philadelphia: University of Pennsylvania Press), 110–43.

Cueto (Santiago Young Lives Project) (2005) *Social Capital and Education Outcomes in Urban and Rural Peru* (London: Save the Children UK).

Daley, Elizabeth and Pallas, Sabine (2014) 'Women and Land Deals in Africa and Asia: Weighing the Implications and Changing the Game', *Feminist Economics*, 20:1, 178–201.

Datta, Kavita, McIlwaine, Cathy, Evans, Yara, Herbert, Joanna, May, Jon and Wills, Jane (2009) 'Men on the Move: Narratives of Migration and Work among Low Paid Migrant Men in London', *Social and Cultural Geography*, 10:8, 853–73.

Davids, Tine and Van Driel, Francien (2010) 'Globalisation and the Need for a "Gender Lens": A Discussion of Dichotomies and Orthodoxies with Particular Reference to the "Feminisation of Poverty"', in Sylvia Chant (ed.) *The International Handbook of Gender and Poverty: Concepts, Research, Policy* (Cheltenham: Edward Elgar), 105–10.

Dávila, Julio, D. (2013) 'Introduction: Urban Mobility and Poverty: Lessons from Medellín and Soacha', in Julio Dávila (ed.) *Urban Mobility and Poverty: Lessons from Medellín and Soacha, Colombia* (London/Medellín: Development Planning Unit, University College London/Faculty of Architecture, Universidad Nacional de Colombia), 9–14.

Davis, Mike (2006) *Planet of Slums* (London/New York: Verso).

D'Cruz, Celine and Satterthwaite, David (2005) *Building Homes: Changing Official Approaches: The Work of Urban Poor Organisations and Their Federations, and Their Contributions to Meeting the Millennium Development Goals in Urban Areas*, Poverty Reduction in Urban Areas Series, Working Paper No. 16, International Institute for Environment and Development, London.

De Brito, Deía (2012) *God is My Alarm Clock: A Brazilian Waste Picker's Story*, WIEGO. (http://wiego.org/sites/wiego.org/files/publications/files/deBrito_WIEGO_WL1.pdf).

De Bruijn, Mirjam (2008) '"The Telephone Has Grown Legs": Mobile Communication and Social Change in the Margins of African Society', Inaugural Address, African Studies Centre, University of Leiden, September. (www.ascleiden.nl/pdf/OratieDeBruijnEng.pdf).

De Bruijn, Mirjam, Nyamnjoh, Francis and Brinkman, Inge (2009) 'Mobile Communication and New Social Spaces in Africa', in Mirjam De Bruijn, Francis Nyamnjoh and Inge Brinkman (eds) *Mobile Phones: The New Talking Drums of Everyday Africa* (Cameroon: Langaa RPCIG), 11–22.

De Certeau, Michel (1994) *The Practice of Everyday Life* (Berkeley: University of California Press).

De Menil, Victoria, Osei, Akwasi, Hill, Allan G., Yaro, Daimak Peter and De-Graft Aikens, Ama (2012) 'Symptoms of Common Mental Disorders and Their Correlates among Women in Accra, Ghana: A Population-based Survey', *Ghana Medical Journal*, 46:2, 952–103. (www.ghanamedj.org/articles/June2012/GMJS06%20Mental%20Health%20Final.pdf).

De Vreyer, Philippe, Gubert, Flore and Rakoto-Tiana, Nelly (2013) 'The Work School Trade-off among Children in West Africa: Are Household Tasks More Compatible with School than Economic Activities', in Philippe De Vreyer and François Roubaud (eds) *Urban Labor Markets in Sub-Saharan Africa* (Washington, DC: World Bank), 349–72.

Deere, Carmen Diana (2010) 'Household Wealth and Women's Poverty: Conceptual and Methodological Issues in Assessing Gender Inequality in Asset Ownership', in Sylvia Chant (ed.) *The International Handbook of Gender and Poverty: Concepts, Research, Policy* (Cheltenham: Edward Elgar), 347–52.

Deere, Carmen Diana, Alvarado, Gina E. and Twyman, Jennifer (2012) 'Gender Inequality in Asset Ownership in Latin America: Female Owners vs Household Heads', *Development and Change*, 43:2, 505–30.

Deere, Carmen Diana and Doss, Cheryl (2006) 'The Gender Asset Gap: What Do We Know and Why Does it Matter?', *Feminist Economics*, 12:1, 1–50.

Díaz Amado, Eduardo, Calderón García, Maria Cristina, Romero Cristancho, Katherine, Prada Salas, Elena and Barreto Hauzeur, Eliane (2010) 'Obstacles and Challenges Following the Partial Decriminalisation of Abortion in Colombia', *Reproductive Health Matters*, 18:36, 118–26.

Dierwechter, Yonn (2008) *Urban Growth Management and Its Discontents: Promises, Practices, and Geopolitics in US City-Regions* (New York: Palgrave Macmillan and Dawson Books).

Drechsler, Denis and Jütting, Johannes (2010) 'Why is Progress in Gender Equality so Slow? An Introduction to the Social Institutions and Gender Index', in Sylvia Chant (ed.) *The International Handbook of Gender and Poverty: Concepts, Research, Policy* (Cheltenham: Edward Elgar), 77–83.

Dobbs, Richard, Smit, Sven, Remes, Jaana, Manyika, James, Roxburgh, Charles and Restrepo, Alejandra (2011) *Urban World: Mapping the Economic Power of Cities*

(Seoul/London/New York: McKinsey Global Institute). (www.mckinsey.com/mgi/publications/urban_world/index.asp).

Dolan, Catherine S., Ryus, Caitlin R., Dopson, Sue, Montgomery, P. and Scott, Linda (2014) 'A Blind Spot in Girls' Education: Menarche and its Webs of Exclusion in Ghana', *Journal of International Development*, 26, 643–57.

Dollar, David and Gatti, Roberta (1999) *Gender Inequality, Income and Growth: Are Good Times Good for Women?*, Policy Research Report on Gender and Development Working Paper Series No. 1 (Washington, DC: World Bank).

Donner, Jonathan (2008) 'Research Approaches to Mobile Use in the Developing World: A Review of the Literature', *Information Society*, 24:3, 140–59.

Doshi, Sapana (2013) 'The Politics of the Evicted: Redevelopment, Subjectivity, and Difference, in Mumbai's Slum Frontier', *Antipode*, 45:4, 844–65.

Duany, Andres, Speck, Jeff and Lydon, Mike (2010) *The Smart Growth Manual* (New York/London: McGraw-Hill).

Dubihlela, Job and Dubihlela, Dorah (2014) 'Social Grants Impact on Poverty among the Female-headed Households in South Africa: A Case Analysis', *Mediterranean Journal of Social Sciences*, 5:8, 160–7.

Ducados, Henda (2007) 'Women in War-torn Societies: A Study of Households in Luanda's Peri-urban Areas', Unpublished M.Phil. Dissertation, Gender Institute, London School of Economics and Political Science.

Dunaway, Wilma A. (ed.) (2014) *Gendered Commodity Chains: Seeing Women's Work and Households in Global Production* (Stanford, CA: Stanford University Press).

Dutta, Shyam (2000) 'Partnerships in Urban Development: A Review of Ahmedabad's Experience', *Environment and Urbanisation*, 12:1, 13–26.

Duvvury, Nata, Callan, Aaife, Carney, Patricia and Raghavendra, Srinivas (2013) *Intimate Partner Violence: Economic Costs and Implications for Growth and Development* (Washington, DC: World Bank).

Dyson, Tim (2010) *Population and Development: The Demographic Transition* (London: Zed Books).

Economic and Social Commission for Southeast Asia (ESCAP) (2002) *Issues, Policies and Outcomes: Are ICT Policies Addressing Gender Equality?* (New York: United Nations). (www.unescap.org/esid/gad/Publication/Issues.pdf).

Economic Commission for Latin America and the Caribbean (ECLAC) (2004) *Roads towards Gender Equity in Latin America and the Caribbean* (Santiago de Chile: ECLAC).

Edström, Jerker (2014) 'The Male Order Development Encounter', *IDS Bulletin*, 45:1, 111–23.

Edström, Jerker (2015) 'Undressing Patriarchy in the Male Order Development Encounter', in Michael Flood and Richard Howson (eds) *Engaging Men in Building Gender Equality* (Cambridge: Cambridge Scholars Publishing), 71–84.

Ekblad, Solvig (1993) 'Stressful Environments and their Effects on the Quality of Life in Third World Cities', *Environment and Urbanization*, 5:2, 125–34.

Elias, Juanita (2013) 'Davos Women to the Rescue of Global Capitalism: Postfeminist Politics and Competitiveness Promotion at the World Economic Forum', *International Political Sociology*, 7, 152–69.

Ellis, Amanda, Manuel, Claire and Blackden, C. Mark (2006) *Gender and Economic Growth in Uganda: Unleashing the Power of Women* (Washington, DC: World Bank). (http://siteresources.worldbank.org/INTAFRREGTOPGENDER/Resources/gender_econ_growth_ug.pdf).

Elson, Diane (1998) 'Integrating Gender Issues into National Budgetary Policies and Procedures: Some Policy Options', *Journal of International Development*, 10, 929–41.

Elson, Diane (1999) 'Labour Markets as Gendered Institutions: Equality, Efficiency and Empowerment Issues', *World Development*, 27:3, 611–27.

Elson, Diane (2013) 'Economic Crises From the 1980s to the 2010s: A Gender Analysis', in Shirin Rai and Georgina Waylen (eds) *New Frontiers in Feminist Political Economy* (London: Routledge), 189–212.

Elson, Diane and Balakrishnan, Radhika (2013) *The Post-2015 Development Framework and the Realisation of Women's Rights and Social Justice* (New Brunswick, NJ: Centre for Women's Global Leadership, Rutgers University). (www.eldis.org/go/home&id=63562&type=Document).

Elson, Diane and Pearson, Ruth (1981) '"Nimble Fingers Make Cheap Workers": An Analysis of Women's Employment in Third World Export Manufacturing', *Feminist Review*, 7, 87–107.

Elson, Diane and Sharp, Rhonda (2010) 'Gender-responsive Budgeting and Women's Poverty', in Sylvia Chant (ed.) *The International Handbook of Gender and Poverty: Concepts, Research, Policy* (Cheltenham: Edward Elgar), 522–7.

Esplen, Emily (2009) *Gender and Care: Overview Report* (Sussex: Bridge).

Esplen, Jessica, Harper, Caroline and Jones, Nicola (2010) 'Crisis, Care and Childhood: The Impact of Economic Crisis on Care Work in Poor Households in the Developing World', *Gender and Development*, 18:2, 291–307.

Essendi, Hildah, Mills, Samuel and Fotso, Jean-Christophe (2010) 'Barriers to Formal Emergency Obstetric Care Services Utilisation', *Journal of Urban Health: Bulletin of the New York Academy of Medicine*, 88:2, 356–69.

Esser, Daniel E. (2014) 'Security Scales: Spectacular and Endemic Violence in Post-invasion Kabul, Afghanistan', *Environment and Urbanization*, 26:2, 373–88.

Evans, Alice (2013a) '"Women Can Do What Men Can Do": The Causes and Consequences of Growing Flexibility in Gender Divisions of Labour in Kitwe, Zambia', Unpublished Ph.D. Thesis, Department of Geography and Environment, London School of Economics and Political Science.

Evans, Alice (2013b) 'Why Do Gender Relations Differ between Rural and Urban Areas of Zambia?', Mimeo, Department of Geography and Environment, London School of Economics and Political Science.

Evans, Ruth (2015) 'Working with Legal Pluralism: Widowhood, Property Inheritance, and Poverty Alleviation in Urban Senegal', *Gender and Development*, 23:1, 77–94.

Fenster, Tovi (1999) 'Space for Gender: Cultural Roles of the Forbidden and the Permitted', *Environment and Planning D: Society and Space*, 17, 227–46.

Fenster, Tovi (2005a) 'The Right to the Gendered City: Different Formations of Belonging in Everyday Life', *Journal of Gender Studies*, 14:3, 217–31.

Fenster, Tovi (2005b) 'Identity Issues and Local Governance: Women's Everyday Life in the City', *Social Identities*, 11:1, 21–36.

Fenster, Tovi and Hamdan-Saliba, Hanaa (2013) 'Gender and Feminist Geographies in the Middle East', *Gender, Place and Culture*, 20:4, 528–546.

Fernando, Priyanthi, and Porter, Gina (2002) 'Bridging the Gap between Gender and Transport', in Priyanthi Fernando and Gina Porter (eds) *Balancing the Load: Women, Gender and Transport* (London: Zed Books), 1–14.

Figueroa Perea, Juan Guillermo (1998) 'Algunos Elementos para Interpretar la Presencia de los Varones en los Procesos de Salud Reproductiva', *Revista de Cadernos de Saúde Pública*, 14, Supplement 1, 87–96.

Filion, Pierre (2010) 'Urban Change on the Horizon? Smart Growth in a Recessionary Context', *Plan Canada*, 50, 38–41.

Fincher, Ruth and Iveson, Kurt (2012) 'Justice and Injustice in the City', *Geographical Research*, 50:3, 231–41.

Fleming, Andrew Sanderlin (2011) 'Making a Place for the Rich? Urban Poor Evictions and Gentrification in Woodstock, South Africa', Unpublished M.Sc. Dissertation, Department of Geography and Environment, London School of Economics and Political Science.

Floro, Maria Sagrario, Tas, Emcet Oktay and Törnqvist, Annika (2010) *The Impact of the Global Economic Crisis on Women's Wellbeing and Empowerment* (Stockholm: Sida).

Folbre, Nancy (1991) 'Women on Their Own: Global Patterns of Female Headship', in Rita Gallin and Ann Ferguson (eds) *Women and International Development Annual*, Vol. 2 (Boulder, CO: Westview), 89–106.

Folbre, Nancy (1994) *Who Pays for the Kids? Gender and the Structures of Constraint* (London: Routledge).

Fontana, Marzia and Eyben, Rosalind (2009) 'Women's Empowerment Needs in a People-centred Economy', Pathways of Women's Empowerment (Sussex: IDS). (www.pathwaysofempowerment.org/IDS_agenda_for_change.pdf).

Fox, Sean (2011) *Understanding the Origins and Pace of Africa's Urban Transition*, Crisis States Working Paper No. 89 (Series 2) (London: LSE). (http://ww2.lse.ac.uk/INternational Development/research/crisisStates/Publications/wpPhase2/wp89.aspx).

Fox, Sean (2013) *The Political Economy of Slums: Theory and Evidence from Sub-Saharan Africa*, International Development Working Paper Series No. 13-146 (London: LSE). (www2.lse.ac.uk/internationalDevelopment/pdf/WP/WP146.pdf).

Fraser, Arabella (2005) 'Approaches to Reducing Maternal Mortality: Oxfam and the MDGs', in Caroline Sweetman (ed.) *Gender and the Millennium Development Goals* (Oxford: Oxfam), 36–43.

Fraser, Nancy (1995) 'From Redistribution to Recognition? Dilemmas of Justice in a "Post-Socialist" Age', *New Left Review*, 212, 68–93.

Fraser, Nancy (2005) 'Mapping the Feminist Imagination: From Redistribution to Recognition to Representation,' *Constellations*, 12:3, 295–307.

Frenk, Julio and Gómez-Dantés, Octavio (2011) 'Women's Health in the City: A Comprehensive Approach for the Developing World', in Afaf Ibrahim Meleis, Eugenie L. Birch and Susan F. Wachter (eds) *Women's Health and the World's Cities* (Philadelphia: University of Pennsylvania Press), 15–27.

Frye, Victoria, Putnam, Sara and O'Campo, Patricia (2008) 'Whither Gender in Urban Health?', *Health and Place*, 14:3, 616–22.

Fukuda-Parr, Sakiko (1999) 'What Does Feminisation of Poverty Mean? It Isn't Just Lack of Income', *Feminist Economics*, 5:2, 99–103.

Gakuru, Mucemi, Winters, Kristen and Stepman, François (2009) *Inventory of Innovative Farmer Advisory Services Using ICTs*, Forum for Agricultural Research in Africa. (www.faraafrica.org/media/uploads/File/NSF2/RAILS/Innovative_Farmer_Advisory_Systems.pdf).

Galea, Sandro and Vlahov, David (2005) 'Urban Health: Evidence, Challenges, and Directions', *Annual Review of Public Health*, 26, 341–65.

Gambia Bureau of Statistics (GBI)/MEASURE DHS ICF International (MDII) (2013) *Gambia Demographic and Health Survey 2013: Preliminary Report* (Banjul/Calverton, MD: GBI/MDII).

Gammage, Sarah (2010) 'Time Pressed and Time Poor: Unpaid Household Work in Guatemala', *Feminist Economics*, 16:3, 79–112.

Gandelman, Nestor (2009) 'Female-headed Households and Homeownership in Latin America', *Housing Studies*, 24:4, 525–49.

García-Moreno, Claudia and Chawla, Manupreet (2011) 'Making Cities Safe for Women and Girls: Integrating a Gender Perspective into Urban Health and Planning', in Afaf Ibrahim Meleis, Eugenie L. Birch and Susan F. Wachter (eds) *Women's Health and the World's Cities* (Philadelphia: University of Pennsylvania Press), 53–69.

Gaventa, John and McGee, Rosemary (eds) (2010) *Citizen Action and National Policy Reform* (London: Zed Books).

Geleta, Esayas Bekele (2013) 'Microfinance and the Politics of Empowerment: A Critical Cultural Perspective', *Journal of Asian and African Studies*, 49, 413–25.

Geller, Alyson L. (2003) 'Smart Growth: A Prescription for Livable Cities', *American Journal of Public Health*, 93:9, 1410–15.

Gender and Development Network (GADN) (2013) *Achieving Gender Equality and Women's Empowerment in the Post-2015 Framework* (London: GADN).

Ghertner, D. Asher (2008) 'Analysis of New Legal Discourse behind Delhi's Slum Demolitions', *Economic and Political Weekly*, 17 May, 57–66.

Ghosh, Jayati (2010) *Poverty Reduction in China and India: Policy Implications of Recent Trends*, DESA Working Paper No. 92 (New York: United Nations Department for Economic and Social Affairs). (www.un.org/esa/desa/papers/2010/wp92_2010.pdf).

Gideon, Jasmine (2014) *Gender, Globalisation, and Health in a Latin American Context* (New York: Palgrave Macmillan).

Gilbert, Alan (2002) 'On the Mystery of Capital and the Myths of Hernando de Soto: What Difference Does Legal Title Make?', *International Development Planning Review*, 24:1, 1–19.

Gilbert, Alan (2003) *Rental Housing: An Essential Option for the Urban Poor in Developing Countries* (Nairobi: UN-Habitat).

Gilbert, Alan (2007) 'The Return of the Slum: Does Language Matter?', *International Journal of Urban and Regional Research*, 31:4, 697–713.

Gilbert, Alan (2009) 'Extreme Thinking about Slums and Slumdwellers: A Critique', *SAIS Review*, 29:1, 35–48.

Gilbert, Alan (2012) 'Viewpoint: De Soto's *The Mystery of Capital*: Reflections on the Book's Public Impact', *International Development Planning Review*, 34:3, v–xvii.

Gilbert, Alan and Gugler, Josef (1982) *Cities, Poverty and Development: Urbanisation in the Third World* (Oxford: Oxford University Press).

Glasier, Anna A., Gülmezoglu, Metin, Schmid, George P., Garcia Moreno, Claudia and Van Look, Paul F. A. (2006) 'Sexual and Reproductive Health: A Matter of Life and Death', *The Lancet*, 368:9547, 1595–607.

Global Campaign for Education (GCE) (2005) 'Ensuring a Fairer Chance for Girls', in Sheila Aikman and Elaine Unterhalter (eds) *Beyond Access: Transforming Policy and Practice for Gender Equality in Education* (Oxford: Oxfam), 36–59.

Goebel, Allison, Dodson, Belinda and Hill, Trevor (2010) 'Urban Advantage or Urban Penalty? A Case Study of Female-headed Households in a South African City', *Health and Place*, 16:3, 573–80.

Goetz, Anne Marie and Hassim, Shireen (eds) (2003) *No Shortcuts to Power: African Women in Politics and Decision-making* (London: Zed Books).

Gondwe, James and Ayenagbo, Kossi (2013) 'Negotiating for Livelihoods beyond the Formal Mzuzu City, Malawi, by the Urban Poor: Informal Settlements as Spaces of Income Generating Activities', *International Journal of Human Sciences*, 10:1, 356–75.

Gonzales de Olarte, Efraín and Gavilano Llosa, Pilar (1999) 'Does Poverty Cause Domestic Violence? Some Answers from Lima', in Andrew R. Morrison and María Loreto Biehl (eds) *Too Close to Home: Domestic Violence in the Americas* (Washington, DC: Inter-American Development Bank), 35–49.

González de la Rocha, Mercedes (1994) *The Resources of Poverty: Women and Survival in a Mexican City* (Oxford: Blackwell).

González de la Rocha, Mercedes (2007) 'The Construction of the Myth of Survival', *Development and Change*, 38:1, 45–66.

González de la Rocha, Mercedes (2010) 'Gender and Ethnicity in the Shaping of Differentiated Outcomes of Mexico's Progresa-Oportunidades Conditional Cash Transfer Programme', in Sylvia Chant (ed.) *The International Handbook of Gender and Poverty: Concepts, Research, Policy* (Cheltenham: Edward Elgar), 248–53.

Gough, Katherine (2010) 'Continuity and Adaptability of Home-based Enterprises: A Longitudinal Study from Accra, Ghana', *International Development Planning Review*, 32:1, 45–70.

Gough, Katherine and Kellett, Peter (2001) 'Housing Consolidation and Home-based Income Generation: Evidence from Self-help Settlements in Two Colombian Cities', *Cities*, 18:4, 235–47.

Gough, Katherine and Yankson, Paul (2011) 'A Neglected Aspect of the Housing Market: The Caretakers of Peri-urban Accra, Ghana', *Urban Studies*, 48:4, 793–810.

Graham, Wendy (2004) 'Exploring the Links between Maternal Death and Poverty', *In Focus* (UNDP International Poverty Centre), 3, 6–8. (www.undp.org/povercentre/newsletters/infocus3May04eng.pdf).

Graham, Stephen and McFarlane, Colin (2015) 'Introduction', in Stephen Graham and Colin McFarlane (eds) *Infrastructural Lives: Urban Infrastructure in Context* (London: Routledge), 1–14.

Greed, Clara (1994) *Women and Planning: Creating Gendered Realities* (London: Routledge).

Grimshaw, Damian and Rubery, Jill (2007) *Undervaluing Women's Work*, EOC Working Paper No. 53 (Manchester: Equal Opportunities Commission).

Grown, Caren (2005) 'Answering the Skeptics: Achieving Gender Equality and the Millennium Development Goals', *Development*, 48:3, 82–6.

Gruffyd Jones, Branwen (2012) '"Bankable Slums": The Global Politics of Slum Upgrading', *Third World Quarterly*, 33:5, 769–89.

Guérin, Isabelle (2006) 'Women and Money: Lessons from Senegal', *Development and Change*, 37:3, 549–70.

Gulis, Gabriel, Mulumba, Joshua Anam Amos, Juma, Olivia and Kakasova, Beatrica (2014) 'Health Status of People in Slums in Nairobi, Kenya', *Environmental Research*, 96, 219–27.

Gupta, Kamla, Arnold, Fred and Lhungdim, H. (2009) *Health and Living Conditions in Eight Indian Cities, National Family Health Survey (NFHS-3), India, 2005–6* (Mumbai/Calverton MD: International Institute for Population Sciences/ICF Macro). (www.measuredhs.com/pubs/pdf/OD58/OD58.pdf).

Gurumurthy, Anita (2004) *Gender and ICTs: Overview Report* (Brighton: Institute of Development Studies, University of Sussex).

Gutmann, Matthew (2007) *Fixing Men: Sex, Birth Control, and AIDS in Mexico.* (Berkeley: University of California Press).

Habib, Tanzima Zohra (2010) 'Socio-psychological Status of Female Heads of Households in Rajsahi City, Bangladesh', *Antrocom: Online Journal of Anthropology*, 6:2, 173–86.

Habitat for Humanity (2009) *Zambia Women Build* (Oxford: Habitat for Humanity). (www. Habitatzam.org.zm/womens_build.htm).

Hamdan-Saliba, Hanaa and Fenster, Tovi (2012) 'Tactics and Strategies of Power: The Construction of Spaces of Belonging for Palestinian Women in Jaffa – Tel Aviv', *Women's Studies International Forum*, 35, 203–13.

Hamilton, Kerry (2001) 'Gender and Transport in Developed Countries', Background Paper for 'Gender Perspectives for Earth Summit 2002: Energy, Information for Decision-making' workshop, Berlin. (www.earthsummit2002.org/workshop/Gender%20Transport%20N%20KH.pdf).

Harper, Caroline, Nowacka, Keiko, Alder, Hanna and Ferrant, Gaëlle (2014) *Measuring Women's Empowerment and Social Transformation in the Post-2015 Agenda* (London: Overseas Development Institute).

Harpham, Trudy (2009) 'Urban Health in Developing Countries: What Do We Know and Where Do We Go?', *Health and Place*, 15, 107–16.

Harris, Leila (2009) 'Gender and Emergent Water Governance: Comparative Overview of Neoliberalised Natures and Gender Dimensions of Privatisation, Devolution and Marketisation', *Gender, Place and Culture*, 16:4, 378–408.

Harris, Richard (2015) 'International Policy for Urban Housing Markets in the Global South since 1945', in Faranak Miraftab and Neema Kudva (eds) *Cities of the Global South Reader* (Abingdon/New York: Routledge), 122–33.

Harriss-White, Barbara, Olsen, Wendy, Vera-Sanso, Penny and Suresh, V. (2013) 'Multiple Shocks and Slum Household Economies in South India', *Economy and Society*, 42:3, 398–429.

Harvey, David (2008) 'The Right to the City', *New Left Review*, 53, 23–40.

Hasan, Arif, Sadiq, Asiya and Ahmed, Suneela (2010) *Planning for High Density in Low-income Settlements, Four Case Studies from Karachi*, Urbanisation and Emerging Population Issues Series Working Paper No. 3 (London: International Institute of Environment and Development).

Hausmann, Ricardo, Tyson, Laura and Zahidi, Saadia (2010) *The Global Gender Gap Report* (Geneva: World Economic Forum).

Hausmann, Ricardo, Tyson, Laura and Zahidi, Saadia (2014) *The Global Gender Gap Report* (Geneva: World Economic Forum). (www3.weforum.org/docs/GGGR14/GGGR_CompleteReport_2014.pdf).

Hawkins, Kate, MacGregor, Hayley and Oronje, Rose (2013) *The Health of Women and Girls in Urban Areas with a Focus on Kenya and South Africa: A Review*, Evidence Report No. 42 (Falmer: Institute of Development Studies, University of Sussex).

Hayes, Shannon for the Huairou Commission (2010) *Valuing and Compensating Caregivers for their Contributions to Community Health and Development in the Context of HIV and AIDS: An Agenda for Action* (New York: Huairou Commission).

Heintz, James (2006) *Globalisation, Economic Policy and Employment: Poverty and Gender Implications*, Employment Strategy Paper No. 2006/3 (Geneva: Employment Policy Unit, Employment Strategy Department, ILO).

Heintz, James (2010) 'Women's Employment, Economic Risk and Poverty', in Sylvia Chant (ed.) *The International Handbook of Gender and Poverty: Concepts, Research, Policy* (Cheltenham: Edward Elgar), 434–9.

Heise, Lori. L., Ellsberg, Mary and Gottmoeller, M. (2002) 'A Global Overview of Gender-based Violence', *International Journal of Gynecology and Obstetrics*, 78, Supplement 1, S5–S14.

Hendriks, Bob (2011) 'Urban Livelihoods and Institutions: Towards Matching Institutions for the Poor in Nairobi's Informal Settlements', *International Development Planning Review*, 33:2, 111–46.

Hernández-Pérez, Amanda (2010) 'Mujeres Indígenas Mixtecas en Oaxaca y Sinaloa: Un Estudio de Jornalerismo Femenino', Unpublished Ph.D. Dissertation, Centre for Latin American Studies, Instituto Ortega y Gasset, Madrid.

Hernández Pérez, Amanda (2012) 'Gender and the Constraints to Co-responsibility in the Context of Seasonal Migration: The Case of Mixtec Women and the Oportunidades Programme in Oaxaca, Mexico', Mimeo, Department of Geography and Environment, London School of Economics and Political Science.

Herrera, Javier, Kuépié, Mathias, Nordman, Christophe, Oudin, Xavier and Roubaud, François (2012) *Informal Sector and Informal Employment: Overview of Data for 11 Cities in 10 Countries*, WIEGO Working Paper (Statistics) No. 9. (http://wiego.org/sites/wiego.org/files/publications/files/Herrera_WIEGO_WP9.pdf).

Herselman, Stephné (2014) 'Creating Meaning through Microfinance: The Case of the Small Enterprise Foundation', *South African Review of Sociology*, 45:1, 45–65.

Hesketh, Therese and Xing, Zhu Wei (2006) 'Abnormal Sex Ratios in Human Populations: Causes and Consequences', *Proceedings of the National Academy of Sciences of the United States of America*, 103:36, 13271–5.

Hinshaw, Drew (2010) 'Senegal's Taxi Sisters Break New Ground', *Global Post*. (www.globalpost.com/dispatch/senegal/100503/taxi-sisters).

Hoa, Dao Thi Mai, Nguyet, Do Anh, Phuong, Nguyen Hoang, Phuong, Dang Thu, Nga, Vu Thu, Few, Roger and Winkels, Alexandra (2013) *Heat Stress and Adaptive Capacity of Low-income Outdoor Workers and Their Families in the City of Da Nang, Vietnam*, Asian Cities Climate Resilience Working Paper Series No. 3 (London: International Institute for Environment and Development).

Holden, Stein with Tefera, Tewodras (2008) 'From Being Property of Men to Becoming Equal Owners? Early Impacts of Land Registration and Certification on Women in Southern Ethiopia', Mimeo, Final Research Report prepared for UN-Habitat, Shelter Branch, Land Tenure and Property Administration Section, Nairobi. (http://arken.umb.no/~steiho/HoldenTefera2008From_Being_Property_of_Men_to_becoming_Equal_Owners.pdf), .

Holmqvist, Göran (2009) *HIV and Income Inequality: If There is a Link, What Does it Tell Us?*, Working Paper No. 54 (Brasilia: International Policy Centre for Inclusive Growth). (www.ipc-undp.org/pub/IPCWorkingPaper54.pdf).

Horn, Zoe Elena (2010) 'The Effects of the Global Economic Crisis on Women in the Informal Economy: Research Findings from WIEGO and the Inclusive Cities Partners', *Gender and Development*, 18:2, 263–76.

House, Sarah, Mahon, Therese and Cavill, Sue (2012) *Menstrual Hygiene Matters: A Resource for Improving Menstrual Hygiene around the World* (London: WaterAid). (www.wateraid.org/uk/what-we-do/our-approach/research-and-publications/view-publication?id=02309d73-8e41-4d04-b2ef-6641f6616a4f).

Hovorka, Alice, de Zeeuw, Henk and Njenga, Mary (eds) (2009) *Women Feeding Cities: Mainstreaming Gender in Urban Agriculture and Food Security* (Leusden: Resource Centers on Urban Agriculture and Food Security Foundation/RUAF).

Huairou Commission (2004) *Local to Local Dialogue: A Grassroots Women's Perspective on Good Governance (Resources on Tools and Methods)* (New York: Huairou Commission).

Huairou Commission (2010a) *Transforming Development: Creating Synergies between Grassroots Women and Institutions of Governance* (New York: Huairou Commission).

Huairou Commission (2010b) *Grassroots Women and Decentralised Governance Change through Partnership* (New York: Huairou Commission).

Huairou Commission (2011) *Global Summit on Grassroots Women's Leadership and Governance* (New York: Huairou Commission).

Huchzermeyer, Marie (2014) 'Troubling Continuities: Use and Utility of the Term "Slum"', in Susan Parnell and Sophie Oldfield (eds) *The Routledge Handbook on Cities of the Global South* (London: Routledge), 86–97.

Hughes, Katherine and Wickeri, Elisabeth (2011) 'A Home in the City: Women's Struggle to Secure Adequate Housing in Urban Tanzania', *Fordham International Law Journal*, 34:4, 788–929. (http://law.fordham.edu/publications/index.ihtml?pubid=300).

Huisman, Henk (2005) 'Contextualising Chronic Exclusion: Female-headed Households in Semi-arid Zimbabwe', *Tijdschrift voor Economische en Sociale Geografie*, 96:3, 253–63.

Hume, Mo (2004) '"It's as if You Don't Know Anything about it, because You Don't Do Anything about it"': Gender and Violence in El Salvador', *Environment and Urbanization*, 16:2, 63–72.

Hunt, Swanee (2014) 'The Rise of Rwanda's Women: Rebuilding and Reuniting a Nation', *Foreign Affairs*, 93:3, 150–7.

Inclusive Cities Project (ICP) (2009) *Home-based Garment Workers: The Impact of the Self Employed Women's Association (SEWA)*. (www.inclusivecities.org/pdfs/IUP_Story_Garment_Workers.pdf).

Institute for Women's Policy Research (IWPR) (2015) *Gender, Urbanisation and Democratic Governance*, White Paper commissioned by the National Democratic Institute (Washington, DC: IWPR).

International Labour Organisation (ILO) (2001) *Report of the Director General: Reducing the Decent Work Deficit – A Global Challenge* (Geneva: ILO). (www.ilo.org/public/english/standards/velm/ilc/ilc89/rep-i-a.htm).

International Labour Organisation (ILO) (2002) *Women and Men in the Informal Economy: A Statistical Picture* (Geneva: ILO). (www.ilo.org/public/libdoc/ilo/2002/102B09_139_engl.pdf).

International Labour Organisation (ILO) (2003) *Report of the Director General: Working Out of Poverty* (Geneva: ILO).

International Labour Organisation (ILO) (2005a) *Decent Work Indicators Database*. (www.oitsial.org.pa/td.paise).

International Labour Organisation (ILO) (2005b) *Gender Equality and Decent Work: Good Practices at the Workplace* (Geneva: ILO). (www.ilo.org/dyn/gender/docs/RES/309/F946263477/WEB).

International Labour Organisation (ILO) (2006) *Global Employment Trends for Youth* (Geneva: ILO). (www.ilo.org/wcmsp5/groups/public/---ed_emp/---emp_elm/---trends/documents/publication/wcm_041929.pdf.

International Labour Organisation (ILO) (2008a) *Youth Employment: Breaking Gender Barriers for Young Men and Women* (Geneva: ILO). (www.ilo.org/wcmsp5/groups/public/@dgreports/@gender/documents/publication/wcms_097919.pdf).

International Labour Organisation (2008b) 'Skills for Improved Productivity, Employment Growth and Development', International Labour Conference, 97th Session, Report V (Geneva: ILO). (www.ilo.org/public/libdoc/ilo/2008/108B09_54_engl.pdf).

International Labour Organisation (ILO) (2009) *Global Employment Trends for Women* (Geneva: ILO). (www.ilo.org/wcmsp5/groups/public/---dgreports/---dcomm/documents/publication/wcms_103456.pdf).

International Labor Organisation (ILO) (2010a) *Women in Labour Markets: Measuring Progress and Identifying Challenges* (Geneva: ILO). (www.ilocarib.org.tt/portal/images/stories/contenido/pdf/Gender/WD-Women2010_123835.pdf).

International Labour Organisation (ILO) (2010b) *Global Employment Trends 2010* (Geneva: ILO). (www.ilo.org/wcmsp5/groups/public/---ed_emp/---emp_elm/---trends/documents/publication/wcms_120471.pdf).

International Labour Organisation (ILO) (2010c) *Maternity at Work: A Review of National legislation Findings from the ILO Database of Conditions of Work and Employment Laws*, 2nd edn (Geneva : ILO). (www.ilo.org/wcmsp5/groups/public/@dgreports/@dcomm/@publ/documents/publication/wcms_124442.pdf).

International Labour Organisation (ILO) (2011) *Global Employment Trends 2011: The Challenge of a Jobs Recovery* (Geneva: ILO). (www.ilo.org/wcmsp5/groups/public/@dgreports/@dcomm/@publ/documents/publication/wcms_150440.pdf).

International Labour Organisation (ILO) (2014) *Global Employment Trends 2014: Risk of a Jobless Recovery?* (Geneva: ILO). (www.ilo.org/wcmsp5/groups/public/---dgreports/---dcomm/---publ/documents/publication/wcms_233953.pdf).

International Telecommunication Union (ITU) (2009) *Measuring the Information Society* (Geneva: ITU). (www.itu.int/itU-d/ict/publications/idi/2009/material/idi2009_w5.pdf).

International Trade Centre (ITC) (2009) *ITC Lends 'Mobile' Hand to Liberian Women*, Press Release (Geneva: ITC). (http://mmd4d.files.wordpress.com/2009/04/tah-pres-release.pdf).

International Trade Centre (ITC) and Ministry of Commerce and Industry of Liberia (MCIL) (2009) *Trade at Hand for Liberia's Market Women: Business Opportunities on Your Cell Phone* (Geneva: ITC). (http://mmd4d.files.wordpress.com/2009/04/090305_tah_factsheet.pdf).

International Trade Union Confederation (ITUC) (2009) *Gender (In)Equality in the Labour Market: An Overview of Global Trends And Developments* (Brussels: ITUC).

International Water Association (IWA) (2014) *An Avoidable Crisis: WASH Human Resource Capacity Gaps in 15 Developing Economies* (Seacourt: IWA). (www.iwa-network.org/downloads/1422745887-an-avoidable-crisis-wash-gaps.pdf).

Izutsu, Takashi, Tsutsumi, Atsuro, Islam, Akramul M., Kato, Seiko, Wakai, Susumu and Kurita, Hiroshi (2006) 'Mental Health, Quality of Life, and Nutritional Status of Adolescents in Dhaka, Bangladesh: Comparison between an Urban Slum and a Non-slum Area', *Social Science and Medicine*, 63, 1477–88.

Ivens, Saskia (2008) 'Does Increased Water Access Empower Women', *Development*, 51:1, 53–7.

Izazola, Haydea (2004) 'Migration to and from Mexico City 1995–2000', *Environment and Urbanisation*, 16:1, 211–29.

Izazola, Haydea, Martínez, Caroline and Marquette, Catherine (2006) 'Environmental Perceptions, Social Class and Demographic Change in Mexico City: A Comparative Approach', in Cecilia Tacoli (ed.) *Earthscan Reader in Rural–Urban Linkages* (London: Earthscan), 252–7.

Izugbara, Chimaraoke O. and Ngilangwa, David P. (2010) 'Women, Poverty and Adverse Maternal Outcomes in Nairobi, Kenya', *BMC Women's Health*, 10:33. (www.biomedcentral.com/1472-6874/10/33).

Izugbara, Chimaraoke O. and Wekesa, Eliud (2011) 'Beliefs and Practices about Antiretroviral Medication: A Study of Poor Urban Kenyans Living with HIV/AIDS', *Sociology of Health and Illness*, 33:6, 869–83.

Izutsu, Takashi, Tsutsumi, Atsuro, Islam, Akramul M., Kato, Seiko, Wakai, Susumu and Kurita, Hiroshi (2006) 'Mental Health, Quality of Life, and Nutritional Status of Adolescents in Dhaka, Bangladesh: Comparison between an Urban Slum and a Non-slum Area', *Social Science and Medicine*, 63, 1477–88.

Jabeen, Huraera (2014) 'Adapting the Built Environment: The Role of Gender in Shaping Vulnerability and Resilience to Climate Extremes in Dhaka', *Environment and Urbanization*, 26:1, 1–19.

Jackson, Cecile (1996) 'Rescuing Gender from the Poverty Trap', *World Development*, 24:3, 489–504.

Jackson, Cecile (2003) 'Gender Analysis of Land: Beyond Land Rights for Women?', *Journal of Agrarian Change*, 3:4, 453–80.

Jacobs, Jane (1996) *The Death and Life of Great American Cities* (New York: Modern Press).

JAGORI in collaboration with Women in Cities International (2010) *A Handbook on Women's Safety Audits in Low-income Urban Neighbourhoods: A Focus on Essential Services* (New Delhi: Jagori). (https://d3gxp3iknbs7bs.cloudfront.net/attachments/f4c63d91-b547-45f7-a656-77103382344a.pdf).

Jagun, Abi, Heeks, Richard and Whalley, Jason (2007) *Mobile Telephony and Developing Country Micro-enterprise: A Nigerian Case Study*, Working Paper No. 29 (Manchester: Development Informatics, Institute for Development Policy and Management, University of Manchester). (www.sed.manchester.ac.uk/idpm/research/publications/wp/di/documents/di_wp29.pdf).

Jahn, Albrecht, Beiermann, Claudia and Müller, Olaf (2013) 'The Prescription for Women's Health: The MDGs and beyond', in United Nations Association (UNA)-UK (ed.) *Global Development Goals: Leaving No-one behind* (London: UNA-UK), 107–11.

Järvelä, Marja and Rinne-Koistinenm, Eva-Marita (2005) 'Purity and Dirt as Social Constructions: Environmental Health in an Urban Shantytown of Lagos', *International Journal of Urban and Regional Research*, 29:2, 375–88.

Jarvis, Helen with Cloke, Jonathan and Kantor, Paula (2009) *Cities and Gender: Critical Introductions to Urbanism and the City* (London: Routledge).

Jeffery, Patricia and Jeffery, Roger (1998) 'Silver Bullet or Passing Fancy: Girls' Schooling and Population Policy', in Cecile Jackson and Ruth Pearson (eds) *Feminist Visions of Development* (London: Routledge), 239–58.

Jennings, Michael (2005) 'Chinese Medicine and Medical Pluralism in Dar es Salaam: Globalisation or Glocalisation?', *International Relations*, 19:4, 457–73.

Jensen, Robert and Oster, Emily (2009) 'The Power of TV: Cable Television and Women's Status in India', *Quarterly Journal of Economics*, 127:2, 753–92.

Jewitt, Sarah and Ryley, Harriet (2014) '"It's a Girl Thing": Menstruation, School Attendance, Spatial Mobility and Wider Gender Inequalities in Kenya', *Geoforum*, 56, 137–47.

Jewkes, Rachel, Vundule, Caesar, Maforah, Fidelia and Jordaan, Esme (2001) 'Relationship Dynamics and Teenage Pregnancy in South Africa', *Social Science and Medicine*, 52, 733–44.

Johnson, Robert (2005) 'Not a Sufficient Condition: The Limited Relevance of the Gender MDG to Women's Progress', in Caroline Sweetman (ed.) *Gender and the Millennium Development Goals* (Oxford: Oxfam), 56–66.

Johnson-Sirleaf, Ellen (2008) 'The Challenge of Gender Equity in Infrastructure Reconstruction in Liberia', Keynote Speech at 'The Role of Infrastructure in Women's Economic Empowerment' workshop, Fourth Tokyo International Conference on African Development, 28–30 May. (http://web.worldbank.org/WBSITE/EXTERNAL/TOPICS/EXTGENDER/0,,contentMDK:21764076~menuPK:336874~pagePK:148956~piPK:216618~theSitePK:336868,00.html).

Johnsson-Latham, Gerd (2004) 'Understanding Female and Male Poverty and Deprivation', in Gerd Johnsson-Latham (ed.) *Power and Privileges: Gender Discrimination and Poverty* (Stockholm: Regerinskanliet) 16–45.

Johnsson-Latham, Gerd (2010) 'Power, Privilege and Gender as Reflected in Poverty Analysis and Development', in Sylvia Chant (ed.) *The International Handbook of Gender and Poverty: Concepts, Research, Policy* (Cheltenham: Edward Elgar), 41–6.

Jolly, Susie and Reeves, Hazel (2005) *Gender and Migration* (Sussex: Bridge IDS). (www.bridge.ids.ac.uk/reports/CEP-Mig-OR.pdf).

Jones, Gareth A. (2011) 'Slumming about: Aesthetics, Art and Politics', *City*, 15:6, 695–707.

Jones, Gareth A. and Chant, Sylvia (2009) 'Globalising Initiatives for Gender Equality and Poverty Reduction: Exploring "Failure" with Reference to Education and Work among Urban Youth in the Gambia and Ghana', *Geoforum*, 40:2, 84–96.

Jones, Gareth A. and Corbridge, Stuart (2008) 'Urban Bias', in Vandana Desai and Robert Potter (eds) *The Companion to Development Studies*, 2nd edn (London: Hodder Arnold), 243–7.

Jones, Gareth A. and Corbridge, Stuart (2010) 'The Continuing Debate about Urban Bias: The Thesis, its Critics, its Influence and its Implications for Poverty-reduction Strategies', *Progress in Development Studies*, 10:1, 1–18.

Jones, Gareth A. and Rodgers, Dennis (eds) (2009) *Youth Violence in Latin America: Gangs and Juvenile Justice in Perspective* (New York: Palgrave Macmillan).

Jones, Gareth A. and Thomas de Benítez, Sarah (2010) 'Youth, Gender and Work on the Streets of Mexico', in Sylvia Chant (ed.) *The International Handbook of Gender and Poverty: Concepts, Research, Policy* (Cheltenham: Edward Elgar), 195–200.

Jones, Harry, Cummings, Clare and Nixon, Hamish (2014) *Services in the City: Governance and the Political Economy in Urban Service Delivery* (London: ODI). (www.odi.org/publications/9115-urban-service-delivery-governance).

Joshi, Deepa (2013) 'Apolitical Stories of Sanitation and Suffering Women', in Tina Wallace and Fenella Porter with Mark Ralph-Bowman (eds) *Aid, NGOs and the Realities of Women's Lives: A Perfect Storm* (Rugby: Practical Action), 215–26.

Joshi, Deepa, Fawcett, Ben and Mannan, Fouzia (2011) 'Health, Hygiene and Appropriate Sanitation: Experiences and Perceptions of the Urban Poor', *Environment and Urbanization*, 23:1, 91–112.

Jovchelovitch, Sandra and Priego-Hernández, Jacqueline (2013) *Underground Sociabilities: Identity, Culture and Resistance in Rio de Janeiro's Favelas* (Brasilia: United Nations Educational, Scientific and Cultural Organization, Brasilia Office).

Jütting, Johannes, Parlevliet, Jante and Xongiani, Theodora (2008) *Informal Employment Re-loaded*, OECD Development Centre Working Paper No. 266 (Paris: OECD). (www.oecd.org/dataoecd/4/7/39900874.pdf).

Kabeer, Naila (2003) *Gender Mainstreaming in Poverty Eradication and the Millennium Development Goals: A Handbook for Policy-makers and Other Stakeholders* (London: Commonwealth Secretariat).

Kabeer, Naila (2008a) *Paid Work, Women's Empowerment and Gender Justice: Critical Pathways of Social Change*, Pathways Working Paper No. 3 (Brighton: Institute of Development Studies, University of Sussex). (www.pathwaysofempowerment.org/PathwaysWP3-website.pdf).

Kabeer, Naila (2008b) *Mainstreaming Gender in Social Protection for the Informal Economy* (London: Commonwealth Secretariat).

Kabeer, Naila (2013) 'The Rise of the Female Breadwinner: Reconfigurations of Marriage, Motherhood, and Masculinity in the Global Economy', in Shirin Rai and Georgina Waylen (eds) *New Frontiers in Feminist Political Economy* (London: Routledge), 62–84.

Kabeer, Naila, Mahmud, Simeen and Castro, Jairo (2010) *NGOs' Strategies and the Challenge of Development and Democracy in Bangladesh*, IDS Working Paper No. 343 (Brighton: Institute of Development Studies, University of Sussex). (www.ntd.co.uk/idsbookshop/details.asp?id=1179).

Kabeer, Naila, Mahmoud, Simeen and Tasneem, Sakiba (2011*) Does Paid Work Provide a Pathway to Women's Empowerment? Empirical Findings from Bangladesh*, IDS Working Paper No. 375 (Brighton: Institute of Development Studies, University of Sussex).

Kabeer, Naila and Natali, Luisa (2013) *Gender Equality and Economic Growth: Is There a Win–Win?*, IDS Working Paper No.417 (Brighton: Institute of Development Studies, University of Sussex).

Kamndaya, Mphatso, Kazembe, Lawrence, Vearey, Jo, Kabiru, Caroline and Thomas, Liz (2015) 'Material Deprivation and Unemployment Affect Coercive Sex among Young People in the Urban Slums of Blantyre, Malawi: A Multi-level Approach', *Health and Place*, 33, 90–100.

Kantor, Paula (2002) 'Female Mobility in India: The Influence of Seclusion Norms on Economic Outcomes', *International Development Planning Review*, 24:2, 145–59.

Kantor, Paula (2010) 'A Gendered Analysis of Decent Work Deficits in India's Informal Economy: Case Study Perspectives from Surat', in Sylvia Chant (ed.) *The International Handbook of Gender and Poverty: Concepts, Research, Policy* (Cheltenham: Edward Elgar), 478–83.

Kar, Kamal with Chambers, Robert (2008) *Handbook on Community-led Total Sanitation* (London/Falmer: PLAN UK/IDS). (www.communityledtotalsanitation.org/).

Kasiira Ziraba, Abdhalah, Madise, Nyovani, Mills, Samuel, Kyobutungi, Catherine and Ezeh, Alex (2009) 'Maternal Mortality in the Informal Settlements of Nairobi City: What Do We Know?', *Reproductive Health*, 6:6, 1–8.

Katz, Cindi (1993) 'Growing Girls/Closing Circles: Limits on the Spaces of Knowing in Rural Sudan and US Cities', in Cindi Katz and Janice Monk (eds) *Full Circles: Geographies of Women over the Lifecourse* (London: Routledge), 88–106.

Keith, Michael, Lash, Scott, Arnoldi, Jakob and Rooker, Tyler (2013) *China Constructing Capitalism: Economic Life and Urban Change* (London: Routledge).

Keiner, Marco, Koll-Schretzenmayr, Martina and Schmid, Willy A. (2005) *Managing Urban Futures: Sustainability and Urban Growth in Developing Countries* (Aldershot: Ashgate).

Kelbert, Alexandra and Hossain, Naomi (2014) 'Poor Man's Patriarchy: Gender Roles and Global Crises', *IDS Bulletin*, 45:1, 21–8.

Kellett, Peter and Tipple, Graham (2011) 'The Home as a Workplace: A Study of Income-generating Activities within the Domestic Setting', *Environment and Urbanization*, 12:1, 203–14.

Kern, Leslie and Mullings, Beverley (2013) 'Urban Neoliberalism, Urban Insecurity and Urban Violence', in Linda Peake and Martina Rieker (eds) *Rethinking Feminist Interventions into the Urban* (London: Routledge), 23–40.

Khan, Md Mobarak Hossain, Khan, Aklimunnessa, Kraemer, Alexander and Mori, Mitsuru (2009) 'Prevalence and Correlates of Smoking among Urban Adult Men in Bangladesh: Slum versus Non-slum Comparison', *BMC Public Health*, 9, 149–62. (www.ncbi.nlm. nih.gov/pmc/articles/PMC2705350/).

Khosla, Prabha, Van Wijk, Christine, Verhagen, Joep and James, Viju (2004) *Gender and Water: Thematic Overview Paper* (The Hague: IRC International Water and Sanitation Centre). (www.irc.nl/content/download/14459/194371/file/Gender.pdf).

Khosla, Rena (2009) *Addressing Gender Concerns in India's Urban Renewal Mission* (New Delhi: UNDP). (http://data.undp.org.in/dg/pub/AddressingGenderConcerns.pdf).

Kinyanjui, Mary Njeri (2014) *Women and the Informal Economy in Urban Africa: From the Margins to the Centre* (Uppsala/London: NordiskAfrikainstutet/Zed).

Kiwala, Lucia (2005) 'Human Settlements: A Concern for Women in the Coming Decade', *Habitat Debate*, 11:1, 4–5.

Klasen, Stephan (2002) 'Low Schooling for Girls, Slower Growth for All? Cross-country Evidence on the Effect of Gender Inequality in Education on Economic Development', *World Bank Economic Review*, 16:3, 345–73.

Klasen, Stephan, Lechtenfeld, Tobias and Povel, Felix (2015) 'A Feminization of Vulnerability? Female Headship, Poverty, and Vulnerability in Thailand and Vietnam', *World Development*, 71, 36–51.

Klein, Michael W., Moser, Christoph and Urban, Dieter M. (2010) *The Contribution of Trade to Wage Inequality: The Role of Skill, Gender, and Nationality* (Cambridge: National Bureau of Economic Research).

Kleine, Dorothea (2013) *Technologies of Choice? ICTs, Development and the Capabilities Approach* (Cambridge, MA: MIT Press).

Knodel, John and Ofstedal, Mary Beth (2003) 'Gender and Ageing in the Developing World: Where Are the Men?', *Population and Development Review*, 29, 677–98.

Kothari, Miloon (2005) 'A "Culture of Silence" on Women's Rights to Housing and Land', *Habitat Debate*, 11:1, 8.

Kovats, Sari, Lloyd, Simon and Scovronick, Noah (2014) *Climate Change and Health in Informal Settlements*, Working Paper (London International Institute of Environment and Development/London School of Hygiene and Tropical Medicine). (http://pubs.iied. org/pdfs/10719IIED.pdf).

Krug, Etienne G., Dahlberg, Linda L., Mercy, James A., Zwi Anthony B. and Lozano, Rafael (2002) *World Report on Violence and Health 2002* (Geneva: World Health Organization).

Kruijt, Dirk and Koonings, Kees (2009) 'The Rise of Megacities and the Urbanisation of Informality, Exclusion and Violence', in Dirk Kruijt and Kees Koonings (eds) *Megacities: The Politics of Urban Exclusion and Violence in the Global South* (London: Zed Books), 8–26.

Kumar, Sunil (2010) 'Gender, Livelihoods and Rental Housing Markets in the Global South: The Urban Poor as Landlords and Tenants', in Sylvia Chant (ed.) *The International Handbook of Gender and Poverty: Concepts, Research, Policy* (Cheltenham: Edward Elgar), 367–72.

Kunieda, Mika and Gauthier, Aimee (2007) *Gender and Urban Transport: Smart and Affordable* (GTZ: Eschborn). (www.itdp.org/documents/7aGenderUT(Sept).pdf).

Langevang, Thilde and Gough, Katherine (2012) 'Diverging Pathways: Young Female Employment and Entrepreneurship in Sub-Saharan Africa', *Geographical Journal*, 178:3, 242–52.

Langevang, Thilde, Namatovu, Rebecca and Dawu, Samuel (2012) 'Beyond Necessity and Opportunity Entrepreneurship: Motivations and Aspirations of Young Entrepreneurs in Uganda', *International Development Planning Review*, 34:4, 439–59.

Larkin, Brian (2013) 'The Politics and Poetics of Infrastructure', *Annual Review of Anthropology*, 42, 327–43.

Larsson, Anita (1989) *Women Householders and Housing Strategies: The Case of Gaborone, Botswana* (Gävle: National Swedish Institute for Building Research).

Lees, Loretta (2004) *The Emancipatory City? Paradoxes and Possibilities* (London: Sage).

Lefebvre, Henri (1986) *Writings on Cities* (Oxford: Blackwell).

Lenoël, Audrey (2014) 'Burden or Empowerment? The Impact of Migration and Remittances on Women Left Behind in Morocco', Unpublished Ph.D. Dissertation, Faculty of Social Sciences and Law, University of Bristol.

Lessinger, Joanna (1990) 'Work and Modesty: The Dilemma of Women Market Traders in Madras', in Leela Dube and Rajni Palriwala (eds) *Structures and Strategies* (New Delhi: Sage), 129–50.

Levine, Ruth (2011) 'Policy for a Better Future: A Focus on Girls and Women', in Afaf Ibrahim Meleis, Eugenie L. Birch and Susan F. Wachter (eds) *Women's Health and the World's Cities* (Philadelphia: University of Pennsylvania Press), 28–34.

Levy, Caren (1992) 'Transport', in Lise Østergaard (ed.) *Gender and Development: A Practical Guide* (London: Routledge), 94–109.

Levy, Caren (1996) *The Process of Institutionalising Gender in Policy and Planning: The 'Web' of Institutionalisation*, Development Planning Unit Working Paper No. 72, (London: The Bartlett, University College London).

Levy, Caren (2009) 'Viewpoint: Gender Justice in a Diversity Approach to Development? The Challenges for Development Planning', *International Development Planning Review*, 31:4, i–xi.

Levy, Caren (2013a) 'Travel Choice Reframed: "Deep Distribution" and Gender in Urban Transport', *Environment and Urbanization*, 25:1, 47–63.

Levy, Caren (2013b) 'Transport, Diversity, and the Socially Just City: The Significance of Gender Relations', in Julio Dávila (ed.) *Urban Mobility and Poverty: Lessons from Medellín and Soacha, Colombia* (London/Medellín: Development Planning Unit, University College London/Faculty of Architecture, Universidad Nacional de Colombia), 23–9.

Li, Bingqin and Shin, Hyun Bang (2013) 'Intergenerational Housing Support between Retired Old Parents and Their Children in Urban China', *Urban Studies*, 50, 3025–44.

Liberian Observer (2009) 'Buying and Selling on Mobile Phones: Market Women and Farmers Connect for Less', *All West Africa*, 21 June. (www.allwestafrica.com/21062009447.html).

Lind, Amy (2002) 'Making Feminist Sense of Neoliberalism: The Institutionalisation of Women's Struggles for Survival in Ecuador and Bolivia', *Journal of Developing Societies*, 18, 228–58.

Lind, Amy (2010) 'Gender, Neoliberalism and Post-neoliberalism: Reassessing the Institutionalisation of Women's Struggle for Survival in Ecuador and Venezuela', in

Sylvia Chant (ed.) *The International Handbook of Gender and Poverty: Concepts, Research, Policy* (Cheltenham: Edward Elgar), 649–54.

Lind, Amy and Farmelo, Martha (1996) *Global and Urban Social Movements: Women's Community Responses to Restructuring and Urban Poverty*, Discussion Paper DP76 (Geneva: UNRISD/UNV). (www.unrisd.org/unrisd/website/document.nsf/0/c59d935ec 5987d6180256b65004ff007/$FILE/dp76e.pdf).

Little, Jo (1994) *Gender, Planning and the Policy Process* (London: Pergamon).

Livingston, Jessica (2004) 'Murder in Juárez: Gender, Sexual Violence, and the Global Assembly Line', *Frontiers: A Journal of Women's Studies*, 25:1, 50–76.

Lloyd, Cynthia B. (2009) *The Power of Educating Adolescent Girls: A Girls Count Report on Adolescent Girls* (New York: Population Council). (www.popcouncil.org/ pdfs/2009PGY_NewLessons.pdf).

Lloyd, Peter Cutt (1979) *Slums of Hope? Shanty Towns of the Third World* (Harmondsworth: Penguin).

Loyka, Mark (2011) 'Inequality and Poverty in Latin America: Can the Decline Continue?', Daily Latin News (Washington, DC: Council on Hemispheric Affairs). (www.coha.org/ inequality-and-poverty-in-latin-america-can-the-decline-continue/).

Lucas, Linda E. (2007) *Unpacking Globalisation: Markets, Gender, and Work* (Lanham, MD: Lexington Books).

Lugo, Jaire and Sampson, Tony (2008) 'E-informality in Venezuela: The "Other Path" of Technology', *Bulletin of Latin American Research*, 27:1, 102–18.

Mabala, Richard (2011) 'Youth and "the Hood" – Livelihoods and Neighbourhoods', *Environment and Urbanisation*, 23:1, 157–81.

Maclean, Kate (2010) 'Capitalising on Women's Social Capital: Gender and Microfinance in Bolivia', in Sylvia Chant (ed.) *The International Handbook of Gender and Poverty: Concepts, Research, Policy* (Cheltenham: Edward Elgar), 569–74.

Maclean, Kate (2014) *The Medellín Miracle: The Politics of Crisis, Elites and Coalitions*, Development Leadership Program Research Paper No. 24 (London: Birkbeck College, University of London).

Madise, Nyovani, Kiraba, Abdalah K., Inungu, Joseph, Khamadi, Samoel A., Ezeh, Alex, Zulu, Eliya M.,Okoth, Vincent and Mwau, Matilu (2012) 'Are Slum Dwellers at Heightened Risk of HIV Infection than Other Urban Residents? Evidence from Population-based HIV Prevalence Surveys in Kenya', *Health and Place*, 18:5, 1144–52.

Mahon, Thérèse and Fernandes, Maria (2010) 'Menstrual Hygiene in South Asia: A Neglected Issue for WASH (Water, Sanitation and Hygiene) Programmes', *Gender and Development*, 18:1, 99–113.

Malaza, Nqobile, Todes, Alison and Williamson, Amanda (2009) *Gender in Planning and Urban Development*, Commonweath Secretariat Discussion Paper No. 7 (London: Commonwealth Secretariat).

Malhotra, Anju (2011) 'Accidental Empowerment', USAID Impact blog. (http://blog. usaid.gov/2011/04/accidental-empowerment).

Manda, Mtafu A. Z., Nkoma, Siku and Mitlin, Diana (2011) *Understanding Pro-poor Housing Finance in Malawi*, Human Settlements Working Paper No. 32, Poverty Reduction in Urban Areas (London: International Institute of Environment and Development).

Martin, Tracey (2003) 'Gambian Schools and the UN Convention on the Rights of the Child', Unpublished Dissertation submitted in part requirement for M.Ed. in Inclusive Education, University of Sheffield.

Martine, George, Eustaquio Alves, José and Cavenaghi, Suzana (2013) *Urbanization and Fertility Decline: Cashing in on Structural Change*, Working Paper (London: International Institute of Environment and Development).

Masika, Rachel with de Haan, Arjan and Baden, Sally (1997) *Urbanisation and Urban Poverty: A Gender Analysis*, Bridge Development–Gender Report No. 54 (Brighton: Institute of Development Studies).

Massey, Doreen (1994) *Space, Place and Gender* (Minneapolis: University of Minnesota Press).

Massey, Doreen (1995) *Spatial Divisions of Labour: Social Structures and the Geography of Production*, 2nd edn (New York: Routledge).

Mayoux, Linda (2006) *Women's Empowerment through Sustainable Micro-finance: Rethinking 'Best Practice'*, Discussion Paper, Gender and Micro-finance website. (www.genfinance.net).

McDowell, Linda (1983) 'Towards an Understanding of the Gender Division of Urban Space', *Environment and Planning D: Society and Space*, 1, 59–72.

McDowell, Linda (1999) *Gender, Identity and Place: Understanding Feminist Geographies* (Minneapolis: University of Minnesota Press).

McDowell, Linda, Ward, Kevin, Fagan, Colette, Perrons, Diane and Ray, Kath (2006) 'Connecting Time and Space: The Significance of Transformations in Women's Work in the City', *International Journal of Urban and Regional Research*, 30:1, 141–58.

McGranahan, Gordon and Satterthwaite, David (2014) *Urbanisation: Concepts and Trends*, Working Paper (London: International Institute for Environment and Development). (http://pubs.iied.org/pdfs/10709IIED.pdf).

McIlwaine, Cathy (2010) 'Migrant Machismos: Exploring Gender Ideologies and Practices among Latin American Migrants in London from a Multi-scalar Perspective', *Gender, Place and Culture*, 17:3, 281–300.

McIlwaine, Cathy (2011) 'Spatial Practices and Super-diversity among Latin American Migrants in London from a Multi-scalar Perspective', in Cathy McIlwaine (ed.) *Cross-Border Migration among Latin Americans: European Perspectives and beyond* (New York: Palgrave Macmillan), 93–117.

McIlwaine, Cathy (2012) 'Overview. Women's Economic Empowerment: Critical Issues for Prosperous Cities', Paper prepared for UN Habitat/Huairou Commission Expert Group Meeting, Cambridge, MA, 11–13 June.

McIlwaine, Cathy (2013) 'Urbanisation and Gender-based Violence: Exploring the Paradoxes in the Global South', *Environment and Urbanization*, 25:1, 65–79.

McIlwaine, Cathy (2014a) 'Gender- and Age-based Violence', in Vandana Desai and Robert Potter (eds) *The Companion to Development Studies* (London: Routledge), 493–9.

McIlwaine, Cathy (2014b) 'Everyday Urban Violence and Transnational Displacement of Colombian Urban Migrants to London, UK', *Environment and Urbanization*, 26:2, 417–26.

McIlwaine, Cathy (2015) 'Gender-based Violence and Assets in Just Cities: Triggers and Transformations', in Caroline Moser (ed.) *Gender, Assets and Just Cities* (London: Routledge), 150–63.

McIlwaine, Cathy and Datta, Kavita (2004) 'Endangered Youth? Youth, Gender and Sexualities in Urban Botswana', *Gender, Place and Culture*, 11:4, 483–512.

McIlwaine, Cathy and Moser, Caroline O. N. (2000) 'Violence and Social Capital in Urban Poor Communities: Perspectives from Colombia and Guatemala', *Journal of International Development*, 13:7, 965–84.

McIlwaine, Cathy and Moser, Caroline O. N. (2007) 'Living in Fear: How the Urban Poor Perceive Violence, Fear and Insecurity', in Kees Koonings and Dirk Kruijt (eds) *Fractured Cities: Social Exclusion, Urban Violence and Contested Spaces in Latin America* (London: Zed), 117–37.

McNay, Kirsty (2005) 'The Implications of the Demographic Transition for Women, Girls and Gender Equality: A Review of Developing Country Evidence', *Progress in Development Studies*, 5:2, 115–34.

McNicoll, George (2013) 'Reflections on Post-transition Demography', in George McNicoll, John Bongaarts and Ethel P. Churchill (eds) *Population and Public Policy: Essays in Honour of Paul Demeny* (New York: Population Council), 3–19.

Meagher, Kate (2010) 'The Empowerment Trap: Gender, Poverty and the Informal Economy in Sub-Saharan Africa', in Sylvia Chant (ed.) *The International Handbook of Gender and Poverty: Concepts, Research, Policy* (Cheltenham: Edward Elgar), 472–7.

Medeiros, Marcelo and Costa, Joana (2006) *Poverty among Women in Latin America: Feminisation or Over-representation?*, Working Paper No.20 (Brasilia: International Poverty Centre). (www.ipc-undp.org/pub/IPCWorkingPaper20.pdf).

Medeiros, Marcelo and Costa, Joana (2008) 'Is There a Feminisation of Poverty in Latin America?', *World Development*, 36:1, 115–27.

Meleis, Afaf Ibrahim (2011) 'Developing Urban Areas as if Gender Matters', in Afa Ibrahim Meleis, Eugenie L. Birch and Susan F. Wachter (eds) *Women's Health and the World's Cities* (Philadelphia: University of Pennsylvania Press), 1–11.

Messias, DeAnne K. Hilfinger (2011) 'The Health and Well-being of Immigrant Women in Urban Areas', in Afaf Ibrahim Meleis, Eugenie L. Birch and Susan F. Wachter (eds) *Women's Health and the World's Cities* (Philadelphia: University of Pennsylvania Press), 144–65.

Meth, Paula (2013) 'Millennium Development Goals and Urban Informal Settlements: Unintended Consequences', *International Development Planning Review*, 35:1, v–xiii.

Meth, Paula (2014) 'Security and Dignity for All: Informal Settlement Upgrading and Experiences of Violence', *SLUMLAB Made in Africa: Sustainable Living Model*, 9, 144–7. (http://u-tt.arch.ethz.ch/wp-content/uploads/2014/02/SLUM-Lab-9-Full-Lo.pdf).

Mills, Sophie (2010) 'Renegotiating the Household: Successfully Leveraging Women's Access to Housing Microfinance in South Africa', in Sylvia Chant (ed.) *The International Handbook of Gender and Poverty: Concepts, Research, Policy* (Cheltenham: Edward Elgar), 373–8.

Ministry for Foreign Affairs of Finland (MFFF) (2011) *Women and Gender Equality in Finnish Development Cooperation* (Helsinki: Unit of Sector Policies Department of Development Policy, Government of Finland). (http://formin.finland.fi/public/download.aspx?ID=71352&GUID=%7BEAC93617-C89E-4461-88E2-7091B5CF960D%7D).

Miraftab, Faranak (2001) 'Risks and Opportunities in Gender Gaps to Access Shelter: A Platform for Intervention', *International Journal of Politics, Culture and Society*, 15:1, 143–60.

Miraftab, Farabak (2010) 'Contradictions in the Gender–Poverty Nexus: Reflections on the Privatisation of Social Reproduction and Urban Informality in South African Townships', in Sylvia Chant (ed.) *The International Handbook of Gender and Poverty: Concepts, Research, Policy* (Cheltenham: Edward Elgar), 644–8.

Mitlin, Diana (2005) 'Understanding Chronic Poverty in Urban Areas', *International Planning Studies*, 10:1, 3–19.

Mitlin, Diana (2008) *Urban Poor Funds: Development by the People for the People*, Poverty Reduction in Urban Areas Series Working Paper No. 18 (London: International Institute for Environment and Development).

Mitlin, Diana and David Satterthwaite (2012) 'Addressing Poverty and Inequality', *Environment and Urbanization*, 24:2, 395–401.

Mitlin, Diana and David Satterthwaite (2013) *Urban Poverty in the Global South: Scale and Nature* (London: Routledge).

Mitra, Amal K. and Rodriguez-Fernandez, Gisela (2010) 'Latin America and the Caribbean: Assessment of the Advances in Public Health for the Achievement of the Millennium Development Goals', *International Journal of Environmental Research and Public Health*, 7:5, 2238–55. (www.mdpi.com/journal/ijerph).

Mitter, Swasti and Rowbotham, Sheila (eds) (1997) *Women Encounter Technology: Changing Patterns of Employment in the Third World* (London: Routledge).

Moghadam, Valentine (1995) 'Gender Aspects of Employment and Unemployment in a Global Perspective', in Mihály Simaj with Valentine Moghadam and Arvo Kuddo (eds) *Global Employment: An International Investigation into the Future of Work* (London: Zed), 111–39.

Molony, Thomas (2009) 'Trading Places in Tanzania: Mobility and Marginalisation at a Time of Travel-saving Technologies', in Mirjam De Bruijn, Francis Nyamnjoh and Inge Brinkman (eds) *Mobile Phones: The New Talking Drums of Everyday Africa* (Cameroon: Langaa RPCIG), 92–109.

Molyneux, Maxine (1984) 'Mobilisation without Emancipation?', *Critical Social Policy*, 4:10, 59–71.

Molyneux, Maxine (2001) *Women's Movements in International Perspective: Latin America and beyond* (Basingstoke: Palgrave).

Molyneux, Maxine (2006) 'Mothers at the Service of the New Poverty Agenda: Progresa/ Oportunidades, Mexico's Conditional Transfer Programme', *Journal of Social Policy and Administration*, 40:4, 425–49.

Molyneux, Maxine (2007) *Change and Continuity in Social Protection in Latin America: Mothers at the Service of the State*, Gender and Development Paper No. 1 (Geneva: United Nations Research Institute for Social Development).

Momsen, Janet Henshall (2002) 'Myth or Math: The Waxing and Waning of the Female-headed Household', *Progress in Development Studies*, 2:2, 141–51.

Momsen, Janet Henshall (2010) 'Gender, Households and Poverty in the Caribbean: Shadows over Islands in the Sun', in Sylvia Chant (ed.) *The International Handbook of Gender and Poverty: Concepts, Research, Policy* (Cheltenham: Edward Elgar), 129–34.

Monk-Turner, Elizabeth and Turner, Charlie G. (2001) 'Sex Differentials in Earnings in the South Korean Labour Market', *Feminist Economics*, 7:1, 63–78.

Montezuma, Ricardo (2005) 'Facing the Environmental Challenge: The Transformation of Bogotá, Colombia, 1995–2000: Investing in Citizenship and Urban Mobility', *Global Urban Development*, 1:1, 1–10.

Montgomery, Mark (2009) 'Urban Poverty and Health in Developing Countries', *Population Bulletin*, 64:2, 1–16.

Montgomery, Mark, Stren, Richard, Cohen, Barney and Reed, Holly (2004) *Cities Transformed: Demographic Change and its Implications in the Developing World* (London: Earthscan).

Moodley, Sagren (2005) 'The Promise of E-development? A Critical Assessment of the State ICT for Poverty Reduction Discourse in South Africa', *Perspectives on Global Development and Technology*, 4:1, 1–26.

Moret, Erica (2008) 'Afro-Cuban Religion, Ethnobotany and Healthcare in the Context of Global Political and Economic Change', *Bulletin of Latin American Research*, 27:3, 333–50.

Moro-Coco, Mayra and Raaber, Natalie (2012) *Getting at the Roots: Re-integrating Human Rights and Gender Equality in the Post-2015 Development Agenda* (Toronto: Association for Women's Rights in Development/AWID).

Morrison, Andrew, Raju, Dhushyanth and Singa, Nistha (2010) 'Gender Equality, Poverty Reduction, and Growth: A Copernican Quest', in Ravi Kanbur and Michael Spence (eds) *Equity and Growth in a Globalising World* (Washington, DC: World Bank on behalf of the Commission on Growth and Development), 103–29. (www.growthcommission.org/storage/cgdev/documents/volume_equity/equityandgrowthsansch8.pdf).

Morrison, Andrew, Ellsberg, Mary and Bott, Sarah (2007) 'Addressing Gender-based Violence: A Critical Review of Interventions', *World Bank Observer*, 22:1, 25–51.

Moser, Caroline O. N. (1986) 'Women's Needs in the Urban System: Training Strategies in Gender-aware Planning', in Judith Bruce and Marilyn Köhn (eds) *Learning about Women and Urban Services in Latin America and the Caribbean* (New York: Population Council), 40–61.

Moser, Caroline O. N. (1989) 'Gender Planning in the Third World: Meeting Practical and Strategic Gender Needs', *World Development*, 17:11, 1799–825.

Moser, Caroline O. N.(1992) 'Adjustment from below: Low-income Women, Time and the Triple Role in Guayaquil, Ecuador', in Haleh Afshar and Carolyn Dennis (eds) *Women and Adjustment Policies in the Third World* (Basingstoke: Macmillan), 87–116.

Moser, Caroline O. N. (1993) *Gender Planning and Development* (London: Routledge).

Moser, Caroline O. N. (1995) 'Women, Gender and Urban Development Policy: Challenges for Current and Future Research', *Third World Planning Review*, 17:2, 223–35.

Moser, Caroline O. N. (1998) 'The Asset Vulnerability Framework: Reassessing Urban Poverty Reduction Strategies', *World Development*, 26:1, 1–19.

Moser, Caroline O. N. (2004) 'Urban Violence and Insecurity: An Introductory Roadmap', *Environment and Urbanization*, 16:2, 3–16.

Moser, Caroline O. N. (2006) *Asset-based Approaches to Poverty Reduction in a Globalised Context*, Global Economy and Development Working Paper (Washington, DC: Brookings Institution).

Moser, Caroline O. N. (2009) *Ordinary Families, Extraordinary Lives, Assets and Poverty Reduction in Guayaquil, 1978–2004* (Washington, DC: Brookings Institution Press).

Moser, Caroline O. N. (2010) 'Moving beyond Gender and Poverty to Asset Accumulation: Evidence from Low-income Households in Guayquil, Ecuador', in Sylvia Chant (ed.) *The International Handbook of Gender and Poverty: Concepts, Research, Policy* (Cheltenham: Edward Elgar), 391–8.

Moser, Caroline O. N. (2011) 'Cancer Note from the Slums', *Environment and Urbanisation*, 23:1, 119–22.

Moser, Caroline (2012) 'Mainstreaming Women's Safety in Cities into Gender-based Policy and Programmes', *Gender and Development*, 20:3, 435–52.

Moser, Caroline O. N. (2014) *Gender Planning and Development: Revisiting, Deconstructing and Reflecting*, DPU Working Paper No. 165/60 (London: Development Planning Unit).

Moser, Caroline O. N. (ed.) (2015) *Gender, Asset Accumulation and Just Cities: Pathways to Transformation* (London: Routledge).

Moser, Caroline and Chant, Sylvia (1985) *The Role of Women in the Execution of Low-income Housing Projects* (Nairobi: United Nations Centre for Human Settlements).

Moser, Caroline O. N. and Felton, Andrew (2010) 'The Gender Nature of Asset Accumulation in Urban Contexts: Longitudinal Results from Guayaquil, Ecuador', in Jo Beall, Basudeb Guha-Khasnobis and Ravi Kanbur (eds) *Urbanisation and Development: Multidisciplinary Perspectives* (Oxford: Oxford University Press), 183–201.

Moser, Caroline, O. N. and McIlwaine, Cathy (2004) *Encounters with Violence in Latin America* (London: Routledge).

Moser, Caroline O. N. and McIlwaine, Cathy (2006) 'Latin American Urban Violence as a Development Concern: Towards a Framework for Violence Reduction', *World Development*, 34:1, 89–112.

Moser, Caroline, O. N. and McIlwaine, Cathy (2014) 'New Frontiers in Twenty-first Century Urban Conflict and Violence', *Environment and Urbanization*, 26:2, 331–44.

Moser, Caroline O. N. and Peake, Linda (eds) (1987) *Women, Human Settlements and Housing* (London: Tavistock).

Moser, Caroline O. N. and Stein, Alfredo (2011) 'Implementing Urban Participatory Climate Change Adaptation Appraisals: A Methodological Guideline', *Environment and Urbanisation*, 23:2, 463–85.

Moser, Caroline, O. N., Winton, Ailsa and Moser, Annalise (2005) 'Violence, Fear and Insecurity among the Urban Poor In Latin America', in Mariane Fay (ed.) *The Urban Poor in Latin America* (Washington, DC: World Bank), 125–78.

Msiyaphazi Zulu, Eliya; Dodoo, F. Nii-Amoo and Chika-Ezee, Alex (2002) 'Sexual Risk-taking in the Slums of Nairobi, 1993–8', *Population Studies*, 56:3, 311–23.

Mughisha, Frederick (2006) 'School Enrolment among Urban Non-slum, Slum and Rural Children in Kenya: Is the Urban Advantage Eroding?', *International Journal of Educational Development*, 26, 471–82.

Mukhopadhyay, Swapna and Sudarshan, Ratna M. (2003) *Tracking Gender Equity under Economic Reforms: Continuity and Change in South Asia* (Ottawa/New Delhi: International Development Research Centre/Kali for Women).

Muñoz-Boudet, Ana Maria, Petesch, Patti and Turk, Carolyn with Thumala, Angelica (2012) *On Norms and Agency: Conversations about Gender Equality with Women and Men in 20 Countries* (Washington, DC: World Bank).

Murphy, Rachel, Tao, Ran and Lu, Xi (2011) 'Son Preference in Rural China: Patrilineal Families and Socioeconomic Change', *Population and Development Review*, 37:4, 665–90.

Musuya, Tina (2011) 'Mobilising Communities to Prevent Violence against Women and HIV in Kampala, Uganda', in Afaf Ibrahim Meleis, Eugenie L. Birch and Susan F. Wachter (eds) *Women's Health and the World's Cities* (Philadelphia: University of Pennsylvania Press), 240–57.

Mwangangi, Francisca (2011) 'Accessibility to Health Care in Urban Environments', in Afaf Ibrahim Meleis, Eugenie L. Birch and Susan F. Wachter (eds) *Women's Health and the World's Cities* (Philadelphia: University of Pennsylvania Press), 227–39.

Myers, Garth (2011) *African Cities: Alternative Visions of Theory and Practice* (London: Zed).

Nakray, Keerty (2010) 'Gender, HIV/AIDS and Carework in India: A Need for Gender-sensitive Policy', in Sylvia Chant (ed.) *The International Handbook of Gender and Poverty: Concepts, Research, Policy* (Cheltenham: Edward Elgar), 333–8.

Nallari, Anupama (2015) '"All We Want Are Toilets Inside Our Homes!" The Critical Role of Sanitation in the Lives of Urban Poor Adolescent Girls in Bengaluru, India', *Environment and Urbanization*, 27:1, 73–88.

National Commission on the Role of Filipino Women (NCRFW) (2004) *Gender and Development Budgeting in the Philippines: Issues, Challenges and Imperatives* (Manila: NCRFW).

Navarrete, Pablo (2015) 'From Survival to Social Mobility: Supporting the Informal Economy in Santiago de Chile', Ph.D. Thesis in preparation, Department of Geography and Environment, London School of Economics and Political Science.

Naved, Ruchira Tabassum, Azim, Safia, Bhuiya, Abbas and Persson, Lars Ake (2006) 'Physical Violence by Husbands: Magnitude, Disclosure and Help-seeking Behaviour of Women in Bangladesh', *Social Science and Medicine*, 62:12, 2917–29.

Nelson, Nici (1997) 'How Women and Men Got by and Still Get by (Only Not so Well): The Gender Division of Labour in a Nairobi Shanty Town', in Josef Gugler (ed.) *Cities in the Developing World: Issues, Theory, Policy* (Oxford: Oxford University Press), 156–70.

Nesbitt-Ahmed, Zahrah (2014) '"I No Go Gree": Everyday Struggles of Domestic Workers in Lagos, Nigeria', Ph.D. thesis in preparation, Department of Geography and Environment, London School of Economics and Political Science.

Newman, Oscar (1972) *Defensible Space* (New York: Macmillan).

Ng, Cecilia and Mitter, Swasti (eds) (2005) *Gender and the Digital Economy: Perspectives from the Developing World* (New Delhi/London: Sage).

Ngwira, Naomi (n.d.) *Women's Property and Inheritance Rights and the Land Reform Process in Malawi* (Blantyre: Institute for Policy Research and Analysis for Dialogue for USAID).

Noh, Hyejin and Kim, Kyo-Seong (2015) 'Revisiting the "Feminisation of Poverty" in Korea: Focused on Time Use and Time Poverty', *Asia Pacific Journal of Social Work and Development*, 24 April, DOI. 1080/02185385.2015.1028430.

Nussbaum, Martha (2000) 'Women's Capabilities and Social Justice', *Journal of Human Development*, 1:2, 219–47.

Obeng-Odoom, Franklin and Stilwell, Frank (2013) 'Security of Tenure in International Development Discourse', *International Development Planning Review*, 35:4, 315–33.

Ochako, Rhoune, Fotso, Jean-Christophe, Ikamari, Lawrence and Khasakhala, Anne (2011) 'Utilisation of Maternal Health Services among Young Women in Kenya: Insights from the Kenya Demographic and Health Survey', *BMC Pregnancy and Childbirth*, 11:1, 1–9. (www.biomedcentral.com/1471-2393/11/1).

Oestmann, Sonja (2007) 'Mobile Operators: Their Contribution to Universal Service and Public Access' (Vancouver: Intelecon Research and Consultancy). (www.inteleconresearch.com/pdf/mobile%20%26%20us%20-%20for%20rru.pdf).

Ofstedal, Mary Beth, Reidy, Erin and Knodel, John (2004) 'Gender Differences in Economic Support and Well-being of Older Asians', *Journal of Cross-cultural Gerontology*, 19, 165–201.

Oostendorp, Remco H. (2004) *Globalisation and the Gender Wage Gap*, Policy Research Working Paper No. 3256 (Washington, DC: World Bank). (www-wds.worldbank.org).

Organisation for Economic Cooperation and Development (OECD) (2009) *Social Institutions and Gender Index* (Paris: OECD). (http://my.genderindex.org/).

Organisation for Economic Cooperation and Development (OECD) (2013) *Transforming Social Institutions to Prevent Violence against Women and Girls and Improve Development Outcomes* (Paris: OECD Development Centre).

Organisation for Economic Cooperation and Development (OECD) (2014) *Social Institutions and Gender Index* (Paris: OECD).

Ortíz Guitart, Anna, Prats Ferret, Maria and García Ramon, Maria Dolors (eds) (2014) *Espacios Públicos, Género y Diversidad* (Barcelona: Icaria Editorial).

Ossome, Lyn (2014) 'Can the Law Secure Women's Rights to Land in Africa? Revisiting Tensions between Culture and Land Commercialisation', *Feminist Economics*, 20:1, 155–77.

Oswin, Natalie (2012) 'The Queer Time of Creative Urbanism: Family, Futurity, and Global City Singapore', *Environment and Planning A*, 44:7, 1624–40.

Overå, Ragnhild (2008) 'Mobile Traders and Mobile Phones in Ghana', in James Katz (ed.) *Handbook of Mobile Communication Studies* (Cambridge, MA: MIT Press), 43–54.

Overman, Henry and Venables, Anthony J. (2010) 'Evolving City Systems', in Jo Beall, Basudeb Guha-Khasnobis and Ravi Kanbur (eds) *Urbanisation and Development: Multidisciplinary Perspectives* (Oxford: Oxford University Press), 103–19.

Oxfam GB and Concern Worldwide (2011) *Walking the Talk: Cash Transfers and Gender Dynamics*, Joint NGO Research Report (Oxford: Oxfam GB). (www.oxfam.org.uk/resources/policy/gender/downloads/rr-walking-the-talk-cash-transfers-gender-120511-en.pdf).

Pain, Rachel (2000) 'Place, Social Relations and Fear of Crime: A Review', *Progress in Human Geography*, 24:3, 365–87.

Pain, Rachel (2001) 'Gender, Race, Age and Fear in the City', *Urban Studies*, 38:5–6, 899–913.

Palermo, Tia Bleck, Jennifer and Peterman, Amber (2013) 'Tip of the Iceberg Reporting and Gender-based Violence in Developing Countries', *American Journal of Epidemiology*, 179:5, 602–12.

Palmer, Ingrid (1992) 'Gender, Equity and Economic Efficiency in Adjustment Programmes', in Haleh Afshar and Carolyne Dennis (eds) *Women and Adjustment Policies in the Third World* (Basingstoke: Macmillan), 69–83.

Panda, Smita Mishra (2007) 'Mainstreaming Gender in Water Management: A Critical View', *Gender, Technology and Development*, 11:3, 321–38.

Parnell, Susan and Pieterse, Edgar (2010) 'The "Right to the City": Institutional Imperatives of a Developmental State', *International Journal of Urban and Regional Research*, 34, 146–62.

Parnell, Susan, Pieterse, Edgar and Watson, Vanessa (2009) 'Planning for Cities in the Global South: A Research Agenda for Sustainable Human Settlements', *Progress in Planning*, 72, 232–40.

Parnell, Susan and Robinson, Jennifer (2012) '(Re)theorising Cities from the Global South: Looking beyond Neoliberalism', *Urban Geography*, 33:4, 593–617.

Parpart, Jane (2009) 'Fine Words, Failed Policies: Gender Mainstreaming in an Insecure and Unequal World', in Jacqueline Leckie (ed.) *Development in an Insecure and Gendered World: The Relevance of the Millennium Development Goals* (Aldershot: Ashgate), 51–70.

Parpart, Jane (2014) 'Exploring the Transformative Potential of Gender Mainstreaming in International Development Institutions', *Journal of International Development*, 26:3, 382–95.

Parpart, Jane (2015) 'Men, Masculinities and Development', in Anne Coles, Leslie Gray and Janet Momsen (eds) *A Handbook of Gender and Development* (London: Routledge), 14–23.

Parreñas, Rhacel (2005) *Children of Global Migration: Transnational Families and Gendered Woes* (Stanford, CA: Stanford University Press).

Patel, Reena (2010) *Working the Night Shift: Women in India's Call Center Industry* (Stanford, CA: Stanford University Press).

Patel, Sheela (2011) 'Are Women Victims, or Are They Warriors?', in Afaf Ibrahim Meleis, Eugenie L. Birch and Susan F. Wachter (eds) *Women's Health and the World's Cities* (Philadelphia: University of Pennsylvania Press), 93–109.

Patel, Sheela and Mitlin, Diana (2004) 'Grassroots-driven Development: The Alliance of SPARC, the National Slum Dwellers Federation and Mahila Milan', in Diana Mitlin and David Satterthwaite (eds) *Empowering Squatter Citizen* (London: Earthscan), 216–41.

Patel, Sheela and Mitlin, Diana (2010) 'Gender Issues and Shack/Slum Dweller Federations', in Sylvia Chant (ed.) *The International Handbook of Gender and Poverty: Concepts, Research, Policy* (Cheltenham: Edward Elgar), 379–84.

Patel, Vikram (2001) 'Cultural Factors and International Epidemiology', *British Medical Bulletin*, 57, 33–45.

Peake, Linda and Rieker, Martina (2013) 'Rethinking Feminist Interventions into the Urban', in Linda Peake and Martina Rieker (eds) *Rethinking Feminist Interventions into the Urban* (London: Routledge), 1–22.

Pearson, Ruth (1997) 'Renegotiating the Reproductive Bargain: Gender Analysis of Economic Transition in Cuba', *Development and Change*, 28, 671–705.

Pearson, Ruth (2000) 'All Change? Men, Women and Reproductive Work in the Global Economy', *European Journal of Development Research*, 12:2, 219–37.

Pearson, Ruth (2010) 'Women's Work Nimble Fingers, and Women's Mobility in the Global Economy', in Sylvia Chant (ed.) *The International Handbook of Gender and Poverty: Concepts, Research, Policy* (Cheltenham: Edward Elgar), 421–6.

Pearson, Ruth (2013) 'Gender, Globalisation and the Reproduction of Labour: Bringing the State Back in', in Shirin Rai and Georgina Waylen (eds) *New Frontiers in Feminist Political Economy* (London: Routledge), 19–42.

Pedwell, Carolyn and Perrons, Diane (2007) *The Politics of Democratic Governance: Organising for Social Inclusion and Gender Equity* (London: One World Action).

Pérez, Orlando J. (2013) 'Gang Violence and Insecurity in Contemporary Central America', in Eric A. Johnson, Ricardo D. Salvatore and Pieter Spierenburg (eds) *Murder and Violence in Modern Latin America* (Chichester: Wiley-Blackwell), 217–34.

Perrons, Diane (2004) *Globalisation and Social Change: People and Places in a Divided World* (London: Routledge).

Perrons, Diane (2010) 'Gender, Work and Poverty in High-income Countries', in Sylvia Chant (ed.) *The International Handbook of Gender and Poverty: Concepts, Research, Policy* (Cheltenham: Edward Elgar), 409–14.

Perrons, Diane and Plomien, Ania (2010) *Why Socio-economic Inequalities Increase? Facts and Policy Responses in Europe*, EU Report commissioned by DG Research (Brussels: European Commission). (http://ec.europa.eu/research/social-sciences/pdf/policy-review-inequalities_en.pdf).

Petchesky, Rosalind P. and Judd, Karen (eds) (1998) *Negotiating Reproductive Rights: Women's Perspectives across Countries and Cultures* (London: Zed).

Peters, Deike (2001) 'Gender and Transport in Less Developed Countries: A Background Paper in Preparation for CSD-9', Background Paper for the 'Gender Perspectives for Earth Summit 2002: Energy, Transport, Information for Decision-Making' workshop, Berlin. (www.earthsummit2002.org/workshop/Gender%20%26%20Transport%20S%20DP.pdf).

Pew Research Center (2015) *Cell Phones in Africa: Communication Lifeline Texting Most Common Activity, but Mobile Money Popular in Several Countries* (Washington, DC:

PewResearchCenter).(www.pewglobal.org/files/2015/04/Pew-Research-Center-Africa-Cell-Phone-Report-FINAL-April-15-2015.pdf).

Pinn, Vivian W. and Corry, Nida H. (2011) 'Women's Health in the Urban Community: National Institutes of Health Perspective', in Afaf Ibrahim Meleis, Eugenie L. Birch and Susan F. Wachter (eds) *Women's Health and the World's Cities* (Philadelphia: University of Pennsylvania Press), 169–87.

Plan International (2009) *Because I Am a Girl: The State of the World's Girls 2009: Girls in the Global Economy: Adding it All up* (London: Plan International). (http://plan-international.org/files/global/publications/campaigns/BIAAG%202009.pdf).

Plan International (2010) *Because I Am a Girl: The State of the World's Girls 2010: Digital and Urban Frontiers: Girls in a Changing Landscape* (London: Plan International). (http://plan-international.org/girls/resources/digital-and-urban-frontiers-2010.php).

Plan International (2011) *Because I Am a Girl: The State of the World's Girls 2011: So, What about Boys?* (London: Plan International) (http://plan-international.org/files/global/publications/campaigns/BIAAG-Report-2011.pdf).

Plan International (2012) *Because I Am a Girl: The State of the World's Girls 2012: Learning for Life* (London: Plan International). (https://plan-international.org/files/global/publications/campaigns/biag-2012-report-english).

Polak, Michele (2006) 'It's a gURL Thing: Community versus Commodity in Girl-focused Netspace', in David Buckingham and Rebekah Willett (eds) *Digital Generations: Children, Young People and the New Media* (London: Laurence Erlbaum), 177–92.

Popli, Gurleen K. (2013) 'Gender Wage Differentials in Mexico: A Distributional Approach', *Journal of the Royal Statistical Society*, A, 176, Part 2, 295–319.

Post-2015 Women's Coalition (2014) *The Post 2015 Development Agenda: What's at Stake for the World's Women?* (www.post2015women.com/).

Potts, Deborah (2012a) *Whatever Happened to Africa's Rapid Urbanisation?* (London: Africa Research Institute). (http://us1.campaign-archive1.com/?u=b7ae4d4d8f18ef3ebd 0323d80&id=d156f00e6f&e=f4e682ed64).

Potts, Deborah (2012b) 'What Do We Know about Urbanisation in Sub-Saharan Africa and Does it Matter?', *International Development Planning Review*, 34:1, v–xxi.

Poulsen, Lone (2010) 'Towards Creating Inclusive Cities: Experiences and Challenges in Contemporary African Cities', *Urban Forum* 21:1, 21–36.

Prada, Elena, Singh, Susheela, Remez, Lisa and Villarreal, Cristina (2011) *Unintended Pregnancy and Induced Abortion in Colombia: Causes and Consequences* (New York: Guttmacher Institute). (https://www.guttmacher.org/pubs/Unintended-Pregnancy-Colombia.pdf).

Prieto-Carrón, Marina, Thomson, Marilyn and Macdonald, Many (2007) 'No More Killings! Women Respond to Femicides in Central America', *Gender and Development*, 15:1, 25–40.

Prügl, Elisabeth (2015) 'Neoliberalising Feminism', *New Political Economy*, 20:4, 614–31.

Purewal, Naviej (2002) 'New Roots for Rights: Women's Responses to Population and Development Policies', in Sheila Rowbotham and Stephanie Linklogle (eds) *Women Resist Globalisation* (London: Zed), 96–117.

Puri, Lakshmi (2013) 'Equality and Empowerment', in United Nations Association (UNA)-UK (ed.) *Global Development Goals: Leaving No-one behind* (London: UNA-UK), 90–1.

Quisumbing, Agnes (2010) 'Gender and Household Decision-making in Developing Countries: A Review of Evidence', in Sylvia Chant (ed.) *The International Handbook of Gender and Poverty: Concepts, Research, Policy* (Cheltenham: Edward Elgar), 161–6.

Rai, Shirin (2009) *The Gender Politics of Development* (New Delhi/London: Zubaan Books/Zed).

Rakodi, Carole (1999) 'A Capital Assets Framework for Analysing Household Livelihood Strategies: Implications for Policy', *Development Policy Review*, 17, 315–42.

Rakodi, Carole (2008) 'Prosperity or Poverty? Wealth, Inequality and Deprivation in Urban Areas', in Vandana Desai and Robert Potter (eds) *The Companion to Development Studies*, 2nd edn (London: Hodder Arnold), 253–7.

Rakodi, Carole (2010) 'Gender, Poverty and Access to Land in Cities of the South', in Sylvia Chant (ed.) *The International Handbook of Gender and Poverty: Concepts, Research, Policy* (Cheltenham: Edward Elgar), 353–9.

Rakodi, Carole (2014) *Expanding Women's Access to Land and Housing in Urban Areas*, Women's Voice and Agency Research Series No. 8 (Washington, DC: World Bank Group).

Ramm, Alejandra (2014) 'Housing Subsidies and Unmarried Mothers in Post-dictatorial Chile, 1990–2010', Paper presented at 'Challenging Gendered Instrumentalism in Latin American Social Policy' panel, Society for Latin American Studies, UK 50th Anniversary Conference, Birkbeck, University of London, 3–4 April.

Rao, Nitya (2011) 'Respect, Status and Domestic Work: Female Migrants at Home and Work', *European Journal of Development Research*, 23, 758–73.

Rao, Vyjayanthi (2006) 'Review Essay: Slum as Theory: The South/Asian City and Globalization', *International Journal of Urban and Regional Research*, 30:1, 225–32.

Rashid, Sabina Faiz (2009) 'Strategies to Reduce Exclusion among Populations Living in Urban Slum Settlements in Bangladesh', *Journal of Health Population and Nutrition*, 27:4, 574–86.

Ravallion, Martin, Chen, Shaohua and Sangraula, Prem (2007) *New Evidence on the Urbanisation of Global Poverty*, World Bank Policy Research Working Paper No. 4199 (Washington, DC: World Bank).

Razavi, Shahra (2007) *The Political and Social Economy of Care in a Development Context: Conceptual Issues, Research Questions and Policy Options* (Geneva: UNRISD).

Razavi, Shahra (2013) 'Addressing/Reforming Care: But on Whose Terms?', in Shirin Rai and Georgina Waylen (eds) *New Frontiers in Feminist Political Economy* (London: Routledge), 114–34.

Razavi, Shahra and Staab, Silke (2010) 'Gender, Poverty and Inequality: The Role of Markets, States and Households', in Sylvia Chant (ed.) *The International Handbook of Gender and Poverty: Concepts, Research, Policy* (Cheltenham: Edward Elgar), 427–33.

Reeves, Dory (2002) 'Mainstreaming Gender Equality: An Examination of the Gender-sensitivity of Strategic Planning in Great Britain', *Town Planning Review*, 73:2, 197–214.

Richter-Devroe, Sophie (2011) 'Palestinian Women's Everyday Resistance: Between Normality and Normalisation', *Journal of International Women's Studies*, 12:2, 32–46.

Roberts, Adrienne (2015) 'The Political Economy of "Transnational Business Feminism": Problematising the Corporate-led Gender Equality Agenda', *International Feminist Journal of Politics*, 17:2, 209–31.

Robinson, Jennifer (2002) 'Global and World Cities: A View from off the Map', *International Journal of Urban and Regional Research*, 26, 531–54.

Robinson, Jennifer (2003) 'Postcolonialising Geography: Tactics and Pitfalls', *Singapore Journal of Tropical Geography*, 24, 273–89.

Robinson, Jennifer (2006) *Ordinary Cities: Between Modernity and Development* (London: Routledge).

Rodenberg, Birte (2004) *Gender and Poverty Reduction: New Conceptual Approaches in International Development Cooperation*, Reports and Working Papers 4/2004 (Bonn: German Development Institute).

Rodgers, Dennis, Beall, Jo and Kanbur, Ravi (2011) *Latin American Urban Development into the 21st Century: Towards a Renewed Perspective on the City*, Working Paper No. 2011/05 (Helsinki: UNU-WIDER).

Rodgers, Dennis, Beall, Jo and Kanbur, Ravi (2012) 'Re-thinking the Latin American City', in Dennis Rodgers, Jo Beall and Ravi Kanbur (eds) *Latin American Urban Development into the 21st Century: Towards a Renewed Perspective on the City* (Basingtoke: Macmillan), 3–33.

Rodríguez-Pose, Andrés and Crescenzi, Riccardo (2009) 'Mountains in a Flat World: Why Proximity Still Matters for the Location of Economic Activity', *Cambridge Journal of Regions, Economy and Society*, 1:3, 377–88.

Roever, Sally and Aliaga Linares, Lissette (2010) *Street Vendors Organising: The Case of the Women's Network (Red de Mujeres), Lima, Peru*, Urban Policies Briefing Note No. 2 (Cambridge, MA/Manchester: Women in Informal Employment, Globalising and Organising). (http://wiego.org/sites/wiego.org/files/publications/files/Roever_Street_Vendors_Organizing-BN2.pdf) .

Rogan, Michael (2013) 'Alternative Definitions of Headship and the "Feminisation" of Income Poverty in Post-apartheid South Africa', *Journal of Development Studies*, 49:1, 1344–57.

Rolnik, Raquel (2009) 'Report of the Special Rapporteur on Adequate Housing as a Component of the Right to an Adequate Standard of Living, and on the Right to Non-Discrimination in this Context', Human Rights Council, Thirteenth Session, 18 December. (www2.ohchr.org/english/bodies/hrcouncil/docs/13session/A-HRC-13-20.pdf).

Rolnik, Raquel (2012) *How to Make Women's Right to Housing Effective* (Geneva: United Nations Special Rapporteur on the Right to Adequate Housing). (http://direitoamoradia.org/wp-content/uploads/2012/01/guia-mulheres-EN.pdf).

Roy, Ananya (2002) *Against the Feminisation of Policy*, Comparative Urban Studies Project Policy Brief (Washington, DC: Woodrow Wilson International Center for Scholars). (www.wilsoncenter.org/topics/pubs/urbanbrief01.pdf).

Roy, Ananya (2003) *City Requiem: Calcutta* (Minneapolis: University of Minnesota Press).

Roy, Ananya (2005) 'Urban Informality: Toward an Epistemology of Planning', *Journal of the American Planning Association*, 71:2, 147–58.

Roy, Ananya (2009) 'The 21st-century Metropolis: New Geographies of Theory', *Regional Studies*, 43:6, 819–30.

Roy, Ananya (2010) *Poverty Capital: Microfinance and the Making of Development* (New York: Routledge).

Roy, Ananya (2015) 'Why India Cannot Plan its Cities: Informality, Insurgence and the Idiom of Urbanisation', in Faranak Miraftab and Neema Kudva (eds) *Cities of the Global South Reader* (Abingdon/New York: Routledge), 310–14.

Ruthven, Orlanda (2002) 'Money Mosaics: Financial Choice and Strategy in a West Delhi Squatter Settlement', *Journal of International Development*, 14, 249–71.

Sabry, Sarah (2009*) Poverty Lines in Greater Cairo: Underestimating and Misrepresenting Poverty*, Human Settlements Working Paper Series Poverty Reduction in Urban Areas No. 21 (London: International Institute for Environment and Development).

Safa, Helen (1995) *The Myth of the Male Breadwinner: Women and Industrialisation in the Caribbean* (Boulder, CO: Westview).

Saith, Ashwani (2006) 'From Universal Values to Millennium Development Goals: Lost in Translation?', *Development and Change*, 37:6, 1167–99.

Samson, Melanie (2003) *Dumping on Women: Gender and Privatisation of Waste Management* (Woodstock, Cape Town: Municipal Services Project and the South African Municipal Workers' Union). (www.gdrc.info/docs/waste/005.pdf).

Samson, Melanie (2009a) *Reclaiming Livelihoods: The Role of Reclaimers in Municipal Waste Management Systems* (Pietermarizberg: groundwork). (www.inclusivecities.org/pdfs/Reclaiming_Livelihoods.pdf).

Samson, Melanie (2009b) 'Wasted Citizenship? Reclaimers and the Privatised Expansion of the Public Sphere', *Africa Development*, 34:3–4, 1–25.

Sancho Montero, Silvia María (1995) *El Programa Hogares Comunitarios en Costa Rica, Sus Primeros Pasos: Primera Parte* (San José: Instituto Mixto de Ayuda Social, Dirección Hogares Comunitarios).

Sanders, Cynthia K. and Porterfield, Shirley L. (2010) 'The Ownership Society and Women: Exploring Female Householders' Ability to Accumulate Assets', *Journal of Family and Economic Issues*, 31:1, 90–106.

Sandler, Joanne and Rao, Aruna (2012) 'The Elephant in the Room and the Dragons at the Gate: Strategising for Gender Equality in the 21st Century', *Gender and Development*, 20:3, 547–62.

Sardenburg, Cecilia (2010) 'Family, Household and Women's Empowerment in Bahia, Brazil, through the Generations: Continuities or Change?', *IDS Bulletin*, 41:2, 88–96.

Sarikakis, Katharine and Shade, Leslie Regan (2011) 'World Media', in Janet Lee and Susan Shaw (eds) *Women Worldwide: Transnational Feminist Perspectives on Women* (New York: McGraw Hill), 62–84.

Sassen, Saskia (2001) 'Women's Burden: Counter-geographies of Globalisation and the Feminisation of Survival', *Journal of International Affairs*, 53:2, 503–25.

Sassen, Saskia (2010) 'Strategic Gendering: One Factor in the Constituting of Novel Political Economies', in Sylvia Chant (ed.) *The International Handbook of Gender and Poverty: Concepts, Research, Policy* (Cheltenham: Edward Elgar), 29–34.

Satterthwaite, David (2007) *The Transition to a Predominantly Urban World and its Underpinnings*, Human Settlements Discussion Paper Series, Theme: Urban Change No. 4 (London: International Institute for Environment and Development).

Satterthwaite, David (2008) 'Urbanisation and Environment in Low- and Middle-income Nations', in Vandana Desai and Robert Potter (eds) *The Companion to Development Studies*, 2nd edn (London: Hodder Arnold), 262–8.

Satterthwaite, David (2009) 'The Implications of Population and Urban Growth for Climate Change', in José Miguel Guzmán, George Martine, Gordon McGranahan, Daniel Schensul and Cecilia Tacoli (eds) *Population Dynamics and Climate Change* (London/New York: IIED/UNFPA), 45–63. (www.unfpa.org/public/site/global/lang/en/pid/4500).

Satterthwaite, David (2010) *Urban Myths and the Mis-use of Data that Underpin Them*, UNU/WIDER Working Paper No. 2010/28 (Helsinki: UNU/WIDER). (http://ideas.repec.org/p/unu/wpaperwp2010/28.html).

Satterthwaite, David (2011) 'Why is Urban Health so Poor Even in Many Successful Cities?', *Environment and Urbanisation*, 23:1, 5–11.

Satterthwaite, David, Bartlett, Sheridan, Cabannes, Yves and Brown, Donald (2013) *Getting the Engagement of Local Institutions in the UN Development Agenda*

Post-2015, Human Settlements Working Paper Series, Poverty Reduction in Urban Areas No. 39 (London: International Institute of Environment and Development).

Satterthwaite, David and Dodman, David (2013) 'Editorial: Towards Resilience and Transformation for Cities within a Finite Planet', *Environment and Urbanization*, 25:2, 291–8.

Satterthwaite, David, Huq, Saleemul, Reid, Hannah, Pelling, Mark and Lankao, Patricia Romero (2007) *Adapting to Climate Change in Urban Areas: The Possibilities and Constraints in Low- and Middle-income Nations*, Human Settlements Discussion Paper Series, Climate Change and Cities No. 1 (London: IIED).

Save the Children (2011a) *No Child Born to Die: Closing the Gap* (London: Save the Children).

Save the Children (2011b) *Missing Midwives* (London: Save the Children Fund).

Schlyter, Ann (1989) *Women Householders and Housing Strategies: The Case of Harare, Zimbabwe* (Gävle: National Swedish Institute for Building Research).

Schmink, Marianne (1986) 'The Working Group Approach to Women in Urban Services', in Judith Bruce and Köhn, Marilyn (eds) *Learning about Women and Urban Services in Latin America and the Caribbean* (New York: Population Council), 30–9.

Schütte, Stefan (2014) 'Living with Patriarchy and Poverty: Women's Agency and the Spatialities of Gender Relations in Afghanistan', *Gender, Place and Culture*, 21:9, 1176–92.

Schuurman, Anna (2009) 'Bangladesh Urban Health Survey: Methods and Results', Paper presented at 'Slums around the World' panel, International Conference on Urban Health, Nairobi, 23–8 October. (www.urbanreproductivehealth.org/system/files/Bangladesh%20 Slums%20ICUH_0.pdf).

Schweitzer, Julian, Makinen, Marty, Wilson, Lara and Heymann, Marilyn (2012) *Post-2015 Health MDGS* (London: ODI). (www.odi.org/sites/odi.org.uk/files/odi-assets/ publications-opinion-files/7736.pdf).

Sclar, Elliott D., Garau, Pietro and Carolini, Gabriella (2005) 'The 21st Century Health Challenge of Slums and Cities', *The Lancet*, 365, 901–3.

Scott, Nigel, Batchelor, Simon, Ridley, Jonathon and Jorgensen, Britt (2004) *The Impact of Mobile Phones in Africa*, Commission for Africa (Reading: Gamos). (http://gamos. org.uk/couksite/Projects/Docs/Mobile%20phones%20in%20Africa/Full%20Report. pdf).

Secor, Anna J. (2004) '"There is an Istanbul that Belongs to Me": Citizenship, Space and Identity in the City', *Annals of the Association of American Geographers*, 94:2, 352–68.

Sedgh, Gilda, Singh, Susheela, Shah, Iqbal H., Åhman, Elisabeth, Henshaw, Stanley K. and Bankole, Akinrinola (2012) 'Induced Abortion: Incidence and Trends Worldwide from 1995 to 2008', *The Lancet*, 379, 625–32.

Self-Employed Women's Association–Indian Institute for Human Settlements (SEWA–IIHS) (2011) 'Inclusive Cities in India', Summary report from 'Inclusive Cities in India' workshop, New Delhi, 7–8 June.

Sen, Amartya K. (1999) *Development as Freedom* (Oxford: Oxford University Press).

Sen, Gita (2008) 'Poverty as a Gendered Experience', in Dag Ehrenpreis (ed.) *Poverty in Focus No. 13: Gender Equality* (Brasilia: International Poverty Centre), 6–7.

Sen, Gita and Ostlin, Piroska (2011) 'Gender as a Social Determinant of Health: Evidence, Policies and Innovations', in Nalini Visvanathan, Lynn Duggan, Nan Wiegersma and Laurie Nisonoff (eds) *The Women, Gender and Development Reader*, 2nd edn (London: Zed), 64–73.

Shekar, Nalini (2009) *From Waste Pickers to University Graduates in One Generation: The Story of the More Family*, Inclusive Cities Project. (www.inclusivecities.org/pdfs/IUP_Story_More_Family.pdf).

Shiva, Vandana (1998) 'Women's Water Rights', *Waterlines*, 17:1, 9–11.

Shrestha, Krishna K., Ojha, Hemant R., McManus, Phil, Rubbo, Anna and Dhote, Krishna Kumar (eds) (2015) *Inclusive Urbanization: Rethinking Policy, Practice and Research in the Age of Climate Change* (London/New York: Routledge).

Simard, Paule and De Koninck, Maria (2001) 'Environment, Living Spaces and Health: Compound Organisation Practices in a Bamako Squatter Settlement, Mali', in Caroline Sweetman (ed.) *Gender, Development and Health* (Oxford: Oxfam), 28–39.

Smith, Daniel Jordan (2004) 'Contradictions in Nigeria's Fertility Transition: The Burdens and Benefits of Having People', *Population and Development Review*, 30:2, 221–38.

Sommer, Marni (2010) 'Where the Education System and Women's Bodies Collide: The Social and Health Impact of Girls' Experiences of Menstruation and Schooling in Tanzania', *Journal of Adolescence*, 33:4, 521–9.

Sommer, Marni, Ferron, Suzanne, Cavill, Sue and House, Sarah (2015) 'Violence, Gender and WASH: Spurring Action on a Complex, Under-documented and Sensitive Topic', *Environment and Urbanization*, 27:1, 105–16.

Song, Shunfeng, Zhu, Erqian and Chen, Zhuo (2011) 'Equal Work Opportunity but Unequal Income Gender Disparities among Low-Income Households in Urban China', *Chinese Economy*, 44, 39–45.

Song, Yan and Ding, Chengri (eds) (2010) *Smart Urban Growth for China* (Cambridge, MA: Lincoln Instiute).

Speak, Suzanne (2012) 'Planning for the Needs of Urban Poor in the Global South: The Value of a Feminist Approach,' *Planning Theory*, 11:4, 343–60.

Spence, Michael, Annez, Patricia Clarke and Buckley, Robert M. (2009) *Urbanisation and Growth* (Washington, DC: Commission on Growth and Development and World Bank).

Spitzer, Denise L. (2005) 'Engendering Health Disparities', *Revue Canadienne de Santé Publique*, 96:2, 578–95.

Standing, Guy (1999) 'Global Feminisation through Flexible Labour: A Theme Revisited', *World Development*, 27:3, 533–50.

Staudt, Kathleen (2008) *Violence and Activism at the Border: Gender, Fear and Everyday Life in Ciudad Juárez* (Austin: University of Texas Press).

Stavropoulou, Maria and Jones, Nicola (2013) *Off the Balance Sheet: The Impact of the Economic Crisis on Girls and Young Women: A Review of the Evidence* (London: ODI/Plan).(http://plan-international.org/files/global/publications/economics/off-the-balance-sheet-english.pdf).

Stevens, Candice (2009) *Draft Report: Green Jobs and Women Workers: Employment, Equity, Equality* (Madrid: Sustain Labour). (www.sustainlabour.org/dmdocuments/en255_2009.pdf).

Stewart-Withers, Rochelle (2011) 'Contesting a Third World Development Category: Female-headed Households in Samoa', *Women's Studies International Forum*, 34, 171–84.

Storper, Michael and Scott, Allen J. (2009) 'Rethinking Human Capital, Creativity and Urban Growth', *Journal of Economic Geography*, 9, 147–67.

Subbaraman, Ramnath, Nolan, Laura, Shitole, Tejal, Sawant, Kiran, Shitole, Shrutika, Sood, Kunal, Nanarkar, Mahesh, Ghannam, Jess, Betancourt, Theresa S., Bloom, David E. and Patil-Deshmukh, Anita (2014) 'The Psychological Toll of Slum Living in Mumbai, India: A Mixed Methods Study', *Social Science and Medicine*, 119, 155–69.

Sujatha, P. and Janardhanam, P. V. S. (2010) 'Urban Health in India: Chennai as a Case Study', *Indian Journal of Science and Technology*, 3:12, 1236–48. (www.indjst.org/archive/vol.3.issue.11-12/dec10sujatha-25.pdf).

Sverdlik, Alice (2011) 'Ill-health and Poverty: A Literature Review on Health in Informal Settlements', *Environment and Urbanisation*, 23:1, 123–55.

Sweet, Elizabeth and Ortiz Escalante, Sara (2010) 'Planning Responds to Gender Violence: Evidence from Spain, Mexico and the United States', *Urban Studies*, 47:10, 2129–47.

Sweetman, Caroline (ed.) (2005) *Gender and the Millennium Development Goals* (Oxford: Oxfam).

Sweetman, Caroline (2008) *How Title Deeds Make Sex Safer: Women's Property Rights in an Era of HIV*, From Poverty to Power Background Paper (Oxford: Oxfam International). (www.oxfam.org.uk/resources/downloads/FP2P/FP2P_How_title_deeds_make_sex_safer_BP_ENGLISH.pdf).

Sweetman, Caroline (2010) 'A Woman and an Empty House Are Never Alone for Long: Autonomy, Control, Marriage and Microfinance in Addis Ababa, Ethiopia', in Sylvia Chant (ed.) *The International Handbook of Gender and Poverty: Concepts, Research, Policy* (Cheltenham: Edward Elgar), 575–80.

Sweetman, Caroline (2012) 'Bringing "Unpaid Care" into Global Policy Spaces Workshop, 18–19 September 2012', *Gender and Development*, 20:3, 618–20.

Tabbush, Constanza (2010) 'Latin American Women's Protection after Adjustment: A Feminist Critique of Conditional Cash Transfers in Chile and Argentina', *Oxford Development Studies*, 38:4, 437–51.

Tacoli, Cecilia (ed.) (2006) *The Earthscan Reader in Rural–Urban Linkages* (London: Earthscan).

Tacoli, Cecilia (2010) 'Internal Mobility, Migration and Changing Gender Relations: Case Study Perspectives from Mali, Nigeria, Tanzania and Vietnam', in Sylvia Chant (ed.) *The International Handbook of Gender and Poverty: Concepts, Research, Policy* (Cheltenham: Edward Elgar), 296–300.

Tacoli, Cecilia (2012) *Urbanisation, Gender and Urban Poverty: Paid Work and Unpaid Carework in the City*, Urbanisation and Emerging Population Issues Working Paper No. 7 (London: International Institute of Environment and Development). (http://pubs.iied.org/10614IIED.html).

Tacoli, Cecilia (2014) The *Benefits and Constraints of Urbanisation for Gender Equality*, Environment and Urbanization Brief No. 27 (London: International Institute for Environment and Development).

Tacoli, Cecilia with Bukhari, Budoor and Fisher, Susannah (2013) *Urban Poverty, Food Security and Climate Change*, Human Settlements Working Paper No. 37, Rural–Urban Interactions and Livelihood Strategies (London: International Institute of Environment and Development).

Tacoli, Cecilia and Chant, Sylvia (2014) 'Migration, Urbanisation and Changing Gender Relations in the South', in Susan Parnell and Sophie Oldfield (eds) *The Routledge Handbook on Cities of the Global South* (London: Routledge), 586–96.

Tacoli, Cecilia and Mabala, Richard (2010) 'Exploring Mobility and Migration in the Context of Rural–Urban Linkages: Why Gender and Generation Matter', *Environment and Urbanization*, 22:2, 389–95.

Tacoli, Cecilia, McGranahan, Gordon and Satterthwaite, David (2015) *Urbanisation, Rural–Urban Migration and Urban Poverty*, IIED Urban Working Paper (London: International Institute of Environment and Development). (http://pubs.iied.org/10725IIED.html?b=d).

Tacoli, Cecilia and Satterthwaite, David (2013) 'Gender and Urban Change', *Environment and Urbanization*, 25:1, 3–8.

Tankel, Yardena (2011) 'Reframing "Safe Cities for Women": Feminist Articulations in Recife', *Development*, 54:3, 352–7.

Tembon, Mercy and Fort, Lucia (eds) (2008) *Girls' Education in the 21st Century: Gender Equality, Empowerment and Economic Growth* (Washington, DC: World Bank). (http://siteresources.worldbank.org/EDUCATION/Resources/278200-1099079877269/547664-1099080014368/DID_Girls_edu.pdf).

Thaker, Roopal (2011) *A Participatory Evaluation of ZanaAfrica's EmpowerNet Club Pilot Program in Kibera Slum Nairobi, Kenya* (Nairobi: ZanaAfrica) (www.zanaafrica.org/wp-content/uploads/2013/02/ZanaAfrica-Evaluation-Report1.pdf).

Thompson, John, Porras, Ina, Wood, Elisabeth, Tumwine, Hames, Mujwahusi, Mark, Katui-Katua, Munguti and Johnstone, Nick (2000) 'Waiting at the Tap: Changes in Urban Water Use in East Africa over Three Decades', *Environment and Urbanization*, 12:2, 37–52.

Tilley, Elizabeth, Bieri, Sabin and Kohler, Petra (2013) 'Sanitation in Developing Countries: A Review through a Gender Lens', *Journal of Water, Sanitation and Hygiene for Development*, 3:3, 298–314.

Titcombe, Kim (2014) 'Gender and Transport in Development: Towards a Gender-responsive Approach to Transport Projects in a Developing Context', Unpublished Dissertation, Certificate of Advanced Studies, Gender, Justice and Globalisation, University of Bern.

Tjon-A-Ten, Varina, Kerner, Brad, Shukler, Shweta and Hochwait, Anne (2011) 'Girls' Health Needs in Urban Environments', in Afaf Ibrahim Meleis, Eugenie L. Birch and Susan F. Wachter (eds) *Women's Health and the World's Cities* (Philadelphia: University of Pennsylvania Press), 36–52.

Tonkiss, Fran (2005) *Space, the City and Social Theory* (Cambridge: Polity).

Touray, Isatou (2006) 'Sexuality and Women's Sexual Rights in the Gambia', *IDS Bulletin*, 27:5, 77–83.

Tran, Hoai Anh and Schlyter, Ann (2010) 'Gender and Class in Urban Transport: The Cases of Xian and Hanoi', *Environment and Urbanisation*, 22:1, 139–55.

Tripathi, Dwijendra (1999) *Slum Networking in Ahmedabad: The Sanjay Hagar Pilot Project*, DPU Working Paper No. 101 (London: UCL Development Planning Unit).

Truelove, Yaffa (2011) '(Re-)conceptualising Water Inequality in Delhi, India through a Feminist Political Ecology Framework', *Geoforum*, 42, 143–52.

Tsenkova, Sasha (2007) 'Urban Futures: Strategic Planning in Post-socialist Europe', *Geojournal Library*, 92, 447–72.

Turner, John F. C. (1976) *Housing by People* (London: Marion Boyars).

Turok, Ivan and McGranahan, Gordon (2013) 'Urbanisation and Economic Growth: The Arguments and Evidence for Africa and Asia', *Environment and Urbanization*, 25:2, 465–82.

Uganda Ministry of Finance, Planning and Economic Development (UMFPED) (2009) *The Contributions of Reduced Gender Inequality to GDP Growth Prospects in Uganda: A Synthesis of an Econometric Analysis Study and a Participatory Investigation* (Kampala: UMFPED).

Unger, Alon and Riley, Lee W. (2007) 'Slum Health: From Understanding to Action', *PLoSMed*, 4:10, 1561–66 (e295).

UNAIDS (2010) *UNAIDS Report on the Global AIDS Epidemic 2010* (Geneva: UNAIDS). (www.unaids.org/globalreport/Global_report.htm).

United Nations (UN) (1994) *Fact Sheet No. 21: The Human Right to Adequate Housing* (New York: UN). (www.unrol.org/files/FactSheet21en.pdf).

United Nations (UN) (2010a) *Millennium Development Goals Report 2010* (New York: UN). (http://mdgs.un.org/unsd/mdg/Resources/Static/Products/Progress2010/MDG_Report_2010_En.pdf).

United Nations (UN) (2010b) *Millennium Development Goals Report 2010: Addendum 2* (New York: UN).

United Nations (UN) (2012) *Millennium Development Goals Report: Gender Chart 2012* (New York: UN).

United Nations (UN) (2014a) 'Adequate Housing as a Component of the Right to an Adequate Standard of Living', orally revised version, Human Rights Council, 25th Session, 26 March, A/HRC/15/L.18.Rev.1 (New York: UN). (http://direitoamoradia.org/wp-content/uploads/2014/03/A_HRC_25_L18-REV1-AS-ORALLY-REVISED.pdf) .

United Nations (UN) (2014b) *Millennium Development Goals Report 2014* (New York: UN). (http://mdgs.un.org/unsd/mdg/Resources/Static/Products/Progress2014/English2014.pdf).

United Nations Children's Fund (UNICEF) (2007) *State of the World's Children 2007: Gender Equality, the Double Dividend* (New York: UNICEF).

United Nations Children's Fund (UNICEF) (2012) *State of the World's Children 2012: Children in an Urban World* (New York: UNICEF). (www.unicef.org/sowc2012/pdfs/SOWC-2012-Main-Report_EN_21Dec2011.pdf).

United Nations Children's Fund (UNICEF) (2015) *Beyond Averages: Learning from the MDGs*, Progress for Children No. 11 (New York: UNICEF). (www.unicef.org/publications/files/Progress_for_Children_No._11_22June15.pdf).

United Nations Children's Fund (UNICEF)/World Health Organisation (WHO) (2012) *Joint Monitoring Programme Report: Progress on Drinking Water and Sanitation, 2012 Update* (New York/Geneva: UNICEF/WHO). (www.wssinfo.org/fileadmin/user_upload/resources/JMP-report-2012-en.pdf).

United Nations Commission on the Status of Women (UNCSW) (2009) 'Report on the Fifty-third Session (1–13 March 2009): The Equal Sharing of Responsibilities between Women and Men, Including Caregiving in the Context of HIV/AIDS' (Geneva: Economic and Social Council, United Nations). (www.un.org/womenwatch/daw/csw/53sess.htm).

United Nations Commission on the Status of Women (UNCSW) (2011) 'Report on the Fifty-fifth Session (22 February–4 March 2011): Access and Participation of Women and Girls in Education, Training and Science and Technology, Including for the Promotion of Women's Equal Access to Full Employment and Decent Work' (Geneva: Economic and Social Council, United Nations). (http://daccess-dds-ny.un.org/doc/UNDOC/LTD/N11/257/33/PDF/N1125733.pdf?OpenElement).

United Nations Department of Economic and Social Affairs (UN-DESA) (2009) *World Urbanisation Prospects: The 2009 Revision* (New York: UN-DESA). (http://esa.un.org/unpd/wup/index.htm).

United Nations Department for Economic and Social Affairs (UN-DESA) (2010) *The World's Women 2010: Trends and Statistics* (New York: UN-DESA).

United Nations Department of Economic and Social Affairs (UN-DESA) (2011) *World Contraceptive Use 2010* (New York: UN-DESA). (www.un.org/esa/population/publications/wcu2010/Data/UNPD_WCU_2010_Contraceptive_RG.xls).

United Nations Department of Economic and Social Affairs (2014a) *World Urbanisation Prospects* (New York: UN-DESA). (http://esa.un.org/unpd/wup/index.htm).

United Nations Department of Economic and Social Affairs (UN-DESA) (2014b) *Demographic Yearbook 2013* (New York: UN-DESA).

United Nations Department for Economic and Social Affairs (UN-DESA)/United Nations Division for the Advancement of Women (UNDAW) (2009) *World Survey on the Role of Women in Development 2009: Women's Control over Economic Resources and Access to Financial Resources, including Microfinance* (New York: UN-DESA/UNDAW).

United Nations Development Fund for Women (UNIFEM) (2008) *Progress of the World's Women 2008/2009: Who Answers to Women? Gender and Accountability* (New York: UNIFEM).

United Nations Development Programme (UNDP) (2005) *En Route to Equality: A Gender Review of National MDG Reports 2005* (New York: UNDP).

United Nations Development Programme (UNDP) (2010) *Human Development Report 2010: The Real Wealth of Nations: Pathways to Human Development* (New York: UNDP). (http://hdr.undp.org/en/reports/global/hdr2010/).

United Nations Development Programme (UNDP) (2014) *Human Development Report 2014: Sustaining Human Progress: Reducing Vulnerabilities and Building Resilience* (New York: UNDP). (http://hdr.undp.org/sites/default/files/hdr14-report-en-1.pdf).

United Nations Fund for Population Activities (UNFPA) (2005) *State of the World's Population 2005: The Promise of Equality: Gender Equity, Reproductive Health and the Millennium Development Goals* (New York: UNFPA).

United Nations Fund for Population Activities (UNFPA) (2007) *State of the World's Population 2007: Unleashing the Potential of Urban Growth* (New York: UNFPA).

United Nations Fund for Population Activities (UNFPA) (2009) *State of the World's Population 2009: Facing a Changing World: Women, Population and Climate* (New York: UNFPA).

UN-Habitat (2005) *Urban Indicators Programme 2005* (Nairobi: UN-Habitat).

UN-Habitat (2006a) *Women's Equal Rights to Housing, Land and Property in International Law* (Nairobi: UN-Habitat).

UN-Habitat (2006b) *The State of The World's Cities 2006/2007: The Millennium Development Goals and Urban Sustainability – 30 Years of Shaping the Habitat Agenda* (London: Earthscan).

UN-Habitat (2007a) *Policy Makers Guide to Women's Land, Property and Housing Rights across the World* (Nairobi: UN-Habitat).

UN-Habitat (2007b) *Global Report on Human Settlements, 2007* (Nairobi: UN-Habitat).

UN-Habitat (2008a) *The State of The World's Cities 2008/2009: Harmonious Cities* (London: Earthscan).

UN-Habitat (2008b) *Gender Equality for a Better Urban Future: An Overview of UN-Habitat's Gender Equality Action Plan (2008–2013)* (Nairobi: UN-Habitat). (www.unHabitat.org/pmss/listItemDetails.aspx?publicationID=2850).

UN-Habitat (2008c) *Factsheet: Gender and Safety and Security in Cities* (Nairobi: UN-Habitat). (www.unHabitat.org/downloads/docs/GenderandSafetyandSecurityinCities factsheet.pdf).

UN-Habitat (2008d) *Gender Mainstreaming in Local Authorities: Best Practices* (Nairobi-UN-Habitat). (www.un.org/womenwatch/ianwge/member_publications/gender_mains treaming_in_local_authorities.pdf).

UN-Habitat (2009) *Planning Sustainable Cities: Global Report on Human Settlements 2009* (London: Earthscan).

UN-Habitat (2010a) *State of the World's Cities 2010/2011: Bridging the Urban Divide* (London: Earthscan).

UN-Habitat (2010b) *Gender Equality for Smarter Cities: Challenges and Progress* (Nairobi: UN-Habitat). (www.unHabitat.org/pmss/listItemDetails.aspx?publicationID= 2887).

UN-Habitat (2010c) 'The Prosperity of Cities: Concept Note for State of the World's Cities Report 2012/13', Mimeo (Nairobi: UN-Habitat).

UN-Habitat (2010d) *Factsheet: Urban Divide: Hunger, Health and Education* (Nairobi: UN-Habitat). (www.unHabitat.org/documents/SOWC10/R10.pdf).

UN-Habitat (2010e) *State of the Urban Youth 2010/2011: Levelling the Playing Field: Inequality of Youth Opportunity* (London: Earthscan).

UN-Habitat (2011a) *Global Report on Human Settlements 2011: Cities and Climate Change: Policy Directions*, abridged edn (Nairobi: UN-Habitat).

UN-Habitat (2011b) *Monitoring Security of Tenure in Cities: People, Land and Policies* (Nairobi: UN-Habitat).

UN-Habitat (2012a) *Gender and Urban Planning: Issues and Trends* (Nairobi: UN-Habitat).

UN-Habitat (2012b) *State of the World's Cities 2012/13: Prosperity of Cities* (Nairobi: UN-Habitat).

UN-Habitat (2013) *State of Women in Cities 2012/13: Gender and Urban Prosperity* (Nairobi: UN-Habitat).

UN-Habitat (2014a) *From MDG to SDG: Towards a New Paradigm at Habitat III* (Nairobi: UN-Habitat). (http://unHabitat.org/wp-content/docs/Communitas%20Coalition%20Habitat %20III%20PrepCom%20Side%20Event_14Aug2014_Website%20Version.pdf).

UN-Habitat (2014b) *Background Paper: World Habitat Day 2014* (Nairobi: UN-Habitat) (http://unHabitat.org/wp-content/uploads/2014/07/WHD-2014-Background-Paper.pdf).

UN-Habitat (2015) *UN-Habitat Policy and Plan for Gender Equality and the Empowerment of Women in Urban Development and Human Settlements GPP 2014–2019* (Nairobi: UN-Habitat).(http://unHabitat.org/un-Habitat-policy-and-plan-for-gender-equality-and-the-empowerment-of-women/).

UN-Habitat/UNECA (2008) *The State of African Cities 2008: A Framework for Addressing Urban Challenges in Africa* (Nairobi: UN-Habitat/UNECA).

UN-Habitat/World Health Organisation (WHO) (2010) *Hidden Cities: Unmasking and Overcoming Health Inequities in Urban Settings* (Nairobi/Geneva: UN-Habitat/WHO).

United Nations Human Rights Council (UNHRC) (2009) *Report of the Special Rapporteur on Adequate Housing as a Component of the Right to an Adequate Standard of Living, and on the Right to Non-discrimination in this Context, Raquel Rolnik*, 4 February 2009, A/HRC/10/7 (New York: UNHRC). (www.unhcr.org/refworld/docid/49a54f4a2.html).

United Nations Millennium Project (UNMP)/Task Force on Education and Gender Equality (TFEGE) (2005) *Taking Action: Achieving Gender Equality and Empowering Women* (London: Earthscan).

United Nations (UN) Open Working Group (2014) *Open Working Group Proposal for Sustainable Development Goals* (New York: UN). (https://sustainabledevelopment. un.org/content/documents/1579SDGs%20Proposal.pdf).

United Nations Research Institute for Social Development (UNRISD) (2010a) *Combating Poverty and Inequality: Structural Change, Social Policy and Politics* (Geneva: UNRISD).

United Nations Research Institute for Social Development (UNRISD) (2010b) *Why Care Matters for Social Development*, Research and Policy Brief No. 9, Political and Social Economy of Care (Geneva: UNRISD). (www.unrisd.org/unrisd/website/document. nsf/8b18431d756b708580256b6400399775/25697fe238192066c12576d4004cfe50/$ FILE/RPB9e.pdf).

United Nations Statistics Division (UNSD) (2008) *Demographic Yearbook* (New York: UN). (http://unstats.un.org/unsd/demographic/products/dyb/dyb2008.htm).

United Nations Statistics Division (UNSD) (2013) *Demographic Yearbook* (New York: UN). (http://unstats.un.org/unsd/demographic/products/dyb/dyb2013.htm).

United Nations Sustainable Development Solutions Network (UNSDN) (2015) *Indicators and a Monitoring Framework for the Sustainable Development Goals* (New York: UNSDN).(http://unsdsn.org/wp-content/uploads/2015/05/150612-FINAL-SDSN-Indicator-Report1.pdf).

UN-Water (2005) *Gender, Water and Sanitation: A Policy Brief* (New York: UN-Water) (www.un.org/waterforlifedecade/pdf/un_water_policy_brief_2_gender.pdf).

UN Women (2011a) *Progress of the World's Women 2011–2012: In Pursuit of Gender Justice* (New York: UN Women). (http://progress.unwomen.org).

UN Women (2011b) *The Gender Dividend: A Business Case for Gender Equality* (New York: UN Women). (www.unwomen.org/~/media/Headquarters/Media/Publications/en/UNWomenTheGenderDividend.pdf).

UN Women (2012) *MDG Gender Chart 2012* (New York: UN Women).

UN Women (2013) *A Transformative Stand-alone Goal on Achieving Gender Equality, Women's Rights and Women's Empowerment: Imperatives and Key Components* (New York: UN Women) (www.unwomen.org/~/media/headquarters/attachments/sections/library/publications/2013/10/unwomen_post2015_positionpaper_english_final_web%20pdf.pdf).

UN Women (2014) *Report of the Expert Group Meeting on Envisioning Women's Rights in the Post-2015 Context* (New York: UN Women), (www.unwomen.org/~/media/headquarters/attachments/sections/csw/59/csw59-egm-report-en.pdf).

UN Women (2015a) *The Beijing Declaration and Platform for Action Turns 20: Summary Report* (UN Women: New York) (www.unwomen.org/~/media/headquarters/attachments/sections/library/publications/2015/sg%20report_synthesis-en_web.pdf).

UN Women (2015b) *In Brazil, New Law on Femicide to Offer Greater Protection* (www.unwomen.org/en/news/stories/2015/3/in-brazil-new-law-on-femicide-to-offer-greater-protection).

UN Women (2015c) *Progress of the World's Women: Transforming Economies, Realizing Rights* (New York: UN Women).

United States Department of State Women's Technology Delegation to Liberia and Sierra Leone (USDS) (2011) 'West Africa's Tech Revolution for Women and Girls', *Daily Beast*, 8 March. (www.thedailybeast.com/articles/2011/03/09/west-africas-tech-revolution-for-women-and-girls.html).

Unterhalter, Elaine (2009) 'Gender and Poverty Reduction: The Challenge of Intersection', *Agenda: Empowering Women for Gender Equity*, 23:81, 14–24.

Uribe-Urán, Victor M. (2013) 'Physical Violence against Wives and the Law in the Spanish World, 1820s–2000s', in Eric A. Johnson, Ricardo D. Salvatore and Pieter Spierenburg (eds) *Murder and Violence in Modern Latin America* (Chichester: Wiley-Blackwell), 49–80.

Valenti, Jessica (2007) 'Is Segregation the Only Answer to Sexual Harassment?', *Guardian*, 3 August. (www.guardian.co.uk/lifeandstyle/2007/aug/03/healthandwellbeing.gender).

Valentine, Gill (1989) 'The Geography of Women's Fear', *Area*, 21:4, 385–90.

Valentine, Gill (2001) *Social Geographies: Space and Society* (London: Pearson).

Valenzuela, María Elena (2005) *Informality and Gender in Latin America*, Working Paper No. 60 (Geneva: International Labour Office, Policy Integration Department).

Van Donk, Mirjam (2006) '"Positive" Urban Futures in Sub-Saharan Africa: HIV/AIDS and the Need for ABC (a Broader Conceptualisation)', *Environment and Urbanisation*, 18:1,155–75.

Van Staveren, Irene (2013) 'Gender as a Macro-economic Variable', in Shirin Rai and Georgina Waylen (eds) *New Frontiers in Feminist Political Economy* (London: Routledge), 135–53.

Varley, Ann (1987) 'The Relationship between Tenure Legalisation and Housing Improvement: Evidence from Mexico City', *Development and Change*, 18, 463–81.

Varley, Ann (2002) 'Private or Public: Debating the Meaning of Tenure Legislation', *International Journal of Urban and Regional Research*, 26:3, 449–61.

Varley, Ann (2007) 'Gender and Property Formalisation: Conventional and Alternative Approaches', *World Development*, 35:10, 1739–53.

Varley, Ann (2013) 'Feminist Perspectives on Urban Poverty: De-essentialising Difference', in Linda Peake and Martina Rieker (eds) *Rethinking Feminist Interventions into the Urban* (London: Routledge), 125–41.

Varley, Ann (2014) 'Gender, Families and Households', in Vandana Desai and Robert Potter (eds) *The Companion to Development Studies*, 3rd edn (London: Routledge), 397–402.

Varley, Ann and Blasco, Maribel (2000) 'Intact or in Tatters? Family Care of Older Women and Men in Urban Mexico', *Gender and Development*, 8:2, 47–55.

Vaswani, Karishma (2010) 'Indonesia Launches Women-only Train Service', BBC News, 19 August. (www.bbc.co.uk/news/world-asia-pacific-11028078).

Venables, Anthony (2009) 'Rethinking Economic Growth in a Globalising World: An Economic Geography Lens', *African Development Review*, 21:2, 331–51.

Vera-Sanso, Penny (1995) 'Community, Seclusion and Female Labour Force Participation in Madras, India', *Third World Planning Review*, 17:2, 155–67.

Vera-Sanso, Penny (2006) 'Conformity and Contestation: Social Heterogeneity in South Indian Settlements', in Geert de Neve and Henrike Donner (eds) *The Meaning of the Local: Politics of Place in Urban India* (London: Routledge/Cavendish), 182–205.

Vera-Sanso, Penny (2010) 'Gender, Urban Poverty and Ageing in India: Conceptual and Policy Issues', in Sylvia Chant (ed.) *The International Handbook of Gender and Poverty: Concepts, Research, Policy* (Cheltenham: Edward Elgar), 220–5.

Vira, Bhaskar and James, Al (2011) 'Researching Hybrid "Economic"/"Development" Geographies in Practice: Methodological Reflections from a Collaborative Project on India's New Service Economy', *Progress in Human Geography*, 35:5, 627–51.

Viswanath, Kalpana and Basu, Ashish (2015) 'SafetiPin: an Innovative Mobile App to Collect Data on Women's Safety in Indian Cities', *Gender and Development*, 23:1, 45–60.

Walker, Julian, Frediani, Alexandre Apsan and Tirani, Jean-François (2013) 'Gender, Difference and Urban Change: Implications for the Promotion of Well-being', *Environment and Urbanization*, 25:1, 111–24.

Walker, Wendy and Vajjhala, Shalini (2009) 'Gender and GIS: Mapping the Links between Spatial Exclusion, Transport Access, and the Millennium Development Goals in Lesotho, Ethiopia, and Ghana', *Community Informatics: A Global E-Journal*, 5:3/4. (http://ci-journal.net/index.php/ciej/article/view/543/513).

Walljasper, Jay (2005) 'Cities of Joy', *Ode Magazine*, 233. (www.resurgence.org/magazine/article518-cities-of-joy.html).

Warschauer, Mark and Ames, Morgan (2010) 'Innovating for Development: Can One Laptop per Child Save the World's Poor?', *Journal of International Affairs*, 64:1, 33–51.

Water Supply and Sanitation Collaboration Council (WSSCC) (2006) *For Her its the Big Issue: Putting Women at the Centre of Water Supply, Sanitation And Hygiene* (Geneva: WSSCC). (www.wsscc.org/sites/default/files/publications/wsscc_for_her_its_the_big_issue_evidence_report_2006_en.pdf).

WaterAid (2014) *Annual Report 2013/14* (London: WaterAid). (www.wateraid.org/uk/who-we-are/annual-reports).

WaterAid (2015) *WASH and Gender Equality: Briefing Note* (WaterAid: London) (www.wateraid.org/se/~/media/Publications/Post%202015/English%20toolkit/8-WASH-and-gender-equality.pdf).

Watts, Cathy and Zimmerman, Charlott (2002) 'Violence against Women: Global Scope and Magnitude', *The Lancet*, 359, 1232–7.

Weiss, Anita (1994) 'Challenges for Muslim Women in a Postmodern World', in Akbar S. Ahmed and Hastings Donnan (eds) *Islam, Globalisation and Postmodernity* (London: Routledge), 123–36.

Weldegiorgis, Tsehaye and Jayamohan, J. K. (2013) 'Livelihoods and Coping Strategies – Looking beyond Poverty: A Study of Female Headed Households in Urban Ethiopia', *Asia Pacific Journal of Social Sciences*, 5:1, 31–51.

Welsh, Patrick (2011) '"Swimming against the Tide is Easier as a Shoal": Changing Masculinities in Nicaragua – a Community-based Approach', in Andrea, Jerker Edström and Alan Greig (eds) *Men and Development: Politicising Masculinities* (London: Zed), 205–18.

Werner, Marion (2012) 'Beyond Upgrading: Gendered Labour and the Restructuring of Firms in the Dominican Republic', *Economic Geography*, 88:4, 403–22.

Whitzman, Carolyn; Legacy, Crystal; Andrew, Caroline; Klodsawsky Fran; Shaw, Margaret and Viswanath, Kalpana (eds) Building Inclusive Cities: Women's Safety and the Right to the City (Abingdon: Earthscan from Routledge).

Whitzman, Carolyn, Andrew, Caroline and Viswanath, Kalpana (2014) 'Partnerships for Women's Safety in the City: "Four Legs for a Good Table"', *Environment and Urbanization*, 26:2, 443–56.

Whitzman, Carolyn, Legacy, Crystal, Andrew, Caroline, Klodsawsky, Fran, Shaw, Margaret and Viswanath, Kalpana (eds) (2013) *Building Inclusive Cities: Women's Safety and the Right to the City* (Abingdon/New York: Routledge).

Whitzman, Carolyn, Shaw, Margaret, Andrew, Caroline and Travers, Kathryn (2009) 'The Effectiveness of Women's Safety Audits', *Security Journal*, 22:3, 205–18.

Widman, Marit (2014) 'Land Tenure Insecurity and Formalising Land Rights in Madagascar: A Gender Perspective on the Certification Program', *Feminist Economics*, 20:1, 130–54.

Wilkinson, Richard and Pickett, Kate (2009) *The Spirit Level: Why More Equal Societies Almost Always Do Better* (London: Allen Lane).

Wilding, Polly (2010) '"New Violence": Silencing Women's Experiences in the Favelas of Brazil', *Journal of Latin American Studies*, 42, 719–47.

Wilding, Polly and Pearson, Ruth (2013) 'Gender and Violence in Maré, Rio de Janeiro: A Tale of Two Cities?', in Linda Peake and Martina Rieker (eds) *Rethinking Feminist Interventions into the Urban* (London: Routledge), 159–76.

Williams, Carolyn (2010) 'Urban Poverty, Heteronormativity and Women's Agency in Lima, Peru: Family Life on the Margins', in Sylvia Chant (ed.) *The International Handbook of Gender and Poverty: Concepts, Research, Policy* (Cheltenham: Edward Elgar), 190–4.

Williams, Colin and Lansky, Mark (2013) 'Informal Employment in Developed and Developing Economies: Perspectives and Policy Responses', *International Labour Review*, 152:3–4, 355–80.

Williams, Glynn, Meth, Paula and Willis, Katie (2009) *Geographies of Developing Areas: The Global South in a Changing World* (Abingdon: Routledge).

Willis, Katie (2002) 'Open for Business: Strategies for Economic Diversification', in Cathy McIlwaine and Katie Willis (eds) *Challenges and Change in Middle America* (Harlow: Longman), 136–58.

Willis, Katie (2010) 'Gender, Poverty and Social Capital: The Case of Oaxaca City, Mexico', in Sylvia Chant (ed.) *The International Handbook of Gender and Poverty: Concepts, Research, Policy* (Cheltenham: Edward Elgar), 385–90.

Wills, Jane, Datta, Kavita, Evans, Yara, Herbert, Joanna, May, Jon and McIlwaine, Cathy (2010) *Global Cities at Work: New Migrant Divisions of Labour* (London: Pluto).

Wilson, Elizabeth (2001) *The Contradictions of Culture: Cities, Culture, Women* (London: Sage).

Winton, Ailsa (2004) 'Urban Violence: A Guide to the Literature', *Environment and Urbanisation*, 16:2, 165–84.

Wojcicki, Janet Maia (2002) '"She Drank His Money": Survival Sex and the Problem of Violence in Taverns of Gauteng Province, South Africa', *Medical Anthropology Quarterly*, 16:3, 267–93.

Women's Campaign International (WCI) (2009) *Women's Campaign International's Trainings in the City of Women, Colombia* (Philadelphia, PA: WCI). (www.womens-campaign-international-org/2009/03/womens-campaign-internationals-training-in-the-city-of-women-colombia).

Wong, Cecilia (2015) 'A Framework for "City Prosperity Index": Linking Indicators, Analysis and Policy', *Habitat International*, 45, 3–9.

Wood, Katherine and Jewkes, Rachel (1997) 'Violence, Rape and Sexual Coercion: Everyday Love in a South African Township', in Caroline Sweetman (ed.) *Men and Masculinity* (Oxford: Oxfam), 41–6.

World Bank (2003a) *ICT and MDGs: A World Bank Group Perspective* (Washington, DC: World Bank). (www-wds.worldbank.org/external/default/WDSContentServer/IW3P/IB/2004/09/15/000090341_20040915091312/Rendered/PDF/278770ICT010mdgs0Complete.pdf).

World Bank (2003b) *Gender in Urban Infrastructure Projects: The Case of the Carácas Slum-upgrading Project* (Washington, DC: World Bank). (http://wb0018.worldbank.org/LAC/lacinfoclient.nsf).

World Bank (2006a) *Gender and Transport Resource Guide* (Washington, DC: World Bank). (www4.worldbank.org/afr/ssatp/Resources/HTML/Gender-RG/index.html).

World Bank (2006b) *Gender Equality as Smart Economics: A World Bank Action Plan (Fiscal Years 2007–10)* (Washington, DC: World Bank).

World Bank (2007) *World Development Report 2007: Development and the Next Generation* (Washington, DC: World Bank).

World Bank (2009a) *Systems of Cities: Harnessing Urbanisation for Growth and Poverty Alleviation: World Bank Urban and Local Government Strategy* (Washington, DC: World Bank).

World Bank (2009b) *World Development Report 2009: Reshaping Economic Geography* Washington, DC: World Bank).

World Bank (2010) *The Little Data Book on Information and Communication Literacy* (Washington, DC: World Bank). (http://siteresources.worldbank.org/EXTINFORMATIONANDCOMMUNICATIONANDTECHNOLOGIES/Resources/LittleDataBook2010.pdf).

World Bank (2011a) *Helping Women Achieve Equal Treatment in Obtaining Land Rights: Gender in Land Administration and Land Certification Projects* Washington, DC: World Bank). (http://siteresources.worldbank.org/EXTPREMNET/Resources/Results2011-PREM-SB-new-Gender-LandTitling.pdf).

World Bank (2011b) *World Development Indicators* (Washington, DC: World Bank). (http://siteresources.worldbank.org/DATASTATISTICS/Resources/wdi_ebook.pdf).

World Bank (2011c) *World Development Report 2012: Gender Equality and Development* (Washington, DC: World Bank). (http://siteresources.worldbank.org/INTWDR2012/Resources/7778105-1299699968583/7786210-1315936222006/Complete-Report.pdf).

World Bank (2012) *World Development Report 2013: Jobs* (Washington, DC: World Bank).(http://siteresources.worldbank.org/EXTNWDR2013/Resources/8258024-13209 50747192/8260293-1322665883147/WDR_2013_Report.pdf).

World Bank (2014) *World Development Indicators* (Washington, DC: World Bank). (http://wdi.worldbank.org/table/2.9).

World Bank (2015) *The Socio-economic Impacts of Ebola in Sierra Leone* (Washington, DC: World Bank). www.worldbank.org/content/dam/Worldbank/document/Poverty%20 documents/Socio-Economic%20Impacts%20of%20Ebola%20in%20Sierra%20 Leone,%20Jan%2012%20(final).pdf).

World Bank and Ellis, Amanda (2007) *Gender and Economic Growth in Kenya: Unleashing the Power of Women* (Washington, DC: World Bank).

World Bank/International Monetary Fund (IMF) (2013) *Global Monitoring Report 2013: Rural–Urban Dynamics and the Millennium Development Goals* (Washington, DC: World Bank/IMF). (http://siteresources.worldbank.org/INTPROSPECTS/Resources/ 334934-1327948020811/8401693-1355753354515/8980448-1366123749799/GMR_ 2013_Full_Report.pdf).

World Health Organisation (WHO) (2002) *World Report on Violence and Health* (Geneva: WHO).

World Health Organisation (WHO) (2005a) *World Health Report 2005: Make Every Mother and Child Count* (Geneva: WHO).

World Health Organisation (WHO) (2005b) *Multi-country Study on Women's Health and Domestic Violence against Women* (Geneva: WHO).

World Health Organisation (WHO) (2009a) *Global Health Risks: Mortality and Burden of Disease Attributable to Selected Major Risks* (Geneva: WHO).

World Health Organisation (WHO) (2009b) *Women and Health: Today's Evidence, Tomorrow's Agenda* (Geneva: WHO).

World Health Organisation (WHO) (2013) *The World Health Report 2013: Research for Universal Health Coverage* (Geneva: WHO).

World Health Organisation (WHO) (2014) *Global Status Report on Violence Prevention 2014* (Geneva: WHO).

World Health Organisation (WHO) and United Nations Children's Fund (UNICEF) (2014) *Joint Monitoring Programme Report: Progress on Drinking Water and Sanitation, 2014 Update* (Geneva/ New York: WHO/UNICEF). (www.wssinfo.org/fileadmin/user_ upload/resources/JMP-report-2012-en.pdf).

Wright, Melissa W. (2013) 'Feminism, Urban Knowledge and the Killing of Politics', in Linda Peake and Martina Rieker (eds) *Rethinking Feminist Interventions into the Urban* (London: Routledge), 41–51.

Yadav, Anil K. and Srivastava, Madhu (2006) *Primary Education in Delhi Slums: Access and Utilisation* (Delhi: Institute of Applied Manpower Research in association with Manak Publications).

Yeh, Anthony G. O., Xu, Jiang and Lio, Kaizhi (2011) *China's Post-reform Urbanisation: Retrospect, Policies and Trends*, Urbanisation and Emerging Population Issues Working Paper No. 5 (London: International Institute for Environment and Development).

Yiftachel, Oren (2006) 'Re-engaging Planning Theory? Towards "South-Eastern" Perspectives', *Planning Theory*, 5, 211–22.

Yonder, Ayse and Tamaki, Marnie for the Huairou Commission (2010) *Our Spaces* (New York: Huairou Commission).

Yorgancioglu, Melisa (2014) 'Low-cost Private Schools: The Solution to Achieving "Education for All" in Africa's Slums? A Case Study of Kenya, Unpublished M.Sc. Dissertation, Department of International Development, London School of Economics and Political Science.

Zahidi, Saaida and Ibarra, Herminia (2010) *The Corporate Gender Gap Report* (Geneva: World Economic Forum). (www3.weforum.org/docs/WEF_GenderGap_Report_2010.pdf).

Zeiderman, Austin (2013) 'Living Dangerously: Biopolitics and Urban Citizenship in Bogotá, Colombia', *American Ethnologist*, 40:1, 71–87.

Zhan, Heying Jenny and Montgomery, Rhonda (2003) 'Gender and Elder Care in China: The Influence of Filial Piety and Structural Constraints', *Gender and Society*, 17:2, 209–29.

Ziraba, Abdhalah K., Mills, Samuel, Madise, Nyovani, Saliku, Teresa and Fotso, Jean-Christophe (2009) 'The State of Emergency Obstetric Care Services in Nairobi Informal Settlements and Environs: Results from a Maternity Health Facility Survey', *BMC Health Services Research*, 9:46. (www.biomedcentral.com/manuscript/1472-6963/9/46).

Zuckerman, Elaine (2007) 'Critique: Gender Equality as Smart Economics: World Bank Group Gender Action Plan (GAP) (Fiscal Years 2007–10)', Mimeo (Washington, DC: GenderAction).

Index